C21st
COOK

21st
COOK

**THE BIBLE OF INGREDIENTS
TERMS, TOOLS & TECHNIQUES**

Angela Nilsen and Jeni Wright

CASSELL
ILLUSTRATED

First published in Great Britain in 2006
by Cassell Illustrated
a division of Octopus Publishing Group Limited
2–4 Heron Quays, London E14 4JP

Distributed in the United States of America by
Sterling Publishing Co., Inc.
387 Park Avenue South, New York,
NY 10016-8810

Managing Editor: Anna Cheifetz
Editor: Robin Douglas-Withers
Art Director: Auberon Hedgecoe
Designer: Austin Taylor
Americanization: JMS Books
Illustrations: Matt Windsor and Abby Franklin (pages 1–326,
395b and c, 397, 431 and 465); Richard Burgess (pages 327–437
with the exception of those listed above).

A CIP record for this book is available from the British Library.

ISBN-13: 978-1-844034-30-7
ISBN-10: 1-84403-430-5

10 9 8 7 6 5 4 3 2 1

Printed in China

CONTENTS

HOW TO USE THIS BOOK

Have you ever wanted to know the best way to roast a chicken, how to prepare the fluffiest couscous, or which potatoes make the smoothest mash?

You'll find the answers to these questions and much more in *21st Century Cook* – the perfect guide to keep on the kitchen shelf or take with you when you go shopping.

Chapter 1 helps you to understand recipe instructions quickly and easily using an A–Z list of terms and techniques, then gives you advice on the best kitchen equipment to buy, and how to choose and use it.

The ingredients chapters tell you everything you need to know about selecting, storing, preparing and cooking all types of food – from basil, star anise, apples and squash to steak, salmon and eggs.

You'll also find basic food preparation and cooking skills, such as how to chop an onion, boil pasta and peel a shrimp, the latest techniques used by chefs, and heaps of handy hints and tips.

With all this, plus some quick and easy recipe ideas, *21st Century Cook* is all you need to become a modern maestro in the kitchen.

CHAPTER 1

Terms, Techniques, and Kitchen Kit

TERMS AND TECHNIQUES

KEEP THIS A–Z BY YOU WHEN YOU COOK. IT GIVES DEFINITIONS OF ALL THE MAIN COOKING TERMS AND TECHNIQUES YOU ARE LIKELY TO COME ACROSS IN RECIPES, BOTH FOR SIMPLE AND STRAIGHT-FORWARD EVERYDAY MEALS AND ALSO FOR MORE ELABORATE SPECIAL-OCCASION DISHES. THE MOST FREQUENTLY USED FRENCH TERMS ARE INCLUDED TOO, AND CHEFS' TECHNIQUES THAT YOU MAY BE LESS FAMILIAR WITH.

Acidulated

Describes a liquid to which acid (usually lemon juice in water) has been added, to prevent the flesh of fruits and vegetables from discoloring.

■ To make acidulated water, fill a bowl or pan with cold water and squeeze in the juice of a lemon, then drop the lemon in too.

■ Apples, pears, and celery root quickly go brown after peeling and/or cutting, so drop them immediately into acidulated water.

■ Cooking cauliflower in acidulated water will help keep it white.

Aerate

A term used in cake, pastry, and batter recipes to describe the technique of incorporating air to give a light result. It is mostly used with flour, although confectioners' sugar can also be aerated.

■ The best way to aerate is by sifting. Even if a flour is labeled "pre-sifted," it can become compacted in its packet, so sift it before use. Hold the sieve high over the bowl and tap gently so the flour cascades slowly down.

■ Flour can also be aerated in cake and pastry recipes when the fat is added (see Rub in, page 40).

Aged

Describes food that has been allowed to mature under controlled conditions.

■ Meat that has been aged is darker and more tender than younger meat (see Meat, page 328).

■ *Aceto balsamico tradizionale di Modena* is balsamic vinegar aged in wooden barrels for at least 10 years.

■ Aging affects cheeses differently— Parmesan becomes stronger, while aged Stilton is mellow and creamy.

Al dente

Italians use this expression when testing boiled pasta to see if it is done "to the bite." This means it should be tender, but with a slight resistance or nuttiness when bitten into. When the drained pasta is mixed with a hot sauce, it will then cook a little more, so boiling to the *al dente* stage makes sure it will not be overcooked when it is served.

AERATE

Bain marie

The term *au bain marie* means to heat or cook in a pan or bowl placed over, or in, a pan of water.

■ A *bain marie* is used when slow cooking or gentle heating is required, such as when setting a custard made with eggs, or melting chocolate.

■ The water in the *bain marie* may be either cold or hot at the beginning of cooking, depending on the degree of gentleness required.

BAIN MARIE

Bake

To cook in the oven. The term is used in two ways: for the cooking of bread, cakes, pastries, and pies, and for cooking in an open baking dish or other ovenproof container. (See also Papillote, page 33.)

TERMS AND TECHNIQUES

Bake blind

To bake a pie shell partially or fully before adding the filling. Line your pan or dish with dough, prick the base all over with a fork (this helps the steam escape and keeps the dough flat), then line the dough with a sheet of foil so that it is covered by the foil and comes about 1 inch above the rim of the pan. Spread a thick, level layer of pie weights (page 70) over the foil and then "bake blind" according to the recipe instructions.

■ Most pie shells are baked blind at 375°F (340°F in fan ovens) on a preheated cookie sheet for 10–15 minutes, then the foil and pie weights are removed, and the pie shell is baked empty for another 15–20 minutes until it is crisp and golden. This will give you a fully baked pie shell, to be used cold when the filling will not require any cooking.

■ When a recipe calls for a partially baked pie shell, bake it blind for 10–15 minutes, then remove the foil and pie weights. Add the filling and carry on baking until both the filling and pastry are fully cooked. Partial baking is good when you are cooking runny fillings that would make the pastry soggy if they were poured over raw dough before cooking.

Baste

To spoon liquid or fat over food during cooking, to make it moist and glossy and help prevent it from drying out.

■ Meat and poultry are usually basted with hot fat during roasting, but if you want crisp cracklings on a pork roast, leave well alone.

Beat

To mix or stir one or several ingredients in a bowl, using a vigorous action and a circular motion, to make smooth and/or incorporate air. It is a similar technique to whipping (page 50) and whisking (page 50).

■ For beating by hand, a wooden spoon or a fork is used; an easy, fast alternative is to use a hand-held or tabletop electric mixer (page 60).

■ Eggs are often beaten by hand, especially for scrambling or omelets.

■ Butter or margarine and sugar are usually beaten by machine to make the batter for cakes and cookies (see Cream, page 17).

Beurre manié

This mixture of butter and flour is used for thickening liquids, especially soups, sauces, and stews, at the end of cooking. It is also called a liaison.

bake blind–blanch

■ Quantities vary, but usually consist of an equal measure of butter and flour. Work them together to a paste on a plate using a metal spatula, then add to the hot liquid a little at a time, and simmer until the liquid has thickened, whisking hard.

Blacken/ Blackened

A technique of pan-frying meat, chicken, or fish over very high heat so the outside is charred, or blackened.

■ Blackening produces a lot of smoke, and is more common in restaurants than at home, but you can use the Cajun technique of rubbing food with "blackened spices," a mix of ground peppers, herbs, garlic, and salt (page 163). As the spices fry, they develop a blackened crust.

Blanch

From the French word *blanchir*, meaning to whiten or purify.

■ Bacon, cured ham, and other cured or salted meats are blanched to remove excess salt, while onions, garlic, and variety meats are blanched to remove strong flavors and/or blood. For this type of blanching, immerse the ingredient in cold water, bring to a boil, and then drain.

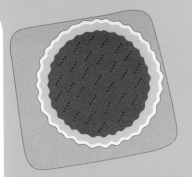

BAKE BLIND

1 *After lining your tin or dish with pastry, prick the bottom all over with a fork (this helps the steam escape and keeps the pastry base flat).*

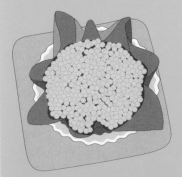

2 *Line the pastry base with foil and fill with a thick, level layer of pie weights (page 10) and "bake blind" according to recipe instructions.*

TERMS AND TECHNIQUES

■ Blanching is also used to keep vegetables a bright color, especially if they are green. Plunge the vegetables into a pan of rapidly boiling water and boil for the time stated in the recipe (rarely more than seconds or a minute or two). As soon as the time is up, drain and rinse under cold running water to stop further cooking. This is a useful technique for getting ahead, as the vegetables need only reheating or short cooking before serving. Fruits and vegetables are often blanched in this way before freezing, to help preserve their quality during storage time in the freezer.

■ To loosen tough skins from fruits and vegetables so that they can be peeled easily, they are blanched by being plunged into boiling water, then into cold. This technique is often used for apricots and peaches (page 238), and tomatoes (page 320).

Blood Heat

see LUKEWARM, *page 30*

Boil

When bubbles break across the entire surface of a liquid, it is boiling—water boils at 212°F.

■ With a rolling boil, the bubbles get larger and break at a rapid pace so they keep bubbling even when stirred.

■ When a recipe gives a boiling time, this should be calculated from the moment the water returns to a boil after the food has been added.

Braise

To cook gently in liquid for a long time in a covered pan or casserole, on the stovetop or in the oven.

■ The ingredients for a braise, usually meat, poultry, or game with vegetables, are cut into large pieces and often browned in fat at the start of cooking, or simply braised from raw.

■ The liquid in a braised dish is usually quite shallow, distinguishing it from a stew, which has more liquid.

■ When cuts of meat or whole birds are braised, they are called pot roasts.

Brochette

The term *en brochette* describes food that is threaded onto skewers and broiled or grilled.

Broil

To cook or brown food under the broiler, which may be in the oven or on top of the stove. It is a healthy cooking method since little or no fat is needed and broiling times are usually short.

■ Preheat the broiler before the food goes under, and move the pan or tray up or down to regulate temperature rather than adjusting the heat.

■ If foods such as steaks and chops are thick, turn them at least once during broiling to help them cook faster and look appetizing on both sides.

Brûlée

Sugar that has been caramelized to give food a shiny glaze, in the oven or under the broiler, or with a blowtorch.

■ Fruits are often brûléed, so are the tops of tarts, especially *tarte au citron*.

■ *Crème brûlée* is said to have been invented at Cambridge University in England.

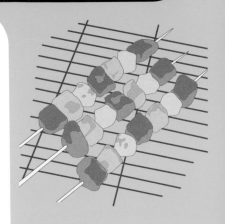

BROCHETTE

Butterfly

To cut through food partially so that it can be opened out flat with butterfly "wings" on either side.

■ The foods most commonly butterflied are lamb (page 342), shrimp (page 431), and sardines (page 413).

■ A spatchcocked bird is also sometimes described as butterflied. (See Spatchcocked, page 46.)

Cappuccino

see FOAM, *page 24*

TERMS AND TECHNIQUES

Caramelize

There are several ways to caramelize:

- To boil sugar to the caramel stage, when it becomes liquid and turns from golden to deep brown. Water can be added to the sugar. The degree of caramelization varies according to the heat used and the boiling time, but it should not exceed 350°F or it may burn. This kind of caramel is used in desserts such as *crème caramel*, and in sauces.
- To sprinkle sugar over food and put it under the broiler, or use a blow-torch, until it is melted and golden.
- To cook ingredients such as onions and shallots over high heat until they are brown and sticky. Oil and butter are good cooking fats for this, and sometimes sugar is added to help the process. This technique gives intense color and flavor, and is often used at the start of meat dishes, especially stews, braises, and casseroles. (See also Deglaze, page 20, and Sear, page 42.)

Cartouche

A disk of waxed paper cut exactly to the diameter of a pan. It is used to cover the surface of ingredients tightly in the pan, to prevent evaporation.

- A cartouche can be used on its own or with the pan lid placed on top, for sweating vegetables, such as onions, and fruits, and for long-cooking stews and casseroles.

Ceviche

A Latin American dish of raw fish marinated in citrus juice (usually lime) until the flesh turns opaque. You may also see it spelled seviche. (See also Marinade/Marinate, page 31.)

Charbroil

To cook on the stove on a ridged grill pan (page 54) so that lightly charred lines are imprinted on the food—the indoor equivalent of grilling on the barbecue. Also known as griddling; the pan may be called a griddle pan.

- Charbroiling is a healthy cooking method for meat, poultry, fish, and vegetables. The food sits across the ridges of the pan, above any fat.
- To prevent sticking, the grill pan must be hot before the food is added.
- Always oil the food not the pan, or the pan will smoke.
- Allow time for the food to char underneath before moving or turning it. If you try to move it too soon, it will stick.
- For a cross-hatch effect, give the food a quarter turn once there are lines on the underside.

Châteaubriand

A small, prime cut for roasting,
enough to serve 2 people. It is cut
from the center of a beef tenderloin.

Chiffonade

Thin strips or shreds of soft, leafy
vegetables, herb, or salad greens.
To make a *chiffonade* of basil leaves,
see page 129.

Chill

When this word appears in a recipe,
it means to place in the refrigerator
for varying lengths of time.

■ Recipes for cold desserts made with
ingredients such as cream, eggs,
chocolate, and gelatin often say "chill
until set." In most cases this will take
at least 4 hours. Desserts set with gelatin should not be chilled longer than
24 hours or they will become rubbery.

■ Very rich pastry dough needs to be
chilled before shaping, or it will be too
soft and sticky to handle. If rolling
out is difficult, even after chilling,
simply press the dough into the pan
with your fingertips.

■ It is a good idea to chill pastry
dough for about 30 minutes after
shaping and before baking. This firms
up the fat so that it does not melt as

TERMS AND TECHNIQUES

soon as the pastry goes in the oven, and helps prevent pastry shrinkage.

■ Chill containers and food before putting them in the freezer. This speeds up the freezing process, helping preserve the quality of the food.

Chine

To remove the backbone (spine) from meat, usually from a rack of lamb or rib of beef, for easy carving.

■ Unless you are proficient with a meat cleaver, chining is best left to the butcher.

Chinois

A conical sieve with a very fine mesh, mostly used by chefs to purée sauces and make ultra-smooth coulis.

Clarify

This term has two meanings, depending on the food in question.

■ Using egg whites and/or shells to make a cloudy liquid clear, as in the making of consommé. Impurities in the stock cling to the egg, which is then removed.

■ Butter is clarified to remove the milk solids (page 455). Older recipes may refer to this as drawn butter. Ghee is a type of clarified butter used in Indian cooking.

Cocotte

see RAMEKINS, *page 59*

Compôte

Fresh and/or dried fruits, poached with sugar, or in a sugar syrup.

■ Wine or liqueur can be used to add flavor to a compôte, as well as sweet spices such as cinnamon, cloves, and star anise.

■ Compôtes are cooked gently, so the fruits retain their shape.

Confit

Preserved duck (page 374) or goose.

Coulis

A sauce that is sieved to a purée.

■ Sweet, red fruits are the most popular, but any soft fruit can be used.

■ Tomatoes can be made into a coulis.

Court bouillon

Poaching liquid for fish, simmered for 30 minutes at the most.

■ A typical *court bouillon* is water delicately flavored with onion, celery, carrot, and bouquet garni, often with lemon juice or vinegar to keep the fish white and firm up the flesh.

Couverture

Chocolate with a high cocoa butter content used by professional pâtissiers for tempering (page 48), to get a silky finish and high gloss for handmade chocolates and decorations.

CHINOIS

Cream

A term used in cake and cookie recipes, meaning to beat fat (usually butter or margarine) and sugar with a wooden spoon or electric mixer, so that they form a creamy mass that is light, fluffy, and pale in color.

■ The purpose of creaming is to incorporate air—the more you cream, the lighter your results will be.

■ You will find creaming easier if the fat is at room temperature, not taken straight from the refrigerator.

■ Creaming can take up to 5 minutes by hand (with a few rests in between); a machine will cut this time in half.

Crème pâtissière

Pastry cream or confectioners' custard that is made very thick with eggs and flour. It is very often used as a filling for pastries, tarts, and buns.

Crêpe

The French for pancake. French *crêpes* are generally thinner and lacier than British or American pancakes, and they can be sweet or savory.

Cross-hatch

To score parallel lines in the surface of food, in one direction, then in the other, to make a diamond pattern.

■ The rind or fat on meat and the skin on poultry (especially duck) are cross-hatched to release fat and let heat penetrate. Cross-hatching fish skin makes fish cook faster and stay flat.

■ Mango flesh is cross-hatched so it is easy to cut into cubes (see page 227).

■ To get a cross-hatch effect by char-broiling (see page 14).

Crudités

Raw vegetables cut into thin batons or small flowerets, often served for dunking in dips.

Crush

Ingredients are described as crushed when they are very finely chopped or smashed with a knife, pounded with a pestle and mortar, or briefly whizzed in a blender or food processor.

■ The term is also used to describe boiled root vegetables that are coarsely crushed with a fork or potato masher (page 71).

Crystallize

When fruits, flowers, and leaves are preserved with a sugar syrup, or egg white and sugar, they are described as "crystallized." It also describes what can happen to sugar syrup when boiling—the sugar may become grainy and "crystallized." To avoid this, do as follows:

■ Make sure every grain of sugar is completely dissolved over low heat before bringing to a boil.

■ Do not stir the syrup.

■ Watch that crystals don't form up the side of the pan. If they do, brush them down with a pastry brush.

Curdle

When custards and sauces made with egg become too hot too fast they curdle or "split" and look grainy.

■ As a precaution against cooking over too high heat, use a *bain marie* (page 9).

■ To rescue a curdled custard, see opposite. Do not substitute skim milk or a low-fat cream for whole unless a recipe says so. They tend to curdle more readily, especially when mixed with an acid ingredient such as citrus juice or onions.

■ When making a custard with eggs, cheat a little by mixing 1–2 teaspoons cornstarch with the cold ingredients at the beginning. Cornstarch is a stabilizer that will help prevent curdling. It cannot be detected in the finished custard.

Dariole
see TIMBALE, *page 49*

Darne
The French word for a cut from a whole round fish, such as salmon or tuna. It is recognizable by its central bone.

Debeard
To remove the beards from live mussels in their shells. The beards are the wispy, hairlike threads protruding from the shell hinges. (See Debearding mussels, page 433.)

Deep-fry
To immerse food briefly in hot deep fat until cooked crisp and golden on the outside, moist and tender inside.

CROSS-HATCH

*TIPS AND TRICKS:
CURDLING*
An effective rescue remedy for an overheated curdled mixture is to remove it immediately from the heat and cool it quickly in an ice bath (see page 28), whisking vigorously until it becomes smooth again.

TERMS AND TECHNIQUES

For safety and best results, use an electric deep-fat fryer with an inbuilt thermometer, and do not put the food in the oil until the oil has reached the required temperature.

Defrost

A term used interchangeably with "thaw," meaning to bring frozen food to room or refrigerator temperature, so that no ice crystals remain.

■ Dairy produce, meat, poultry, and fish, should be defrosted in the refrigerator, especially in warm weather when bacteria grow rapidly. A sudden change in temperature can also spoil the texture of set desserts.

■ The microwave is good at rapid defrosting. Follow the manufacturer's instructions for best results, and cook/reheat immediately after defrosting.

Deglaze

When meat and poultry cook (especially during roasting), juices, sediment, and fat collect underneath, often caramelizing and sticking to the pan. Deglazing is the technique of dislodging them.

■ Remove the meat from the pan, pour or spoon off any excess fat, then put the pan on the stove over high heat, and pour in a few spoonfuls of liquid —stock, wine, or water. Boil the liquid until it has reduced and the base of the pan is clean, stirring vigorously to dislodge all the bits stuck to the base. Serve poured over the meat, or use to make gravies and sauces.

Dégorger

To remove impurities.

■ When meat, variety meats, poultry, or fish are soaked in cold water, sometimes with vinegar or salt, it is called *dégorging*. The technique is used to remove blood from meat and the muddy taste from freshwater fish.

■ The same word is used to describe sprinkling salt over vegetables such as eggplants, zucchini, and cucumber, to draw out the juices.

Degrease

To remove fat from the surface of liquids, especially gravies, stocks, sauces, soups, and stews.

There are four effective methods:

■ Slowly draw a metal spoon or ladle across the surface of the liquid to skim off the fat, tilting the pan when you get to the edge (see illustration, right). Repeat as many times as it takes until the liquid is grease-free.

■ Blot the surface with a wad of absorbent paper towels. Discard and repeat until all the grease has gone.

■ Drop an ice cube into the hot liquid
—the fat will cling to it—then quickly
scoop it out.
■ If the recipe allows for cooling and
reheating, chill the liquid until the fat
rises to the surface and sets in a solid
layer (this is best done overnight),
then lift or scrape off.

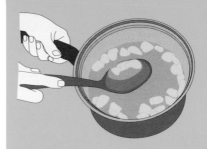

DEGREASE

Demi-glace

A classic brown sauce, very often used
as a base for other sauces. Enriched
and reduced with Madeira, sherry, or
red wine, it has a shiny glaze and an
intense flavor.

Deseed

see SEED, *page 42*

Devein

Shrimp and lobsters have a black vein
running the length of their backs.
Although perfectly safe to eat, the
vein looks unsightly and is best
removed. The deveining technique for
shrimp is shown on page 431.

Dice

To cut food into equal cubes. Dicing
is a more precise technique than
simple chopping.

■ The size of the cubes may or may not be given in a recipe but, as a general rule, the longer the cooking time, the larger the dice. Small dice are about ¼ inch square, and the largest dice are about 2 inches square.

■ The French term *mirepoix* (page 32) refers to a mixture of cooked, diced vegetables.

Discoloration

The process by which the flesh of certain fruits and vegetables turns brown or black on exposure to air—the technical term is oxidization.

■ Avocados and globe artichokes discolor when they are cut, and the best way to prevent this is to rub or coat the cut surfaces with lemon juice immediately after cutting.

■ Acidulated water (page 8) can also be used when preparing fruits, such as apples, and vegetables that discolor, such as Jerusalem artichokes.

Drain

Not to be confused with strain (page 48). When food is drained, excess liquid or fat is poured off, usually using a sieve, strainer, colander, or slotted spoon. In most cases, the drained food is used and the fat or liquid discarded.

Dredge

To coat liberally with flour or sugar.

■ Food that is to be fried is often dredged with flour, to form a protective layer around it. Use a flour sifter or a sieve to dredge straight onto the food, or spread the flour out on a flat plate and dip and turn the food in it until evenly coated on all sides (see illustration, opposite). In both cases, shake off the excess flour before cooking.

■ Confectioners' sugar is often dredged through a sieve over cakes, pastries, and cookies before or after baking, and over desserts before serving for a pretty presentation. When it is dredged before baking, it melts and makes the topping shiny.

Dressed

A term with four culinary meanings.

■ A salad is described as dressed when it has been tossed in a dressing.

■ Dressed poultry and game have been hung and prepared for cooking. In other words, they are oven-ready.

■ A dressed crab has had the white and dark meat removed from the shell, the inedible parts discarded, then the meat returned to the cleaned shell.

■ Blanched tripe (page 360) is described as dressed.

Dry-fry/dry-roast

To heat food without fat or liquid, on the stove or in the oven. Also called toasting. Used for nuts, which are tossed in a pan until golden brown, and for spices (page 162). Also used for cooking duck breasts, and for cooking or heating up flat breads and tortillas. For best results, use a nonstick or heavy cast-iron skillet.

DREDGE

Dry marinade

see RUB, *page 39*

Duxelles

Very finely chopped mushrooms cooked with shallots and butter until quite dry. The mixture is used to flavor savory dishes, or as a stuffing or garnish.

Egg wash

Used for glazing pastry and bread and applied with a brush, this can be a whole, beaten egg or just the yolk or white, often diluted with a little milk or water. Brush on before or during baking, depending on the recipe.

■ The more concentrated the egg yolk, the darker the color of the glaze.

■ For a high gloss finish, add the egg wash in layers during baking.

Emulsify

To combine ingredients that do not usually mix well to form an emulsion. Two of the best-known are mayonnaise (egg and oil) and hollandaise (egg, butter, and lemon juice). There are three keys to success:

■ Make sure all the ingredients are at a similar temperature.

■ Add one ingredient to another a little at a time, letting them combine before adding more.

■ Beat or mix vigorously, to help disperse the ingredients so they come together readily as a smooth whole.

Flake

A term often used with fish, to describe two different techniques.

■ In fish recipes you will often see "the fish is done when it flakes with a fork." Tease a small section of the flesh apart with a fork—if it separates easily into flakes without any resistance, it is done.

■ When you require small pieces for a dish such as a pie, you can flake a whole cooked fish or a large piece of fish by pressing on it gently with your fingers. The fish will separate into flakes of its own accord. Alternatively, you can use a fork. (See illustration, opposite.)

Flame

There are two ways of flaming food:

■ Setting light to food with alcohol, usually a spirit or liqueur, is called flaming or flambéing. The alcohol is warmed, ignited, and poured over the food. As the flames burn, the alcohol burns off. Flambéing gives depth of flavor to a dish, but take care when doing it. Stand back from the pan and don't have the alcohol too hot—it will ignite when just warm.

■ When cooking on a gas stove, chefs often have the heat so fierce that flames lick up the sides of the pan. When liquid is added and the pan tilted, the fat in the pan catches light. This type of flaming intensifies flavors, and works especially well with stir-frying in a wok. It cooks the food in seconds rather than minutes, so natural colors and nutrients are retained, but it is not a technique for the novice cook.

Foam

Food served topped with a "foam" produced by frothing or syphoning was made popular by Catalan chef Ferran Adrià for his restaurant El Bulli. Some foam dishes, especially soups, are described as "cappuccino," for obvious reasons.

Fold

To combine two mixtures together, one of which is usually lighter, or less dense. A gentle action used where you need to retain volume and air. (See page 450.)

■ Whipped cream and/or whisked egg whites are folded into a fruit purée or melted chocolate to make a mousse or soufflé.

■ Whisked egg whites are folded into a cake batter to make it lighter.

■ To make meringues, sugar is folded into whisked egg whites.

FLAKE

Fondant

A term with two meanings. A paste made from sugar syrup used by pâtissiers for decorating and filling confectionery and chocolates. Diluted, it is used to frost cakes and pastries.

■ Chocolate fondant is a steamed or baked chocolate pudding with a liquid chocolate center.

Fondue

This French word for "melted" is used for two traditional dishes. It describes the pot of melted cheese and wine served with cubes of bread for dipping, and the meat version (known as *fondue bourguignonne*), in which cubes of steak are dunked into hot oil.

■ The modern, healthier version of *fondue bourguignonne* uses stock instead of oil, and chicken and vegetables for dipping.

■ Chocolate fondue consists of melted chocolate and cream, with fruits and cubes of cake as dippers.

■ Tabletop fondue sets with skewers for spearing the food are suitable for all kinds of fondue.

Freezer burn

When food in the freezer is insufficiently wrapped and/or air is not excluded from the packaging before freezing, it turns white and looks dry —a condition known as freezer burn. Food with freezer burn is safe to eat, but you may want to cut the burn off to make the food look more appetizing.

Fry

To cook in a skillet in hot, shallow fat over medium or high heat. Also called pan-frying, and most often used for ingredients that cook quickly.

■ For healthy frying, use a small amount of oil to cover the base of the skillet. Be sure it is hot before adding the food—hold your hand over to feel the heat rise. If not hot from the start, fat can seep into the food making it greasy, and the food may stick.

Fumet

An intensely flavored fish stock, although the term is sometimes used to describe a game stock.

Galette

A flat cake or tart made from flaky pastry, sometimes raised with yeast.

Gaufre

The French for "waffle," a *gaufrette* is the fan-shaped wafer often served with ice cream.

Gigot

Gigot d'agneau is a leg of lamb, but it is often shortened to *gigot*.

Glaze

A shiny coating that covers food, to protect and moisten it and make it look appetizing.

■ Egg wash (see page 23) is used to glaze both sweet and savory foods.

■ Aspic and jellied stock are for glazing savory dishes only, which can also be glazed with melted butter, oil, sauces, melted jellies, or dressings.

■ Melted fruit jellies, sieved jam and chocolate make good sweet glazes.

■ For a very smooth finish, always spoon a glaze on slowly and wait until completely set before serving. Brush strokes will show and will spoil the glossy effect.

Gluten

A mixture of proteins that gives dough its stretch and spring. When bread dough is kneaded, the gluten strengthens and becomes elastic, helping the dough rise and expand.

■ The stronger the gluten, the lighter and more spongy the texture of the bread, which is why you should use a high-gluten flour milled from hard wheat in breadmaking—described as "strong" or "bread" flour on the bag. Flour labeled "very strong" is even richer in gluten—good for breads such as sourdough that need a long fermentation time.

■ Ordinary all-purpose flour made from soft wheat is low in gluten. It is suitable for making cakes, cookies, and pastries, not bread. (See also Flour, page 87, and Knead, page 30.)

Gratin

Food cooked under the broiler or in the oven until it has a golden crust is described as a gratin, or cooked *au gratin*. Often, grated cheese or bread crumbs are sprinkled on top before cooking. (See also Tian, page 49.)

Griddle

This term has evolved over the years.

■ The traditional griddle is a flat, rimless pan made of a heavy metal such as cast iron. It is used for cooking griddle scones and flat breads.

■ A modern griddle is a ridged, heavy pan that is either made of cast iron or is nonstick. It is sometimes called a grill pan. This is used to cook meat, poultry, fish, and vegetables and to give charred lines on the food characteristic of grilling on the barbecue. (See also Charbroil, page 14, and Charbroil pan, page 54.)

■ When food on a restaurant menu is described as "griddled" or cooked "on the griddle," it invariably means it has been cooked on a very hot metal plate on the stove, or on a grid or rack over charcoal as on a barbecue.

Grill

To cook on a barbecue of charcoal or gas-fired coals, with or without a lid. Grilling is a quick, dry cooking method and the heat is intense, so the food benefits from being marinated, basted, and/or glazed to help make it moist and succulent.

Grilling

The British term for broiling. Grill is the word for the broiler itself.

Grind

To cut, chop, or pound food into very small pieces, sometimes as fine as powder.

■ Grind meat by fine chopping with a blade, either with a very sharp knife or in a mechanical grinder or electric food processor.

■ Nuts and spices can be ground with a pestle and mortar (page 65), or you can use a special electric grinder or the mini bowl of a food processor (page 60).

Hull

To remove the leafy green calyx and stalk of soft fruit, especially strawberries. (See illustration, opposite, and page 208.)

Ice bath

This is a bowl of ice and water. Half fill a wide bowl with ice and pour in cold water until it is about three-fourths full.

■ When you need to cool a hot mixture quickly, sit it in its bowl or pan in the ice bath. This technique is invaluable for speeding up the preparation of custard, cream, and gelatin-based mousses, and for rescuing a curdled custard.

■ After draining blanched, boiled, or parboiled vegetables, plunge them into an ice bath to stop cooking from continuing. This is called refreshing (see page 36).

HULL

Jerk

A Jamaican term meaning to rub food (originally pork but now frequently chicken) with a jerk seasoning, then cook over charcoal so it forms a charred spicy crust.

■ You can buy commercial jerk seasoning (see page 164), or make it at home. Traditional recipes usually include a mixture of spices and herbs, such as Jamaican allspice, hot chilies and thyme, plus bay, nutmeg, cinnamon, and cloves.

Julienne

Very thin batons of vegetables with squared-off edges, cut with precision. Carrots, celery, celery root, and bell peppers are often cut into *julienne*, and are used in cooked dishes and salads, or to make a neat and stylish garnish.

Jus

The juices that collect in the base of the pan when roasting meat. If a dish is described as *au jus*, it means it is served with these juices poured over, or that the juices have been diluted and reduced with stock or wine.

Knead

There are two ways of kneading. In pastry making, it describes the way dough is gathered lightly and gently to bring it together as a smooth ball. In breadmaking, it is the working of the dough so that the gluten in the flour stretches and becomes elastic, and helps the dough rise. It also distributes the air in the dough so that it will rise evenly. Kneading bread dough can be done by hand or machine, and instructions and times vary from one recipe to another, but the basic technique is as follows:

■ To knead by hand, lightly flour the counter, then hold the dough in one hand, and push it away from you with the heel of the other hand (see illustration, opposite). Fold the dough back on itself and give it a quarter turn. Repeat this action for about 8–10 minutes (with rests in between) until the dough is smooth and springy to the touch.

■ In an electric mixer fitted with a dough hook, kneading should take about 5 minutes to get the dough to the smooth, springy stage. Take care not to overwork the dough or it will collapse and you will have to start again with fresh ingredients.

■ To test if you have kneaded a dough enough, press a finger into it—the dough should spring back straightaway when the finger is withdrawn.

Knock back

see PUNCH DOWN, *page 36*

Liaison

Mixture of two ingredients, used to thicken hot liquids like soups or stews.

■ Common liaisons are *beurre manié* (butter and flour, see page 10), egg yolks and cream (see page 467), and cornstarch or arrowroot and water mixed to a paste.

Lukewarm

Also called blood heat, this term is often used for water and/or milk in breadmaking. The liquid should be at blood temperature, just below 100°F, which means it will feel lukewarm or tepid when you dip a finger into it.

■ For quick lukewarm, combine one-third boiling water and two-thirds cold water.

Macédoine

Mixed diced fruits or vegetables used as decoration or garnish. Fruit is often soaked in sugar syrup or liqueur; vegetables are coated with butter and herbs, or sometimes cream.

Macerate

To soak food in liquid so it softens and takes on the flavor of the liquid. It often refers to fruit in alcohol, such as prunes in armagnac or peaches in brandy.

Marinade/ Marinate

To marinate is to soak, or steep, food in a marinade. Recipes for marinades vary, but are usually a blend of oil and lemon juice or wine vinegar, some-times combined with plain yogurt, plus a mixture of herbs, spices, onion, and garlic to give added flavor.

■ The purpose of marinating is to flavor, moisten, and tenderize. It is most often used before cooking by a dry heat, such as broiling, grilling, or roasting.

KNEAD

On a floured counter, hold the dough in one hand and push it away from you with the heel of other hand.

■ Meat, poultry, and game are the most common foods to be marinated, followed by fish and vegetables.

■ Food that is marinated is usually raw, although occasionally it can be seared beforehand.

■ For a marinade to be effective at softening tough fibers in meat, an acid ingredient such as lemon juice or vinegar is essential. Plain yogurt is also used for this reason. Fresh pineapple and papaya contain enzymes that tenderize, so you may see these in marinades for tough meat.

■ The longer food is left in a marinade, the more successful the result will be. Overnight in the refrigerator is generally recommended, although some meat and game recipes may suggest up to 3–4 days. The exception to this is fish, which should not be left for more than 4 hours, or the acid will start to "cook" the delicate flesh, as in Ceviche (see page 14).

Mash

To crush cooked root vegetables until they have been broken down into a lump-free "mash."

■ You can use a fork or a potato masher, but a ricer will produce a smoother result. See Kitchen Kit (page 70) for information on these. When the mash is pushed through a sieve or a food mill, it becomes a purée (page 36).

Médaillon

A medallion-shaped piece of meat that may be round or oval.

■ Traditionally, it was cut from a tenderloin of beef (and also called *filet mignon* or *tournedos*), but now most prime cuts of meat and poultry are used. You will also see *médaillons* of fish on restaurant menus.

■ To moisten the lean meat during cooking, fat is sometimes wrapped around the edges and tied with string.

Mille-feuille

Layers (French for "one thousand leaves") of puff pastry traditionally sandwiched with jam and whipped cream, or *crème pâtissière* (page 17), but now used to describe any layered puff pastry shape with either a sweet or savory filling.

Mirepoix

Diced vegetables, usually onion, celery, and carrot, sweated in butter and/or oil and used as a base for stocks, soups, sauces, stews, and braised dishes. The size of the dice varies according to the length of cooking (see Dice, page 21.)

Noisette

French for "hazelnut," but in cookery it has two other meanings:

■ It describes the round nugget or "eye" of prime-quality meat—tenderloin of beef, veal, and pork, and the fillet from the loin of lamb. Fat is often tied around the sides of these to help moisten the lean meat as it cooks.

■ *Beurre noisette* is butter that has been heated to a nut-brown color. It is used for drizzling over fish.

Oxidization

Describes the deterioration that occurs when a cut or peeled ingredient is exposed to air. (See Acidulated, page 8, and Discoloration, page 22.)

Pan-fry

see FRY, *page 26*

Papillote

Meat, poultry, fish, or vegetables baked or steamed in a packet of waxed paper, baking parchment, or foil are described as en papillote (see illustration, right). Grape and banana leaves can also be used as wrappers.

■ Cooking *en papillote* is healthy— little or no fat is required.

TIPS AND TRICKS: MARINADES

As marinades usually contain acid, always use nonmetallic containers for marinating.

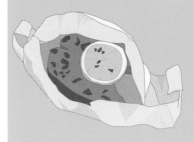

PAPILLOTE

TERMS AND TECHNIQUES

■ Flavorings packed inside the packet insure that the food emerges moist and tasty.

Parboil

To partially cook food in boiling water. Most often used to soften vegetables, especially potatoes before roasting.

■ Parboiling times vary and should be given in individual recipes, but they are generally quite short and never more than half the full cooking time. This distinguishes parboiling from blanching (page 11), when food is boiled for a much shorter time.

Pare

This means to peel fruits and vegetables very thinly, for which you will find a paring knife (page 72) most helpful. The zest of citrus fruits is described as pared when the thin outer colored part is removed (page 51).

Pass
see SIEVE, *page 44*

Poach

Strictly speaking, poaching is to cook in liquid at a slightly lower temperature than simmering.

■ Poaching can be done on the stove or in the oven. The liquid should barely simmer—the surface should murmur and break with the occasional bubble.

■ It is a gentle method, best suited to delicate foods like fish, and soft fruits that would fall apart if simmered or boiled, and for tough cuts of meat and mature birds that need long cooking at a low heat to make them tender. For poaching eggs see pages 54 and 466.

Pod
see SHELL, *page 44*

Pot roast
see BRAISE, *page 12*

Pourable consistency

In cake, cookie, and dessert recipes, beating a batter or creamed mixture to a "pourable consistency" means that the mixture will drop off the spoon or whisk when you shake it.

■ A soft, pourable consistency has a higher ratio of liquid or eggs to dry ingredients than a pourable consistency, and is therefore slightly slacker. It will drop when you lift the mixture out of the bowl, without shaking.

Preheat

- When a recipe calls for a specific oven temperature, you should allow time for the oven to heat up. Without preheating, you will not get a reliable result, especially when baking.
- The usual time for preheating is 15–20 minutes, but ovens vary in the time they take to reach temperature, so consult your oven handbook. Some fan ovens do not need preheating.
- When cooking pastry, bread, and pizza on a flat cookie sheet or stone, you will get the best results if it is hot when the dough is placed on it, so you should preheat it at the same time as you preheat the oven.
- Preheating is essential before broiling, so the food starts to cook as soon as it is put under the broiler.
- To prevent food sticking, preheat woks and cast-iron grill pans (when charbroiling) before any ingredients are added.

Proving

A term used in breadmaking for the second, or last, rising of the dough before baking. Proving lightens the dough, but it is not always necessary. You should only prove the dough if the recipe says so. Dough made with fast-action yeast will not need proving.

■ To prove, shape the dough in its pan or straight onto a cookie sheet, then leave in a warm place, usually for half the time of the first rise. It will not double in size as it does with the first rise; it will just increase to the size it will be when baked.

■ To prevent dough from drying out, most recipes say to cover with oiled plastic wrap or a dish towel during proving, but instructions do vary.

■ To test if the dough is ready to put in the oven, press it with a finger—the dough should spring back instantly.

Punch down

To knock the air out of bread dough after the first rise, also called "knocking back." This prevents the baked loaf from having large holes in the crumb. (Open-textured breads like ciabatta are not punched down—one of the reasons why they have so many holes.) The technique is the same as kneading, but for a much shorter time: half a minute at most.

Purée

A smooth mixture that is made by whizzing, or puréeing, ingredients in a machine (a blender or food processor), or by pushing through a sieve, or using a food mill. If a machine is used and you want the purée to be completely smooth, it will need to be sieved afterward.

Quenelle

A small, soft, oval dumpling of puréed or ground meat, poultry, or fish bound together with eggs and/or a sauce, then poached in stock. This is the traditional quenelle from the Lyon region in eastern France, but now the term is used to describe oval shapes of many different foods, such as mashed potato, vegetable purées, and ice cream.

Reduce

To boil a liquid in an uncovered pan so that it evaporates and reduces in volume, to become a reduction. Wine, stock, and cream are often reduced in sauces, making them thicker and more concentrated in flavor.

■ For the quickest results, use a wide, shallow pan rather than a narrow one as this will speed up evaporation.

■ Reducing intensifies the saltiness of stock, so wait until after reduction before tasting and adding seasoning.

Refresh

Vegetables are refreshed after blanching, boiling, or parboiling to stop

cooking from continuing and to keep their colors bright. There are two ways to refresh, both equally effective:
■ Drain the vegetables in a sieve or colander and hold under cold running water until they cool down.
■ Drain and plunge into an ice bath (see page 28).

Rehydrate

Dried fruits such as prunes and raisins, and dried vegetables such as mushrooms and sun-dried tomatoes, are full of concentrated flavor, but often too chewy or hard to be eaten or cooked as they are. Before you use them, you need to rehydrate them so they plump up and become tender.
■ Hot water is a quick and effective way of rehydrating, although some-times tea, alcohol, or fruit juice may be used to add flavor.
■ Soaking times vary and should be specified on the packet or in the recipe. For general guidelines, see Dried fruit (page 84), Mushrooms (page 95), and Sun-dried tomatoes (page 118).

Relax

This is when food is allowed to rest, either before or after cooking.
■ Pastry dough should be relaxed in

the refrigerator after shaping to help prevent it from shrinking in the oven. Roasts should be left to relax after cooking, to make carving easier (see Meat, Poultry, and Game, pages 333 and 368).

Rémoulade

When mayonnaise is mixed with mustard, capers, and dill pickles it becomes a *rémoulade*. This is a piquant cold sauce that goes well as an accompaniment to meat, poultry, and fish, and with raw vegetable *julienne*, especially celery root. Recipes vary, and often include chopped parsley and/or anchovies.

Render

When the fat in meat melts and becomes liquid, this is called rendering.
■ Duck and goose fat renders during roasting. Both have a distinctive flavor, and are excellent for roasting potatoes.
■ To render the fat from a piece of meat or bacon, put the meat or bacon in a pan over a very low heat and let the fat melt out slowly. Strain the rendered fat to remove any sediment or crispy pieces, leave until cool, then keep in a covered container in the refrigerator. It can be used in cooking like any other fat.

Rest
see RELAX, *page 37*

Ribbon trail

A term used in dessert and cake making, describing the stage when eggs and sugar are whisked to such a thick consistency that they leave a trail on the mixture when the whisk is lifted across it (see opposite). Instructions are usually "whisk until the mixture leaves a ribbon trail" or "to the ribbon stage." With an electric mixer this takes about 10 minutes, depending on the quantity of mixture and the whisking speed; with a hand beater or balloon whisk it can take up to 20 minutes. Standing the bowl over a pan of hot water will speed up the thickening process.

Rib steak

A beef steak from between the ribs. (See Beef, page 334.)

Roast

To cook food uncovered in the oven, usually with some extra fat, until it is brown on the outside and tender within.
■ Prime cuts of meat and young birds are best for roasting, as are fish and certain vegetables.

- To prevent food stewing in its own fat or juices, place it on a rack in the roasting pan, or on a bed of vegetables or herbs.
- Always preheat the oven before starting to roast, so that cooking times can be calculated accurately.
- Basting during roasting helps prevent food from drying out, but there are exceptions (see Baste, page 10).
- When roasting meat, a thermometer (page 58) will help get good results. For internal meat temperatures, see page 333.

RIBBON TRAIL

Roux

A mixture of butter and flour cooked together to a paste, used as a thickening base for sauces and soups before the liquid is added.

- The amount of flour and butter varies according to individual recipes, but is usually equal volumes.
- A *roux* can be cooked to different colors, from white to blond and brown, and this will give the color of the finished sauce.

Rub

A mixture of dried herbs or ground spices that is rubbed over food before cooking are known as "rubs" or "dry marinades."

■ Using a rub is a quick way to inject flavor and/or give a flavored crust to meat, poultry, and fish. The longer it is left, the more effective it will be.

■ You can buy ready-mixed spices to use as rubs (see page 163) or you can make your own, but do not add salt until just before cooking or it will draw out the juices from the food and make it dry.

Rub in

In cake, biscuit, and pastry recipes, you may see the instruction "rub the fat into the flour until the mixture resembles fine bread crumbs." This technique distributes the fat in tiny pieces in the flour so that it melts evenly during baking.

■ Make sure the fat (usually butter or margarine) and your hands are cold, or the fat will stick to your fingers and/or clog in the flour. Take the fat out of the refrigerator and let it come to room temperature. Hold your hands under cold water and dry them.

■ Cut the fat into small cubes and drop them over the surface of the flour. With your fingertips, gently and lightly work the cubes into the flour, lifting the flour up above the top of the bowl, to incorporate air.

■ As an alternative to using your fingertips, you can use a pastry blender.

Sauté

From the French verb *sauter* meaning to jump, this means to fry food quickly in hot, shallow fat (usually butter and/or oil), turning and tossing it frequently so that it "jumps" about, rather similar to stir-frying.

■ For best results, use a sauté pan or skillet with deep, sloping sides that allow room for the food to move without jumping out of the pan.

■ Don't add too much food at once as this lowers the temperature in the pan and the food will stew rather than fry.

Scald

To bring a liquid (usually milk) to just below boiling point, when bubbles start to appear around the edge. Watch carefully and catch it just at this point or the liquid may boil over and scorch. Milk is scalded when it is steeped with aromatics—see Steep (page 46).

Scallop

A thinly cut slice of tender, prime-quality meat, poultry, or fish without bones. Pork, veal, and chicken scallops are tenderized by pounding gently with a meat bat before being cooked (page 48).

Score

When shallow cuts or slashes are scored in the surface of food with a sharp knife, often in parallel lines or as a diamond pattern (see Cross-hatch, page 18). Scoring makes food look attractive, but the main purpose of this technique is to help with the cooking process in the following ways:

RUB IN

■ Scoring or slashing opens up food so that it cooks more quickly.

■ Liquids such as marinades, dressings, and sauces penetrate the flesh through the slashes to make the food moist and inject flavor. They can also help tenderize (see Marinade/ Marinate, page 31).

■ Herbs and garlic are often pushed into the slashes in meat and fish to flavor the flesh. Asian flavorings can be used in this way too.

SCORE

■ Scored lines in the skin of pork help make cracklings crisp (page 347). In the skin of duck, they help release the fat underneath. When fish is scored, it helps it to lie flat during cooking.

■ In the oven, steam escapes from a pastry lid that is slashed before baking, preventing it from becoming soggy.

■ Bread dough that is scored or slashed on the top before baking— whether on a cookie sheet or in a loaf pan—will rise evenly without the loaf bursting apart.

Sear

To pan-fry or roast food for a short time over high heat, or in a very hot oven, so it becomes dark brown on the outside. Foods most often seared are meat and poultry, and whole fish.

■ Searing does not seal in juices. It releases juices onto the surface of the food where they become caramelized, making the food look appetizing, and giving a depth of flavor from the start.

■ A heavy cast-iron skillet or griddle is ideal for searing as it retains heat well. Get the pan hot over a high heat before the food is added.

■ Make sure the food is thoroughly dry before searing by patting it with paper towels, then brush with oil. Always oil the food, not the pan—if you oil the pan it will smoke.

■ Do not overcrowd the pan, as it will lower the temperature. It is better to sear in several small batches rather than in one large one.

■ Do not move, stir, or turn the food until it is browned underneath. Once one side is seared, turn and sear the others (including the edges).

■ After searing, deglaze the pan (page 20) so the caramelized juices are not wasted. If the food stays brown when liquid is added, you have seared it successfully—if the color washes off, you have not.

■ After searing, cooking is usually finished at a lower temperature, often with liquid added (see Braise, page 12, and Stew, page 47).

Seed

To remove and discard the seeds or pits from fruits and vegetables, sometimes called deseeding.

Seize/seized

A term used to describe melted chocolate that has solidified or "seized" into a lump with an unpleasant grainy texture. Seizing occurs for two reasons—when the chocolate is melted too quickly over too high heat, and/or if moisture (even steam) gets into the chocolate while it is melting. There are a few ways to prevent seizing:

■ Break chocolate into small pieces and melt it in a bowl over a *bain marie* (page 9) of hot, not boiling, water.

■ Do not let the base of the bowl touch the water and do not let the water get too hot—it is better to melt it slowly.

■ If the bowl seems to be getting too hot and/or if you see steam rising around it, remove the bowl from the *bain marie* and let it cool down, stirring gently from time to time. The chocolate will melt gradually, even off the heat.

■ Do not cover the bowl at any time, as this will cause droplets of moisture to fall into the chocolate.

■ To rescue seized chocolate, remove from the heat and beat in 1–2 teaspoons flavorless vegetable oil. Or start again and melt more chocolate, then beat this into the chocolate that is seized

Separate

This term has three culinary meanings:

■ If a recipe calls for an egg to be separated, it means that the shell should be cracked in half and the white separated from the yolk. This technique is shown in Dairy, page 465.

■ Custards and egg-based sauces are often described as having separated or "split" when they have curdled (see Curdle, page 18). To rescue a custard that has curdled, see Ice bath (page 28).

■ When you are making mayonnaise, it may separate if the ingredients are not at the right temperature and/or if the oil is added too quickly to the egg. For a foolproof mayonnaise recipe, see page 467.

Seviche
see CEVICHE, *page 14*

TIPS AND TRICKS: SEED
A word of caution: contrary to what you may think, grapes labeled "seeded" have their seeds in them. Grapes without seeds are described as "seedless."

Shell

To remove the outer covering of fruits, vegetables, nuts, eggs, and shellfish—see the individual entries for specific techniques. Removing peas and beans from their shells is also called podding.

Shred

Food that is cut into thin strips is described as shredded.

■ Use a very sharp chef's knife. Leaves can be stacked on top of each other and shredded together, either kept flat or rolled into a cigar shape if they are soft enough (see Herbs, page 129). *Chiffonade* (page 15) is the French term for leaves that have been finely shredded in this way.

■ The large holes of a grater, or a food processor with a shredding disc, make light work of shredding hard foods like carrots and white cabbage.

■ For very fine shredding, use a mandoline (a tabletop metal slicer that slices and shreds to a professional standard—see page 70).

Shuck

Removing shellfish from their shells is called shucking. The term is most often used for oysters, but it can also be used for shelling mussels, clams

and sea scallops. Oysters and sea scallops are raw when they are shucked, which is difficult to do at home, so let the fish supplier do the job. Mussels and clams are usually shelled after cooking, which is easier although still fiddly—the technique is shown on page 432.

Sieve

To sieve is to press food through a sieve (see Kitchen Kit, page 66) to make a smooth purée. The contents of the sieve are pushed through the mesh by pressing and rotating a metal spoon or ladle (or a pestle) against the inside; solids such as skins and pips are left behind in the sieve. Chefs often use a special chinois sieve (page 16) for this technique, which they refer to as "passing."

Sift

To shake food through a sieve or strainer, or a special sifter that may have large holes or a fine wire mesh. The term is most often used for dry ingredients such as flour and sugar.

■ Sifting incorporates air (see Aerate, page 8) and, in recipes with ingredients such as flour, unsweetened cocoa powder, and salt, it combines them.

■ Tap firmly on the rim of the sieve

while shaking to help food go through.

■ To remove lumps, press down hard with the back of a metal spoon.

Simmer

To cook food in liquid at just below boiling point (185–200°F for water). A few small bubbles should break on the surface of the liquid, so that food is cooked more gently, and often for a longer time, than by boiling.

Skim

To remove fat, froth or scum from the surface of a liquid. Special spoons called skimmers can be used, but you can just as easily use an ordinary metal spoon which isn't perforated.

■ When stock or jam is boiling, or if you are clarifying butter (page 16), a frothy scum often rises to the surface. Scoop it off gently without disturbing the liquid underneath.

■ To skim fat off gravies, stocks, and stews (see Degrease, page 20).

■ For information on skim milk, see page 442.

Smoke point

This describes the stage at which fat starts to smoke when it is heated. Never heat fat beyond this point or it may reach "flash point" and burst into flame.

■ Butter has a low smoke point, but it is raised slightly when the butter is clarified (page 455).

■ If you like to use butter, combine it with oil to help prevent smoking.

■ Grapeseed and peanut oils have very high smoke points, so are good for deep-frying.

■ Extra virgin olive oil has a low smoke point, but it is too good for frying. Use for dressings and for sprinkling over food before serving.

■ Do not re-use any oil that you have used for frying. Throw it away.

Spatchcocked

Also known as butterflying (see page 13), this term is applied to birds, usually chickens and Cornish hens, which have had their spines removed and are opened out flat.

■ Spatchcocked birds are excellent for grilling and broiling because they cook faster than a whole bird.

■ It is very easy to spatchcock a bird (see Poultry, pages 368 and 387), but they are often available ready spatch-cocked at supermarkets.

■ For ease of handling and to help keep the bird flat, insert skewers through its wings and legs prior to cooking (see illustration, opposite, and page 387).

Split

see SEPARATE, *page 43*

Steam

To cook in the vapor produced by boiling water. Place the food in a perforated container above the water, then cover with a lid so the steam will surround the food and cook it gently. For information on steamers, see page 54.

■ Steaming is a healthy method of cooking as no fat is used, and vitamins and minerals don't leach out into the water, as they do in boiling, simmering, and poaching.

Steep

To soak aromatics in hot liquid to extract flavor from them. Steeped liquids are usually strained of their flavorings before use.

■ To steep milk with vanilla for a custard, split a vanilla bean lengthwise in half, scrape the seeds into the pan of milk, and drop in the bean halves. Scald the milk (page 40), cover, and let it stand until cool.

■ For flavored milk for white or bread sauce, stud a small peeled onion with cloves and place it in a pan of milk with 1–2 bay leaves. Bring to a boil, cover, and let it cool.

■ To make a perfumed sugar syrup for a fruit salad, add a few pieces of pared citrus zest and a few whole spices such as star anise, cinnamon, and cloves to the syrup.

■ Steep also means to soak an ingredient in liquid so that it plumps up, softens, and/or takes on the flavor of the liquid. (See Marinade, page 31, and Rehydrate, page 37.)

A SPATCHCOCKED BIRD

Stew

Stewing is similar to braising in that food is cooked gently in liquid in a covered pan for a long time, either on the stove or in the oven, but the ingredients are usually cut into smaller pieces and more liquid is used. Stewing is an especially good way of cooking tough cuts of meat.

■ When all the raw ingredients and liquid are put in the pan together at the start, this is called a white stew.

■ To make a brown stew, the main ingredients are browned in fat before the liquid is added.

Stir-fry

To cook food fast in a wok or other deep-sided pan by stirring and tossing over fierce heat.

■ Originally an Asian technique, stir-frying is healthy and nutritious.

It uses a small amount of oil and the food is cut thinly so that it cooks in a very short time and retains maximum nutrients.

■ For successful stir-frying, get the wok and oil hot before adding the ingredients, and let the food sizzle and color on the base of the pan in between stirring.

Strain

To let a liquid pass through a sieve (see Kitchen Kit, page 66) or strainer to separate it from any solids such as skins, seeds, or bones. In most cases the liquid is used and the solids are discarded (the opposite of draining, see page 22), although sometimes both liquid and solids may be kept and used, depending on the recipe.

Sweat

An unfortunate term for a frequently used technique, it means to cook food slowly and gently so that it softens without coloring. Sweating also concentrates the flavor of the food.

■ Onions, celery, garlic, and carrots are often sweated and used as a flavoring base for soups, sauces, and stews.

■ Butter is a favorite fat for sweating because it gives a good flavor and color. To stop it burning, add a spoonful of vegetable or olive oil.

■ Duck and goose fats are excellent for sweating because they give a good flavor, but they do not burn like butter.

■ For the ingredients to cook as gently as possible, use a heavy pan over low heat. You can also use a heat-diffusing mat under the pan as an extra precaution.

■ To stop evaporation and help concentrate juices, press a round of waxed paper over the vegetables (see Cartouche, page 14).

Tempering

This is the technique of melting, cooling, and re-warming chocolate so that it becomes malleable and sets hard with a gloss. It can be done at home, but it is more often used by pastry chefs working with a special kind of chocolate called couverture (page 17).

Tenderize

To break down tough connective tissue in meat and poultry before cooking so that it will be more tender to eat. There are two methods—you can use either, or both together:

■ Cover the meat with plastic wrap and pound with a meat bat or rolling

pin. If you do not have either of
these, you can use the base of a heavy
pan or skillet.

■ Soak in a marinade (page 31).

Tepid
see LUKEWARM, *page 30*

Thaw
see DEFROST, *page 20*

Tian
A *tian* is both the French name for
a baking dish and the food that is
cooked in it, usually a creamy vegetable gratin topped with cheese.
Traditional *tian* dishes are square or
rectangular, and are made from
earthenware.

Timbale
A small, round, metal mold used for
baking or steaming both sweet and
savory mixtures. The mold lends its
name to the food cooked in it, which
is always served turned out.

■ *Timbales* have straight tapering
sides, while a dariole mold, which is
used in much the same way as a *timbale,* has rounded sides and looks like
a mini pudding bowl.

Toast

see DRY-FRY, *page 23*

Tournedos

see MÉDAILLON, *page 32*

Tranche

The French word for a slice. Frequently used to describe a rectangle of puff pastry, or a thick piece of boneless fish.

Truss

To keep poultry and game birds in shape by tying them with string or securing them with skewers. Birds are often sold ready trussed, which looks neat and tidy, but they will cook better if the strings or skewers are removed before roasting (page 38).

Turn/Turned

To pare vegetables, especially potatoes, carrots, and turnips, into torpedo shapes. A classic chef's technique that is rarely used at home.

Whip

To beat vigorously in a wide and sweeping circular motion, to incorporate air into an ingredient or mixture so it increases in volume. The term is most often used with cream or creamy mixtures, and the whipping may be done by hand with a fork or balloon whisk (page 68), or by machine with a "wand" blender or an electric mixer (page 60).

■ Always use a large, deep bowl for whipping. This will allow for maximum volume without splattering.

■ Contrary to what you may think, you will get more volume by hand with a balloon whisk than with an electric machine, and the mixture will hold its shape better—and longer.

Whisk

Using a whisk (see Kitchen Kit, page 68) to beat an ingredient, or a mixture of ingredients, incorporating varying amounts of air.

■ A coiled whisk is used for dressings and sauces so the ingredients come together and emulsify.

■ A balloon whisk is used for whisking egg whites to incorporate as much air as possible (see Dairy, page 465).

Wilt

To cook vegetable leaves very briefly so they lose their springiness and become soft. Cabbage and spinach are often wilted (see Vegetables, pages 270 and 312), and the same technique is used with leaves like arugula and radicchio in warm salads.

Zest

This is the outer, colored part of the rind or skin of citrus fruit, not including the bitter white pith underneath. It contains aromatic oils that have an intense flavor, especially when heated (see Steep, page 46).

ZEST

■ If you know you are going to use the zest, buy unwaxed fruit. Scrub in hot water, then dry well.

■ The zest can be removed in strips with a vegetable peeler or paring knife and then cut into thin strips, or you can use a zester (see right, and Kitchen Kit, page 72).

■ In recipes calling for "grated zest," rub the fruit against the fine holes of a grater, moving it around frequently so that you do not grate too deeply and include any of the pith. Use a brush to remove the zest stuck to the grater's teeth, both inside and out.

KITCHEN KIT

ALWAYS BUY GOOD-QUALITY EQUIPMENT. IT WILL BE A PLEASURE TO USE, AND WILL HELP YOU PREPARE FOOD EFFICIENTLY AND WELL, WHICH WILL GO A LONG WAY TO MAKING YOU A GOOD COOK. START WITH A FEW BASIC ESSENTIALS AND COLLECT EXTRA PIECES AS AND WHEN YOU NEED THEM. THIS WILL SPREAD THE COST, AND MAKE SURE THAT YOU DO NOT BUY THINGS YOU WILL NEVER USE —CLUTTERED SURFACES AND CUPBOARDS WILL HINDER YOUR WORK AND SLOW YOU DOWN, SO TOO WILL CHEAP EQUIPMENT, WHICH WILL NOT LAST.

ON THE STOVETOP

Before buying any equipment to use on top of the stove, check to see what types of stove it is suitable for. Induction stoves require special pots and pans.

MUST HAVE

Saucepans

Essential for all cooking that involves liquid, especially boiling vegetables, rice, and pasta, and making sauces and soups.

■ A basic set of three sizes should cover most of your needs: one small 6½-inch pan will hold 6¼ cups, one medium 7-inch pan will hold 8¾ cups, and one large 8-inch pan will hold 12½ cups.

■ Stainless steel is the most durable metal and an excellent conductor of heat. It is also easy to clean after use. Look for a heavy gauge pan with a ¼-inch base.

■ Lids are a must, but are not always included in the price of the pan.

■ Long handles are good as they stay cooler than short ones, but pans with two stubby ovenproof handles (also called stockpots) are more versatile as they can double as casseroles in the oven. Check if the lids are oven-proof—if not, use foil instead.

■ When buying a large pan, consider choosing a pasta pot with an inset drainer. Apart from safely boiling and draining pasta, it can be used as a stockpot and steamer, and for cooking bulky or large quantities of vegetables (especially potatoes and spinach).

Skillet

A great complement to a wok or stir-fry pan, a shallow skillet is essential for frying food that needs to be crisp and/or flat. Cast iron is a popular metal for skillets as it is heavy duty and will not buckle over high heat, but nonstick is lighter and easier to use. Titanium is the best, and it can be used with metal utensils, which is a real bonus. A useful size (to take 4 fried eggs) is 10–12 inches.

STIR-FRY PAN

WOK

Wok/ Stir-fry pan

Woks are very versatile, as they are shallower and wider than saucepans, with curved or rounded sides. Their open shape cooks many things quickly and easily, such as pasta sauces, risotto, curries, pan-fried or sautéed chicken, meat or fish in a sauce, and stir-fries, of course. An Asian-style wok with a long handle is ideal, but it may have an unstable, round base and no lid. A wok with two short handles, a flat base, and ovenproof lid is safer and more useful. Sometimes called a "stir-fry pan", it can double as a flameproof casserole, so you can start cooking on the stove and transfer to the oven. An 11-inch pan is ideal.

GOOD
TO HAVE

Charbroil pan

Also called a grill pan, this is a heavy pan with ridges on the base that imprint charred lines on the food. Food is raised above any fat so charbroiling is a healthy way to cook— see Charbroil (page 14) for more information.

■ Cast iron is the traditional material for these pans, but it can be very heavy, so you may prefer nonstick.

■ A pan with a rim is useful. It will let you add liquid at the end of cooking, to make a sauce or gravy.

Egg poacher

Poaching eggs is not the easiest of techniques, so if you like poached eggs a lot, invest in one of these. The best kind has nonstick cups that fit into an insert. When the insert is lifted out, the pan doubles as a deep skillet or sauté pan. To poach eggs with or without a poacher, see page 466.

Small skillet

A 6–8-inch pan is good for one person, and the best size for a 2- or 3-egg omelet.

■ Choose a pan with shallow, curving sides so that you can slide omelets out easily. This will also come in useful for crêpes.

■ Nonstick is the most practical, with a thick base. For tossing and flipping, it should not be too heavy.

Steamer

If you do a lot of steaming, buy a tiered steamer so that you can cook several different things at once. For occasional steaming, a collapsible basket is a cheaper alternative—it will fit inside a pan of any size and fold flat for compact storage when not in use.

■ Tiered or stacking steamers in stainless steel are hygienic and easy to clean. Bamboo steamers are less expensive. They look good and can be used over a wok, but food tends to stick in them (unless they are lined with leaves) and they tend to retain smells and flavors, so they are not the most practical choice.

IN THE OVEN

MUST HAVE

Baking dish

Oven-to-table ceramic baking dishes are invaluable as they are so versatile. Use to make dishes like baked pasta, fish and shepherd's pies, gratins, and puddings, for roasting, reheating, and serving. Most baking dishes are strong enough to resist the fierce heat of a broiler (useful for gratins and browning dishes before serving), but aren't usually flameproof and can't go on the stove. A good/useful size is 10 x 8 inches—2 inches deep.

Cookie sheet/tray

Strictly speaking, a cookie sheet is completely flat, so it is easy to slide things off, and it usually has one shallow raised edge for easy handling, while a baking tray has raised edges on all sides (see page 57). Makers are generally unaware of this distinction, so choose by appearance and choose the largest that your oven will take. The best material is nonstick hard

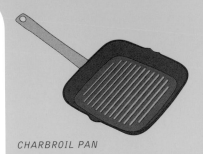

CHARBROIL PAN

COLLAPSIBLE STEAMER

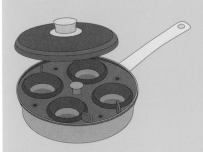

EGG POACHER

KITCHEN KIT: IN THE OVEN

anodized metal, as it is very sturdy, conducts heat evenly, and does not buckle in extreme heat.

Cooling rack

Allows air to circulate under food, making cooling quicker and preventing food from getting soggy. Most cakes, cookies, and pastries benefit from being cooled on a rack (if left in their pans they can stick). It is also useful if you are dredging them with sugar—excess falls through the rack and gives the food a clean edge.

Flameproof casserole

If you don't have a stubby-handled saucepan or stir-fry pan that will go in the oven (page 53), you will need a casserole dish. Make sure it is flameproof, i.e. it can be used on top of the stove and in the oven (if the label says "heatproof" or "ovenproof", it can't be used on the stove). For a casserole to serve 4–6, a diameter of 11–12 inches with a capacity of 15–17½ cups is a good size.

■ A casserole should heat up quickly on the stove and not stick, then retain its heat in the oven. Cast iron fills the bill, is durable, and looks good to serve from.

Oven mitts

These protect hands and wrists from hot oven racks and pan handles. They should not be so thick that they make handling difficult. Gauntlets that cover your forearms are best.

■ Look for the word "insulated" on the label. The type made of flexible silicone can withstand temperatures up to 570°F.

Roasting pan

Heavy duty is essential, so the pan stays rigid and does not buckle or warp in a very hot oven, or when making gravy on the stovetop.

■ Pans with ridges in the base prevent food from sitting in its own fat, and a corner spout is handy for draining off fat and pouring out gravy.

■ Buy the largest pan your oven will take, about 14 x 11 inches, and perhaps a medium-sized one for smaller amounts. These should cover you for most occasions.

■ Choice of material is up to you— stainless steel or a nonstick hard anodized metal will serve you well.

Roasting rack

Many roasting pans come complete with their own rack. If not, an adjustable or hinged V-shaped rack is a good buy. It acts as a cradle for meat and poultry, holding it securely in position throughout roasting and stopping it sitting in fat.

GOOD TO HAVE

Cake pans

Sturdy, nonstick, springform, loose-based pans are best for easy removal of delicate cakes, cheesecakes, and cakes and desserts that are set in the refrigerator or freezer.

■ Most recipes for 4–6 people specify an 8-inch or a 9-inch pan, so it is unlikely you will need more than these two sizes. A depth of 3 inches is good for most purposes. Always use the pan size specified in the recipe. Using the wrong-sized pan is one of the main reasons for failure when baking cakes.

Dariole molds

Also called mini pudding bowls, these are made of metal for good heat conduction. Use them for baked or steamed sponge puddings, custards, and *crème caramel* that are served turned out. The usual capacity for a bowl or mold is ¾ cup.

COOKIE SHEET

BAKING TRAY

SPRINGFORM CAKE PAN

KITCHEN KIT:IN THE OVEN

Loaf pan

For breads, cakes, pâtés, and terrines.

■ Heavy-gauge nonstick is best. The sturdiest ones are made of hard anodized metal.

■ They come in two sizes—a small one is 1 pound, and a large one is 2 pounds.

Meat thermometer

For cooks who worry whether meat is properly cooked, especially when roasting, this is an essential confidence booster. Meat thermometers measure internal temperature, which is the best guide to doneness—cooking times can never be accurate as ovens vary so much. Dial thermometers are pushed into the meat at the beginning of cooking and left there until they reach the correct temperature; instant-read digital thermometers can be inserted at any time. For an accurate reading with either type, insert the probe into the thickest part of the meat, away from any bones.

Muffin pan

Not just for muffins; also for cup cakes, buns, deep fruit tarts, Yorkshire puddings, and individual deep-dish quiches. Cup depths vary, as does the number of cups—the choice is usually between 6, 12, and 24 cups. Deep, flexible, silicone-rubber ones are completely nonstick and easy-release, and won't rust. Metal muffin pans with nonstick coatings are also good, but are best lined with paper cases to insure they do not stick.

Quiche pan

For cooking tarts and quiches, with fluted sides and a lift-out base. Look for silver anodized metal with a satin finish—this conducts heat well and evenly, and won't warp, giving a crisp, professional finish to pastry.

■ Deep pans are the most versatile, especially for quiches and savory flans. Shallow pans make European-style dessert tarts look stylish.

■ The most useful size is 9 inches, which will serve 4–6 people.

■ Individual 4½-inch pans are perfect for appetizer-size portions.

■ A ceramic tart dish looks good for taking from oven to table, but ceramic is not so good a conductor of heat as metal, so pastry bases may be soggy, and the first slice is difficult to get out without breaking.

Removal is easier with a loose-based metal pan, and you can always serve the tart from the metal base.

Ramekins

These small ceramic baking dishes, also called cocottes, are used for individual portions of soufflé, custard, baked eggs, mousses, and dauphinois potatoes. They come in handy as serving bowls too; in fact you will find yourself using them again and again for all sorts of things. Sizes vary enormously, so it is a good idea to buy more than you need to allow for breakages—you may not be able to get the same size again. The most useful size is ⅔ cup.

Traybake

A tray-cum-pan useful for baking, roasting, and heating things up, a tray-bake is more versatile than a jelly roll pan because it is deeper, usually about 1½ inches deep. The best ones are made of hard anodized metal, which is nonstick, and a useful size is 12 x 9 inches or 13 x 8 inches.

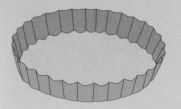

QUICHE PAN

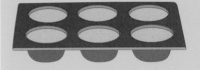

MUFFIN PAN

ELECTRICS

There is a huge range of electrical equipment to choose from, most of which you will never need and which will only clutter your kitchen. Electric machines are expensive, so buy with caution and think about the type and amount of cooking you do. Many of the machines duplicate functions.

MUST HAVE

Blender

Choose between two types:
■ A hand-held "wand" works directly in your pan or bowl, without the need to decant the mixture into a machine. Apart from speed and convenience, this saves on clearing up. Good-quality wands come with many attachments, and will beat, blend, whip, purée, chop, grind, and whisk—and make smoothies and crush ice.
■ A more expensive option is a free-standing blender. This performs the same functions as the wand, but has a more powerful motor, making it easier to blend or purée large quantities quickly. More cumbersome to store than a wand, this type of blender is not good for small quantities that do not cover the blade.

GOOD TO HAVE

Food processor

For the serious cook, this expensive machine will soon pay for itself—it is a multitasking workhorse. A powerful motor will make light work of chopping, slicing, grinding, and grating large quantities, and it will also make pastry and knead dough for bread, as well as purée, whisk, and extract juice. Buy one with a separate mini bowl, for chopping small quantities of herbs, and grinding spices and nuts.

Mixer

If you have a wand blender with attachments and/or a food processor, you may not need an electric mixer. There are two types, hand-held and tabletop, both of which whisk and whip air into egg whites and cream, and cake and cookie mixtures.
■ The hand-held mixer does little more than a good-quality wand blender, so you will not need both, but a heavy-duty freestanding mixer beats air into cake batters more efficiently, and is better for large quantities. It will also make pastry, bread, and pasta doughs and, if you buy the right attachments, will grind, slice, peel, and shred.

PREP TOOLS

MUST HAVE

Brushes

There are many different types. These two are the most useful:

■ A soft pastry brush is indispensable for glazing, sealing dough edges, and greasing pans and molds. A small, flat paint brush with natural bristles is just as effective as a pastry brush bought from a kitchenware store—and less likely to have wayward bristles.

■ For scrubbing vegetables such as potatoes and artichokes clean, and removing the zest from the teeth of graters, you need a brush with hard bristles. A sturdy nail brush will do the job, but do not use it for cleaning delicate vegetables such as mushrooms as it will damage their fragile gills.

Can opener

Not all cans have ring pulls, so you are bound to need a can opener at some time or other. Choose a practical one that has a good grip and is easy to use, not a gimmicky gadget.

HANDHELD
"WAND" BLENDER

TABLETOP MIXER

SOFT PASTRY BRUSH

Corkscrew

The simplest but most efficient is the screw-pull. It screws into the cork, then, as you keep screwing, the cork pulls out. Keep one in the kitchen, so you know where it is when you need it.

Cutting boards

Food scientists say wooden cutting boards are more hygienic than plastic, as long as they are scrubbed in hot water and dried thoroughly after use.

■ You really need three boards—one for raw meat and poultry, one for strong ingredients such as onions and garlic, and a third for everything else. Color-coded sets are practical, or buy a selection of wood and plastic to help distinguish between them.

■ Boards with a dip, for use with a mezzaluna (a half-moon-shaped blade with a handle at either end), are good for chopping herbs.

■ To prevent your board slipping during use, put a special mat or a folded dish towel underneath.

Grater

Apart from the mandoline, there are two basic types:

■ A traditional box grater is inexpensive to buy and has different cutters on each surface. Choose one with a comfortable handle and a wide, stable base. Some have special grippers on the base to keep them in place, which is helpful.

■ Expensive, flat, stainless-steel graters with double-edged, super-sharp blades are good for very fine grating, especially hard ingredients like citrus zest, Parmesan cheese, fresh ginger root and bittersweet chocolate. There are coarse versions for softer ingredients, and there is also a type with a single blade for shredding and shaving. For safety's sake, they should have long handles, nonslip "feet," and a guard to protect your fingers.

Ladle

Indispensable for decanting liquids from one container to another, especially hot liquids that can be messy and/or dangerous. One small and one large ladle are the most you will need. Some have pouring spouts, which are useful but not essential.

Lemon squeezer

You can squeeze juice out of halved citrus fruit by inserting a fork and twisting and squeezing, but a lemon squeezer will make the job easier and less messy. There are many to choose from—try not to be tempted by looks alone. The traditional reamer is most efficient at squeezing out lots of juice, but the kind that has a strainer to catch the seeds and a container underneath to hold the juice is more practical. Stainless steel is both hygienic and sturdy.

BOX GRATER

Measuring cups

Both solids and liquids are measured in cups, which are always leveled off in the cup measure. For ingredients such as sugar and flour, do this by over-filling slightly and then leveling with the blade of a knife. Sets of measuring cups are widely available and there are usually four of them—1 cup, ½ cup, ⅓ cup and ¼ cup—but additional measures may be included. Some also have further graduations on the sides. They are made from a variety of materials. For measuring liquids in a graduated cup, a transparent material is best. Do not use plastic cups for measuring hot or boiling liquids unless you are sure that they are heatproof. Metal measuring cups are long lasting and easy to clean.

Measuring jugs

Canadian and British cooks will find a measuring jug—a pitcher marked in ml and/or fl oz graduations—useful. See page 471 for conversions to cups.

■ Toughened or tempered glass is both heat-resistant for boiling liquids and microwave-proof.

■ Plastic, angled jugs allow you to read the measurements by looking into them from above, which makes measuring easier and more accurate than with a conventional jug.

Measuring spoons

For successful results, especially in baking recipes, always use proper measuring spoons.

■ Nesting sets usually contain four spoons—1 tablespoon, 1 teaspoon, ½ teaspoon, and ¼ teaspoon— although others may be included.

■ Stainless steel is the most practical material, and slim-line spoons are good for fitting into the narrow necks of small herb and spice jars.

■ When spoon measures are specified in recipes, the ingredient should be leveled off with a knife. Occasionally you will read "rounded" or "heaping," which means what it says—it is not intended to be an exact measure. The term "scant" is also used sometimes, meaning slightly less than level.

Metal spatulas

These should be flexible and thin with a rounded end. Useful for all spreading jobs and for turning and lifting delicate foods, as well as helping to release cakes and desserts from pans and molds. Two sizes (large and small) will be sufficient; stainless steel will last longest.

Mixing bowls

A nest of different sizes is the most practical choice, as it will take up the least amount of storage space. A set of four bowls should be enough for most cooks.

■ Heatproof glass and stainless steel are more versatile and robust than plastic, and some come with lids that make them airtight for storage.

■ If you use the microwave a lot, look for tempered glass bowls suitable for microwave use.

Peeler

There are two basic types of peeler for you to choose from. To decide which you prefer, check whether it feels comfortable in your hand and that you can get a good grip. Stainless-steel blades are best as they will not rust.

■ A fixed-blade vegetable peeler is

good for peeling most fruits and vegetables. If it has a sharp, pointed end,
it will double as a corer, and can also
be used for removing stems and hulls
from soft fruits, and digging out the
"eyes" in potatoes.

■ Swivel-bladed peelers are quick
to use once you get the hang of
them. They are good at sliding over
curved or knobby vegetables to
remove the skin.

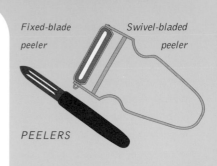

Fixed-blade peeler   *Swivel-bladed peeler*

PEELERS

Perforated spatula

Flat and wide, made from stainless
steel, a perforated spatula is used to
lift and turn delicate foods like fish
fillets and eggs, and for draining fat
and/or liquid through the perforations
or slots. It is also good for pressing
food flat when cooking—charbroiling
steaks, for example.

*PERFORATED
SPATULA*

Pestle and mortar

The heavier, larger, and deeper the
mortar is, the better, so you can use
force without spillage when crushing
and grinding. A pouring spout is useful for homemade mayonnaise, pesto,
and other sauces.

PESTLE AND MORTAR

■ Granite is the heaviest and best. Rock solid, it will not slip on the counter, and an unpolished bowl is perfect for getting a good grip.

■ Frosted glass is tough and heavy, surprisingly good for the job.

■ Unglazed ceramic or porcelain is less heavy than granite or glass, but it is the classic choice with its comfortable wooden handle, and it does the job well. Some have angled or elliptical mortars, others are conical, but there is nothing to beat the traditional round bowl—a bowl 8 inches in diameter is a good size.

Salt and pepper mills

So often chosen for their looks, but other features are more important.

■ Ceramic mechanisms last longer than metal because they do not rust or corrode when they get wet (if you grind salt or pepper into hot food the steam can damage the mechanism just as easily as water).

■ Electronic mills are excellent, although they can be noisy.

■ An adjustable grind, from fine to coarse, is a must.

■ To prolong the life of your mills, do not screw them too tightly at the top.

Scales

For precision when weighing small amounts, electronic digital scales are best, and they take up the least amount of storage space too. Buy the ones which convert from metric to imperial at the touch of a button, and that you can return to zero when weighing more than one ingredient in the bowl at the same time.

Scissors

Keep a pair for kitchen use only, so you know where they are when you need them. Apart from using them for opening packets, you can also use them for snipping herbs, shredding leafy greens, trimming beans and snow peas, and cutting bacon and pancetta into lardons.

Sieve/colander

Stainless steel is the most practical material for sieves and colanders, and is easy to clean. Choose a large sieve that has one or two hooks opposite the handle, so it will stay in position when you are using it over a bowl or pan. Colanders are freestanding with larger holes than sieves, and are useful for rinsing and draining vegetables and pasta, especially when you are cooking

pestle–spatulas

large quantities. If storage space is tight in your kitchen, a large sieve may be more versatile. A small sieve is handy for sifting small amounts of dry ingredients like confectioners' sugar, and for straining tea.

■ For rinsing, draining, and straining, a round bowl with a medium mesh is best, and can also be used for purée-ing if you do not have a blender or food processor.

■ A conical sieve (called a chinois, see Terms and Techniques, page 16) with fine mesh is good for straining or puréeing sauces into pitchers.

■ A fine mesh is best for sifting dry ingredients.

COLANDER

SIEVE

Spatulas

They may be made from wood, plastic, or rubber.

■ A wooden spatula does almost the same job as a wooden spoon, but is more effective at scraping around bowls and pans. As they are flat, spat-ulas can also be used to turn food.

■ Plastic and rubber spatulas are flexible, so they are good for folding in whipped cream and whisked egg whites, and are also indispensable for scraping pans and bowls clean. Rubber is more bendy than plastic, but there is little to choose between them.

Spoons

Apart from measuring spoons (page 64), there are three types of spoon that you will need repeatedly.

■ Wooden spoons are essential for stirring, mixing, beating, and creaming. For use on the stove, a long-handled spoon will protect hands from heat, while short-handled ones are best for beating and creaming. A useful wooden spoon is one with an angled edge, for scraping around the base of bowls and pans.

■ Wash and dry wooden spoons well, especially after using strong ingredients like onions and garlic, as wood retains smells and flavors.

■ A slotted spoon, sometimes called a perforated or draining spoon, is a metal spoon with holes—for lifting and draining food from liquid and fat, and for skimming. A wide, round, fairly flat one is best to lift large and/or heavy food from deep liquid. A curved, oval one with a pointed tip will lift food out of fat or liquid.

■ A large, stainless steel spoon with a slightly curved bowl and pointed tip is perfect to scoop, skim, and serve.

Timer

Get into the habit of using a timer, no matter what you are cooking and for how short a time. Digital timers can be set for the longest number of hours and minutes, and they are the most accurate. The type you can hang around your neck or clip onto your clothes is the most practical, and the longer and louder the ring, the better.

Tongs

These are the best implement for lifting and turning food without piercing so that no juices escape, and are especially useful when frying or broiling. The simpler the design, the better—don't bother with gimmicky extras like spring-action hinges as these are likely to break. Stainless steel is the most practical material.

Whisk

Although you can whisk with a fork, it takes ages and is very hard work, so it pays to buy at least one or two whisks as they are inexpensive. You will find both of the following useful:

■ A stainless steel balloon whisk with large, springy coils makes light work of whisking air into egg whites and cream, and is indispensable for beating lumps out of sauces and batters.

■ For making dressings and gravy and whisking small quantities, buy a flat coil whisk.

GOOD TO HAVE

Blowtorch

Gas-powered and simple to refill with gas lighter fluid, this is far better than the broiler for bruléeing the tops of custards and getting gratins a good golden brown—it gives a quick, even color without scorching and melting, and you can direct the flame to a specific area with great accuracy.

Carving board

You can use a cutting board for carving meat and poultry, but if you often cook roasts and like to carve them at the table, a carving board with prongs to steady the meat will give greater stability, and the channel running round the edge will catch the juices.

Cutters

Even if you don't make cookies very often, a set of round, stainless steel cutters will come in useful for other jobs when you want a professional finish. Use them to get a sharp edge on disks of pastry, potato, and bread, and to serve neat individual portions of vegetables and rice. The ones that are double-sided (plain and fluted) are the most useful.

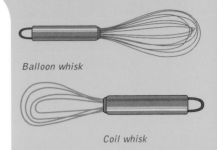

Balloon whisk

Coil whisk

WHISKS

Garlic crusher/press

For speed, and to avoid garlicky fingers, a well-designed garlic press is a good gadget to have. Make sure it has a detachable grill for easy cleaning. Another gadget that works well is a garlic peeler—a simple rubber tube in which you roll garlic cloves until the skins slip off. It makes light work of this awkward job.

Ice cream scoop

Serving hard ice cream can be difficult without a good scoop, which can be used to shape mash and vegetable purées as well. A stainless steel scoop with an angled or sculptured blade is a good choice as it will glide easily through the ice cream. A short rubber handle helps to get a good grip. If you dip the scoop in warm water between each portion, it will work better.

Mandoline

For very fine slicing and shredding, nothing beats the ultra-sharp blade of a mandoline. Traditionally used only by professional chefs, especially the Japanese, mandolines are now widely available in kitchenware stores and are not expensive. Choose from wood, stainless steel, or plastic frames—they all have very sharp blades that adjust for fine or coarse shredding (some even have rippled blades for fancy cutting). A mandoline with a "carriage" is a good buy. It will steady the food while you slice, and protect your fingers at the same time.

Meat bat

Made of either metal or wood, a meat bat is useful for pounding poultry and meat to tenderize and flatten—so that it cooks more quickly and evenly. Always protect food by covering it with plastic wrap or dampened waxed paper before pounding, or the food may tear. If you do not have a meat bat, pounding with a rolling pin or the base of a heavy pan makes a good substitute.

Pie weights

For baking pastry blind (page 10). Re-usable and heavy in weight, they do a good job of keeping the bases of pie shells flat. Dried peas or beans can be used instead, as can rice. Alternatively, line the dough with foil and insert a smaller pan inside the pan you are baking in—it will hold the pie shell in shape.

Potato masher

Of course you can mash potatoes and other root vegetables with a fork, but a potato masher makes the job easier.

■ The classic design with round perforations, a sturdy handle and a good rubber grip is best—though modern mashers look more stylish, and most perform well.

■ An alternative is a potato ricer, a perforated metal drum with a metal disk attached that forces the potato through (the same principle as a garlic press only larger). Although more expensive than conventional mashers, potato ricers are exceptionally effective and will give you light and fluffy, lump-free mash every time.

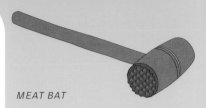

MEAT BAT

Rolling pin

For rolling out pastry dough, and pounding poultry and meat. Choose a straight wooden pin that is smooth and heavy, without handles.

■ A large empty jelly or pickle jar can be used as a substitute.

Salad spinner

After washing salad greens, the best way to shake off the water is in a salad spinner. When you turn the handle on the lid, the basket of leaves

KITCHEN KIT:PREP TOOLS

spins inside the drum so that they dry without bruising. Choose a sturdy one (they are all made of plastic) with a well-fitting lid.

Skewers

Use these not only for kabobs and brochettes, but also for piercing food to see if it is cooked.

■ Flat metal skewers are best used for cooking meat and vegetables. They are good conductors of heat, and the food will not swivel when you turn the skewers around under the broiler or on the barbecue.

■ Bamboo skewers look good and can also be used for cooking meat and vegetables, but you need to soak them in cold water for at least 30 minutes before use or they will char.

Zester

A nifty cutting tool with a row of tiny holes, for removing the zest (the outer colored part of the rind) from citrus fruit in long, thin strips. A canelle knife does the same job, but its V-shaped blade removes the zest in one wide strip. (See also Terms and Techniques, page 51.)

KNIFE BOX

Knives are a major investment, so choose carefully and build up your collection according to your needs. Good-quality knives will last for years if you look after them properly. Keep them on a magnetic strip or in a block, and wash them by hand rather than in the dishwasher. A steel is the professional choice for sharpening, but if you find it awkward to use, you may prefer to use a sharpener. Good makes of knives generally have a sharpener in their range. Remember that a sharp knife is much safer than a blunt one that can slip easily.

Apart from a serrated bread knife and a carving knife for roasts, a good basic "starter set" of three knives will be adequate for most jobs.

■ A large chef's knife with a 7–8 inch blade is a good all-rounder for chopping and slicing, and it can also double as a carving knife.

■ For peeling fruits and vegetables a small paring knife with a 3–4 inch blade is best.

■ A small serrated knife is useful for all sorts of jobs, like cutting soft tomatoes and slicing cheese.

Pantry Staples

PANTRY STAPLES

AS YOU BUILD UP THE CONTENTS OF YOUR PANTRY IT WILL BECOME A SOURCE OF TASTY, QUICK SUPPERS, EXCITING FLAVOR BOOSTERS, RELIABLE STAPLES, AND HEALTHY SNACKS. BUY IN BULK ONLY IF YOU HAVE ROOM AND KNOW YOU WILL USE THE ITEM. BUYING IN SMALLER AMOUNTS WILL MAKE SURE THAT NOTHING WILL BE WASTED. KEEP SMALLER, MORE FREQUENTLY USED ITEMS AT THE FRONT OF THE PANTRY SO YOU DON'T FORGET WHAT YOU HAVE IN STOCK.

Anchovy

Slim little fillets of fish which can be chopped, mashed, or left whole to add a sophisticated burst of flavor to your food. They will keep for ages in your pantry.

CHOOSE Available packed in oil in cans or jars, or packed in salt, which gives a great flavor. Anchovies in jars are very tightly packed—use a little gentle persuasion to lure them out carefully so they don't get broken. The most foolproof way is to tip them straight into a sieve, then, if you want to wash the salt off, you can rinse them straight under the faucet.

COOK Anchovies don't need cooking—they are ready to eat straight from the jar or can. You might need to use only a couple of anchovies to give the salty bite you require, so after opening, tip the rest into a plastic container. They will keep for up to a week in the refrigerator.

USE FOR

- Livening up a take-out pizza.
- Snipping a few with scissors and sprinkling over a salad (especially one with crisp greens and Parmesan cheese, such as Caesar), or stirring into a pasta sauce (they break down and flavor the sauce as they cook).
- Mash one or two with some butter and let it melt over broiled or pan-fried lamb or fish.
- Creating a no-cook appetizer—arrange in a casual cluster on a platter, drizzle with oil, sprinkle with chopped parsley, and surround with broiled vegetables and olives.

Beans

Collectively known as legumes, beans are a great and cheap way to increase your protein, especially if you are a vegetarian. There are many types with both subtle and striking differences in looks, texture, and taste, but basically they all add a certain "meaty" texture

anchovy–beans

to a dish. Dried beans will keep for up to a year in an airtight container, although once they get too hard they won't cook so well.

CHOOSE AND USE Canned beans are easy and convenient, while dried ones give you more choice and tend to have more taste and texture. It really depends how organized you are, as dried need soaking before they can be cooked. As there are so many types to choose from, it's good to experiment to find your favorites.

Borlotti: Recognizable by their attractive, pinky-red freckles.
■ Mix with rice and pasta or use in stews and soups.

Cannellini: Pale cream in color, oval in shape.
■ Use in similar ways to navy.

Flageolet: Looks like a slimmed-down, pale green version of the red kidney bean. Keeps its shape well while cooking.
■ A pretty addition to salads (canned are handy for this), flageolets are also good with lamb and in stews. They can be used instead of navy beans.

Garbanzo bean: A little, knobby, round bean with a chunky texture; looks a bit like a skinned hazelnut.
■ Adds a sturdy crunch to salads, or toss with oil, lemon juice, parsley, and finely chopped garlic as a simple side

PANTRY STAPLES STARTER KIT

Ten top ingredients you'll find it hard to do without:
■ Bouillon
■ Flour
■ Mustard
■ Olive oil
■ Pasta
■ Rice
■ Soy sauce
■ Sugar or honey
■ Tomatoes (canned)
■ Vinegar

salad. Blend to a purée for hummus, or as a great alternative to mashed potato by mixing with a little oil and garlic to serve with fish or chicken. Garbanzo beans are often used in Moroccan dishes and are a great meat substitute in Indian vegetarian curries.

Lima bean: This flat, creamy colored bean is softer in texture than most, so purées easily, but can break down if overcooked.

■ Purée in soups, or add to stews and salads.

Navy: In its naked form this is a white bean, and is the one used for canned baked beans.

■ Good in slow-cooked stews, soups, and casseroles such as cassoulet or Boston baked beans, as it is quite sturdy and keeps its shape well.

Red kidney bean: The most colorful edible bean, kidney-shaped.

■ Integral to chili con carne, red kidney beans are used a lot in Mexican cooking where they are mashed to a paste for refried beans. They also add a splash of color and texture to salads, especially when combined with rice, corn, or paler-colored beans.

COOK

Canned: Drain and rinse them first. For salads they are then ready to eat, or heat them up in the dish you are cooking so they take on the flavor.

Dried: To be safe and to remove their (natural) toxins, soak the beans first in plenty of cold water for at least 12 hours, or overnight if that's more convenient. Beans expand a lot in liquid so make sure the bowl is big enough to allow them room to increase by at least double. Before cooking, it's worth noting that there are a couple of things that can toughen the skins of dried beans—prolonged boiling, or adding too much salt early on (that includes salty ingredients like soy sauce and bouillon, as well as any acidic ingredients such as tomatoes, lemon juice, vinegar). To cook, drain and rinse the soaked beans, then tip them into a large pan. Cover with about 2 inches of cold water, bring to a boil, scoop off any foam, then boil hard for 10 minutes. Skim off any more foam and add a pinch of salt. Half cover with the pan lid, turn the heat down and simmer gently for the suggested time, skimming and adding more water if needed. Cooking times for dried beans vary, so check the packet instructions—it's usually about 1–1½ hours. Drain when done.

Bouillon

This is stock in an easily accessible, concentrated form that has a long shelf life.

beans–caper

CHOOSE Available as either a paste, a powder, or as a compact cube. Bouillon powder has a subtle herby taste. The rule of thumb is always to buy the best quality you can, such as organic and low-salt, as a good stock should be something you can enjoy drinking on its own if it's going to do its job properly.

COOK Dissolve in the required amount of boiling water, then use as your recipe suggests.

USE FOR
■ Giving an instant flavor base for soups, risottos, stews, gravies.
■ Sprinkling or crumbling into ground dishes like bolognese sauce or shepherd's pie, to enhance the taste.

Caper

If you like the sharp taste of things pickled in vinegar, these little green flower buds are a culinary treasure.

CHOOSE You can buy really petite capers called *nonpareille* that are about the size of a peppercorn. More commonly available are the slightly larger ones. Capers come in jars, either pickled in vinegar or preserved in salt. The salted ones need rinsing first. If they are still too salty for your

PANTRY STAPLES VEGGIE SNACK
Serves 2–3; ready in 10 minutes

For a quick hummus, tip a rinsed and drained 14-ounce can garbanzo beans into a food processor or blender, add ½ teaspoon crushed garlic (from a jar or fresh), a few pinches of ground cumin, 2–3 teaspoons lemon juice (bottled or fresh), 2 tablespoons olive oil, and whizz all ingredients together. Whizz in enough water (a few tablespoons) to make it as soft as you prefer, and season with salt. Serve with a drizzle of oil and a sprinkling of ground cumin or paprika, pita bread, and raw vegetables for dipping into the hummus.
■ Optional extras: Add 1 tablespoon tahini (or enough to taste), and a handful of finely chopped parsley.

QUICK-SOAK BEANS
If short of time when soaking dried beans, speed things up by tipping them into a bowl and pouring in enough boiling water to cover them by 2 inches. Cover and leave until doubled in size, about 1½ hours. Drain, rinse, and continue to cook as described opposite. NB This does not apply to red kidney beans.

taste, rinse again and soak in water for a while. For real caper flamboyance, try caperberries. They are the seed pods of the caper plant and are bigger and bolder than the bud. They are handsome, have an elegant stem, and a milder and slightly sweeter taste.

USE FOR

■ Sprinkling over meat and fish dishes —they go well with tuna and anchovy. They also look pretty, so can be a garnish as well as supplying a flavor hit.
■ Adding to sauces or vegetables to give a lively tang.
■ Italian and Spanish dishes, such as *spaghetti puttanesca* made with capers, anchovies, tomatoes, and olives, as well as in provencal *tapenade*.

USE INSTEAD Dill pickles.

Chili (dried)
see SPICES, *page 169*

Chocolate

Made from cocoa beans found in the big pods that hang from the cacao tree. The beans are roasted, then ground to extract the chocolate liquor. This liquor contains cocoa butter, and the more of this a chocolate has, the more expensive and better it will be.

CHOOSE Check out the wrapping to find the information you need. Cooking chocolate shouldn't have too much sugar added, as it is the taste you are after, not sweetness. But the most important thing to look for is the amount of cocoa solids. You could say the more, the merrier, as cocoa solids are what give the chocolate its delicious flavor and richness, but if you go very high, over 70%, you may find the taste too bitter; 50% is middle of the road, whereas 60–70% is a good-quality all-rounder. Taste it and see which percentage suits you— if you like the way it tastes fresh out of its wrapper, you'll like the way it tastes when cooked. Chocolate keeps well as long as it's dry, so a cool place is better than the refrigerator. Moisture can give it a white, frosty-looking film on its surface. If the chocolate feels gritty in the mouth, it's past its best.

Bittersweet: Great for cooking. It will give the richest flavor, as it has more cocoa solids and less sugar.
Milk: Sweeter than bittersweet, with less cocoa solids (about 30–40%) and some milk, so it is lighter both in flavor and color. It isn't so good to cook with as it doesn't withstand high temperatures as well as bittersweet.
White: Not technically chocolate at

caper–chocolate

all as it has no cocoa solids, but is made up of cocoa butter, milk solids, vanilla, and a lot of sugar, so it tastes less chocolaty than bittersweet chocolate. A good-quality white chocolate has lots of cocoa butter and a good vanilla taste. White is trickier to melt as it can easily seize (see right).

TO MELT

On the stove: Pour 1–2 inches water into a small pan. Rest a heatproof bowl over the pan, one that will sit above the water rather than in it. (Chocolate doesn't get along well with water if it comes in direct contact.) Break the chocolate into pieces and put into the bowl, turn the heat to medium so the water just simmers gently, and let it sit and melt in the warmth from the water. When the chocolate feels soft, give it a stir and take off the heat when melted.

In the microwave: Break the chocolate into a nonmetallic bowl. Microwave, uncovered, in spurts of 30 seconds on defrost, stirring between each—timing depends on how much chocolate you are melting. Chocolate melted in the microwave keeps its shape, so you need to stir to check if it's done or not.

USE FOR (apart from in desserts and baking):

FIX IT: CHOCOLATE

Overheating or letting any moisture get into the chocolate can cause it to "seize"—which means it tightens and thickens. To rescue it, try stirring in a teaspoon or two of vegetable cooking oil—if that works the chocolate can be used in a sauce. If it's too far gone or if it gets really overheated and burns, the best thing is to throw it away and start again. (See also page 42.)

■ Dropping a square or two into Mexican meat recipes such as chilies and stews. You don't taste the chocolate, but it adds an exotic richness.

■ A mug of hot chocolate for a cosy bedtime drink: melt grated bittersweet chocolate, then whisk in hot milk and sugar to taste.

■ Making a fondue for dipping fruit— melt a 7-ounce bar of bittersweet or milk chocolate, take off the heat, and stir in about 6 tablespoons milk.

Chutney

A spicy Indian relish with a sweet-savory kick, its name comes from the Indian word *chatni*. Since it is made with a base of sugar and vinegar, both of which are preservatives, chutney has a long shelf life, lasting up to 2 years in the pantry, or, once opened,several months in the refrigerator. Chutney comes in many flavors, such as mango, apple, and tomato.

USE FOR It's handy to have a jar to accompany an Indian curry or make a cheese snack, but it has other uses.

■ An instant creamy dressing for a cold chicken salad: stir a little tropical fruit chutney into mayonnaise with a dash of curry powder, then thin with milk until it's the thickness you like.

■ Adding a spoonful to flavor a sauce for pan-fried chicken and pork: deglaze the pan with some stock or water (or wine if you have a bottle open), then stir in some heavy cream and a spoonful of chutney. Or omit the cream and flavor with tomato chutney for fish, chops, and steaks.

Coconut milk, cream

Indispensable for Thai, Indonesian, and Indian food. Coconut milk is not the thin liquid found in a fresh coconut, but the liquid pressed from the snowy white coconut flesh. By soaking grated coconut flesh in boiling water, then squeezing out the liquid, a thick milk is produced from the first squeezing, a thinner one from the second, and the cream is what rises to the top of the milk when it is cold. So having it readily available in a can saves an awful lot of work.

CHOOSE Coconut milk is available in cans and the thicker cream can be bought in small cartons. There is also a reduced-fat version of the milk. The cream keeps for up to a year and the milk for 2 years. Once opened, both will keep in the refrigerator for up to 1–2 days.

COOK Coconut milk and cream are ready to use straight from their containers. Give coconut milk a good stir before using.

USE FOR

■ As well as for enriching and flavoring Indian and Thai curries and soups (lovely with fish), it can be used instead of milk and cream for homemade ice cream.
■ Giving custard a change of flavor by using coconut milk instead of milk.
■ Try substituting coconut milk for ordinary milk in rice pudding.
■ Pouring coconut cream over a tropical fruit salad.
■ Mixing coconut milk, yogurt, and chopped fresh mango to make a mango smoothie.

USE INSTEAD Heavy cream will give you the creaminess, but not the unique flavor.

Corn

see also VEGETABLES, page 280
Available in cans as kernels of corn, or creamed corn, which adds a creaminess as well as texture to soups. Mix with other vegetables and rice in salads and use in Mexican cooking. Use the kernels to make corn fritters.

PANTRY STAPLES THAI SUPPER
Serves 2 generously; ready in 20–25 minutes

The only fresh thing you need to buy is chicken; everything else can come from your pantry.

Heat 1 tablespoon vegetable oil in a wok or large pan. Drop in 1 rounded tablespoon Thai chili paste (red or green), 3 freeze-dried lime leaves, and a pinch of crushed, dried chilies and fry for 1 minute. Tip in a 1¾-cup can coconut milk, ⅓ can water (measured in the coconut milk can), 1 tablespoon Thai fish sauce, and 1 teaspoon sugar and bring to a simmer. Add 10–12 ounces skinless, boneless chicken breast portions (cut into bite-size chunks) and an 8-ounce can bamboo shoots, drained. Simmer for 10 minutes until the chicken is cooked. Serve with Thai rice or noodles.
■ *Optional extras: Add a handful of frozen peas just before the chicken is cooked, or some torn fresh cilantro at the end.*

Cornmeal

see POLENTA, *page 108*

Cornstarch

This is a fine, white, powdery starch made from corn. Unlike flour made from wheat it contains no gluten (protein). Rub it between your fingers and see how silky and fine it feels—this is the smooth texture it will give to your cooking, and it is less likely to create lumps when used to thicken certain sauces, unlike flour.

COOK Cornstarch needs to be mixed to a paste with a liquid first. When using it to thicken a sauce, gravy, or stew that is too runny, mix 1 teaspoon cornstarch with 1 teaspoon water, stir it into the sauce gradually, off the heat, then put it back on, and keep stirring until the sauce thickens. Keep doing this until you get the thickness you want. Once the sauce has thickened take it off the heat quite quickly—if you cook cornstarch for too long it can break down and go thin again.

USE FOR

■ Thickening sauces, both sweet and savory, such as custards and gravies; also stir-fries, soups, and stews.

■ Baking: when mixed with flour it gives an extra-light texture to cookies such as shortbread.

■ Whisking into a meringue mixture for a gooey inside: use ½ teaspoon cornstarch to each egg white.

USE INSTEAD All-purpose flour, but cornstarch blends in more easily and the mixture turns slightly clearer when cooked, so it is better than flour for sweet sauces, such as the one used as a base for lemon meringue pie.

Corn syrup

It's the cheapest syrup to buy and keeps for ages—up to a year. It is available in both light and dark forms, the latter having a stronger flavor.

COOK The advantage of corn syrup is that it doesn't crystallize and go grainy when heated. The disadvantage is that it is difficult to measure out because it is so sticky—brush your measuring spoon with a little oil first and the syrup will just glide off.

USE FOR

■ Making cakes and cookies—it helps make flapjacks and gingerbread sticky and deliciously moist.

■ Pouring over waffles, pancakes, or porridge.

cornmeal–couscous

■ Giving a shiny gloss to a simple homemade chocolate sauce by stirring in a spoonful as the chocolate melts.

USE INSTEAD Maple syrup, although it's more expensive, thinner, and has a more distinctive flavor.

Couscous

This tiny yellow grain is actually a type of pasta usually made from semolina and used in North African dishes. It becomes light and fluffy after a quick soak and, since it has hardly any flavor of its own, it loves being mixed with other tasty ingredients.

CHOOSE You can add your own flavorings to plain couscous, or buy the more expensive pre-flavored couscous.

COOK Couscous traditionally had to be slowly steamed; now it is available precooked and, after soaking, is ready to eat in minutes. Tip the couscous into a large bowl and pour in boiling water or stock (see right for quantities). Stir, cover with plastic wrap, and let it stand for 5 minutes. Once all the liquid is absorbed, use a fork to break and lighten up the couscous. Enrich and moisten with a drizzle of olive oil or a pat of butter, if you like.

FIX IT: CORNSTARCH
If you end up with a lumpy sauce, give it a vigorous whisk with a wire whisk until you've got it back to a smooth texture. If that doesn't work, push the sauce through a fine sieve.

PANTRY STAPLES
PUDDING SAUCE
For a quick butterscotch sauce, drop a couple of spoonfuls of corn syrup into a pan with the same amount of light or dark Barbados sugar and butter. Heat through gently, stirring until everything blends and goes saucy, then pour swiftly over ice cream, sliced bananas, pancakes, or sticky toffee pudding.

HOW MUCH COUSCOUS?
FOR 2: ⅔ cup couscous to ⅔ cup liquid
FOR 4: 1½ cups couscous to 1¼ cups liquid
FOR 6: 2 cups couscous to 2¼ cups liquid

USE FOR

■ Bulking out salads.

■ Tossing with different flavorings such as toasted pine nuts, raisins, lemon zest, olives, and parsley and serving with lamb, chicken, or fish.

■ A base for stuffing instead of rice or bread.

■ An accompaniment in place of rice, pasta, or mashed potatoes.

USE INSTEAD Rice or a small shaped pasta.

Curry paste

When you find one that you are happy with, whether it is based on Indian or Thai spices, you will see that these ready mixed pastes really cut corners when it comes to adding authentic flavor to a speedily made curry.

CHOOSE There are so many to choose from that experimentation is the best way to find those that suit your taste buds.

Indian: On a heat scale, these include:

■ MILD: Biriyani, Jalfrezi, Korma, Tikka Masala.

■ MEDIUM: Balti, Rogan Josh, Dhansak.

■ HOT: Madras, Vindaloo.

Thai: Green and red curry paste—both are a fragrant blend of chilies, herbs, and spices such as cilantro, lemongrass, lime leaves, garlic, galangal, cumin, and coriander, the difference being that green is made with a pounded base of green chilies, red with red chilies. Both can be used interchangeably.

COOK AND USE Curry pastes are usually fried off first when making curries, to bring out all their intricate flavors. When not cooking with Indian curry pastes (if adding a spoonful to flavor a dressing or mayonnaise, for example), you still need to heat them through briefly rather than using them straight from the jar.

Dried fruit

As a group these are a healthy alternative to many other snacks since they contain no fat or cholesterol and are very low in sodium (salt)—and a handful can be counted as one of the "five a day" fruit and vegetables (see page 326). If well wrapped, they will keep for up to a year.

CHOOSE Go for the plumpest-looking fruit with a good, even color. Apricot: the plump and moist ready-to-eat soft, dried apricots can be used straight away. They go well with chicken, beef, and lamb dishes.

couscous–dried fruit

Cherries and berries: A summery mix of sharp and sweet blueberries, cranberries, cherries, and raisins. Or buy them individually. Check on the packaging that they aren't coated in sugar.

Currant: Not a dried currant, but a type of small dried grape.

Date: Medjool dates are a prize variety—deliciously sweet, sticky, and succulent. Hand them around at the end of a meal with cups of espresso.

Fig: Dried figs are a lot sweeter than fresh. Some get quite flattened after drying, so if you are after plumpness look for the ready-to-eat soft ones.

Golden raisin: These are golden or dark in color, depending on the variety of grape they are dried from.

Prune: A dried plum, containing fiber, iron, and potassium. *Mi-cuit* prunes are semi-dried, so have a lovely soft, creamy texture, Agen prunes are also very succulent.

Raisin: This is a dried, usually seedless grape.

Tropical fruits: Often available in bags of mixed fruits such as mango, papaya, pineapple, and melon. Mango is a good source of vitamin E and carotene.

COOK All dried fruits can be used straight away, but to add flavor and extra juiciness to recipes like fruit

PANTRY STAPLES
MOROCCAN SALAD
Serves 4; ready in 10 minutes

Soak 1½ cups couscous (see page 83). Tip in a rinsed and drained 14-ounce can garbanzo beans, a couple of handfuls each of toasted whole almonds, raisins, and chopped apricots, and a handful of pistachio nuts (or toasted pine nuts). Combine 2 rounded teaspoons harissa (see page 89) with 4–5 tablespoons olive oil, a pinch of dried mint, and seasoning to taste and toss everything together. Pile into bowls and drizzle with extra olive oil. Serve as is, or with grilled or roast chicken breast portions.

PANTRY STAPLES
DRIED FRUIT APPETIZER
Figs and prosciutto make good partners. Slit ready-to-eat dried figs and stuff with a thin slice of goat cheese, wrap the prosciutto around, and serve on a bed of salad greens drizzled with an herb dressing.

cakes and tea breads, you can plump
the fruit up first by soaking in tea,
wine, fruit juice, rum, or brandy,
depending on the recipe.

USE FOR

■ Nibbling.

■ Mixing into baking recipes.

■ Adding a natural sweetness to
savory stews, or salads.

■ Apricots, dates, figs, and prunes are
good with Moroccan spicings and, in
addition, help to bulk out and thicken
stews.

■ A quick appetizer (see page 85).

■ Chop prunes into couscous with
toasted pine nuts and mint.

■ Soaking in rum to liven up a winter
fruit salad. Figs also go well in fruit
compôtes.

■ Mixing into stuffings or rice salads
—cranberries, apricots, and raisins
go particularly well with pine nuts.

■ Slit Medjool dates and stuff with a
soft cream cheese for a party snack.

USE INSTEAD If you can't find the
fruit you are looking for, follow this
list of substitutes:

APRICOT: peach

CRANBERRY: raisin, cherry

CURRANT: snipped raisin

DATE: fig or raisin

FIG: prune, apricot, date, or raisin

MANGO: papaya

Fish sauce

Used throughout Southeast Asia
as we might use salt, particularly in
Thailand (where it is known as *nam
pla*) and Vietnam (where it is known
as *nuoc cham*). It is made from salted,
fermented dried fish (usually shrimp
or anchovy). Once you have acquired a
taste for it, you'll want to spoon it
into all sorts of things.

CHOOSE A little goes a long way,
so, as you need only a splash to have
an effect, the small bottles are very
handy. The lighter-colored sauce
usually indicates a finer, more refreshing, salty flavor than the darker one.
If you notice the color dramatically
darkening once the bottle has been
opened it means it's getting rather
old, so it is best to discard it.

USE FOR

■ Capitalize on its very fishy, salty
taste to perk up stir-fries, noodle
dishes, and salad dressings.

■ A dipping sauce sprinkled with a few
chopped chilies and a little sugar to
give a sweet/sour taste—goes with
fish cakes, or cold chicken or beef.

■ Leave the bottle on the table and
use sparingly as a seasoning.

USE INSTEAD No substitute.

Flour

Wheat flours are made from two types of wheat, "hard" and "soft." Hard wheat contains a lot of gluten (a mixture of proteins) which becomes elastic, so the flour produced from this makes good bread and pasta, as it creates a dough that will stretch and rise. Flour from soft wheat has less gluten, so it is better for making cakes, cookies, and sauces. The three basic types of flour are brown, white, and whole-wheat (see right). White flour keeps for up to 9 months, whole-wheat or brown for about 3 months. Don't mix old flour with new—it will just go off more quickly.

CHOOSE AND USE (see top right)
All-purpose: A mix of hard and soft flours with no rising agent added. It has only a small amount of gluten, so it is no good for breadmaking.
■ Use in pastry, sauces and gravies, and cookies, or as a coating.

Self-rising: All-purpose flour with a rising agent added.
■ Use in cakes, cookies, teabreads, and sponge puddings.
USE INSTEAD All-purpose flour with baking powder added—2 teaspoons baking powder to 2 cups flour.

BASIC FLOUR TYPES
WHITE: About 75% of the wheatgerm is left.
BROWN: Some of the bran and wheatgerm have been removed, about 85% of the original grain is left. It is a little lighter than whole-wheat flour.
WHOLE-WHEAT: 100% of the wheat grain is used to make this flour—nothing is added, nothing taken away.

LABELS ON FLOUR: WHAT THEY MEAN
MULTIGRAIN: A malted wheat grain flour with wheat grains added.
ORGANIC: Flour that has been milled by registered growers and millers, from grain grown to organic standards.
STONEGROUND: Whole-wheat flour that has been traditionally ground between two stones.
WHEATGERM: White or brown flour, with about 10% wheatgerm added.

GLUTEN-FREE
For a gluten-free flour, use buckwheat, gram, or rice flour.

Spelt: Made from a very nutritious variety that has more protein, fat, and fiber than wheat. Nothing else is added to make spelt flour.
■ Good for pizzas, cakes, and bread.

Strong: Available in white, brown, and whole-wheat, this is made from hard wheat. Whole-wheat used on its own gives a heavy texture, but can be easily lightened by mixing it half and half with strong white bread flour.
■ Suitable for bread (use in bread-making machines), pizza dough, Yorkshire puddings, puff pastry.

Italian "00" and "0" flour:

"00" is most common, "0" is more likely to be found in an Italian deli. "00" is milled finer and has less bran.
■ Use for pasta, pastry, Italian cakes, pizza dough, and other breads.

Garbanzo bean

see BEANS, *page 75*

Ginger (in syrup)

Tender round nuggets of fresh ginger root that have been simmered in syrup and preserved in jars. The syrup takes on a gingery flavor, the ginger takes on sweetness from the syrup, so everything can be used. Lasts for ages.

USE FOR
■ **Ginger:** Chopping into cookie and cake mixes, or chopping and sprinkling over cake frostings as a flavorful decoration (goes well with lemon, orange, and chocolate).
■ **Syrup:** Soaking a sponge cake to flavor and moisten, then serving with fresh fruit and whipped cream. Stir a spoonful or two into a crushed cookie base for creamy desserts such as cheesecake.
■ **Both:** Spooning over ice cream and adding to fresh fruit salads, especially ones made from exotic or tropical fruits. Cooking with poached rhubarb or pears.

USE INSTEAD Candied ginger (no syrup, though). It is available in boxes and jars.

Ginger (pickled)

A Japanese accompaniment of wafer-thin slivers of fresh ginger root that are pickled in vinegar, sugar, and salt.

CHOOSE Available in a delicate shade of pink (dyed with food coloring) or in a natural pale golden color.

USE FOR
■ Accompanying sushi or anything else you care to try it with.

- Serving with broiled or pan-fried fish (especially salmon and tuna), or chicken.
- Chopping into salads with bean sprouts and cold beef or cooked shrimp.
- Tossing into noodle stir-fries, or piling on top as a garnish.
- Sprinkling between slices of smoked salmon on a bed of arugula as a quick and easy appetizer.

Harissa

A fiery red paste with a fiery red flavor to match. Its hot base is due to chilies which have been pounded to a paste, then enlivened further with ingredients such as coriander, caraway, cayenne, garlic, cumin, and salt, plus beet and carrot. It is spicy, fragrant and hot all at once—if you have a jar of this, your food will never taste dull again. It crops up a lot in Moroccan, Tunisian, and other North African recipes.

CHOOSE It is available in jars, cans, or tubes as a paste (you also might find it as a powder which just needs oil and garlic added). Once opened, it will keep in the refrigerator for about 5–6 weeks. Make sure that the surface of the harissa is covered with oil to prevent it from drying out.

USE FOR There's no end to the possibilities, but don't go mad with it

RICH PIE CRUST PASTRY

Makes about 11 ounces dough, enough to line a 9–10 inch quiche pan; takes 10–15 minutes

BY HAND
Tip scant 1½ cups all-purpose flour into a large bowl and stir in pinch salt. Rub in ¾ stick butter (see page 40), until the mixture is evenly colored and resembles fine bread-crumbs. Lightly beat 1 medium egg in a bowl. Make a well in the center of the flour mixture and add the beaten egg, a little at a time, mixing it into the flour mixture with a round-bladed knife. Add the egg gradually until sufficient has been added that the dough begins to hold together. Gather the dough into a smooth ball with your hands. Do not overwork or you will toughen it, and use according to your recipe.

IN THE FOOD PROCESSOR
Put the flour, salt, butter, egg, and 1 teaspoon of water into the processor. Process just until the mixture combines together, adding a little more water if necessary. Gather into a smooth ball as above.

PANTRY STAPLES

unless you know how hot you like it.

■ Stirring a teaspoonful into a tomato-based pasta sauce, or livening up a soup, stir-fry, or couscous.

■ Diluting with olive oil, and drizzling over summer veg, new potatoes, chicken, or fish before roasting.

■ Spreading neat onto chicken or fish before grilling or roasting, or adding to a marinade before cooking.

■ Putting a small spoonful on the side of your plate as an ultra-spicy version of tomato ketchup.

■ Brightening up a dip—just swirl a little into mayonnaise, crème fraîche, yogurt, or sour cream and serve with potato wedges or raw veggies.

USE INSTEAD Chili paste, although flavorings and spices vary.

Herbs
see pages 128–160

Hoisin sauce

Some find this reddish-brown sauce rather overpowering, while others couldn't eat Peking duck without it. Made from soybeans, spices, vinegar, sugar, and garlic, it can't be beaten if you want to add an authentic sweet and spicy Chinese flavor.

CHOOSE Sold in bottles, it is cheaper to buy from Chinese supermarkets. Keep in the refrigerator once open.

USE FOR

■ A dipping sauce straight from the bottle with Chinese food, in particular Peking duck and spring rolls.

■ Spooning into marinades, stir-fries, vegetable dishes (especially good with broccoli).

■ The perfect Asian barbecue sauce.

Honey

Honey is a natural sweetener and can give a unique flavor to both sweet and savory dishes.

CHOOSE You can buy it pourable and runny, so thick you have scrape it out of the jar, or as a honeycomb which you have to work at a little to retrieve the delicious sweet liquid. There are also many different flavors. Taste and color are determined by which flowers the bees have visited when collecting the nectar. If the honey is pale in color, the chances are it will be more delicate in flavor, like acacia. For a more robust taste, go for a darker honey such as Greek or Scottish heather. Other flavors to try include eucalyptus from Australia and orange blossom from Spain and Mexico.

USE FOR

■ Drizzling over a bowl of thick yogurt for a super-quick dessert (the Greek way), or over scoops of ice cream.

■ Mixing into marinades.

■ Adding a little sweetness and flavor to salad dressings, desserts, and baked dishes.

■ Spooning into Moroccan savory dishes, especially tagines.

■ Squirting into your favorite fruit smoothie.

■ A quick lunch or appetizer—toast slices of French bread, top with slices of goat cheese and a drizzle of honey. Broil until melting and caramelized and serve on a bed of dressed salad greens.

USE INSTEAD Sugar, depending on the recipe. Honey is sweeter and also stronger, so, if you are experimenting, try replacing half the quantity of sugar with honey.

Kidney bean
see BEANS, *page 76*

Lentils

Like beans, lentils are an excellent vegetarian food and a good substitute for meat as they contain lots of protein and fiber.

FIX IT: HONEY

Clear honey can go cloudy after a while. To restore its clarity, stand the jar in a bowl of very hot water.

CHOOSE You can buy green lentils in cans; the rest are mostly sold dried. If you want lentils that break down more as they cook, or some to purée, choose red lentils. If you want lentils that keep their shape and bite, go for the speckled French Puy lentils—check the packet to insure you are buying the authentic ones, which are grown in the Puy region of France. Lentils keep for a good year, and are less likely to deteriorate after opening if you transfer them to an airtight container.

COOK Unlike beans, lentils don't need soaking before cooking. Simmer red lentils for about 20 minutes; after that they can turn quite mushy. Simmer Puy lentils for about 25 minutes, green ones for about 40–45 minutes. Don't add salt during cooking.

USE FOR

Green: Adding to soups and stews, salads and vegetarian versions of lasagne and moussaka instead of meat.
Puy: Serving as a vegetable in their own right, flavored with a little onion, carrot, and herbs (good with fish). When simmered with red wine they go really well with any meat, especially game. Also good in salads.
Red: Thickening wintry soups and stews; in Indian cooking, especially vegetarian dishes (used to make dhal).

Maple syrup

A classic Canadian sweetener with a distinctive taste, made by collecting sap from the maple tree which is then boiled and reduced down. It is thinner than corn syrup, so pours easily. Keep in the refrigerator after opening.

CHOOSE The genuine syrup is the most expensive and will say "pure" maple syrup on the label. "Flavored" maple syrup is a cheaper imitation.

USE FOR

■ Pouring over pancakes or waffles.
■ Sweetening North American cake batters such as muffins and tray bakes, also pumpkin pie.
■ Adding a lovely flavor and shine when glazing vegetables (good with carrots and squash) and for pork, especially spareribs.
■ Deglazing a pan, particularly when cooking pork. Pour in 1 tablespoon each maple syrup and balsamic vinegar with some stock for a rich gravy.
■ Pouring over hot cakes and bacon, for breakfast, or over porridge with a handful of blueberries sprinkled on the top.
■ Marinades (see opposite).

USE INSTEAD Runny honey, although the flavor is quite different.

Mayonnaise

CHOOSE Available in a jar or a handy, squeezable container. Apart from the classic plain mayonnaise, you can get a variety of flavors, such as mustard, lemon, and garlic, as well as a reduced-calorie (light) version. Mayonnaise will keep fresh for a year unopened. Once it's opened you need to put it in the refrigerator, then use it within a couple of months.

USE FOR

■ Serving as a sauce on its own with salads or fish (for an instant tartar sauce chop up and stir in a few capers and dill pickles, or add some crushed garlic for the French dip aioli).

■ A dressing for tossing over boiled new potatoes—flavor with a little horseradish sauce and some chopped chives, and thin with milk.

■ Making a dip by stirring in one of your favorite flavorings, such as pesto, mustard, or harissa, to serve with raw vegetables or tortilla chips.

Mirin

Not to be confused with sake, the Japanese rice wine, mirin is a sweet, spirit-based rice liquid designed specifically for use in Japanese cooking, never for drinking.

PANTRY STAPLES
MAPLE SYRUP
MARINADE FOR CHICKEN
Serves 2; ready in 45 minutes

Combine 2 tablespoons maple syrup, 1 tablespoon soy sauce, and 2 teaspoons sesame oil, 2 crushed garlic cloves, ½ teaspoon ground ginger, and a generous grinding of black pepper in a shallow ovenproof dish. Add 2 chicken breast portions, turn to coat in the marinade, and leave for 5–10 minutes. Roast at 375°F (340°F in fan ovens) for about 30 minutes or until the chicken is cooked, basting halfway through. Serve with rice and the juices poured over.

USE FOR

- Bringing a sweet taste to Japanese marinades such as teriyaki. Its high sugar content gives food a lovely shine.
- Adding to dressings and stir-fries.

USE INSTEAD Sherry—sweet is best (although not really the same). If you have only dry sherry, throw in a little sugar for the required sweetness.

Miso soup

Japanese, made from soybean paste.

CHOOSE AND USE Just mix the mustardy-colored paste sold in envelopes with boiling water.

- Making soup—mix miso with boiling water, then combine with pre-soaked rice noodles, cubed tofu, shredded spinach, watercress or bok choy, cooked chicken, and a splash of soy sauce.
- Dilute and use instead of stock.
- As a glaze for spreading over broiled chicken or fish—mix 2 envelopes miso with 1 tablespoon sugar and mirin.

Molasses syrup

A concentrated, dark, intensely fla-vored syrup, best used sparingly.

USE FOR

- Giving color and flavor to ginger-bread, sticky sponge puddings.
- Making Boston baked beans.
- Spooning into Christmas cake and pudding mixtures for a dark color and rich taste.
- Drizzling over a bowl of porridge.

USE INSTEAD Black treacle—it's cheaper, but not so rich-tasting.

Moroccan lemons

Whole juicy lemons that have been preserved and pickled in salt. They have a zesty, almost sweet-and-sour taste.

CHOOSE Whole lemons are packed snugly into big jars. There's no need to store them in the refrigerator, even after opening, as the salt will preserve them for about a year.

USE FOR Use whole, in wedges, diced, sliced, or zest only.

- Flavoring Moroccan tagines (good with fish and chicken) and soups, or Mediterranean dishes.
- A salad—chop the zest only into little pieces and sprinkle over torn strips of roasted red bell pepper,

crumbled feta cheese, and a generous drizzle of olive oil.

■ Adding to stuffings for fish.

■ Stirring into couscous with lots of chopped fresh parsley, mint, and sliced scallions.

■ Tucking a whole lemon into the cavity of a chicken ready for roasting so it flavors as it roasts.

■ Cutting into wedges and roasting with a mix of Mediterranean vege-tables and bay leaves for an unusual and refreshing fragrance.

■ Serving as part of an antipasto— mix strips of lemon with green olives, chopped cilantro, and olive oil.

■ A colorful, zingy salsa—chop and mix with chopped tomatoes and cilantro and a drizzle of olive oil, and serve with fish.

USE INSTEAD Fresh lemons, but the flavor isn't quite the same.

Mushrooms
(dried)

see also VEGETABLES, *page 295*

Some look so shriveled you may be forgiven for thinking they are past their best. But it's the drying that preserves them and really concen-trates the flavor. Their meaty texture makes them popular with vegetarians.

CHOOSE Among the varieties you will find are shiitake, ceps/porcini (the strongest tasting), and morels. All taste slightly different, but all add a rich and wonderful mushroom flavor to a dish. They are expensive to buy, but you need add only a few pieces to get your money's worth of flavor. If you don't use the whole packet up at once, keep it tightly sealed, or their amazing aroma may take over your pantry.

COOK Soaking the mushrooms for 20–30 minutes in water or stock (use hot if you want to speed things up a little), or wine, will quickly bring them back to life. Their soaking liquid becomes like a concentrated stock, so you can use that too. If it tastes rather too strong, add some more water or stock.

USE FOR
■ Livening up scrambled eggs and omelets (chop and fry in butter first), as well as stuffings (chop a few and mix into the stuffing for the Thanksgiving turkey).
■ Adding to casseroles and stews, especially ones with gutsy flavors made with game or beef.
■ Tucking slices into potato gratins.
■ Stirring them fried into risottos.
■ Tossing with freshly cooked pasta

(fry first with olive oil, garlic, and some thyme or parsley).
■ Mixing with fresh mushrooms to intensify their flavor. Ideal for a fresh mushroom soup.

USE INSTEAD Fresh mushrooms, but the flavor isn't nearly so intense so you will need more.

Mustard

Made by grinding mustard seeds to a paste, the taste and color varying from strong to mild according to the type of seeds used and the other flavorings added.

COOK Mustard, especially Dijon, can taste bitter if it cooks too long, so best to add toward the end.

CHOOSE AND USE It's useful to have more than one type of mustard in your pantry as each has something different to offer.
English: The hottest of mustards, buy as a powder or ready-made. Livens up simple English dishes, giving a real bite to cured ham, roast beef, sausages, and anything with cheese. To make up the powder (which is more potent than ready-made), mix with an equal amount of cold water, then let it sit for about 15 minutes so

the flavor can develop. It is best to mix small amounts as needed—you don't need much to get the effect, and freshly made tastes so much better.

Wholegrain: The mustard seeds are not completely crushed, so the grains give texture and look attractive, making it a good mustard for stirring into salad dressings, sauces, or creamy mashed potato.

American: This is a bright yellow color with a sweeter, milder taste than English mustard, so it can be used much more liberally.

German: Not quite so hot as English mustard, but still very bold in taste. Try it in the traditional German style—with sausages.

French: The most famous is Dijon which is blended with white wine and is used in sauces (especially cheese sauces), salad dressings, and for serving with steaks. It has a sharp, fresh taste, and is milder than English mustard. There is also Bordeaux (smooth and mild), and Moutarde de Meaux (grainy).

USE INSTEAD Despite their differences in strength of flavor, mustards can be used interchangeably. If you are unsure of the strength of the one you are substituting, the best thing is to add it cautiously to begin with and keep tasting.

Noodles

Noodles are the Asian version of pasta. They should last 1–2 years in the pantry.

CHOOSE AND COOK Chinese and Japanese noodles can be made from several different types of flour—rice, buckwheat, or wheat—and can also be found in a variety of sizes. They just need to be soaked in boiling water. If they are going to be tossed into a salad, tip them into a colander after soaking and then run them under cold water. This will cool them and stop them from sticking together.

Bean thread noodles: Also called cellophane noodles, these are very thin and almost see-through, so all they need is a quick soak before using. Put in a large pan, cover with boiling water, and leave for 3 minutes. Add to things like soups and stir-fries rather than serving as an accompaniment.

Chinese egg noodles: Made from wheat flour and eggs, they come in various widths—fine, medium, and broad. Cook the fine in boiling water for 3 minutes, medium for 4 minutes, and broad for 7 minutes.

Rice noodles: Soak in boiling water for 4 minutes before using.

Rice vermicelli: A very fine delicate noodle, soak in boiling water for 4 minutes before using.

Soba noodles: Also Japanese, they look a bit like whole-wheat spaghetti and are made from buckwheat and whole-wheat flours. Boil them for 5–7 minutes.

Stir-fry rice noodles: A thin noodle, often packaged in separate bundles. Soak in boiling water for 4 minutes, then drain.

Udon noodles: Fat, white Japanese noodles. The ones sold fresh in vacuum packs are ready in 1 minute. They will keep in the refrigerator for a few days.

USE ALL FOR

■ Adding to soups, stir-fries, and salads with Asian flavors.
■ As an accompaniment instead of rice, tossed with a little sesame oil.

USE INSTEAD Pasta noodles of a similar size.

Nuts

Nuts are bursting with protein and, although high in calories, give you lots of energy. Once opened, they are best kept in the refrigerator or freezer. They will go off more quickly if left in the pantry because of all the fat that they contain.

noodles–nuts

CHOOSE Buy them in well-sealed containers so that they stay fresh for the longest possible time. Nuts in their shells are fun to have around, but go stale more quickly.

COOK To really bring out the flavor of nuts, toast them first. Tip into a heavy pan (no need to add oil as the nuts will give off their own when heated, so they won't stick). Keep the pan moving the whole time so the nuts color evenly without burning. To keep their crunchy texture in savory dishes, sprinkle them onto whatever you are making at the end of cooking, particularly if there is a sauce involved, or they will tend go a little soft.

USE FOR

- Snacking on while you prepare supper (any type).
- Tossing into a pan of stir-fried vegetables (cashew and almond).
- Giving a crunch to pasta dishes (pine nut, walnut, and almond).
- Adding extra protein to vegetarian dishes (any type).
- Sprinkling over salads and cooked vegetables (almond, pine nut, walnut, hazelnut).
- Slicing and sprinkling over fruit desserts (pistachio, hazelnut, pecan, almond).

PANTRY STAPLES NOODLE SOUP
Serves 3–4; ready in 10 minutes

Soak 4 ounces stir-fry, rice or medium egg noodles in boiling water for 4 minutes. Break up with a fork, then drain, and tip into a pan. Pour in about 4 cups hot chicken or vegetable stock, an 11-ounce can corn, drained, a 7-ounce can crabmeat, drained and flaked, a few splashes of soy sauce, and a few pieces of pickled ginger and warm through. Serve sprinkled with a little sesame oil.

- *Optional extras: Add sliced bok choy or spinach leaves when warming through, and coarsely torn cilantro or parsley at the end.*

THE FOUR MOST USEFUL NUTS
- *ALMOND*
- *CASHEW*
- *PECAN (and/or walnut)*
- *PINE (not technically a nut, but used like one, so it is fine to use if you have a nut allergy)—toast for best flavor.*

■ Baking—for special-occasion cookies and cakes try the luxurious Australian macadamia nut (creamy flavor, crunchy texture) or pistachio (for its lovely green color).

Oats

Oats are the most nutritious of grains, rich in soluble fiber, vitamins, and minerals, so starting the day with a bowl of porridge helps keep your energy levels up.

CHOOSE Rolled porridge oats are ultra-quick to cook, so you can have a bowlful of porridge ready in approximately 10 minutes. Bigger oat flakes are called "jumbo" oats, and oats that have been ground are called oatmeal, which is available in varying degrees of coarseness.

USE FOR
■ Adding to crumble toppings.
■ Stirring into cakes and cookie mixtures for added texture.
■ Mixing into stuffings.
■ A crunchy coating for fish.

Oil

A pantry is the perfect place to store oil, especially if it's cool, as a bottle of oil deteriorates if it gets too hot sitting on the kitchen counter, or standing for a time in bright sunlight. Once opened, the oil should be used as soon as possible.

CHOOSE AND USE
Argan oil: A very nutritious oil (high in vitamin E), made from nuts of the Moroccan argan tree. It therefore has a nutty flavor, and is a bit milder than some of the other nut oils such as walnut and hazelnut. It is not suitable for cooking.
■ Drizzle over salads or mix with lemon juice to make a dressing.
■ Flavor Moroccan tagines and vegetable soups, such as pumpkin, at the end of cooking, or drizzle over couscous to moisten and enrich it.
■ Make a spread for toast by mixing the oil with crushed almonds and honey—a little like peanut butter.

Avocado oil: This is an extra virgin oil extracted from avocados and has a smooth, rich taste and color.
■ Use as a dipping oil with crusty bread, or for marinades.
■ Great for stir-frying as it can be used at high temperatures.
■ Adds a splash of green color to your plate when drizzled over salads, broiled fish, and chicken.

Corn oil: A good all-round cooking oil.

nuts–oil

■ Especially good for deep-frying.
USE INSTEAD Peanut oil.

Flavored oils: Oils that have been
steeped with flavorings such as chili,
basil, garlic, and lemon. Truffle oil is
a more expensive treat, a few drops
will elevate risottos, pasta dishes,
potato salad, or mashed potatoes.
■ As a lively addition to salad dressings and marinades. Lemon oil is
good marinated with cubes of feta
cheese, rosemary, and crushed dried
chilies.
■ For drizzling over pasta and
risottos, as well as simply cooked
broiled or grilled meats, fish (shrimp
and lemon or chili oil make great
partners), and steamed or broiled vegetables—try lemon oil with asparagus,
basil oil with bell peppers.
■ Stir garlic oil and a few chopped
chives into crushed new potatoes.

Grapeseed oil: Very mild in flavor,
almost bland, and best used for
cooking.
■ Its lack of flavor makes it perfect
for frying mild-flavored foods like
fish, as it doesn't overpower.
■ Good for deep-frying.
USE INSTEAD Peanut oil.

Peanut oil: Also known as groundnut
oil, this is a good, light, all-purpose

COOKING WITH OIL

*First, check the oil you are using
is suitable to cook with (see the
individual oils). Some, like sesame,
are splashed on at the end of
cooking as a flavoring since they
can burn if overheated.*

*When frying, heat the oil before
adding any food—you want to
hear that instant sizzle as the food
goes in. If the ingredients go into
cold oil the fat gets absorbed
rather than creating a golden outer
color and crust, which give so
much flavor.*

FIX IT: NUT OILS

*Nut oils have a lot of flavor, so
if you find it too strong, tone it
down for a salad dressing by
diluting with a little olive, sunflower, or peanut oil—about
1 part nut oil to 2 parts other oil.*

oil, very mild in flavor.

■ Can be heated to a high temperature, so good for Chinese stir-fries—in fact for any frying, shallow or deep. To flavor it for stir-frying, fry a few pieces of sliced ginger, garlic, or scallion in the oil before using.

■ Mixes well with olive oil for dressings to give a light taste.

USE INSTEAD Sunflower oil, corn oil, grapeseed oil.

Nut oils: The most popular ones are walnut (rich and nutty) and hazelnut (a bit lighter). They don't last as long as other oils (about 6 months), after which time they can turn rancid.

■ Great served in a little dish as a dipper for bread.

■ In salad dressings and for leafy-based salads—walnut oil goes well with cheese and Belgian endive, hazelnut with pears and arugula or watercress.

Olive oil: Choosing olive oil is a bit like choosing wine—the choice is wide and the different types vary in taste, smell, and color, so it all boils down to what flavor you like. The styles are judged on fruitiness, bitterness, and pepperiness. "Extra virgin" olive oil tends to be more expensive. This is pressed from the fresh fruit of the olive and then the water is taken away—very pure. If an olive oil is not good enough to be extra virgin, it goes to the refinery to be cleaned up, and because it is bland and tasteless some extra virgin oil is added for flavor. This is called simply "olive oil." You can use extra virgin olive oil for everything except cooking at a very high temperature, and olive and olive pomace oil (see opposite) can be used for all culinary purposes, including high- temperature cooking.

Olive oil is produced in several countries, mainly Greece, Spain and Italy. The typical characteristics are:

■ Greek: Fruity and herby in flavor. Great for salads, not good for making mayonnaise. A good all-purpose oil.

■ Italian: Italy produces the biggest range of flavors. Oil that comes from the north is more gentle and nutty in flavor and goes well with fish. Oil from central Italy is more aggressive in taste, with lots of grassy flavor, so tastes good drizzled over things like steak on an arugula or watercress salad. Southern Italy (especially Sicily) produces oil that has more "tomato-on-the-vine" type flavors, and complements all sorts of vegetable salads.

■ Spanish: Fruity and sweet, with very little bitterness—tastes more of melon, passion fruit, and nuts. A good all-rounder. Not so good as a dipping

oil

oil but goes especially well with salads that include fruit.

■ Olive pomace oil: When the olives have been pressed and the juice is extracted, a paste is left called pomace. The oil that is extracted from the pomace is called pomace oil. It is the cheapest of all the olive oils and is a healthy choice for using when deep-fat frying.

Palm oil: Used in African cooking. High in saturated fat.

■ Gives a rich red color to fish and meat stews.

USE INSTEAD Vegetable oil, but you won't get the authentic color.

Sesame oil: This has an intense, concentrated sesame flavor, especially the darker "toasted" version, so a few drops are often all that's needed to give a superb exotic taste. Not good for cooking with as it burns easily, but ideal for adding at the end of cooking to give flavoring.

■ Toss with cooked noodles and rice—it is good in salads too.

■ Splash sparingly over stir-fries.

■ Add to marinades.

■ Drizzle over steamed fish with a few slices of fried garlic and ginger.

USE INSTEAD Olive oil—it adds the richness, but not the flavor.

SALAD DRESSINGS IN SECONDS

Tip 2 tablespoons white wine or cider vinegar into a small bowl with a pinch each of salt and pepper. Slowly whisk in 6 tablespoons olive oil (or use half olive and sunflower oil for a lighter taste), so everything mixes in together.

You can enhance this in one of the following ways:

■ *NUTTY: Substitute walnut oil for half the olive oil and sprinkle a couple of tablespoons of finely chopped toasted walnuts on top just before serving. Good with cheese salads.*

■ *MUSTARD AND HONEY: Combine 1 tablespoon cider vinegar with 1 teaspoon honey and 1 teaspoon wholegrain mustard. Whisk in 5 tablespoons extra virgin olive oil as above. Goes well with chicken.*

■ *DELICIOUSLY DARK: Combine 2 teaspoons balsamic vinegar with 1 small finely chopped garlic clove and a pinch of salt and pepper. Slowly whisk in 4 tablespoons olive oil. Goes well with tomatoes.*

■ *CHEESE: Mix 4 tablespoons sunflower oil with 1 tablespoon wine vinegar, salt, and pepper. Mash 3 ounces blue cheese with a fork, then slowly add the dressing until creamy. Good with salad greens and nuts, or on crisp leaves with burgers.*

Stir-fry oil: A blend of oils mixed especially for the high temperatures of stir-frying, plus flavorings such as ginger, pepper, and garlic.
USE INSTEAD Peanut oil, flavored (see page 101), and a splash of sesame oil at the end.

Sunflower oil: A light, thin oil, extracted from sunflower seeds.
■ An excellent cooking oil, better for shallow- rather than deep-frying.
■ Good for mixing with olive oil for salad dressings.
USE INSTEAD Peanut oil.

Vegetable oil: Often a blend of oils, usually including canola.
■ A good, cheap frying oil.

Olives

Olives can be green or black, and many shades in between. Their color reflects their age when they were picked: green ones are the youngest and first off the tree, purple are picked half ripe, while wrinkly, brownish-black ones have been left longer to ripen. Because they aren't fully ripe when picked, green olives are actually too bitter to eat, so have to be soaked, washed and cured. Canned or bottled olives keep for up to a year. After opening transfer to the refrigerator in a plastic container, and use quickly.

CHOOSE You will find olives from many Mediterranean countries, mostly Italy, Spain, Greece, and also France. When deciding which ones to buy, it depends on what color, size, and strength of flavor you are after (see below). Olives with their pits in are juicier and fresher than pitted olives.
Black: These have had longer on the tree to ripen, so contain more oil, making them softer and milder in flavor. Look for glossiness in a black olive, the good ones are small and wrinkled. The almost ink-black (usually pitted) olives are actually green olives that have been dyed.
Green: The younger green olives tend to be plumper and firmer and often have a sharper taste. Varieties include the Spanish Manzanilla and the plump Italian Cerignola.
Kalamata: This is the large Greek olive with a wonderful tinge of purple and a fruity flavor which makes it ideal for a classic Greek salad.
Stuffed: Being firmer in texture and sharper in taste, it is usually green olives that are stuffed—with all sorts of things, including anchovies, capers, pimientos, and nuts—more for handing around as a party nibble than for use in cooking.

USE FOR

- Tossing into rice and pasta dishes.
- Making your own tapenade.
- Sprinkling over pizzas and salads.
- Adding to rich stews, especially chicken and beef.
- Chopping and adding to a tomato salsa for topping pan-fried fish.

Oyster sauce

You would think this thick, brown Chinese sauce would taste of the oysters of which it's made, yet its taste is quite different—salty like soy sauce, but richer and tangier. It's not so strong, however, that it overpowers other foods.

CHOOSE Sold in bottles. After opening, keep in the refrigerator.

COOK You can cook with it, but more often it's added at the end of cooking as a last-minute flavoring, rather like any thick bottled sauce.

USE FOR

- Flavoring chicken and other meat dishes.
- Thinning down with a little oil and serving drizzled over stir-fried or steamed vegetables such as broccoli or bok choy, or over an omelet.

Pasta (dried)

Most pasta is made with flour and water, and a simple sauce is all it needs for serving. Pasta that has been made with eggs is richer both in taste and color, so is better suited to richer, creamier sauces. Once the packet of pasta has been opened, use within a month or two as dried pasta can become quite brittle.

CHOOSE

Cannelloni: Longish, wide tubes of egg pasta into which a filling, such as spinach and ricotta, is spooned. You can make your own cannelloni by folding cooked lasagne sheets around a filling.
Conchiglie: Shell-shapes, the larger ones can be stuffed. Orechiette can be used instead.
Farfalle: Little bows that look pretty in salads. Often sold in packs that contain a mix of green, red, and white pasta.
Fusilli: Available as short spirals, or long ones called *fusilli lunghi* which are a bit like a curly spaghetti and can be used instead of it.
Lasagne: Broad, flat sheets of (usually egg) pasta, used in baked dishes. For convenience buy the type that doesn't need cooking first.
Linguine: A flat version of spaghetti, which can be used instead of it.
Macaroni: Tube-shaped pasta, like a very small version of cannelloni.
Orecchiette: These look like mini ears. You could use small conchiglie instead.
Orzo: Look like fat grains of rice, and the texture ends up quite creamy, rather like risotto. Go well in salads. You can use small pasta shapes instead (the type used for soup).
Pappardelle: Very wide ribbons of pasta that sometimes have frilly edges. Like a slimmer version of tagliatelle.
Penne: Small tubes of pasta, sliced off diagonally at each end. Similar to rigatoni and fusilli.
Rigatoni: A plumper, ridged, slightly curvaceous version of penne.
Spaghetti: Long strands of pasta, also sold in shorter lengths. If your pan isn't big enough to take the very long strands, just snap in half—easier to eat this way too. Similar to linguine.
Tagliatelle: Can be bought in tight bundles shaped like nests, which makes it easy to add them to the pan. Also available in straight lengths. Similar to pappardelle, only thinner.
Tortellini: These look like tightly pinched little bonnets, and because they have a filling, usually of spinach or cheese, will keep for only about 3 months in the pantry. Store in the refrigerator after opening.

COOK Use a big pan and plenty of water (fill the pan until it is at least half full) so that the pasta has enough room to move around and cook evenly. Bring the water to a boil, add a pinch of salt, then drop the pasta in, and give it a stir to stop it clinging together. Keep the water boiling so the pasta keeps moving. Check the packet for timings—the pasta should be *al dente* (that is, have a little bite in the center), so test a piece by eating it before draining off the water. Drain well if adding to a runny sauce otherwise, if just serving with something like pesto or cheese, keep back half a cup of the cooking water so you can moisten the sauce if you need to. Mix the pasta and its sauce together while both are still hot—if the pasta sits on its own getting cold, it will stick to itself. To use the pasta for a salad, cool it quickly in a colander or strainer under cold running water and toss with olive oil.

Pesto

This wonderfully fragrant Italian sauce, made from the magical combination of fresh basil, Parmesan or pecorino cheese, pine nuts, garlic, and olive oil, transforms the flavor of whatever food or dish it comes into contact with.

WHICH SAUCE FOR WHICH SHAPE?
LONG AND THIN, such as spaghetti or linguine: Use a medium-thick sauce, or an oil-based one like pesto that clings to the strands, rather than a chunky one that slides off.
SHORT AND RIBBED, such as fusilli: you need a little more sauce for these shapes, but not so chunky that it catches in the little ribs.
HOLLOW TUBES, such as macaroni, penne, and rigatoni: Choose a sauce that won't clog the tubes too much, such as tomato or creamy cheese.
RIBBONS, such as tagliatelle or pappardelle: Use thinner sauces— creamy ones that will coat the pasta.
FANCY SHAPES, such as farfalle, orecchiette, conchiglie: These can take chunky meat sauces or creamy ones that get caught in their shapes.

HOW MUCH PASTA?
FOR 1: 3–3½ ounces
FOR 2: 5–7 ounces
FOR 4: 10–14 ounces
FOR 6: 1 pound–1 pound 5 ounces

FIX IT: PASTA
If pasta sticks, tip into a colander, pour in boiling water to loosen it, drain, then toss in a little olive oil.

PANTRY STAPLES

CHOOSE All pesto adds a bonus flavor to your cooking. Basil-based pesto is the most versatile, but you can also buy it made with arugula, bell pepper, and eggplant. After opening, store pesto in the refrigerator where it will keep for a couple of weeks. If it starts to dry out, top it up with olive oil.

USE FOR

■ Tossing with pasta—splash in a little of the pasta cooking water as well to give a extra sauciness.

■ Spreading on chicken breast portions before roasting or broiling them.

■ Mixing with olive oil and a squirt of lemon juice to make a speedy dressing for drizzling over new potatoes, salads, fish, or broiled tomatoes on toast.

■ Spreading generously over a ready-made pizza base before piling on your choice of fillings.

■ Stirring into mayonnaise for a dip, or spreading on bread instead of butter, especially good on Italian bread for a mozzarella and tomato sandwich.

■ Livening up your mashed potatoes.

Polenta

Made from cornmeal which is either coarsely or finely ground. It has a slightly sweet taste. In Italian kitchens it is as common as all-purpose flour is in American ones. Polenta can be creamy and sloppy, or so firm that you can slice and fry it. The terms cornmeal and polenta can be used interchangeably.

CHOOSE The quickest way to make polenta is to use instant polenta flour (precooked cornmeal) which can be made up in under 10 minutes. Regular cornmeal takes about 30 minutes to cook. Polenta can also be bought ready-made—it simply has to be sliced and heated up.

COOK Follow the instructions on the packet for the type of polenta you are using. For added flavor, replace half the water with stock or milk. At the end of cooking, stir in a pat of butter and season to taste.

USE FOR

■ As an accompaniment instead of potatoes, rice, or pasta. Try flavoring it with cheese, such as grated Parmesan or cubes of Gorgonzola.

■ Spread the cooked polenta on a cookie sheet and let it set, then cut it into squares, broil or fry, and use as a base for fried mushrooms, roasted bell peppers, and cheese.

■ A colorful coating for protecting chicken or fish when frying.

Pulses

see BEANS, *page 74*

Red currant jelly

CHOOSE You can also buy red currant and cranberry jelly, which has more of a sweet-tart taste.

USE FOR

- Stirring into sauces and gravies to give them a slight sweetness and glossiness, especially good with lamb.
- Livening up pan-fried sausages and onions—just bubble in some stock and 1 tablespoon red currant jelly at the end of frying.
- Making a snack—spread on toasted French bread, top with slices of goat cheese, and melt under the broiler.

Rice

There are three kinds of grain: long (basmati and American long-grain), medium (Thai and risotto), and short (pudding and sushi rice). Each of the many varieties has its own character-istics. A lot are interchangeable, but if you are cooking a specialty, such as an Italian risotto, Spanish paella, or Indian biriyani, it's best to stick to the

PANTRY STAPLES

right rice. All rice will keep for about a year in the pantry.

CHOOSE, COOK, AND USE Rice is cooked by boiling it in a pan of lightly salted water. You can simply place the rice in a pan two thirds full of boiling water, and drain off the water when the rice is cooked. Or, you can measure out exact quantities of rice and water so that the rice absorbs all the water during cooking. The proportions are generally 1 part rice to 2 parts water—measure the rice in a measuring cup and measure double that volume of water, then tip both into a pan. Bring to a boil, stir, then cover, and cook on a low heat until the water is absorbed. Don't lift the lid to peek, or stir while cooking. Take it off the heat, cover, and leave it to stand for 3–5 minutes to help prevent it being soggy. A quick fluff up with a fork and it's ready to serve. Alternatively you can use the microwave: there's less mess, but it's no speedier (see opposite).

American long-grain: The good quality has a slightly sweet aroma, almost like popcorn.
■ Very good for salads, stuffings, or on its own. It is the rice to serve with chili con carne and other Mexican food.

COOK Boiling: 12 minutes.
Absorption: 1 part rice to 2 parts water, 15 minutes.

Basmati: An elegant long-grained rice from India, this has a fluffy texture and an aromatic fragrance when cooked that perfectly complements the spiciness of Indian food.
■ Apart from using for Indian dishes, try it instead of long-grain rice in spicy salads, or whenever you want to serve rice with a distinctive flavor.
COOK It helps to rinse basmati rice thoroughly before cooking, not to clean it, but to get it going and give a fluffier, lighter texture.
Boiling: 10–12 minutes.
Absorption: 1 part rice to 1½ parts water, 12–15 minutes.
Flavor it: Drop in a few cardamom pods, cinnamon sticks, star anise, or strips of lemon or lime zest as it cooks. Or for Thai and Indian dishes, cook in half water, half coconut milk.
Color it: Sprinkle and stir ½ teaspoon turmeric into the water after you've added the rice (for 4 servings). If you add too much, the rice can taste bitter.

Brown: Tastes nuttier than white long-grain rice and takes quite a lot longer to cook.
■ With its chewier texture, it's a good base for vegetarian dishes and salads.

rice

COOK Boiling: 30–35 minutes.
Absorption: generous ½ cup rice to
1 cup water, 25 minutes.

Camargue red: This is wine red in
color when cooked and tastes nutty.
■ It makes a stunning-looking salad,
or can be served as an accompaniment to gutsy meat dishes.
COOK Boiling: 30 minutes. Take off
the heat and let stand for 15 minutes.
Absorption: generous ½ cup rice to
1¼ cups water, 20 minutes.

Easy-cook: A useful option, this
rice, whatever the type, has been
steamed very briefly, which makes it
easier to cook so that you are always
assured of a nonstick grain. The
disadvantages are that it takes longer
to cook and, as it loses some of its
natural flavor in the steaming
process, the taste is not so good as
pure rice.
COOK Follow the packet instructions.

Paella: This rice is to Spain what
risotto rice is to Italy. It has a slightly
chewy texture when cooked.
COOK Follow the packet instructions
or your recipe. Paella rice should be
shaken, not stirred, so when you want
to move it around, just shake the
pan—there's no need to use a spoon.
USE INSTEAD Arborio rice.

HOW MUCH RICE?
FOR 1: ¼–½ cup
FOR 2: ⅔–¾
FOR 4: 1¼ cups
FOR 6: 1⅓–1¾ cups
FOR 8–10: 2½ cups

WHEN IS RICE DONE?
*To check, lift a grain of rice from
the pan with a fork, let it cool, then
take a bite. It should be tender but
with a little firmness. If it's crunchy
and the center looks hard and
uncooked, it's not quite done.*

REHEATING
LEFTOVER RICE
*Leftover rice must be cooled quickly
after cooking. If it is left at room
temperature, it can cause mild food
poisoning. Tip the hot leftover rice
into a strainer and run cold water
through it. Drain and put it in a
covered container in the refrigerator, and it will keep for up to
2 days. To use, steam, microwave,
or fry until piping hot—but reheat
only once.*

PANTRY STAPLES

Pudding: These plump grains absorb a lot of liquid as they cook and give a soft, slightly sticky texture. A lot of good pudding rice comes from Italy.
■ Traditionally used for rice pudding.
COOK Follow the recipe or packet instructions.

Risotto: This plump Italian rice absorbs a lot of liquid when cooking, which gives it its characteristic creamy texture. Italy has many varieties of risotto rice, all of which are interchangeable for making risotto. The most popular are:
Arborio: A softer grain, and the easiest to overcook.
Carnaroli: Easier to cook, so good for beginners.
Vialone nano: A smaller, slightly harder grain, often favored for seafood risottos.
COOK Follow the recipe or packet instructions as the amount of liquid needed can vary.

Sushi: A short-grained white Japanese rice with a slightly sweet flavor.
■ Making sushi. It becomes sticky and malleable when cooked, so it can be shaped around the sushi filling easily to make an edible wrapper.
COOK Check the packet, but soaking for 30 minutes is often recommended before cooking for a lighter grain.
Boiling: 10–12 minutes.
Absorption: 1 part rice to 2 parts water, 10 minutes. Drain but don't rinse.

Thai fragrant: Another aromatic rice like basmati. It goes very slightly sticky when cooked, so it's easy to pick up with chopsticks. Also known as "jasmine" rice.
■ Use as for basmati, or as an accompaniment with Thai, Indonesian, and Chinese dishes.
COOK Boiling: 10 minutes.
Absorption: 1 part rice to 1½ parts water, 12 minutes.

Wild: Very nutty in taste and chewy in texture, and smells a bit like a freshly mown lawn as it cooks—which is not surprising as this slender, black grain is not really a rice but a North American semi-aquatic grass that grows in shallow water. This makes harvesting difficult, so true wild rice (which has a longer, bigger grain than the cultivated rice) is expensive. To lighten it up and give color contrast, it is often sold mixed with white rice and this mix cooks more quickly.
■ Excellent with salmon. Also good in stuffings with lots of herbs, nuts, and dried cranberries, blueberries, or raisins (try it with the Thanksgiving turkey), in salads (it goes well with

rice

Chinese flavors), and with gutsy stews and casseroles.

COOK Unlike most rice that keeps its shape when cooked, wild rice starts to burst open when tender. If the grains begin to curl it means they are over-cooked, but wild rice doesn't go soggy so it is still edible. If you soak wild rice for 1 hour before cooking, you can reduce the cooking time to 30 minutes. Boiling: 45–50 minutes.

Absorption: 1 part rice to 3 parts water, 40 minutes (stir after 30).

OTHER GRAINS TO TRY

Buckwheat: A staple in Russian cooking, often sold toasted, used to make the Russian porridge-type dish *kasha*. Sometimes also referred to as *kasha*. Like rice it can be served on its own or added to salads or stuffings.

Bulgur wheat: Wheat grains that have been cooked, dried, and cracked. Used a lot in Middle Eastern cooking, it is the main ingredient for tabbouleh salad. Treat it like couscous: simply tip it into a bowl, pour over boiling water or stock sufficient to cover, leave for 15 minutes, drain, and dry on paper towels. Use instead of rice in salads.

Quinoa: A tiny South American gluten-free grain with a mild taste. It is high in protein, so it is great for vegetarians. Cook like rice and use in a similar way to rice and couscous.

MICROWAVING RICE

It's no quicker to cook rice this way, but there is less mess. Use the right amount of water and follow the timing given below for your type of rice. There is no need to stir during cooking.

1 Tip 1¼ cups rice into a deep (to avoid spills) microwave-safe bowl.

2 Stir in the right amount of boiling water (see below), ½ teaspoon salt, and a pat of butter if you wish.

3 Cover with microwave-safe plastic wrap, leaving a little vent on one side.

4 Cook on full power (750W) for 6 minutes.

5 Continue to cook on medium (350W) for the time given below.

6 Let the rice stand for 5 minutes, then uncover, and fluff up.

AMOUNT OF WATER AND TIMINGS
(from step 5 on 350W)

- *American long grain: 2½ cups water, for 10 minutes.*
- *Basmati: 2 cups water, for 10 minutes.*
- *Easy cook long grain American: 2½ cups water, for 14 minutes.*
- *Thai fragrant: generous 2 cups water, for 10 minutes.*
- *Wild: 3 cups water, for 35 minutes.*

Rice wine

A Chinese wine which you can use both for drinking and cooking, made from rice, yeast, and water. Not to be confused with sake, the Japanese version of rice wine which you drink, or mirin with which you cook (see page 93).

CHOOSE Many consider Shaoxing rice wine to be the best. Store as you would any other wine, making sure the cork is seated tightly.

USE FOR
■ Flavoring Chinese marinades, sauces, and stir-fries.

USE INSTEAD A pale dry sherry, although the taste is harsher.

Salt

CHOOSE AND USE

Rock salt: Large crystals of salt for putting in a salt mill for grinding.
Sea salt: Available as coarse or mild grades, or in flakes. These pure flakes of salt are strong in taste, so you don't need to use much. It looks pretty sprinkled over food.
Table salt: A finely ground salt, this contains anti-caking agents to stop it from clogging.

COOK If you are cooking foods that are already salty, such as bacon, ready-made stocks, and cheese, taste before adding extra salt. When cooking a dish with lots of flavors and spices, add salt lightly and gradually: the flavors will develop as they cook, affecting how much salt you need.
Salt before: Salting fish before frying or broiling helps firm up the flesh. When cooking pasta, salt the water before adding the pasta—it makes the water boil more furiously and the pasta move around more quickly so it is less likely to stick. If you are cooking with onions, add a pinch of salt as they fry and they are less likely to burn. When frying meat, salt just before cooking—if done too early, the salt will draw out the moisture and the meat will stew rather than fry.
Salt after: Salt roast potatoes at the end of roasting—if added too early, salt will draw out their moisture so they won't go crispy. Salt dishes that have dried beans and fresh fava beans (unless you are going to skin these) at the end of cooking, as too much salt added too soon can toughen their skins.

USE FOR
■ Flavoring.
■ Preserving food, such as Moroccan lemons.
■ Helping bread rise.

USE INSTEAD To use less salt in your cooking, flavor dishes with herbs, lemon juice, vinegar, and spices.

Soy sauce

Made by fermenting soybeans, wheat, and water with salt, then leaving the mix to age for a few months.

CHOOSE Between dark and light soy sauce. The dark has been left to age for longer; it is also thicker and slightly sweeter. Light soy is paler in color, thinner in consistency, and saltier in taste. Dark gives more depth of color to slowly cooked meat dishes, or a darker-looking marinade, stir-fry, or dipping sauce. Both keep well for about a year.

COOK Because soy sauce contains so much salt, it's best to taste food before adding extra seasoning.

USE FOR
■ Sprinkling over Chinese rice dishes, rather as you would use Worcestershire sauce.
■ Splashing over steamed vegetables to flavor them, as well as into heartier meat and chicken dishes, to give both color and flavor.

FLAVORED SALT

By mixing salt with a few other ingredients from your pantry, you can create imaginative flavor combinations:

■ *RED HOT: Mix in some dried crushed chilies—use with beef, chicken, ground meat dishes, and roast vegetables, or for tossing through a simple pasta dish.*

■ *NICE AND SPICY: Stir in equal amounts of toasted cumin and coriander seeds—sprinkle over roast squash or lamb.*

■ *NUTTY: Grind with sesame seeds and use to season rice, or use as a crunchy, nutty coating for chicken and fish before pan-frying.*

■ *FRAGRANT: Grind with a dried lime leaf and use for sprinkling on fish.*

■ *PEPPERY: Mix with ground black pepper and dried thyme, and sprinkle over new potatoes as they roast.*

FIX IT: SALT

If you have over-salted a casserole, curry, or stew, adding a few raw chopped potatoes will help reduce the salty taste.

Spices

see pages 162–198

Stock cubes

see BOUILLON, *page 76*

Strained tomatoes

Also known as passata, this is made from tomatoes that have been puréed and sieved to get rid of all the seeds and skin, and then bottled.

CHOOSE AND USE Available in bottles and cartons, it will keep for a year in the pantry, and in the refrigerator for 4–5 days after opening.

USE FOR

■ Giving a creamy smoothness to soups, casseroles, and Italian-based sauces.
■ Curries where you want the tomato taste without the tomato texture.
■ Spreading over pizza bases—add more flavor by stirring in some herbs and garlic.

USE INSTEAD If you don't have bottled, strained tomatoes, you can simply whizz a can of tomatoes in a blender or food processor, then sieve

them. It's a more time-consuming method, but achieves the same result.

Sugar

The choice of sugars ranges from pure white and powdery (refined confectioners') to dark and sticky molasses. Most sugar is extracted from sugar cane. The range of flavors, colors, and textures depends on how much molasses the sugar has and how much it has been refined. The more molasses there is, the darker, stickier, and more flavorsome the sugar will be. After opening, sugar will keep longer if it is placed in an airtight container.

CHOOSE AND USE
Barbados sugar (unrefined): A moist sugar full of natural molasses, hence its color. The refined version is milder in taste and called soft brown sugar.
■ Brings a rich taste to baking, sauces, and marinades.
Brown (unrefined): This has a well-balanced taste and is milder than Barbados sugar. The refined version is called light soft brown sugar.
■ Gives a mild, fudgy flavor to cakes, cookies, sweet sauces (toffee), or can be used in marinades and savory sauces. Use as for Barbados sugar.
Confectioners': Available as golden

spices–sugar

confectioners' (unrefined) and confectioners' (refined).

■ To sift over cakes and desserts as a decoration. When using for cake frostings, refined confectioners' sugar gives a sparkling white frosting for wedding or Christmas cakes, whereas golden confectioners' sugar gives a mild butterscotch flavor and color.

Granulated: Available as golden granulated (unrefined) or granulated (refined). Granulated is coarser than superfine, finer than raw sugar.

■ Good for making caramel and crunchy dessert toppings.

Molasses: The darkest of all sugars with the most flavor, owing to the high quantity of molasses that it contains, so it is usually used in small amounts.

■ Adds richness to marinades and sauces (especially barbecue), fruit cakes, chocolate cakes, and chutneys.

Palm: Known as jaggery in Southeast Asia, this brown sugar has a distinctive caramel flavor and is often sold in a solid block. Frequently produced from the syrup of palm trees.

■ To sweeten savory and sweet Thai and other Southeast Asian dishes.

Pectin: This is sugar with pectin added. Pectin helps preserves to set, and so reduces the boiling time.

■ Use for jellies and other preserves.

Preserving: Its large sugar crystals dissolve quickly as they don't stick

PANTRY STAPLES
EASY STIR-FRY SAUCE
Make an instant sauce for stir-fries by splashing some soy sauce and a little stock or water into your wok at the end of stir-frying meat or vegetables. This works well, especially if you start by frying a little garlic, onion, and ginger, which are great cooking partners to soy.

WHAT THE LABEL
MEANS: SUGAR
Sugar is labeled either "refined" or "unrefined" on the packet. All sugar cane goes through some refining process to extract the sugar; unrefined just goes through less. Because of this, unrefined sugars lock in rather than refine out the molasses of the sugar cane during production, which gives them a natural color and flavor.

Refined soft brown sugar is white refined sugar sprayed with molasses and sometimes caramel coloring, so it is brown on the outside only.

together when mixed with liquid.

■ Use for Jams, marmalades, jellies.

Raw sugar: This has a crunchy texture and the small amount of molasses it contains imparts a delicate flavor.

■ Adds a crunchiness to toppings for fruit crumbles and pies, and in a coating for roast cured hams. Its flavor makes it ideal for sweetening coffee.

Rock: Big yellow chunks of Chinese sugar that you need to break into smaller pieces with a rolling pin or meat bat (page 70).

■ Gives a shiny glaze to slow-cooked Chinese dishes and sauces.

Superfine: Available as golden superfine (unrefined) or superfine (refined). Golden superfine sugar has a good flavor and a pale butterscotch color. Refined superfine sugar is pure white in color, so it is popular for making meringues.

■ Its fine texture makes it especially suited for baking. Use it as a quick-dissolving sweetener for fruits and desserts—if you sprinkle some over a bowl of strawberries, it dissolves and draws out the natural fruit juices to create an instant syrup.

Vanilla: Superfine sugar made fragrant and speckled with vanilla seeds.

■ Cakes, cookies, sprinkling over pies and fruits, making vanilla ice cream.

USE INSTEAD Use the following sugars interchangeably:
Superfine: granulated (although not as suitable for cake making).
Brown: Barbados sugar.
Palm: brown or Barbados sugar.
Preserving: granulated.
Rock: granulated or coffee crystals.

Sun-dried tomatoes

CHOOSE The dried kind sold in packets might look a bit wrinkly, but are chewy and full of sweet flavor. Or you can buy them preserved in oil in jars. Both keep for about a year; put those in oil in the refrigerator after opening. *Mi-cuit* sun-dried tomatoes are semi-dried, plump and soft.

COOK Sun-dried tomatoes in oil are softer, so can be snipped into dishes straight from the jar. You can cook with the oil from the jar too. The dried kind (not *mi-cuit*) are best softened before cooking by soaking in warm water for about 15 minutes.

USE FOR

■ Snipping two or three into a tomato sauce or soup while it cooks, or into a pasta dish at the end of cooking.

■ Eating as a snack instead of candies.

■ Brightening up roast chicken breast portions or fish fillets—place a few on top toward the end of cooking and drizzle with a little oil from the jar.
■ Adding to a tomato and mozzarella salad sprinkled with basil.

Tabasco

Just a few drops of this hot, fiery sauce made from Tabasco chili peppers, vinegar, and salt, will liven up anything you care to add it to, whether it's vodka for a Bloody Mary or scrambled eggs.

USE FOR

■ Livening up pasta sauces, especially those that are tomato-based.
■ Adding both heat and chili flavor to burgers and fish cakes.
■ Salad dressings—add a drop or two to dressings to serve with chicken, shrimp, eggs, vegetables, or rice.
■ Splashing tentatively (or not—as you like!) on to plain broiled or pan-fried fish, chicken, or pork, or even onto poached eggs.

USE INSTEAD Chili sauce.

Tapenade

An olive-based paste which is further flavored with other ingredients, including anchovies and vinegar.

FIX IT: SUGAR

Sugar has a habit of going solid. If it has dried out, put it in a mixing bowl, lay a slice of bread on top, sprinkle with a little water, cover, and place in the microwave for 30–40 seconds on high. Let it stand for 5 minutes, then throw away the bread, and put your now-loosened sugar in an airtight container. (This doesn't work for confectioners' sugar.)

Alternatively, put the sugar in a bowl, cover with a clean damp cloth, and leave overnight. Then store as above.

SHORT CUT: VANILLA SUGAR

To buy vanilla sugar is expensive. You can make your own cheaply at home by tucking a vanilla bean into a jar of superfine sugar. In a couple of days it will have soaked up the vanilla scent, and will then keep for ages.

USE FOR

■ Serving as it is as a dip with crisp raw vegetables, or diluted by mixing with mayonnaise to soften the intense taste.

■ As an appetizer. Spread on French bread that has been drizzled with olive oil, then bake the bread in the oven until crisp.

■ Putting a spoonful straight from the jar on top of grilled or griddled shrimp, or scallops just before serving.

■ Spreading over a pizza base instead of tomato sauce.

■ Mixing with a little olive oil, then brushing over salmon or other fish fillets just before broiling or roasting.

■ Spreading over a lamb roast before putting it in the oven.

■ Spreading a thin layer under the skin of a whole chicken before roasting.

■ Stirring a teaspoonful into gravies or sauces for meat or fish.

■ Mixing a few spoonfuls into a bean salad with herbs, olive oil, and finely chopped red onion.

Tomatoes

Canned tomatoes are one of the most useful and versatile ingredients to have in your pantry. No peeling is required—just open the can and tip them out. They keep at least a year. If you don't use the whole can in one go, tip the rest into a plastic container and keep in the refrigerator for up to 4 days.

CHOOSE AND USE The different types can all be used in similar ways, but these are their strengths:

Chopped: A convenient short-cut for making a sauce, but more expensive and the quality may not be as good as that of whole tomatoes.

Crushed: Canned crushed tomatoes are mixed with tomato paste to form a chunky sauce. They are perfect for soups, pasta sauces, and pizza toppings.

Whole cherry: Toss them into simple pasta dishes when fresh ones are not at their peak, or into sauces.

Whole plum: Give a rich taste and texture to sauces, casseroles, stews, and curries.

COOK A pinch of sugar added to a dish made with canned tomatoes will bring out their naturally sweet flavor.

Tomato sauce and purées

CHOOSE AND USE

Tomato ketchup: A very sweet mix of tomatoes, vinegar, sugar, and spices. Once opened, it should be stored in the refrigerator and used within 2 months.

Tomato paste: Adds concentrated tomato flavor to your cooking. Available in a can, tube, or jar. The can is great if you are going to use it all at once, but if you need only a small amount, a tube or jar is more practical, as it can be resealed and used at a later date. Tomato paste thickens and adds color to curries, chili and Bolognese sauce, or whenever you want extra tomato flavor. Once opened, keep in the refrigerator; the tube and jar will last for longer than the can, up to 4 weeks.

Sun-dried tomato paste: Gives a richer taste and color than tomato paste, so use sparingly. Useful for Italian sauces, soups, and marinades.

Tuna (canned)

The canning process gives this a different taste from fresh tuna, but it is handy as a form of ready-to-use cooked protein for flaking and adding to dishes. (For fresh tuna, see Fish and Shellfish, page 417.)

COOK Simply drain before using.

CHOOSE AND USE Available in cans packed in oil, brine, or water, or in meatier chunks packed in jars.

PANTRY STAPLES
EASY TOMATO SAUCE
For tossing with pasta, spreading on pizza, or as a sauce for fish or chicken.

Finely chop a small onion and a plump garlic clove. Heat 2 tablespoons olive oil in a pan, add the onion and garlic with a pinch of salt, and stir-fry until softened and golden. Tip in a 14-ounce can whole plum tomatoes, some pepper, and a pinch of sugar. Bring to a boil, then stir, turn the heat down, and let it gently bubble away for about 5–10 minutes (depending on how thick you want it), stirring every now and then, until the tomatoes break down to a rich sauce. To bump up the flavor, sprinkle in any or all of the following: a pinch of dried oregano, a good squirt of tomato paste, a handful of torn fresh basil.

TIPS AND TRICKS:
CANNED TOMATOES
Add a pinch of sugar to a dish made with canned tomatoes to help bring out their natural sweet flavor.

If you don't use the whole can, tip the rest into a nonmetal container and keep in the refrigerator for up to a day.

■ Flaking into cooked pasta tossed with finely grated lemon zest, a little fried garlic, a few crushed chili flakes, a small bag of arugula, and a good drizzling of olive oil.

■ Combining with mayonnaise and chives or scallions and using as a topping for baked potatoes, or flaking on top of pizza with tomato sauce, cheese, and olives.

■ Mixing with a jar of tomato-based pasta sauce and tossing with pasta.

■ For making quick fish cakes instead of using fresh fish.

Vinegar

Most vinegars are made from wine, cider, or other alcohol. Although this gives them different characteristics, they can be used interchangeably. Vinegars flavor, preserve, and tenderize your food, and it is fun to build up an interesting selection. Light and heat can spoil the flavor of vinegar, so store it in a cool dark place.

CHOOSE AND USE

Balsamic (dark): Made from grape juice, this deliciously rich, sweet, and syrupy vinegar varies in color, taste, and consistency. The genuine article comes from Modena in Italy. If it has *"tradizionale"* on the label, it indicates it is top-of-the-range, and the most expensive. Usually the more expensive balsamic is, the longer it has been aged and the sweeter and more syrupy it will be. Balsamic needs to be flavored by aging (you won't find its age on the label, but cost is a good clue). So whatever your price range when choosing, check that additives such as caramel haven't been included to give it flavor instead. Cheaper balsamics are fine for using in cooking, but it's worth spending a little more for one that will be drizzled on dishes such as salads.

■ Brushing over chicken or duck breasts as they roast for a crisp, slightly sweet-tasting skin.

■ Tossing a spoonful with pasta and roasted vegetables, or stirring into a tomato sauce for pasta.

■ Drizzling neat over salads that have been tossed with olive oil, especially those that are tomato-based.

■ Using the thick syrupy type as a decoration—trickle a few flavorsome droplets around plates of salad.

■ Adding a few drops to a bowl of summer strawberries.

Balsamic (white): This has a sweet but delicate taste.

■ Because of its pale color, it can be added to marinades, sauces (when deglazing pans, see page 20), and dressings where you don't want the color to affect the food, as with fish, shellfish, and chicken, or simple steamed vegetables.

Cider: This has a golden color and delicate flavor and is less overpowering and more subtle than some other vinegars. Use it in a similar way to white wine vinegar.

■ In salad dressings it complements fruit—try it with arugula and pear.

■ Use in marinades—it's especially good with pork.

■ For making fruit chutneys.

Fruit: Summer berries, sometimes plums, are used to flavor red or white wine vinegar. These vinegars should be flavored with fresh fruits, so check the label to see which have been used.

■ Dressings—the flavors of fruit vinegars and nut oils combine really well.

■ Deglazing pans for gravies and sauces to add a hint of fruitiness to a dish.

Herb: Made from white wine vinegar and herbs. Tarragon vinegar is useful as it goes well with chicken and fish.

■ Dressings.

■ Marinades.

Malt: The cheapest vinegar you can get, also the crudest, strongest-tasting.

■ Splashing, British-style, on your French fries.

■ For making rich, dark chutneys.

Rice: A clear, mild-flavored vinegar distilled from rice, with a hint of sweetness.
- Use for dipping sauces, salad dressings, and sweet-and-sour flavors in Chinese and Japanese dishes—.

Sherry: It has a deliciously rich, sweet taste, and can be sprinkled directly onto food in the same way as balsamic vinegar.
- Deglazing pans for making a sauce.
- Sprinkling onto salads.

Wine: Both red and white wine vinegars can be used interchangeably, but each has its own strength. You may come across an aged red wine vinegar in specialty shops: it is wonderfully fruity and less sharp-tasting.
- Red has a stronger taste, so is especially good for cooking, such as when deglazing pans for meat sauces, or in rich-flavored dressings and marinades.
- White is particularly popular for the classic oil and vinegar dressing.

Wasabi

Made from Japanese horseradish, this has a spicy hot taste, quite different from the Western version. Wasabi is a green paste that can give you quite a shock if you take too much, but elevates the taste of mild-flavored Japanese dishes if you get the balance right.

CHOOSE Comes in a tube and keeps for at least a year.

USE FOR
- Dabbing on your sushi.
- Using sparingly to flavor salad dressings and Japanese noodle dishes.
- Adding a couple of teaspoons to a soy sauce-based marinade for fish.
- Serving with salmon or tuna—it is especially good if the fish has been pan-fried in a coating of sesame seeds.

Worcestershire sauce

Although the actual recipe for this is a secret, its ingredients include tamarind, vinegar, soy, molasses, spices, anchovies, sugar, and garlic.

USE FOR
- Splashing a few drops over fish, for using in a punchy dressing to serve with meat, or in a Caesar salad.
- Bringing depth of flavor to a meat stew, soup, or gravy.
- Adding a teaspoon or two to cheese dishes, such as cauliflower cheese.
- Mixing with soy sauce in a stir-fry.
- Livening up stroganoff, Bolognese, beef burgers, or shepherd's pie.
- Serving just as it is to accompany a juicy steak sandwich.

Yeast (dried)

Fresh yeast is not always easy to buy, so dried yeast is handy to have in the pantry. However, it doesn't last forever. Although inactive until introduced to warmth and liquid, yeast is a living thing and, once it becomes stale, it will not do its job properly, which is to make bread rise.

CHOOSE Available in packets or cans in dried granular form (needs dissolving in lukewarm water with sugar first, and leaving to go frothy), or powdered dried rapid-rise yeast (no dissolving required, can be mixed straight into the flour). Both do the same job—easy-blend is quicker and easier to use.

COOK Just as gentle warmth allows yeast to grow, the intense heat needed to bake it kills it off, so make sure your bread has risen sufficiently before it goes into the oven.

USE FOR
- Raising sweet and savory breads.

USE INSTEAD
Fresh yeast. Use twice the weight of fresh to dried, so for ¼ ounce dried yeast granules (1½ teaspoons), use 2 ounces fresh (1 tablespoon).

TIPS AND TRICKS: YEAST

2 teaspoons dried yeast is sufficient to raise 4 cups flour.

STORING DRIED YEAST

Check the can or packet for the best-before or use-by date. The yeast should always be used by that date, or the dough may not rise. You can tell when granular dried yeast is stale, as it doesn't froth up when mixed with sugar and lukewarm water.

PANTRY STAPLES HOOCH HOARD

With a few bottles tucked away, you'll always have something punchy to slip into your cooking.

■ **Di Saronno (Amaretto)** If you love flavored coffees or cooking with chocolate, one of the Italian nut liqueurs is ideal and great for sipping too. It goes beautifully in chocolate cheesecake. Or, to make a five minute dessert—sandwich soft Italian amaretti cookies together with scoops of coffee ice cream and serve drizzled with amaretto.

■ **Angostura bitters** Don't forget this little bottle from Trinidad. A few drops will refresh a fruit salad, spice up a tonic, or perk up a Bolognese sauce perfectly.

■ **Baileys** This creamy liqueur is brilliant for drizzling over ice cream and lovely in homemade chocolate truffles.

■ **Crème de cassis** This is the essence of black currants. Put a dash at the bottom of a glass, then top off with sparkling wine.

Drizzle over or through ice cream or add a dash to boost a summer fruit salad or to fruits for summer pudding.

■ **Limoncello** The flavor of Italian lemons in a bottle, tart and sweet all at the same time. Serve in small chilled glasses as an after-dinner liqueur. Or drizzle lightly over store-bought lemon tarts to smarten them up.

■ **Ruby port** Not as old-fashioned as you might think. It's a fantastic drink loaded with fruity taste. Top it off with cranberry juice, ice, and a dash of lemon for a cooling summer drink. You could also poach pears and plums in it, then serve with crème fraîche or put them in a crumble, or add a dash to boost the richness of gravy.

■ **Vodka** The great thing about vodka is that, flavored vodka apart, it is a spirit without any taste. The advantage is that you can add an alcoholic boost to any dish where you don't want to change the flavor base, as in a beet soup, or a bell pepper jelly served in a glass as an appetizer. As part of the base liquid for fruit jellies, citrus vodka is great.

Herbs and Spices

HERBS

KNOWING HOW TO RECOGNIZE AND USE FRESH HERBS, AND HOW TO PREPARE AND STORE THEM, WILL HELP YOU ENJOY THEM TO THEIR FULL. MANY HERBS CAN BE BOUGHT FRESH IN SUPERMARKETS, BUT IF YOU WANT TO GROW THEM YOURSELF, HERBS IN CONTAINERS CAN BE FOUND IN HORTICULTURE STORES AND OTHERS SELLING PLANTS. THE CREATIVE WAYS GIVEN FOR USING HERBS AND SUGGESTIONS FOR INGREDIENTS THAT GO WELL WITH EACH HERB WILL MAKE IT EASY TO BRING INSTANT FLAVOR TO YOUR FOOD.

STORING FRESH HERBS

CHILL OUT

Delicate herbs, such as cilantro, dill, chervil, tarragon, and chives, will keep fresh and perky in the refrigerator for several days, depending on the individual herb. Give them a quick rinse only if they need it and pat dry with a dish towel (or use a salad spinner). Lay the herbs on a bed of dampened paper towels, tuck them into a plastic bag so they have plenty of room, and keep in the salad drawer of the refrigerator.

KEEP FRESH IN THE FREEZER

If you end up with a glut of herbs, some can be frozen in individual blocks of ice. Chop or shred the leaves, pack into ice-cube trays to fill loosely, then top off with cold water. Once the cubes have frozen, put them into freezer bags. They will remain fragrant for up to 3 months—very handy for dropping into all sorts of things such as sauces, soups, and stews. Parsley freezes best if frozen in sprigs on a tray first, then it's easy to crumble into a freezer bag for storing.

PREPARING FRESH HERBS

Herbs are used whole, in sprigs, or chopped in various ways depending on the type and how it is to be used.

CHOP When you want the flavor to mingle completely with that of other ingredients, or for sprinkling over food as a fresh garnish at the end of cooking. Chopping immediately releases the herbs' flavor; whether it's done finely or coarsely is up to you and the dish you are making.

■ Strip the leaves from their stems onto a board. Hold a sharp knife in one hand (a blunt blade bruises rather than chops) and lay the fingers of your other hand on the pointed end. Keeping the pointed end in one position, move the knife backward and forward over the herbs in a continuous rocking motion. Keep scooping back into a pile and chopping until done (see illustration, right).

CHOPPING HERBS

SHREDDING HERBS

POUND To make a paste or sauce, such as Thai curry paste or pesto.
■ Use a pestle and mortar (see Kitchen Kit, page 65), or mini food processor to crush to the desired consistency.

SHRED If you want to add texture to a dish, or to use as a garnish (Chiffonade, see page 15). Use for bigger leaves such as basil or mint.
■ Lay several leaves on top of each other and roll them up like a cigar. Cut thinly across the width with a sharp knife and the slices will fall into fine shreds (see illustration, right).

SNIP Some herbs, especially chives, are more successfully chopped with scissors than with a knife.
■ Snip chives with scissors in small pieces for flavoring, or into long strands for use as a garnish. This method is handy for cutting small

BOUQUET GARNI

This is a little bundle of herbs, traditionally a few sprigs of parsley and thyme and a bay leaf, wrapped in cheesecloth or a fresh bay leaf, and tied up with string. It is used to flavor slow-cooked dishes such as stews and soups and is thrown away at the end of cooking. The herbs used can be added to or varied, depending on the dish in which the bouquet garni is being used. For example, rosemary goes well with lamb dishes or sage with pork dishes.

amounts of parsley too—drop parsley sprigs into a cup or small bowl and snip them finely with scissors. Or snip other herbs such as cilantro, mint, or parsley straight over a dish to get the full flavor effect.

COOKING WITH HERBS

When cooking with herbs, taste before serving, remembering that packets of fresh herbs from supermarkets often have a milder flavor than home-grown.

DRIED HERBS are mostly added at the beginning of cooking, both to soften them and release their flavor.

FRESH HERBS with sturdy stems, such as thyme and rosemary, are added early on for flavor, or later to give color. Soft, leafy herbs, such as cilantro, chervil, chives, basil, and dill, have more flavor when raw so are better sprinkled on at the end of cooking to keep their vibrancy.

FRYING HERBS

Some herbs, such as parsley, basil, and sage, make wonderful garnishes when they are briefly fried until crisp. Make sure the leaves are really dry first, then heat about 1 inch vegetable, sunflower, or peanut oil in a small, heavy pan. To test if it's ready, drop a leaf in and it should sizzle immediately. When the oil is hot enough, drop in the herbs, a few leaves at a time to give them room (parsley can be fried in sprigs), and after a few seconds, when they are crisp and just turning color, lift them out with a slotted spoon, and drain on paper towels. Fried herbs are delicious scattered on risottos and pasta.

DRIED HERBS

Nothing matches the flavor that fresh herbs give to a dish, but dried are handy to be able to use at a moment's notice and are especially good in slow-cooked dishes. Robust herbs keep their flavor best when dried. The top five to have in your pantry are:

- Bay
- Oregano
- Rosemary
- Sage
- Thyme

SUBSTITUTING FRESH FOR DRIED:

1 tablespoon fresh = 1 teaspoon dried.

basil

HERBS A–Z

Basil

Think of basil and you invariably think of Italy. But this herb has a lot more going for it than pesto. You'll find it in many Thai, Malaysian, Indonesian, and other Southeast Asian recipes.

CHOOSE Available fresh (for the varieties you are most likely to find, see below). Also freeze-dried, dried, or in sunflower oil.

TASTE The different fresh varieties have similar taste characteristics to the most common sweet basil. Generally Mediterranean basils tend to be milder and sweeter, Asian ones more pungent.

Mediterranean:

- Sweet basil: Its large, bright green leaves are a must for making traditional pesto. The taste is peppery with a hint of cloves, mint, and anise.
- Greek basil: Its small leaves are perfect for nipping off the stem and tossing into salads. Peppery in taste.
- Purple basil: A dark, rich color that is stunning mixed into salads. Similar in taste to sweet basil, just a little milder.

Asian:

- Lemon basil: Looks a little like

BASIL

MAKE YOUR OWN PESTO

There are many ways to make pesto. This is an easy one with loads of flavor that includes parsley as well as basil.

Drop ½ cup basil leaves and ⅓ cup flat-leaf parsley leaves into a food processor with ½ cup pine nuts, 1 ounce Parmesan cheese (cut into small cubes), and 1 coarsely chopped garlic clove. Process until mixed, then gradually pour in ¼ cup olive oil, keeping the machine running until you have a moist paste.

The pesto will keep in the refrigerator for up to a week—if it starts to dry out, just pour a little more olive oil on top to keep it well covered.

oregano. Its fresh, citrusy taste and fragrance make it a good partner for fish and shellfish.

■ Thai basil: This has all the flavors of sweet basil, but more so.

■ Holy basil: More intense, aromatic, and spicy and, unlike sweet basil, its flavor is better when cooked than raw. Used a lot in Thai cooking.

STORE Keeps only briefly in the refrigerator as the leaves soon wilt and darken. Lasts longest when bought in a pot. Put in a sunny but sheltered spot, water, and use it; new leaves should keep coming to supply you with basil for several months (see Storing Fresh Herbs, page 128).

PREPARE Keep leaves whole and strew over dishes just before serving. For a more casual look, tear them with your fingers. Thin shreds of basil leaves (see page 129) look pretty sprinkled on soups or rice dishes such as risotto.

COOK Basil is a tender herb and loses its flavor and color if added too soon, so it's best to sprinkle it over a dish after cooking.

USE FOR

■ Making pesto (see page 131).

■ Sprinkling over salads and pizzas, adding to pasta and noodle dishes,

sauces and stir-fries, sprinkling over fish before steaming.

■ Tucking a few leaves under chicken skin before roasting.

■ Frying whole leaves to use as a garnish (see Frying Herbs, page 130).

■ Flavoring cream for using in savory custards or sauces—chop the basil, then heat it in the cream, and let it take on the flavor for about an hour. Strain and use.

■ Making flavored butter (see opposite).

■ Adding to summer fruit, especially raspberries and strawberries.

GOES WITH Tomatoes and garlic, mozzarella cheese, zucchini, eggplants, new potatoes, fish, chicken, raspberries, and strawberries.

USE INSTEAD All the basils can be used interchangeably. Use dried basil instead of fresh only if you have to, as the flavor is nowhere near so vibrant. Replace with fresh mint if using basil in Thai recipes, oregano in tomato recipes, or use parsley or cilantro for a different-flavored pesto.

Bay

The shiny, elegant-looking leaf from an evergreen tree is one of the hardiest of herbs. It is used a good deal

basil–bay

in Mediterranean cooking and many other cuisines too.

CHOOSE Fresh (available all year around), freeze-dried, or dried.

TASTE When picked straight from the tree, bay leaves have a slightly bitter aftertaste, but this quickly fades as the leaf wilts, so it's better to use them dried or semi-dried. The bay leaf should not be eaten, so when it has given its flavor to a dish, throw it away. Adds a complex, slightly sweet, spicy, almost astringent flavor, dried bay being more intense.

STORE Fresh leaves will keep that way for up to 4–5 days. To dry your own, just lay them flat, away from direct light, and leave for a few days until brittle and a dull green color. Dried bay will keep in an airtight container for about 9 months. Once the leaves turn brown, the flavor is lost.

PREPARE The leaves are usually used whole, although tearing them into a couple of pieces helps to release the flavor more quickly.

COOK Bay is the opposite of basil— cook it long and slow in a dish and it loves it. You usually don't need to add more than a couple of dried leaves for

HERB BUTTERS

These are great to have for melting over fish, into mashed or crushed potatoes, over steaks and chicken, spreading on toast to go with scrambled eggs, or to make herbed garlic bread. Beat the herbs with softened butter, tip onto a piece of plastic wrap, and shape into a log. Wrap tightly with another piece of plastic wrap. The butter will keep in the refrigerator for up to 5 days, or in the freezer for up to 2 months.

WITH ½ CUP SOFT BUTTER YOU CAN MAKE:

■ *SUMMER HERB BUTTER Beat in 3–4 tablespoons chopped, mixed herbs such as parsley, basil, and marjoram.*

■ *CHIVE AND GARLIC BUTTER Beat in 2–3 tablespoons snipped chives and 1 crushed plump garlic clove (or use just garlic chives, omitting the fresh garlic).*

■ *HOT TARRAGON BUTTER Mix in 1 teaspoon chopped tarragon and 1 tablespoon whole-grain mustard or ½ teaspoon crushed dried chili flakes.*

■ *LEMONGRASS BUTTER Mix in 1 finely sliced stalk of lemongrass, 2 teaspoons finely grated lime zest, and a handful of chopped cilantro. Goes well with chicken or fish.*

a gutsy stew, but if using fresh, one or two more won't go amiss.

USE FOR

■ Flavoring stews (especially beef or fish), soups, stocks, tagines, sauces (lovely with tomato), marinades, steeping savory white sauces, even in a sweet custard.

■ Sprinkling among potatoes, fish, or chicken fillets while they roast, or inside the cavity of a whole chicken or fish for fragrance.

■ Threading onto skewers between chunks of fish, meat, chicken, or vegetables to flavor kabobs.

■ Dropping into the cooking water of rice (for taste), cabbage or cauliflower (to help eliminate the smell).

■ A garnish with melted butter on top of meat or fish pâtés.

GOES WITH Beef, chicken, lamb, legume and rice dishes, fish, shellfish, lemons, tomatoes.

USE INSTEAD Juniper berries (page 180), for slow-cooked meat dishes, or thyme sprigs (page 159)— they will give a different flavor.

Borage

The best thing about borage is its perky little star-shaped vibrant-blue flowers, although the leaves can be used too. Used in European dishes.

CHOOSE Fresh is the only kind of borage available.

TASTE Quite mild, often likened to cucumber. Use the leaves sparingly.

STORE Use flowers soon after picking. The leaves don't last much longer—up to a day or two in the refrigerator (see Storing Fresh Herbs, page 128). Flowers can be frozen in ice cubes for dropping into drinks (see Storing Fresh Herbs, page 128).

PREPARE The leaves are best used when tender and young, and, as they are rather prickly and hairy, they need to be finely chopped.

COOK Not a cooking herb—but great in salads.

USE FOR

Flowers: Floating in tall glasses of Pimms or other summer drinks, sprinkling over fruit or leafy salad greens, decorating cakes and desserts. Leaves: Ripping into soups (such as cucumber, spinach, and pea) and tossing into salads (especially potato). Whole leaves can go with the flowers in a glass of Pimms.

USE INSTEAD Baby spinach leaves (only for savory dishes).

BORAGE

Chervil

One of the more delicate herbs, its fine stems hold up sprigs of feathery leaves. It is used mostly in European cooking, particularly French, and is sometimes called French parsley.

CHERVIL

CHOOSE Fresh chervil.

TASTE Delicate in appearance and flavor, so use quite generously. Has a hint of parsley and anise about it.

STORE Fresh chervil stores for up to 2 days in the refrigerator (see Storing Fresh Herbs, page 128).

PREPARE A coarse chop, including the stems, is all that is needed.

COOK Stir into sauces or any other hot dish at the end of cooking for the most flavor, or throw over warm cooked vegetables just before serving.

USE FOR
- Combining with parsley, chives, and tarragon for the classic *fines herbes* mix in French cooking.
- Adding to salads, omelets, creamy sauces, and dressings.

HERBS A–Z

■ Mixing with melted butter, lemon zest, and juice for pouring over fish.

GOES WITH Eggs, fish, shellfish, chicken, asparagus, peas, carrots, potatoes, beet, fava beans.

USE INSTEAD Parsley, dill, chives, tarragon, fennel leaves (although all offer different flavors).

Chives

A delicately flavored member of the onion family. The pale purple flowers can be used as well as the stems, which look like plump, long blades of grass. Chives were used in China thousands of years ago—there is a variety called garlic chives that is also known as Chinese chives.

CHOOSE Fresh, dried, or freeze-dried. For fresh, the stems should look pert and crisp. Garlic chives, traditionally used in Chinese and Indian cooking, are broader and flatter.

TASTE Use chives generously for a mild, slightly sweet and spicy onion flavor. They are one of the classic French herbs. The initial taste of garlic chives is mild and grassy, followed by a sudden mighty garlic kick that lingers. Use these more cautiously.

STORE Keep in the refrigerator for up to 3 days (see Storing Fresh Herbs, page 128).

PREPARE The easiest way is to gather a bundle of stems together and snip with scissors—cut them short and fine for mixing and sprinkling, long for using as an edible garnish.

COOK To keep their crispness and oniony flavor, snip them over food at the end of cooking rather than during.

USE FOR
Flowers:
■ Sprinkling over salads. They are edible, but used more as a garnish.
Stems:
■ Livening up the flavor of omelets, sauces, soups, rice, salsas, cheese dishes, and salad dressings.
■ Making flavored butter (see Herb Butters, page 133).
■ Stirring into savory biscuit, pancake, and muffin mixes.
■ Mixing with sour cream and folding into crushed potatoes, or into soft cheese for baked potato toppings.

GOES WITH Eggs, potatoes, tomatoes, smoked fish (especially salmon), salad greens, chicken, sour cream and cream cheese, avocados, beet, carrots, globe artichokes.

USE INSTEAD The green tops of scallions.

Cilantro

Every last bit of this herb gets used: even the root is prized in Thai cooking. It's a global herb, cropping up in Mexican, Latin and North American, Thai, African, Indian, Middle Eastern, Asian, and Mediterranean (especially Portuguese) cooking. It looks a little like flat-leaf parsley only floppier, and is also known as Chinese parsley.

CHOOSE Fresh, freeze-dried, dried, or in sunflower oil. The seeds of cilantro form the spice coriander, and are available as dried seeds and powder (see Spices, page 174).

TASTE Cilantro is a mix of flavors —hints of lemon, sage, mint, pepper, and ginger—all of which give a unique refreshing taste. If you love it, add loads. The root is more pungent than the leaves and stems.

STORE Keeps in the refrigerator for up to 4–5 days (see Storing Fresh Herbs, page 128). Outer leaves can turn yellow, so check regularly.

PREPARE A large bunch may need a good rinse to get rid of any gritty

CHIVES

CILANTRO

soil. Chop the tender part of the stems along with the leaves, or just tear the leaves off the stems and sprinkle in whole. The roots are traditionally pounded in a curry paste.

COOK The roots and stems are cooked in curry pastes or dishes that are simmered. The more fragile leaves are best stirred in at the end so their distinctive flavor is not lost.

USE FOR
■ Adding flavor to Thai curry pastes (the root) and *chermoula*—a spicy Moroccan marinade (leaves and stems).
■ Flavoring Indian lentil dishes, such as *dhal* (stems).
■ Stirring into salsas (good with tomato or mango), fresh chutneys, and relishes (goes well with corn), also hummus.
■ Tossing at the last minute into stir-fries, noodle and rice salads, and slow-cooked braises.
■ Making a cilantro pesto.
■ Piling in profusion onto noodle soups for a garnish.

GOES WITH Coconut milk, chilies, ginger, garlic, lime, rice, noodles, chicken, lamb, pork, fish, shrimp.

USE INSTEAD Flat-leaf parsley—you'll get the look but not the flavor.

Curry leaf

This looks a little like a miniature bay leaf, but is less sturdy and is used in greater quantities. It grows mainly in India and Sri Lanka where it is used to flavor curries. Also found in Malaysian and Indonesian cooking.

CHOOSE Fresh (from good Indian specialty stores) or freeze-dried.

TASTE When very fresh, the leaves are incredibly aromatic with a sweet, spicy taste of curry. They give a mild curry flavor to dishes rather than heat. The flavor becomes more muted after drying.

STORE Fresh leaves can be kept for 3–4 days in the refrigerator. They freeze well, so if you have too many, pack the rest flat in a plastic bag and store them in the freezer for up to 3 months.

PREPARE Simply strip the leaves from the stems in a single motion.

COOK Curry leaves may be fried, often with mustard seeds, at the start of a dish to bring out their aroma, or sprinkled in at the end. As the dried leaf tastes milder than the fresh, you may need to use more.

USE FOR

■ A flavor base for curries.

■ Chopping and mixing into fresh chutneys and relishes (fresh only).

GOES WITH Chicken, lamb, fish, most vegetables (especially root vegetables), mangoes.

USE INSTEAD No substitute.

Curry plant

This has silvery-green leaves that look a little like those of a rosemary plant. If you rub them between your fingers, or brush past the plant, the curry aroma is intoxicating—far stronger than the taste.

USE FOR

■ Flavoring rice, vegetables, or salads.

Dill

Dill has long been associated with Scandinavian cooking where it is popular with fish, but it is also used a lot in Russia, Iran, Germany, and Turkey. Its light, feathery sprigs are similar to those of fennel, just a little spikier.

CHOOSE Fresh, dried, or freeze-dried. Dill seeds are available as a spice (see Spices, page 176).

DILL

TASTE Mild with a slight touch of aniseed.

STORE Fresh in the refrigerator for up to 3 days (see Storing Fresh Herbs, page 128). Once it starts to droop, it is past its best.

PREPARE Strip the fronds from the tougher main stalk, and tear, snip, or chop.

COOK Will lose its flavor if added too early to a dish.

USE FOR
■ Stirring into creamy sauces for fish and chicken.
■ Marinating for pickles or with salmon for gravad lax.
■ Salad dressings—delicious in a potato salad.
■ Snipping over vegetables just before serving—try on buttered carrots or fresh beans.
■ Stuffing whole sprigs into fish before baking.

GOES WITH Fish (especially salmon, mackerel, trout, tuna), eggs, beet, fava beans, green beans, potatoes, cucumber.

USE INSTEAD Fennel fronds or tarragon (gives a different flavor).

Elderflower
see EDIBLE FLOWERS, *page 161*

Fennel
Green fennel has frond-like leaves that look much like dill, although the foliage is a bit more dense on thicker stalks. Not to be confused with the fennel bulb.

CHOOSE Fresh, as green or bronze fennel (the leaves are best when young). Fennel seeds are available as a spice (see Spices, page 176).

TASTE Fennel has an even more defined aniseed taste than dill. Bronze fennel is milder.

STORE In the refrigerator for up to 3 days (see Storing Fresh Herbs, page 128).

PREPARE Chop, using the stalks as well as the leaves.

COOK Stirring it into a dish toward the end of cooking will soften it as well as bring out the flavor.

USE FOR
■ Livening up sauces for fish, chowders, and fishy soups.

- Roasting fish—make an herb bed with the whole stalks.

FENNEL

GOES WITH Oily fish, (especially mackerel, trout, sardines, salmon), potatoes, rice, beet.

USE INSTEAD Dill, or fronds from the fennel bulb.

FENUGREEK

Fenugreek

Used a lot in Indian and Iranian cooking, fenugreek (or *methi* as it is called in India) has a leaf shape that is similar to clover, but with larger gaps between the leaves. In Indian cooking, the leaves are often used in salads.

CHOOSE Fresh (usually available in Indian and Iranian specialty stores). Fenugreek seeds are available as a spice (see Spices, page 177).

TASTE This leaf has an extremely mild, slightly bitter, grassy flavor when raw.

STORE Fresh fenugreek will keep in the refrigerator for up to 3 days (see Storing Fresh Herbs, page 128).

PREPARE A little chopping is all that's required.

COOK The bitterness is reduced by cooking, which also releases a curry-powder aroma and taste.

USE FOR

■ Stirring into fish curries and *dhal*.

■ Giving a spicy flavor to burgers and Indian *seekh* kabobs.

■ Mixing into an herb omelet.

■ Tossing with cooked potatoes or into salads.

■ Adding to Indian bread such as *chappati*.

GOES WITH Potatoes and rice, lamb, chicken, cauliflower, green beans, tomatoes, mushrooms, shrimp, yogurt, garlic, ginger.

USE INSTEAD Fresh curry leaves.

Filé powder
see SASSAFRAS, *page 155*

Lavender

Not just a pretty flower that is found in the garden, lavender is popular in cooking in Mediterranean countries as well as in England. It is used mainly to give flavor to sweet dishes, but also to some savory recipes. You can eat both the leaves and the flowers, but the flowers are the best.

CHOOSE Fresh. For use in cooking, it's best to grow your own if you can, as plants bought in a florist or horticulture store may have been sprayed with pesticides.

TASTE Lavender has a powerful flavor and sweet fragrance that is a mix of floral with citrus. The flowers give a stronger flavor than the leaves, and are more commonly used. But, be sure to use very cautiously—too much will give an overpoweringly perfumed taste to your food.

STORE Will keep for up to a week in the refrigerator (see Storing Fresh Herbs, page 128).

PREPARE Rinse and carefully dry the lavender on paper towels. Chop the leaves finely (if using them); chop the flowers finely or carefully pull the petals out separately.

USE FOR

■ Flavoring superfine sugar for use in cakes, cookies, meringues, chocolate cake or muffins, ice cream, jellies, rice pudding, custard, and *crème brûlée*. Nestle a few dried flower heads into a jar of sugar and leave for a week or two for the flavor to develop. Sift them out before using the sugar.

fenugreek–lemon

■ A substitute for rosemary (the spiky leaves) for adding to bread, or use the lavender stems as skewers for fruit or lamb kabobs.

■ A flavorsome decoration in salads (the flowers), sprinkled on desserts, or dropped into a chilled glass of champagne or white wine.

■ Chopping and adding just a few sprigs straight into cake and cookie mixes.

■ Steeping in milk or cream for creamy desserts.

GOES WITH Lamb, game (especially good with pheasant), rabbit, cream, raspberries, straw-berries, apricots and other summer fruits, rhubarb.

USE INSTEAD Rosemary, although the flavor is different.

Lemon balm

This herb is a member of the mint family, which it resembles closely.

CHOOSE Fresh only. Leaves will either be variegated with splashes of yellow, or plain green. Younger leaves have a better flavor.

TASTE A mild combination of lemon and mint.

LEMON BALM

STORE Will keep in the refrigerator for about 4 days, or freeze in ice cubes for dropping into drinks (see Storing Fresh Herbs, page 128).

PREPARE Chop, shred, or use the leaves whole or as sprigs (like mint) for adding to drinks.

COOK Best used with cold dishes, as heat kills its flavor, although it can also be added to a dish at the end of cooking.

USE FOR

■ Tearing or chopping into tomato salsas or salads, or whole in mixed salad greens.
■ Sprinkling over cooked vegetables such as carrots and zucchini.
■ Adding chopped to sauces, stuffings, or marinades.
■ Steeping a sugar syrup for use in fruit salads.
■ Flavoring creams and custards.
■ Making herbal tea.
■ Decorating and giving flavor to a glass of iced tea or other summer coolers.

GOES WITH Chicken, veal, fish, creamy sauces, tomatoes, vegetables, summer fruits and berries.

USE INSTEAD Lemon zest.

Lemongrass

Adds the exotic fragrance to Thai, Indonesian, and Vietnamese food, but it crosses the culinary divide well and is wonderful in Western dishes too. It looks a bit like a drier, firmer version of a scallion stalk—it is the pale green part of the stem that holds the key to its flavor.

CHOOSE Fresh or freeze-dried. Also available crushed in sunflower oil, a convenient and concentrated way to buy it. Fresh stalks should feel firm and heavy—if they feel light, the chances are the whole thing has dried out too much.

TASTE Unique. Not exactly lemony, more like a refreshingly tart perfumed citrus essence. Not added for its looks, just for its flavor.

STORE Keeps in the refrigerator in a plastic bag for about a couple of weeks. Or freeze, tightly bound in plastic wrap, for several months.

PREPARE Lemongrass is used whole, sliced, or pounded to a paste. To release the flavor, remove the outside of the stalk, slice off the bottom, then peel off any dry outside layers. Give a hefty bash with a rolling pin

lemon–lemongrass

to bruise it and you will smell the scented oils being released. If using to flavor a stew or curry, the whole stalk can be dropped in, then removed at the end as you would a bay leaf. For adding to marinades or salads, cut the bottom part of the stalk into very fine slices. As soon as it starts to feel hard stop slicing, as the top part can be rather woody. Or, for a curry paste, pound the sliced stalk to a paste using a pestle and mortar. If using dried lemongrass, it helps to soak it in hot water for an hour or so before using to soften it, unless it is going to be cooked in liquid for a longish time.

COOK The whole stalk is added at the beginning of slow-cooked dishes for the flavor to steep, then removed at the end.

USE FOR
- Flavoring Thai curries, especially with fish and chicken.
- Adding to the water used for steaming fish, chicken, or vegetables, along with some ginger and other aromatics such as star anise, for a gentle scent.
- Flavoring marinades (finely chopped), soups (goes well with tomato), noodle broths, or stocks.
- Mixing raw finely chopped into salads (especially chicken or shellfish)—use the lower tender white part of the stem.

LEMONGRASS

- A skewer for kabobs—wrap ground meat around a whole stem for broiling or grilling. Or cut each stem into four lengthwise and use as a skewer on which to thread pieces of food.
- Flavoring cream for *crème brûlée*.
- Bringing a fragrance to fruit salads, especially tropical fruit salads, by flavoring a syrup (see opposite).

GOES WITH Chicken, fish, shellfish, pork, beef, chili, tomato, coconut, ginger, galangal, lime leaves, cilantro, basil, most fruits and vegetables.

USE INSTEAD Lemon zest—although don't expect the unique intense fragrance of lemongrass.

Lemon verbena

Native to Chile, lemon verbena is a plant worth growing. As well as providing an herb for culinary use, you can also enjoy its fragrance.

CHOOSE A fresh herb you are more likely to find in a horticulture store.

TASTE Fresh, lemony, and fragrant. Use generously.

STORE Once picked, the leaves last a couple of days in the refrigerator (see Storing Fresh Herbs, page 128).

PREPARE Use finely chopped or as sprigs.

USE FOR
- Adding to rice to serve with chicken or fish.
- Flavoring salads and drinks—whole leaves are especially good in iced tea.
- Steeping in cream for making ice cream.

GOES WITH Chicken, pork, duck, fish, carrots, rice.

USE INSTEAD Lemongrass or lemon zest.

Lime leaf

The kaffir lime leaf, also known as makrut, is dark green and glossy, shaped like an elongated heart with two leaves joined at their base, and grows on an evergreen tree which also bears the fresh kaffir lime fruit used in Asian cooking. Gives a special and unique citrus flavor to the cooking of Southeast Asia, particularly to that of Thailand and Indonesia.

CHOOSE Fresh and freeze-dried.

TASTE Aromatic with an intensely fragrant citrus flavor, and a strong scent of lime.

lemongrass–lime leaf

STORE The fresh leaves will keep for several weeks in a plastic bag in the refrigerator and freeze well, too, for up to a year.

PREPARE Use whole, or shred very finely with a pair of scissors or a small, sharp knife.

COOK Use lime leaves as you would bay—drop them in at the beginning of cooking, and take them out before serving. Shred as above for adding more last-minute flavor to a stir-fry.

USE FOR
- Sprinkling into stir-fries (good with pork and chicken).
- Adding to Thai fish cakes, curries, and stir-fries (finely chopped).
- Tossing into salads (shredded).
- A garnish for soups and curries— very finely shredded.
- Dropping into cool summer drinks.
- Steeping with milk or cream for custards and other creamy desserts.

GOES WITH Chicken, pork, salmon, shrimp, fish, rice, coconut, lemongrass, Thai basil, cilantro, ginger, blueberries.

USE INSTEAD Strips of lime zest—will give the citrus taste but not the unique perfume.

LEMONGRASS SYRUP

Stir 1 generous cup boiling water into ½ cup golden superfine sugar and stir until the sugar has dissolved. Add 1 bruised, halved lemongrass stalk and let cool. Pour the syrup into jars and chill for 2–3 days. Remove the lemongrass before serving. Use for fruit salads.

LEMON VERBENA

LIME LEAF

Lovage

This slightly resembles the leaves of celery, and is used mostly in European dishes. If you want to use this herb, you will probably have to grow it.

CHOOSE Fresh lovage is not often available commercially, but it is easy to grow in a pot.

TASTE Like celery, only much stronger. If added in large quantities, it can overpower, so use sparingly.

STORE Fresh will keep for 3–4 days in the refrigerator (see page 128).

PREPARE Both leaves and stems are used, but if the stems are thick they will be tough, so discard. Use chopped or finely shredded (page 129).

COOK Despite its similarity to celery, it is not so robust when cooked, so it is best added at the end.

USE FOR

■ Adding to chowders, especially fish chowder.
■ Tossing a few leaves into an apple and cheese, or leaf salad.
■ Making soup (on its own or with potatoes and carrots), stock, sauces, marinades.

GOES WITH Legumes, lamb, pork, fish, root vegetables, apples, rice.

USE INSTEAD Parsley or celery leaves, or an equal mix of both.

Marigold

see EDIBLE FLOWERS, *page 161*

Marjoram and oregano

These herbs are closely related. They both look similar and have a similar taste. (Oregano is sometimes known as wild marjoram.) They are popular in Italian, Greek, and Mexican cooking, especially when tomatoes are among the ingredients.

CHOOSE Fresh, freeze-dried, and dried.

TASTE A warm, aromatic spiciness pervades both herbs. Marjoram tends to be milder and sweeter, especially sweet marjoram; oregano is a little stronger, more peppery.

STORE Fresh will keep for about 3 days in the refrigerator (see Storing Fresh Herbs, page 128), dried for up to a year in an airtight container.

lovage–mint

PREPARE Use the leaves whole or chopped. Sprigs of the little pink or white flowers make a pretty garnish.

COOK Add toward the end of cooking to preserve their flavor.

USE FOR
- Chopping into Greek salad.
- Sprinkling over pizzas, into sauces (popular in souvlaki), and over roast vegetables.
- Stuffings, especially for chicken and lamb.
- Roasting with lamb—just sit the roast on top of a big bunch.
- Making a marinade for chicken by mixing with olive oil, lemon juice, and crushed dried chilies.

GOES WITH Lamb, tomatoes, olives, garlic, lemons.

USE INSTEAD Use marjoram and oregano interchangeably.

LOVAGE

MARJORAM/OREGANO

Mint

Traditionally a familiar herb in the United States (think of mint julep and many popular candies), although it is also used in many other countries, such as India (mixed into raw chutneys), Morocco (mint tea), and France (crème de menthe liqueur).

HERBS A–Z

CHOOSE Fresh, freeze-dried, or dried, although dried lacks that refreshing minty flavor. Dried mint is used more in Mediterranean countries, often mixed with oregano. There are numerous mint varieties, but the one most commonly grown is spearmint, also known as garden mint. Peppermint and apple mint are popular too. In addition, there is Moroccan mint with its smaller leaves, and Indian mint with its very powerful flavor. For Vietnamese mint, see opposite.

TASTE Spearmint is menthol-fresh, slightly sweet, and slightly sharp. Peppermint and apple mint are milder, apple mint combining mint and the sweetness of apple. Moroccan mint is quite spicy, but not so sweet as spearmint.

STORE Keeps for up to 3 days in the refrigerator (see Storing Fresh Herbs, page 128), or keep in water like a small bunch of flowers

PREPARE Strip the leaves from the stems (which can be tough, so discard) and use whole or torn, shredded or chopped. Smaller leaves at the top of the stem tend to be sweeter and tastier, so they are good to save for garnishing.

COOK Best sprinkled onto food raw at the end of cooking, although it is also added to boiling potatoes or peas.

USE FOR
- Mixing into yogurt with grated cucumber and a little cumin for a spicy raita dip, or without the cumin for tzatziki.
- Tossing into an omelet with crumbled feta.
- Adding a sprig or two to boiling water as you cook new potatoes or peas.
- Flavoring salads (great with couscous, tomatoes, and new potatoes), and fruit or vegetable salsas.
- Stirring into ground meat for meatballs, kabobs, or burgers.
- Adding to the water when steaming white fish.
- Dropping into a glass of Pimms or a pitcher of punch.
- Sprinkling over slices of sweetened strawberries.

GOES WITH Lamb, chicken, duck, shrimp, feta or halloumi cheese, beet, spring vegetables (especially new potatoes, peas, and fava beans), zucchini, tomatoes, cucumber, peaches, strawberries and raspberries, oranges, watermelon, apples, chocolate, yogurt, oregano.

USE INSTEAD No real substitute.

Nasturtium
see EDIBLE FLOWERS, *page 161*

Nettle
This traditional herb is collected wild; make sure the area where you pick it has not been sprayed with pesticides.

CHOOSE Young, tender leaves in the spring.

TASTE Similar to spinach. Not to be eaten raw because of its sting.

STORE Best used as soon after picking as possible as it wilts quickly.

PREPARE AND COOK Cook as you would spinach (see Vegetables, page 314). The leaves lose their sting after cooking.

USE FOR
■ Adding to soups.
■ Mixing into bread dough—gives a lovely green fleck to the bread.

USE INSTEAD Spinach.

Oregano
see MARJORAM AND OREGANO, *page 148*

MOROCCAN MINT TEA
Mint tea is a national drink in Morocco. To make enough for 6, heat the teapot with boiling water first. Throw out the water, add 2–3 teaspoons green tea leaves, ½ teaspoon dried mint, and 4–5 sugar cubes, then tuck in several sprigs of washed, fresh mint so the pot is tightly filled. Fill up with boiling water, let it steep for about a minute, then serve immediately (traditionally in small, heatproof glasses)—if the tea sits too long it starts to taste bitter.

VIETNAMESE MINT
Despite its name, this is not actually mint. It is a spicy and aromatic Asian herb that tastes more like cilantro. It is quite hard to find, but traditionally used a lot in salads, stir-fries, soups, and noodle dishes and for wrapping inside spring rolls. It is also called Rau Ram and Vietnamese coriander

HERBS A–Z

Parsley

A real all-rounder and a most useful herb for adding a splash of color as well as flavor to many European, American, and Middle Eastern dishes. It is both hardy and readily available.

CHOOSE Fresh—between curly and flat-leaf. Curly is the traditional parsley in northern countries and is a brighter green than the darker, more open, flat-leaf parsley that is often referred to as Italian parsley. Dried and freeze-dried are also available.

TASTE Curly parsley has a fresh, grassy flavor, flat-leaf parsley has a stronger flavor.

STORE Keeps for about 5 days in the refrigerator, or freeze (see Storing Fresh Herbs, page 128).

PREPARE The leaves are used finely chopped (if you want to have parsley as a background flavor and texture), or whole or coarsely chopped for a dish such as a salad, where the parsley is an important part of the taste. The stalks can flavor stocks.

COOK For the best flavor, add at the end of cooking. Fried parsley is used as a garnish

USE FOR
- Mixing with grated lemon zest and finely chopped garlic for Italian *gremolata*—sprinkling over fish, veal, chicken, or lamb before serving.
- Bulking out basil for making pesto.
- Sprinkling into soups, stews, and sauces (the most traditional being parsley sauce) at the end of cooking, for color and tangy taste.
- Stirring or tossing into meatballs, hamburgers, fish cakes, omelets, marinades, salsas.
- Adding flavor to salads, especially tabbouleh.
- Chewing if you've eaten garlic or onion to help get rid of the odor.

GOES WITH Most things, especially chicken, cured ham, fish, rice, pasta, eggs, tomatoes, most vegetables (it goes well with crushed potatoes), garlic, lemon, chives, basil.

USE INSTEAD Traditionally, use curly with north European recipes and flat-leaf with other cuisines—but there are no hard-and-fast rules. Chervil or cilantro make good substitutes.

Rosemary

A hardy herb that thrives in the warmth of the Mediterranean, but also grows well in cooler parts of

parsley–rosemary

Europe and America. It is an essential ingredient in *herbes de Provence* (a French blend of herbs which also includes marjoram, tarragon, thyme, savory, bay, lavender, and basil).

CHOOSE Fresh and dried are available all year around. Dried keeps its flavor quite well.

TASTE A very aromatic herb, with hints of pine and a bittersweet taste.

STORE For 5–6 days in the refrigerator (see Storing Fresh Herbs, page 128), or put stems in a vase of water.

PREPARE Sprigs and leaves are used whole to give flavor, but are hard and tough to eat, so chop finely if the herb is to be eaten. Use cautiously and taste when adding, as it can be overpowering if too much is used.

COOK Unlike that of other herbs, the taste does not fade with cooking.

USE FOR
Chopped: Flavoring Mediterranean stews, sauces, and gravies, sprinkling over pork and lamb chops or roasts before cooking, adding sparingly to shortbread.
Individual leaves: Sprinkling over breads before baking, especially

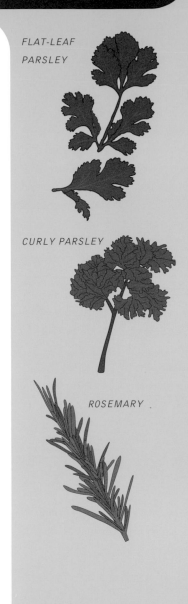

FLAT-LEAF PARSLEY

CURLY PARSLEY

ROSEMARY

Italian breads such as focaccia, also over meat and vegetables for roasting.

Sprigs and stems: Use the sprigs to brush olive oil over vegetables, then rest them on the vegetables as they roast or grill. Use sprigs to flavor oil or vinegar, or steep in cream or sugar syrup for desserts and fruit salads; throw onto barbecue coals and let the fragrance flavor the food as it cooks. Use older, firmer stems, stripped of leaves, as skewers for kabobs, sea scallops, or small bacon rolls to serve with turkey.

Flowers: Adding to drinks for decoration by freezing in ice cubes (see Storing Fresh Herbs, page 128).

GOES WITH Lamb, pork, duck, game, sausages, oily fish (especially salmon), monkfish, scallops, goat cheese, potatoes, legumes, tomatoes, olives, mushrooms, eggplants, pumpkin, squash, garlic, oranges, apricots, nectarines, and peaches.

USE INSTEAD Fresh thyme—although the taste is different.

Sage

Sage is a popular herb particularly in Italian cooking. It goes really well with oily foods and fatty meats as it cuts the richness.

CHOOSE AND TASTE Fresh, freeze-dried, or dried. There is a number of fresh varieties, the best known being common sage (silvery green leaves), which is strong and earthy. Other varieties include purple sage (milder in taste), pineapple sage (smells more of the fruit than it tastes) and tricolor sage (variegated leaf with pink, cream, and green patches, milder taste).

STORE Best eaten freshly picked, but keeps in the refrigerator for 2–3 days (see Storing Fresh Herbs, page 128).

PREPARE Use the leaves whole, or strip from the stems and chop finely.

COOK Sage is only used cooked—its flavor develops and doesn't disappear over time. Because of its powerful taste, it is not an herb to be added in large handfuls.

USE FOR

■ In the Italian tradition—to flavor butter for tossing with pasta (drop a few leaves into butter as it melts), mushrooms, or squash.

■ In the British tradition—to flavor meat and poultry stuffings.

■ In the Greek tradition—stirring into meat stews.

■ Frying the leaves for a crisp fragrant garnish (see Frying Herbs, page 130)—it goes really well on risotto and pasta, especially with pumpkin and squash.

GOES WITH Pork, duck, goose, liver, sausages, bacon, cheese, legumes (especially lentils), onions, pumpkin or squash, mushrooms, apples, thyme, and parsley.

USE INSTEAD Dried is a good substitute for fresh sage. Or you can use another hardy herb such as rosemary or thyme—but expect a different taste.

SAGE

Sassafras

The North American sassafras tree bears the leaves that are dried and ground to make filé powder which is used in Cajun and Creole cooking, a specialty of Louisiana. It both flavors and thickens stews—most famously, Creole gumbos.

CHOOSE Dried filé powder, some-times called gumbo filé.

TASTE Citrus and sour. It gives Creole gumbo (a spicy meat, fish, or vegetable stew) its distinctive taste.

HERBS A–Z

STORE Will keep for up to 6 months in an airtight container.

COOK Cooking or boiling makes the texture of filé powder go stringy, so, with the pan off the heat, stir it in just before serving. Doesn't reheat well.

USE FOR
■ Cajun and Creole cooking when you are thickening and flavoring soups and gumbos.
■ Serving separately as a flavoring like salt.

USE INSTEAD No substitute.

Savory

In Germany this herb is referred to as *Bohnenkraut*, the "bean herb"— it is happy to be paired with fava beans, wax beans, and lentils. Winter savory is robust and tough with thin, glossy leaves to see it through the cold; summer savory has longer, softer leaves.

CHOOSE Between summer and winter savory.

TASTE As its name suggests, savory is full of flavor. It has a slight, not unpleasant, bitter taste, so shouldn't be used with a heavy hand, especially winter savory. Summer savory is a little more delicate, tastes a little like thyme with a hint of marjoram, and is tender in texture. Winter savory is altogether more robust, has tougher leaves and a stronger flavor that is closer to that of sage.

STORE Being hardier, winter savory will last for about 10 days in the refrigerator, twice as long as summer savory (see Storing Fresh Herbs, page 128).

PREPARE Use it finely chopped, or as sprigs to give flavor to bean dishes as they cook.

COOK The taste is powerful raw, but mellows and improves with cooking.

USE FOR
■ Enhancing slow-cooked, robust, meaty stews and vegetables.
■ Flavoring stuffings along with other herbs such as thyme, mint and marjoram.
■ Stirring into bean or potato salads.

GOES WITH Lamb, pork, rabbit, oily fish (good with trout), most beans, peas, mushrooms, cabbage, root vegetables, beet.

USE INSTEAD Thyme or marjoram.

Sorrel

A member of the dock family (it looks like spinach) that grows wild in parts of Asia and Europe.

CHOOSE Between garden sorrel and the smaller French sorrel (also called buckler leaf sorrel). You are unlikely to find sorrel in supermarkets, but try looking in horticulture stores as it is an easy herb to grow.

TASTE A little like spinach, with a slight tartness and a bitter edge.

STORE For a day or two in the refrigerator (see Storing Fresh Herbs, page 128).

PREPARE Only the large leaves are used (stripped from the stalks), often shredded into ribbons (see page 129).

COOK You can cook it like spinach (see page 314)—briefly, until wilted and losing its vibrant-green color. It loses a lot of its volume when cooked.

USE FOR
- Shredding into omelets.
- Adding younger, raw leaves, shredded, to salad greens.
- Flavoring creamy soups, sauces, and purées for fish.

WINTER SAVORY

SUMMER SAVORY

GOES WITH Chicken, eggs, fish
(especially salmon).

USE INSTEAD Spinach.

Tarragon

An herb that some cooks just can't do
without. The French love it and it's
essential in *sauce béarnaise*. Although
the slender, floppy leaves appear delicate, they give a great flavor.

CHOOSE Available fresh, freeze-
dried, and dried. French tarragon is
the preferred variety—there is also
a Russian tarragon which lacks the
subtle, refined flavor of the French.

TASTE Strongly aromatic with a
touch of spicy pepper and licorice.
You need only a little of this delicate-
looking herb to give a lot of flavor to
a dish, so use cautiously and taste as
you go.

STORE Fresh keeps in the refrigerator for up to 5–6 days, or it freezes
well (see Storing Fresh Herbs,
page 128).

PREPARE Use whole leaves
stripped from the stalks, chopped
leaves, or as sprigs. It can be used
both raw or cooked.

COOK Cooking tarragon brings out
its best side and the flavor remains,
whether it is used in a dish that is
cooked for a long or short time.

USE FOR
- Most chicken dishes—tarragon
and chicken are a great combination.
Try tucking a few sprigs under the
skin of the bird before roasting.
- Adding to a potato salad.
- Stirring into mayonnaise and
serving alongside cold chicken or
poached salmon.
- Mixing 2–3 chopped leaves with
chives and chervil, or parsley, for a
fresh herb omelet—or with a few
fried mushrooms.
- Laying a sprig or two with lemon
slices in the cavity of a fish such as
trout or salmon before cooking, or
on top of fish or chicken fillets to be
cooked in paper packets.
- Flavoring white wine vinegar.
- Making herb butter (see Herb
Butters, page 133).

GOES WITH Chicken, prosciutto, fish
(especially salmon and trout), shellfish,
eggs, cream, potatoes, asparagus,
tomatoes, mushrooms, beet, carrots,
mayonnaise, lemon, mustard.

USE INSTEAD Fennel leaves,
although the flavor is different.

Thyme

An herb used in many dishes, favored by cooks around the world including British, Caribbean, Mediterranean, Mexican, Middle Eastern, and North American. It's perfect for flavoring rich, earthy dishes.

CHOOSE Fresh or dried. There are many varieties, the most familiar being common thyme. The second most popular is lemon thyme. Unlike many other herbs, dried thyme keeps its flavor well.

TASTE The tiny thyme leaves give off a sweet fragrance and a spicy, earthy taste. Lemon thyme blends the flavor of thyme with the fresh taste of lemons.

STORE Fresh will keep in the refrigerator for about a week (see Storing Fresh Herbs, page 128). Dried thyme keeps for about a year in an airtight container.

PREPARE As the leaves are very small, they can be stripped from the stems and thrown straight into a dish, or whole sprigs can be added. The tiny flowers can also be used as a garnish. Tie together with parsley and bay to make a *bouquet garni*.

TARRAGON

THYME

HERBS A–Z

COOK Thyme is one of the few herbs that can survive in the cooking pot for a long time. The stems can be a little tough and twig-like, so remove them prior to serving.

USE FOR

■ Enhancing the taste of robust dishes (such as Irish stew, steak and kidney pie, Cajun gumbos, French *cassoulet*), soups, sauces, casseroles, and roasts.
■ Adding to stuffings with other herbs such as parsley and rosemary.
■ Stirring into marinades, or dropping a few sprigs into stocks.
■ Giving flavor to fried or roast potatoes, or onions—sprinkle in a handful of leaves, or a few sprigs as they cook.
■ Stuffing into whole fish before cooking (lemon thyme).
■ Flavoring cookies (lemon thyme) and bread.
■ Mixing with goat cheese.

GOES WITH Most meats (especially lamb, pork, and game), poultry, fish, vegetables, beer and wine, legumes, feta, goat cheese.

USE INSTEAD Dried thyme instead of fresh, or *herbes de Provence* which includes thyme.

Verbena

see LEMON VERBENA, *page 146*

Vietnamese mint

see MINT, *page 149*

EDIBLE FLOWERS

Before using edible flowers, make sure they are clean and dry and haven't been sprayed with pesticide.

■ **Borage** See page 134.

■ **Elderflower** Catch elder while you can—it is in flower for a few weeks only in May. If picking from wild hedges, choose elderflower as far away as possible from the road to avoid any pollution, and use it on the day of picking. Whole heads can be used to make elderflower cordial, or they can be steeped in sugar syrup to extract their perfumed taste before using the liquid to make desserts such as sherbets and jellies.
USE INSTEAD: Elderflower cordial.

■ **Marigold** Pluck off the bright-yellow petals (don't use the centers) and use them straight away for sprinkling over salads. But don't stop there—they can add taste and color to custard or rice, instead of saffron.

■ **Nasturtium** Nasturtium flowers have a peppery taste, a little like cress, and look very pretty tumbled into salads, or tossed into summer fruit punches. The leaves are even more peppery, like arugula, and can be used in salads too.

■ **Rose** Sprinkle petals onto poached peaches or apricots for a Middle Eastern dessert, or over cakes and creamy desserts for an instant decoration. Individual petals can be frosted for a longer-lasting decoration. Gently brush each petal with lightly beaten egg white using a clean paint brush. Sprinkle all over with superfine sugar, shake off any excess, then lay the coated petals on waxed paper to dry and become crisp. They will keep for a week or more in an airtight container.

SPICES

FROM THE EXOTIC TO THE FAMILIAR, SPICES GIVE AUTHENTICITY TO CUISINES FROM AROUND THE WORLD. ALL HAVE A UNIQUE FLAVOR, AND IT'S GOOD TO KNOW HOW THEY CAN BE USED TO BRING OUT THEIR BEST CHARACTERISTICS. TO HELP YOU USE THEM AT THEIR BEST, BEFORE THEY LOSE THEIR POTENCY, THERE ARE ALSO SOME QUICK IDEAS FOR SPICING UP YOUR COOKING. AND IF YOU DON'T HAVE THE RIGHT SPICE, YOU'LL FIND SUGGESTIONS FOR ALTERNATIVES.

GRINDING WHOLE SPICES

Bought ground spices are convenient, but their flavor disappears quickly. For top taste and aroma you can't beat freshly ground. It's best to grind just the amount you need or that you can use up soon, as the flavor soon fades after grinding. Dry-fry first (see right) if you wish, then use any of the following grinding methods:

- Pestle and mortar—easy to crush, make as coarse or fine as you like.
- Rolling pin or heavy pan—put the whole spices into a strong freezer bag, seal the end, and bash them with a rolling pin or pan until crushed.
- Electric grinder—if you want to grind whole spices on a regular basis, buy a special spice grinder or keep a small coffee grinder just for this purpose, so your coffee won't be spicy or your spices coffee-flavored.

BRINGING OUT THE FLAVOR

Heat brings out the flavor of spices, whether they are to be used whole or in preparation for grinding.

Dry-frying: To get the fullest flavor from spices or seeds, they are often dry-fried first in a pan with no oil. Heat a small, heavy skillet (without any oil), tip in the spices, and fry them over medium heat, stirring or tossing around frequently for a minute or two, lowering the heat if they brown too quickly. When they start to turn brown and smell rich and nutty, remove from the heat and cool. Use whole or crushed.

Tarka: A special Indian technique where spices such as mustard and cumin seeds are fried in hot oil. This intensifies the flavor of both the seeds and the oil. Heat a thin layer of oil in

cajun spice

a heavy pan until very hot. Add the seeds—they will sizzle and jump around in the pan. Watch carefully and remove once they start to deepen in color. This takes only a few seconds.

SPICE MIXES

Ready-blended spice mixes bring the exotic and exciting flavors of other countries to your food and save you having to buy lots of different spices. (You can, of course, make them yourself too.) Use them to sprinkle into food, or as a spice rub on meat or fish before pan-frying, broiling, roasting, or grilling.

Cajun spice

A blend of herbs and spices that usually includes pepper, chili, paprika, garlic, thyme, oregano, and cumin. It may also include cayenne pepper.

TASTE Bold and hot with chili, sweet with herbs for a Louisiana-style taste.

USE FOR Flavoring gumbos and jambalaya, rubs for fish and meat, or stirring into yogurt to make a quick dip for raw vegetables, roast potato, potato skins, or sweet potato wedges.

TOP 10 STARTER KIT

When starting to build up a spice collection, these 10 spices in your pantry will give your food plenty of global flavors.

- Cinnamon
- Chili
- Chinese five spice
- Cumin
- Garam masala
- Mustard seeds
- Paprika
- Peppercorns
- Saffron or turmeric
- Vanilla

Caribbean mix

A blend of garlic granules, celery salt, pepper, paprika, curry powder, and sugar, found throughout the Caribbean.

TASTE Warming and lively with a hint of sharpness.

USE FOR Adding to vegetables such as mashed sweet potato and dusting fish before frying. It's also used to flavor substantial meat stews.

Chinese five spice

Made of star anise, Sichuan pepper, cinnamon, fennel, and cloves.

TASTE Exotic, with a complex blend of sweet, bitter, and pungent flavors.

USE FOR Tossing into stir-fries or rice, or in oil and soy sauce marinades.

Dukkah

An Egyptian mix which usually includes roasted sesame, coriander, cumin seeds, and hazelnuts.

TASTE Adds Middle Eastern flair with its spicy, nutty flavor.

USE FOR Sprinkling over salads, coating meats, fish, and vegetables before roasting, nibbling on its own as a snack, dipping (dip bread into olive oil, then into the dukkah mix), mixing with honey for a sandwich filling.

Garam masala

This Indian blend literally translates as "hot spices." Recipes vary—Indian cooks make their own—but it usually includes chili, coriander, fennel, cardamom, black pepper, cumin, cloves, nutmeg, and cinnamon.

TASTE Garam masala gives an authentic Indian taste to your food.

USE FOR Adding to curries as they cook, but it is more often sprinkled over at the end as a seasoning, a little like salt and pepper.

Jamaican jerk seasoning

A blend of allspice and hot chili peppers with thyme, bay, cinnamon, cloves, or nutmeg for using in Caribbean cooking. "Jerk" refers to the dry mix of herbs and spices used to flavor meat and fish, as well as describing the style of cooking, usually grilled.

TASTE Hot and spicy Caribbean taste.

USE FOR Sprinkling over oiled meat (especially pork), chicken, or fish before cooking.

Ras-el-hanout

A Moroccan blend of rose petals or buds, black peppercorns, ginger, cardamom, nigella seeds, cayenne, allspice, lavender, cinnamon, cassia, coriander seeds, mace, nutmeg, cloves.

TASTE A complex mix of spicy, herbal, and floral flavors.

USE FOR Tossing into rice, tagines, game dishes, and couscous for an aromatic Moroccan hit.

Seven-spice powder
(shichimi togarashi)

This Japanese mix of spices, flavorings, and seeds can contain white sesame seeds, pieces of dried mandarin zest and nori (seaweed), poppy seeds, hemp seeds, chili flakes, and pepper. Look for it in specialty stores

TASTE Hot and aromatic, peppery.

USE FOR Seasoning meat and fish.

SPICES A–Z

Allspice

Sometimes called Jamaican pepper, the berry is similar but slightly bigger than a peppercorn and comes mostly from Jamaica where it grows on an evergreen tree native to the Caribbean and Central America. Caribbean cooks grind it to make jerk seasonings and rubs (see Spice Mixes, page 164). but elsewhere it is usually used whole in pickles and ground in baking and desserts.

CHOOSE Whole berries or ground.

TASTE Tastes of a combination of spices, cloves being dominant, with a hint of cinnamon, nutmeg, and pepper.

STORE The berries keep almost indefinitely in an airtight jar.

USE FOR
- Flavoring Jamaican jerk dishes and giving authentic flavor to other Caribbean dishes, plus broiled pork chops, poached fish, and stewed fruit.
- Flavoring the meat for moussaka.
- Mixing into pickles (whole).
- Adding to marinades for meat.
- Spicing up your Christmas cooking— sprinkle some into applesauce for apple pies, Christmas pudding or cake, mulled wine (use whole), or spiced red cabbage.

GOES WITH Beef, pork, chicken, sausages, root vegetables, fruit (particularly oranges), honey, chocolate.

USE INSTEAD Equal parts of cloves, cinnamon, and nutmeg.

Asafetida

Sometimes called "stinking gum" because of its strange smell when raw. Asafetida is a gum resin from the stem and roots of a giant, fennel-like plant which grows in India and Iran, and is used mostly in Indian cooking.

CHOOSE In its whole, solid form it looks like lumps of shiny brown sugar, but it is usually available dried and ground as a beige-, brown-, or mustard-colored powder.

TASTE When the solid pieces are crushed, they smell quite unpleasant, but once fried, they have a pleasant garlicky-onion aroma. The ground version is milder in flavor as it is mixed with a starch to stop it sticking together. Use only in small amounts.

STORE Whole asafetida lasts for many years, the ground for up to 1 year. Keep in a very tightly closed container or the smell will overpower your pantry.

PREPARE Grind the solid version before using.

USE FOR
- Enhancing the flavor of Indian dishes (especially curries and pickles) and spice mixes.
- A replacement for onion and garlic.

GOES WITH Fish, legumes, vegetables.

USE INSTEAD Garlic or onions.

Caraway

A curvy little seed with ridges that flavors cakes, cookies, and breads in North European cooking, and is in spice blends in North African cuisine (essential to harissa, see Pantry Staples, page 89).

CHOOSE Dried whole seeds.

TASTE Aromatic, warm, and nutty, with a hint of anise and citrus.

STORE Keeps for about 6 months in an airtight jar.

COOK If you dry-fry the seeds for a minute or two in a small skillet, this will bring out their aroma (see Bringing out the Flavor, page 162).

USE FOR

- Flavoring breads and seed cakes.
- Adding to stews such as Hungarian goulash.
- Stirring into cheese biscuit or cheese cracker mixtures.

GOES WITH Pork, beef, cabbage and other vegetables, cheese.

USE INSTEAD Fennel or dill seeds (milder).

Cardamom

These pale green pods grow on bushes in the rain forests of southern India, Sri Lanka, and Guatemala. They are hand-picked and dried, and so cost rather more than most spices. Russians and Scandinavians tuck them into pastries, cakes, cookies, and breads, and Indians into tea, rice, and meat dishes.

CHOOSE Pale green pods (white ones have been bleached) that hold about a dozen tiny black seeds. The stickier the seeds, the fresher they are. Available ground, but this is harder to find.

TASTE The seeds have a perfume and flavor that's all their own—it is

hard to describe but there is quite a strong taste of eucalyptus, with hints of ginger and citrus, slightly bitter and sweet all at the same time. The outer pods merely protect the seeds, so should not be eaten.

STORE The fresh pods will keep for about a year in an airtight jar. For ground cardamom, crush the seeds just before you need to use them as the flavor will diminish quickly once they have been ground.

PREPARE When adding cardamom pods whole to dishes, give them a quick sharp bash with a rolling pin first, to crush lightly or bruise them to expose the seeds and their flavor. The pods are usually discarded after cooking, or left in for decoration only. To obtain the seeds, slit the papery pods lengthwise with a sharp knife, so that you can open them up and tease out the seeds.

USE FOR

- Flavoring rice dishes (especially pilafs or rice pudding) and slow-cooked meat dishes.
- Giving fragrance to vanilla ice cream or Indian ice cream (kulfi) and custards, and to lassi, Indian tea, Moroccan coffee, and mulled wine.
- Adding to fruits being poached in sugar syrup.

caraway–chili

GOES WITH Lamb, rice, cream, yogurt, chocolate, coffee, apples, pears, figs, mangoes, oranges.

USE INSTEAD No real substitute.

Cassia
see CINNAMON, *page 171*

Cayenne
see CHILI, *below*

Chili

One of the most widely used spices around the world, chili is particularly popular in the cuisines of India, Mexico, South America, Southeast Asia, the Caribbean, Africa, and southern Italy, especially Sardinia and Sicily.

CHOOSE AND TASTE Chilies vary in taste from mild and sweet to scorchingly hot. As a general rule with fresh chilies, the plumper the chili, the milder the taste. But chilies aren't only about heat: each variety, of which there are hundreds, has its own unique flavor.

Fresh: These should be firm and glossy. For mild heat try the large, sweet-tasting, green Anaheim or greeny-yellow banana chili, for medium heat

CARDAMOM

TIPS AND TRICKS: CHILI

■ *Cool it—if your mouth burns from using too much chili in a dish, water or beer won't cool you down. Instead reach for something from the dairy counter, such as a glass of milk or some yogurt. If the dish itself is too hot to eat, mellow the flavor with a spoonful or two of yogurt or cream.*

the torpedo-shaped jalapeño, and for fiery heat the fruity habanero (Scotch bonnet) or the tiny Thai bird's-eye.

Whole dried: For adding whole or broken in pieces to a cooked dish.

Dried crushed: Made from crushed whole chilies including the seeds, they have a concentrated taste that gets more intense with cooking. Add early on for the hottest heat; sprinkle over at the end for a milder effect.

Cayenne: Made by grinding the smallest chilies to a hot powder, this is pure chili—what Indians call chili powder. This causes confusion with Western chili powder, which is milder, being a blend of spices originally devised for Mexican dishes. Hot and strong, cayenne packs a mighty punch. Use cautiously, in pinches.

Chili powder: Whereas cayenne is pure chili, this is a diluted blend of chili peppers with spices, oregano, and salt, that is available hot or mild.

STORE Fresh chilies will keep in a plastic bag in the refrigerator for up to 2 weeks. Dried chilies will keep for ages in an airtight container, the powder for up to 6 months as it loses its strength over time.

PREPARE

It is the inner parts of the chili—the ribs and seeds—that hold the heat, so remove them if you want to calm things down. Because these parts can burn sensitive skin, deal with them carefully. Halve the chili lengthwise, then lift and scrape out the central rib and seeds with a sharp knife (see illustration, opposite). Slice or chop the chili, then wash your hands. If you put your hands to your face or eyes, it can cause stinging.

COOK Start timidly by adding small amounts and get braver as you find out how much heat you enjoy. To add flavor, rather than heat, drop whole chilies into your dishes at the start of cooking, then lift them out at the end.

USE FOR

■ Stirring into salsas, salads, mash; sprinkling over fish and chicken before roasting to add a spicy kick.

■ Grinding fresh to make Thai curry paste (green or red).

■ Dropping whole (fresh or dried) into stews, curries, and casseroles for a spicy flavor, or into sugar syrups to make sherbet (fresh).

■ Adding a pinch when you want to add heat to a dish, especially good in chowders, kedgeree, smoked salmon, sauces, pasta (cayenne, dried crushed chilies).

■ Giving a spicy flavor to Mexican dishes such as tacos, chili con carne, tortillas; to Bolognese and tomato-based sauces; to marinades, dips, and dressings (fresh, chili powder).

■ Flavoring a mild cooking oil such as peanut before using to stir-fry vegetables. If you drop a couple of whole dried chilies with a few slices of garlic and ginger into the hot oil and let them fry for a couple of minutes, they flavor it beautifully (see Pantry Staples, page 101).

■ Serving as a special seasoning—offer dried crushed chili in a little dish as an alternative to salt and pepper.

GOES WITH Chicken, beef, lamb, shrimp, fish, coconut, cilantro.

USE INSTEAD Tabasco adds a kick.

SEEDING CHILI

Cinnamon and cassia

CINNAMON

Native to Sri Lanka, cinnamon is the inner bark stripped from an evergreen tree and which curls into sticks (quills) as it dries. It is used in sweet and savory dishes all over the world, from India and Morocco to North America and Mexico. Cassia is very similar although less aromatic, but is native to Burma. It is most important in Chinese cooking, and one of the spices that make up Chinese five spice (see page 164).

CHOOSE Either the curled-up, thin sticks of bark, or ground powder. The paler the color, the better the quality. Cassia is closely related to cinnamon but looks and tastes a little coarser— less curled and more bark-like. It is harder to find than cinnamon.

TASTE The flavor and aroma of cinnamon are easily recognizable, being sweet and fragrant and slightly woody. Cassia has a slightly stronger taste.

STORE Sticks of cinnamon keep for several years in an airtight container. Ground cinnamon loses its flavor more quickly, but keeps for several months.

COOK When cooking with cinnamon, use whole sticks when you want a subtle flavor without the flecks of spice, or release more flavor from the sticks by breaking them in pieces. Use the ground for a spicy look and extra flavor.

USE FOR

- Flavoring desserts such as apple pie, poached pears, fruit crumbles, rice pudding, ice cream, fruit and spice cakes, breads, and cookies (sticks or ground).
- Stirring hot chocolate (sticks).
- Dropping into mulled wines, fruit punches, fruit salads, and compotes (sticks).
- Adding spicy fragrance to fruit and vegetable chutneys (sticks or ground).
- Bringing sweet spiciness to savory dishes such as Indian curries and pilafs, Greek moussaka, Moroccan tagines, Mexican stews (sticks or ground).
- Livening up French toast or buttermilk pancakes (ground).
- Pairing with more robust flavors, such as duck and pork, figs and prunes, root vegetables (cassia).
- Tying in bundles to decorate the Christmas tree (sticks).

GOES WITH Poultry, lamb, rice, couscous, beet, bananas, oranges, apricots, apples and pears, figs, rum, chocolate, coffee, red wine.

USE INSTEAD Cinnamon and cassia can be used interchangeably.

Cloves

These unopened buds of a small tropical evergreen tree get their name from the French *clou*, meaning nail, which they resemble. As well as being used alone, cloves also crop up in spice mixes, including Chinese five spice and garam masala.

CHOOSE Whole cloves or ground. When buying whole, look for plump cloves that haven't been broken up.

cinnamon–cloves

TASTE Quite pungent and over-powering with hints of camphor and pepper, it is a taste that numbs the mouth if too much is used. Whole cloves are not eaten, so take them out before serving, or warn people of their presence. Use cautiously.

STORE Whole cloves can be kept for up to a year in an airtight jar, ground cloves for up to 6 months.

USE FOR

■ Flavoring Middle Eastern, African, Indonesian, and Indian rice dishes, also curries and other meat dishes, including French veal *blanquette*.

■ Poking into onions to flavor milk for savory sauces such as bread sauce, into cured ham to flavor and decorate, into oranges or apples to float in mulled wine or hard cider (whole).

■ Spicing up apple pie (add two or three at the most) and pickles (whole). Studding baked apples (whole).

■ Adding to baking recipes (ground)—many countries use cloves in baking.

GOES WITH Pork, lamb, cured ham, chicken, root vegetables, onions, red cabbage, apples, oranges, and dried fruits.

USE INSTEAD Allspice (instead of ground cloves).

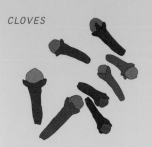

CLOVES

Coriander

see also HERBS (Cilantro),
page 137

These small, round and brittle seeds
from the herb cilantro are included in
spice mixes such as Moroccan harissa,
Egyptian dukkah, and Indian garam
masalas (in India, coriander is called
dhaniya), as well as being used on
their own in cuisines worldwide.

CHOOSE Dried seeds and ground.

TASTE Unlike the fresh leaves of the
herb, the spice is mild and sweet with
floral and orange touches.

STORE The seeds will keep for about
a year in an airtight container, the
ground for several months.

COOK The seeds benefit from being
dry-fried before use (see Bringing out
the Flavor, page 162).

USE FOR
■ Adding to casseroles (pork and
chicken), soups (root vegetables), and
curries (dry-fry first, see page 162).
■ Flavoring pickles and chutneys.
■ Mixing into marinades and stocks.
■ Crushing the seeds and sprinkling over
potatoes before roasting, or mixing with
cumin for a spicy crust for roast lamb.

GOES WITH Pork, chicken, fish,
carrots, parsnips, rutabaga, legumes.

USE INSTEAD Cumin.

Cumin

These small oval seeds, similar in
look to caraway, only less round, find
themselves spicing up chili recipes in
Tex-Mex cooking, in Indian curries
(in India cumin is known as *jeera*),
as well as in North African and some
European dishes.

CHOOSE Seeds or ground.

TASTE Strong, slightly sweet as well
as bitter—nice and spicy. Cumin is
best used in small amounts.

STORE The seeds will keep in an
airtight container for up to 6 months,
but ground cumin loses its flavor
rather more quickly.

COOK Dry-fry the seeds (see
Bringing out the Flavor, page 162)
before grinding, or fry them whole in
oil briefly before using them to bring
out their flavor.

USE FOR
■ Flavoring kabobs (great with lamb)
and couscous dishes.

- Making Indian lamb curries such as rogan josh.
- Sprinkling over pumpkin and potatoes or other root vegetables when roasting.
- Spicing up meatballs and burgers.
- Mixing with yogurt to make *raita*.

GOES WITH Most meats especially lamb, chicken, cheese, lentils, rice, couscous, potatoes, cabbage, cauliflower, eggplant, yogurt, coriander.

USE INSTEAD Coriander.

Curry powder

A convenient blend of spices used for Indian cooking in the West. It is not used in India where cooks blend their own spices.

CHOOSE Ground powder—mild, medium, or hot.

TASTE Different blends vary, but all usually include coriander and cumin, and sometimes fenugreek, along with other spices such as turmeric, ginger, and mustard. The hotter blends have varying amounts of ground chilies added. All are aromatic.

STORE Curry powder keeps in an airtight jar for several months.

USE FOR

- Mild curries such as korma and tikka masala (mild powder).
- Medium curries such as rogan josh (medium powder).
- Spicier curries such as madras and vindaloo (hot powder).
- Sprinkling into sauces, marinades, soups, or over vegetables as they roast.

USE INSTEAD Garam masala.

Dill seeds

see also HERBS, page 139

Flat, oval dill seeds are popular in European and North American cooking.

CHOOSE Seeds.

TASTE A little like caraway, but milder and sweeter.

STORE Dill seeds keep in an airtight jar for about 2 years.

USE FOR

- Pickling, as in American dill pickles.
- Adding to breads and cakes.

GOES WITH Shellfish, cured fish, vegetables, especially beet, cabbage, and cucumber.

USE INSTEAD Caraway seeds.

Dukkah

see SPICE MIXES, page 164

Fennel seeds

see also HERBS, page 140

Fennel seeds are used in Chinese five spice (see page 164), as well as in the Indian five-spice mix *panch poran*. The dried seeds come from the fennel plant that can be found growing in India and Asia, South America, Australia, and the United States, as well as the Mediterranean. They look like a greener version of cumin seeds.

CHOOSE Only the seeds are available as a spice.

TASTE They have an aniseed flavor.

STORE The seeds will keep in an airtight container for about 2 years.

COOK Dry-frying them (see Bringing out the Flavor, page 162) will draw out the sweetness.

USE FOR

- Flavoring savory breads, pickles, and chutneys.
- Meat, fish, and vegetable curries.
- Chewing at the end of a meal as a mouth freshener.

GOES WITH Oily fish such as salmon, chicken, lamb, lentils, tomatoes.

USE INSTEAD Caraway or dill seeds.

Fenugreek seeds

see also HERBS, *page 141*

These mustard-yellow seeds look a bit like miniature corn kernels and come from the fresh fenugreek herb. They are widely used in Middle Eastern cooking. In India they are called *methi* and are often fried in oil with onion, cumin, and mustard seeds to bring out the flavor at the start of making a curry.

CHOOSE The seeds are found in Indian specialty stores.

TASTE The smell is similar to that of curry powder (they are often used in commercial curry powders)—they give a nutty, earthy, and bitter taste.

STORE The seeds will keep in an airtight container for about a year.

COOK A brief spell in the skillet to dry-fry (see Bringing out the Flavor, page 162) is important to bring out their nutty taste. If they outstay their welcome in the pan, or get too hot while frying, they turn bitter.

USE FOR

- Flavoring meat and vegetable curries.
- Adding to Indian pickles, chutneys, and sauces.
- Sprouting the seeds for salads.

GOES WITH Fish, lamb, rice, tomatoes, potatoes, and other root vegetables.

USE INSTEAD There's no substitute (not even the fresh leaf of the fenugreek plant)—just leave it out of your recipe if you can't obtain it.

Five spice, Chinese

see SPICE MIXES, *page 164*

Galangal

This is the Southeast Asian cousin of ginger root, sometimes called Thai ginger, that is used a lot in Thai, Malaysian, and Indonesian cooking. It has the same knobby look as root ginger but its shoots are tinged pink when young, and it has a more translucent skin, whiter flesh, and tougher texture.

CHOOSE Fresh roots, dried (sliced), and ground. The type most available

in the West is "greater" galangal—*laos*—which is native to Java. The smaller, "lesser" galangal—*kenchur*—is native to China. Look for galangal in specialty grocers, some supermarkets, and Asian stores.

TASTE A mild blend of ginger and pepper with a hint of citrus.

STORE Keep fresh galangal in the refrigerator in a perforated plastic bag for at least a week, possibly two. Or freeze for 2–3 months. The dried will keep for about a year, ground for up to 3 months.

PREPARE Peel fresh galangal first, then pound, grate, thinly slice, or chop according to the recipe, as you would ginger root (see page 181). Dried galangal needs soaking in hot water for at least 10 minutes.

USE FOR

- Dropping a few slices into Asian noodle soups, or the classic Thai chicken and coconut soup *tom ka gai*.
- Pounding with other flavorings such as chilies, lemongrass, and cilantro to make Thai curry pastes.
- Adding to sauces for fish.

GOES WITH Chicken, fish and shellfish, noodles, coconut.

USE INSTEAD Fresh ginger root (not quite the same—more gingery).

Garam masala
see SPICE MIXES, *page 164*

Ginger

Ginger is one of those spices that has never been out of fashion, and is prized for its medicinal as well as culinary virtues. It was once so popular in Europe that it was put on the table just like salt and pepper. Although fresh ginger is called ginger root, it is really an underground stem (rhizome), and its irregular, knobby shape gives each piece a lively character all of its own.

CHOOSE Fresh root, ground, and dried, or crystallized. Or preserved ginger in syrup, or pickled ginger (see Pantry Staples, page 88). Fresh gives the best ginger flavor, but ground is used for baking. Fresh ginger root should be plump and heavy rather than light and wrinkled. Choose pieces with not too many knobs as they are easier to work with. Once wrinkled they are more likely to be fibrous inside. Ready-grated ginger in sunflower oil is also available in jars.

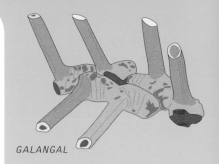

GALANGAL

TIPS AND TRICKS: GALANGAL

1 teaspoon powdered galangal is equivalent to about ¼-inch piece of the fresh root.

TASTE Fresh ginger is warm and rich with a hot, tangy bite. Ground ginger is hotter, more potent, and less aromatic, very different from fresh.

STORE To stop fresh ginger drying out or going moldy, put it in a perforated plastic bag in the refrigerator where it will keep for at least 2 weeks. Or freeze whole (or peeled and grated into ice cube trays) for up to 2 months. Ground keeps for about 6 months.

PREPARE The knobs are easy to snap off in pieces, so you can prepare the size you need. Peel off the brown outer skin with a sharp knife (not necessary if the ginger is to be discarded after cooking), then slice, grate, shred, or chop (see opposite).

USE FOR

■ Storing in sherry (fresh), then using both the ginger and the sherry in Chinese cooking.

■ Adding to marinades, jams and marmalades (fresh, preserved in syrup, and crystallized).

■ Livening up ice cream mixtures or fresh fruit salads (chopped fresh, preserved in syrup, or crystallized).

■ Shredding fresh into batons, then frying briefly with thin slices of garlic and scallion, for garnishing Chinese-style steamed fish.

■ Partnering with garlic for a sweet-pungent combination at the beginning of cooking Chinese stir-fries or Indian curries (chopped fresh).

■ Baking—goes well in shortbread, flapjacks, fruit cakes and puddings, crumble toppings (mostly ground, but other types too).

■ Making a soothing cup of ginger tea—grate a small knob of peeled ginger into a cup. Pour boiling water over and let it steep for 5 minutes. Strain if you want, add a squeeze of lemon juice, and sweeten with honey.

■ Dipping into melted chocolate for a sweet treat (crystallized).

■ Sprinkling over fresh melon chunks or wedges as an appetizer (ground).

GOES WITH Pork, beef, duck, chicken, shrimp, scallops, fish (especially salmon), onions, rhubarb, pears, apples, lemons, oranges, melons, chocolate, honey.

USE INSTEAD Galangal for fresh ginger. Ground ginger doesn't make a good substitute for fresh.

Juniper

Gin would be nothing without the dark purple juniper berries that flavor it. Europeans also find many other uses for juniper berries—Germans

ginger–juniper

mix them into sauerkraut, while Scandinavians use them when pickling beef as an aromatic. The berries, which also grow in North America, look like small, dark blueberries, and have the smell of a pine forest when they are crushed.

CHOOSE Dried berries, which should be plump with a chalky bloom like blueberries.

TASTE Slightly bitter with a refreshing hint of pine and reminiscent of gin. You don't need many berries to add flavor: four to six are usually enough.

STORE In an airtight container where they will keep for a couple of years. When they go hard and dry they will be past their best.

PREPARE Crush first to release their flavor.

USE FOR
- Giving rich flavor to game dishes (including pâtés), beef casseroles, and stews.
- Giving a venison-like flavor to other strong-flavored meats such as beef or pork.
- Adding to marinades, especially red wine marinades for game.

PREPARING FRESH ROOT GINGER

PEEL: Snap off the amount you need, then peel off the skin with a small, sharp knife.
SLICE: For rounds, cut across the piece of ginger in thin slices. For shredding into batons, make a small pile of the rounds, then cut across them into thin batons.
CHOP: For finely chopped, cut as for batons, then continue chopping as for finely chopped herbs (see page 128).

SHREDDING GINGER

TIPS AND TRICKS: GINGER

If fresh ginger is particularly fibrous, it's easier to grate rather than slice or chop. It's even easier to grate if you freeze it first.

■ Making a rub for meats, mixed with garlic and salt.

GOES WITH Game, venison, pork, goose, cabbage, apples, hard cider.

USE INSTEAD If adding to sauces or marinades, use 1 teaspoon of gin for every couple of berries required.

Mace

see also NUTMEG, *page 184*
This is the lacy orange helmet that fits snugly over the hard nutmeg seed, part of the fruit of the tropical nutmeg tree. Once it has been picked, the nutmeg seed dries and shrinks in its protective sheath, and the mace can then be cracked and removed. It is traditionally used to flavor potted meats and fish.

CHOOSE As blades (pieces of the lacy sheath) of mace, or ground.

TASTE Like a slightly bitter version of nutmeg.

STORE The blades have a long life span if kept in an airtight container.
COOK If using the whole blades in cooking, remove them before serving.

USE FOR
■ Adding a pinch to melted butter when making potted shrimp.
■ Flavoring milk puddings, fruity chutneys, and quiches.
■ Steeping in milk for béchamel, onion, or cheese sauces, or adding to stock liquid for soup (especially fish and shellfish).
■ Giving a warm spiciness to mulled wine or tropical punches.

GOES WITH Lamb, fish, shellfish, onions, carrots, spinach, cheese, red wine.

USE INSTEAD Ground nutmeg.

Mustard seed

Small, round seeds that are popular in both European and Southeast Asian cooking. Crush them and their flavor leaps out at you; fry them whole and they can be very subtle and sweet. Used to make a variety of mustards (see Pantry Staples, page 96).

CHOOSE Dried yellow (sometimes referred to as white), brown, or black seeds.

TASTE The brown seeds have a hotter, more bitter taste than the

juniper–**m**ustard

sweeter yellow ones. The tiny black seeds are the strongest and most pungent of all of them.

STORE Mustard seeds have a long shelf life if kept airtight and dry.

COOK Many Indian recipes call for dry-frying the seeds first or frying them in a little oil until they pop, to draw out their nutty flavor (see Bringing out the Flavor, page 162).

USE FOR
- Adding to chutneys (lovely in mango chutney), pickles, and marinades.
- Frying with garlic and ginger to start off a vegetable stir-fry.
- Mixing into a syrupy glaze for spreading over cured ham.
- Sprinkling over potatoes, squash, or root vegetables as they roast (coat with oil first).
- Flavoring Indian vegetable and *dhal* dishes.
- Sprouting the seeds for salads

GOES WITH Chicken, pork, lentils, spinach, cauliflower, cabbage, root vegetables, mango, maple syrup, and honey.

USE INSTEAD No real substitute.

MACE/
NUTMEG

TIPS AND TRICKS: JUNIPER
An easy way to crush the soft juniper berries (if you don't have a pestle and mortar), is in a small bowl with the back of a spoon.

TIPS AND TRICKS: MACE
Mace is extremely hard, so to grind your own, break the blades into smaller pieces and grind in a small coffee grinder. Or buy it ready ground.

Nigella (kalonji)

Also sometimes called black onion seeds or even occasionally black cumin, these tiny jet black seeds are mainly produced in India, and are used a lot in Indian and Middle Eastern cooking.

CHOOSE Dried seeds—although sometimes labeled as black cumin or black onion seeds, this is incorrect as Nigella is a completely different plant species.

TASTE Slightly bitter and peppery—with a crunchy texture.

STORE The seeds will keep for up to 2 years in an airtight container.

COOK Dry-fry first (see Bringing out the Flavor, page 162).

USE FOR

■ Sprinkling into or over bread doughs before baking, or over savory crackers such as cheese crackers.
■ Flavoring rice pilafs and curries.
■ Adding to pickles and chutneys.
■ Sprinkling over root vegetables as they roast.

GOES WITH Most vegetables, rice, lentils.

USE INSTEAD Cumin seeds, sesame seeds, cracked pepper (each will give a different character to your dish, however).

Nutmeg

see also MACE, *page 182*

England went crazy for nutmeg in the 18th century, and it was sprinkled into both sweet and savory dishes. Today it is popular in many European dishes as well as North African ones, especially Moroccan and Tunisian. Fresh from the tree, nutmeg comes well padded. It is found snuggled inside a fleshy fruit with its own outer shell of mace. Nutmeg is more popular than mace, partly because it is cheaper and generally easier to obtain.

CHOOSE Whole nutmeg or ground. Ground is very convenient, but freshly grated has more flavor.

TASTE Warm, spicy, and bittersweet.

STORE Whole nutmeg keeps for years in an airtight container. Ground loses its aroma and taste quite quickly (it keeps for about 6 months).

PREPARE The most efficient way to grate a nutmeg is to have a special nutmeg grater that gives you a fine, fragrant powder. Use carefully—for most dishes, a pinch or two is enough.

USE FOR

■ Adding a little to a savory quiche, fish pie, or chowder.

■ Mixing into pasta sauces, especially creamy ones, or sauces with spinach; also absolutely essential for a classic béchamel sauce.

■ Adding to Mediterranean meat sauces for lasagne, moussaka, and Bolognese, and Middle Eastern lamb dishes.

■ Giving fragrance to mulled wine, punches, and eggnog.

■ Flavoring milk-based desserts and sauces, especially rice puddings and set custards.

■ Stirring a pinch into fruit compotes.

■ Perking up cookies, fruit cakes, and teabreads.

GOES WITH Chicken, lamb, cheese, eggs, milk, pumpkin and squash, carrot, broccoli, cauliflower, cabbage, spinach, honey.

USE INSTEAD Mace.

Paprika

Take a special variety of sweet red bell peppers, dry, then grind them, and you have paprika. It's the spice Hungarian cooking couldn't do without (think

TIPS AND TRICKS: NUTMEG

■ *Nutmeg is quite oily, so tends to stick in clumps in the jar. If this happens, just give the jar a good shake.*

■ *From one whole nutmeg, you should get 2–3 teaspoons of ground powder.*

of goulash). The Spanish version of paprika is used in chorizo and many fish, rice, egg, and potato dishes. It also adds color and spice to some Indian dishes and Moroccan tagines. In Europe, Spain and Hungary are the main producers.

CHOOSE Dried ground paprika. The degree of sweetness or heat depends on the type of peppers used, as well as how much of the hot parts of the pepper (seeds and veins) are added. It is not so hot as chili, however, as paprika's main purpose is to add color and flavor, not heat. When recipes call for paprika they usually refer to Hungarian paprika. You can also buy Spanish paprika, smoked or not.

TASTE

Hungarian: Often called "sweet paprika" after its taste—sweet and well balanced.

Spanish: Can be slightly milder than Hungarian. Spanish paprika is graded as *dulce* (sweet and mild), *agridulce* (bittersweet), and *picante* (hot).

Smoked: This striking, red Spanish paprika is made from peppers that have been wood-smoked before grinding, giving it a wonderful new depth of flavor. You may see it sold as smoked paprika or *picante pimentón*. It's easy to get addicted to its robust, smoky flavor.

STORE Will keep in an airtight container for a few months. Its color can deteriorate quickly.

COOK Take care when frying with paprika, as overheating makes it bitter.

USE FOR

■ Boosting the color and taste of homemade tomato sauce, chili con carne, meat stews, or curries.
■ Sprinkling a little over chunks of chicken or pork before stir-frying, or even over a whole chicken before roasting.
■ Mixing with salt, rosemary sprigs, and oil, then tossing with potatoes ready for roasting.
■ Coloring and flavoring a salad dressing.
■ Coating roasted almonds—after roasting, toss in oil, then paprika and salt, and eat as a snack.
■ Sprinkling a pinch or two over soups, broiled fish, canapés, salads, sauces, and dips (such as hummus), to garnish and flavor.

GOES WITH Chicken, sausages, beef, pork, rice, most vegetables, yogurt.

USE INSTEAD Cayenne pepper (for heat and color—not the flavor), but use a fraction of the amount called for as it is far hotter and not so sweet.

Pepper

see also SICHUAN PEPPER,
page 192.

Black, white, or green pepper comes
from peppercorns, the fruit (berries) of
the pepper plant. Pink peppercorns are
similar but come from a different
plant. Green peppercorns are picked
while unripe, black ones are picked
when turning from green to red, then
dried in the sun until black, hard, and
wrinkly. Pepper is grown mainly in
India, Vietnam, Indonesia, and Brazil.

CHOOSE Whole dried peppercorns,
black, white, green (also in brine),
pink (also in brine), or as a mix. Or
as ground (black or white).
Black: Good all-rounder. Grind whole
peppercorns yourself for the freshest
peppery flavor.
White: Choose for lighter-colored
dishes, such as fish, or where you
don't want the specks of black to spoil
the look, as in light sauces or soups.
Green: Often used for sauces with
steak, lamb, or duck.
Pink: Popular for fish dishes in the
south of France, also goes well with
poultry and vegetables.

TASTE Black pepper is hot and fiery
(less so when used whole); white is
less aromatic and milder in taste, but

quite strong in heat; green is milder than black and fresher; pink is milder than green and sweeter.

STORE Peppercorns keep for ages in an airtight container.

PREPARE Peppercorns are used whole or crushed with a pestle and mortar (see Grinding Whole Spices, page 162, and Kitchen Kit, page 65). Pink peppercorns are a little soft for grinding, so are usually used whole. Any in brine should be rinsed first.

COOK For the best flavor, add pepper toward the end of cooking.

USE FOR
■ Flavoring soups or slow-cooked dishes (whole or freshly ground).
■ Crushing and patting onto meat, especially steak, before broiling, grilling, or roasting.
■ Mixing into herb butters or anything that will benefit from a peppery taste.
■ Elevating the taste of strawberries by sprinkling a good grinding of black pepper over the top.

GOES WITH Smoked fish, most vegetables, most meats.

USE INSTEAD No exact substitute.

Poppy seed

Versatile, minute seeds from the opium poppy (opium is not found in the seeds, though). Can be used in cooking, to be decorative, or to add crunch or flavor to both sweet and savory dishes.

CHOOSE Seeds. The most common are dark blue-black and easy to buy. Harder to find are the white ones favored in Indian cooking.

TASTE Faintly nutty.

STORE The seeds are best kept in the refrigerator for up to a few months as they can go rancid, or in the freezer.

COOK Dry-frying (see Bringing out the Flavor, page 162) enhances their taste.

USE FOR
■ Adding to or sprinkling over muffins, cookies, cakes, pancakes, and breads.
■ Tossing with noodles—great for noodle salads.
■ Mixing into salad dressings (goes well with lemon) or sprinkling over steamed and buttered vegetables.

GOES WITH Breads, feta, salad greens (especially spinach and arugula), cauliflower, carrots, lemon.

USE INSTEAD Sesame seeds
(different flavor, though).

Ras-el-hanout
see SPICE MIXES, *page 165*

Saffron

The dried stigmas from the saffron
crocus may not look like much, but
introduce them to liquid and they
explode with color and flavor.
Hand-harvesting the huge amounts
required makes it the most expensive
of spices. It is mainly produced in
Spain, India, and Iran, but also in
Greece, and Italy, although centuries
ago it was grown in Saffron Walden
in Essex, England, which took its
name from the spice. Use it for both
sweet and savory dishes.

CHOOSE Stigmas (threads). As a
general rule, the deeper the color, the
better the saffron—the best being
deep red with orange tips. Lack of
orange on the tips could indicate the
saffron has been dyed. Cheaper
saffron, apart from not having the
intense red-to-orange glow about it,
can also look a bit ragged. Good
saffron will always be expensive, so
when buying unbranded cheap saffron
from markets in other countries, look

out for fakes—if it's too yellow, the chances are it's not the real thing. Ground saffron is sometimes available, but has often been adulterated with other ingredients.

TASTE Easier to recognize than describe—but very pungent and aromatic, slightly bitter, and almost musty with floral hints. You don't need to use much saffron to have an effect—a pinch (about a dozen threads) is usually enough for a dish to serve 4. Too much makes food taste too bitter and rather medicinal.

STORE Saffron will keep in an airtight container for several years.

PREPARE To tease the color from the threads and insure the color is evenly distributed, they are usually steeped in a few tablespoons of warm water, white wine, stock, or milk for 30 minutes or so before using. You can then add the liquid with or without the threads, but straining them off is tiresome, and they look good too.

USE FOR

■ Giving flavor and color to traditional dishes such as Spanish paella, Moroccan tagines, French fish stews (*bouillabaisse*), Italian risottos, Cornish saffron cake, and Swedish saffron buns.

■ Zapping up a tomato sauce to go with pasta.

■ Sneaking some into a tortilla—soak a few threads in a spoonful of boiling water and add with the eggs.

■ Adding a pinch to a creamy sauce for fish or spaghetti, or to the water when boiling rice.

■ Steeping in a little butter and beating into mashed potato.

■ Mixing into a spiced syrup for fresh fruits such as figs, nectarines, and plums.

GOES WITH Fish and shellfish (especially mussels), lamb, chicken, rice, polenta, carrots, fennel, garlic, white wine.

USE INSTEAD Turmeric is cheaper and will give you a yellow color (fine for rice), but doesn't go with all food, and the flavor is very different.

Sesame seeds

These tiny, flat, oval seeds, from the seed pods of a tropical plant, certainly get around. You'll spot them being sprinkled into or over Asian dishes (stir-fries and sesame shrimp toasts), Middle Eastern breads and sweetmeats (*halvah*) and crushed into pastes (tahini, the base for hummus), or sprinkled over American burger rolls.

saffron–sesame

CHOOSE Seeds—white (the most common), black (hard to get), or brown (unhulled white) depending on the variety of plant the seeds come from. Or as sesame oil (see Pantry Staples, page 103).

TASTE Can be used raw but their wonderful nutty taste comes into its own after dry-frying (see Bringing out the Flavor, page 162). A lot of flavor is packed into each tiny seed; black sesame seeds contain the most.

STORE Best kept in the refrigerator for up to 6 months, or in the freezer.

COOK Dry-frying is really worth it to release their nuttiness and fragrance (see Bringing out the Flavor, page 162). Heat the white and brown ones until just turning golden and starting to jump in the pan for the best flavor, and the black ones until you can start to smell the fragrance. Sesame seeds burn quickly, so watch them. If sprinkling over food before baking, there's no need to fry first.

USE FOR
- Giving crunch to stir-fries.
- Coating tuna and salmon fillets before frying.
- Sprinkling over cookies and breads.
- Mixing into Asian dressings.

- Sprinkling over salads before serving, especially chicken salads.
- Sprinkling over root vegetables, such as carrots or parsnips, after roasting.

GOES WITH Chicken, fish, shrimp, Chinese greens, noodles, tofu, rice.

USE INSTEAD Poppy seeds (although the flavor is not so nutty).

Sichuan pepper
(*also spelt* SZECHUAN)

Although similar in look to pepper, this isn't from the pepper family at all but is a dried berry from a shrub native to the Sichuan province of China. It is one of the ingredients used to make Chinese five spice (see Spice Mixes, page 164).

CHOOSE Whole berries or coarsely ground.

TASTE Fragrant, spicy, and pungent, slightly peppery.

STORE Whole berries will keep indefinitely in an airtight container, ground for up to 6 months.

COOK Dry-fry to bring out their oils for 4–5 minutes until they start to smoke (see Bringing out the Flavor, page 162), but watch the heat and throw away any that get too blackened.

USE FOR
- Stir-fries.
- Seasoning crispy duck.

GOES WITH Chicken, duck.

USE INSTEAD Black peppercorns (less pungent).

Star anise

Among the prettiest of spices (each one is a starry-flower-shaped, dried seed pod), star anise is native to China and Vietnam and one of the spices used in Chinese five spice. Western cooks are latching onto its merits and drop it into all sorts of dishes, including syrups, preserves, and even poaching broths, to give an exotic flavoring.

CHOOSE Whole star anise (shiny brown seeds within the pod), or pieces.

TASTE Like licorice, with an added fragrance and warmth. The taste is fairly intense, so don't overdo it.

STORE If kept in an airtight container in the pantry, whole star anise will keep for many months.

PREPARE It's very simple—just drop the whole thing into whatever dish you are making. Take it out before serving, or leave in as a decoration (but take care not to eat it).

USE FOR
- Steeping in a syrup for fruit salads.
- Flavoring marinades for chicken.
- Adding to broth for steaming fish or chicken with other aromatics, such as ginger, lemongrass, or cinnamon, or into stocks for Asian dishes.
- Dropping into rice while it cooks to accompany Chinese dishes.
- Giving flavor to stewed fruits such as pears and rhubarb.

GOES WITH Chicken, pork, duck, beef, rice, tropical fruits, peaches, pears, plums, rhubarb, leeks, soy sauce, lemongrass, ginger, Sichuan pepper.

USE INSTEAD Chinese five spice (see Spice Mixes, page 164) for savory dishes where it's all right to use a ground spice.

Sumac

Used a lot in Arabic, Lebanese, and Turkish cooking, sumac is the fruit of a small shrub. It is used to add sourness to a dish in the same way as lemon, vinegar, or tamarind.

STAR ANISE

CHOOSE Ground powder (brick red) from Middle Eastern or Greek shops.

TASTE Tart, almost lemony.

STORE Sumac will keep for several months in an airtight container.

USE FOR
■ Rubbing over cubes of fish, chicken, or lamb for kabobs before broiling to add flavor and color.
■ Flavoring stuffings, stews, and casseroles.
■ Mixing the powder into yogurt with mint or cilantro for a dipping sauce.

GOES WITH Chicken, lamb, fish and shellfish, rice, lentils and legumes, eggplants, sesame, yogurt, nuts.

USE INSTEAD Lemon juice or vinegar for an acidic flavor (only if adding to stews or salads). Lemon zest and salt if using for sprinkling.

Tamarind

Also known as Indian date, this is the fruit of the tamarind tree which grows inside pods that look rather like large peanuts in their shells. Inside the pods is a sticky, brown pulp wrapped around numerous seeds. Commercially this pulp is semi-dried and shaped into blocks or made into paste. Much loved in Indian, Middle Eastern, and Southeast Asian dishes, it is used to add an acidic tang much as lemon juice or vinegar is used in the West.

CHOOSE The pulp in various guises —as paste in jars, pulp in blocks, and concentrate.

TASTE A complex mouthful of sour, sweet, fruity, and tangy flavors.

STORE Both the paste and blocks will keep for up to a year in the refrigerator.

PREPARE
Paste in jars: The paste is the crushed, strained pulp, so everything has been done for you. Just get out your spoon—the label or recipe will advise how much you need.
Pulp in blocks: Thai or Indonesian is moist and soft, so simply cut off a piece and mash it with hot water to make your own paste. Use as is or strain for just the liquid. If it is to go into something that simmers, just chop the tamarind finely, add as is, and let it dissolve in the dish. Indian tamarind is harder and more compressed, so it is not so easy to work with.
Cut off a 1-ounce piece and soak in $\frac{2}{3}$–$1\frac{1}{4}$ cups hot water for 30 minutes.

sumac–turmeric

Strain, pressing the tamarind well down to extract all the liquid.
Concentrate: This is like a very dark syrup. Use sparingly and cautiously. Not so fresh-tasting as paste.

COOK The flavor softens when added early on in a dish.

USE FOR
- Giving a mild fruity taste to rice— add a little to the water as it cooks.
- Flavoring salad dressings instead of lemon juice or vinegar.
- Using in marinades, especially for chicken, pork, or shrimp.
- Adding a spoonful to tomato or mango relishes for a sweet-sour taste.
- Making chutney (tamarind has a lot of pectin, so helps it set).
- Stirring into curries, especially vegetable or chicken.

GOES WITH Fish and shellfish, chicken, pork, potatoes, cauliflower, legumes, mangoes.

USE INSTEAD Lime or lemon juice, or vinegar (not such complex flavors).

Turmeric

This tropical root, a member of the ginger family, looks like ginger root but has orange flesh. After drying it turns yellow, and will give a distinctive color to many curry and rice dishes, that is deeper and more ocher yellow than saffron. The main producer is India, where it forms the basis of many masalas and curry powders. Turmeric is also used throughout Southeast Asia and in Moroccan tagines and stews.

CHOOSE Ground turmeric. The whole root is available from Indian specialty stores, but the powder is more commonly used. Handling the raw root may stain your hands and the kitchen counter.

TASTE Musky and pungent, slightly harsh. If you add too much, both color and flavor can get too intense.

STORE Ground will keep in an air-tight container for about 9 months.

PREPARE If using the root, peel it like ginger root, then slice, chop, or grate.

COOK Turmeric is often fried with other spices to draw out the flavor, but be careful not to let it burn.

USE FOR
■ Giving color and fragrance to both fish and meat curries.

■ Mixing a little into kedgeree and other savory rice dishes.
■ Making spicy chutneys and pickles (it's what gives piccalilli its characteristic color).
■ Adding a pinch or two to a fish chowder or to savory pancake batter.
■ Sprinkling over potatoes as they roast for a golden glow.

GOES WITH Chicken, lamb, fish, vegetables (especially potatoes, cauliflower, and spinach), legumes, rice, coconut milk, yogurt, ginger.

USE INSTEAD You might be tempted to substitute saffron, but saffron is more expensive and has a different flavor, so use it instead only when a yellow color is needed and not the flavor of turmeric.

Vanilla

There's something exotic about vanilla. It's nearly as expensive as saffron but its tantalizing flavor makes it worth paying the price. The beans are the fruit of a Mexican orchid which have been sun-dried so that they shrivel and turn a deep brown. Vanilla is exported from tropical countries such as Mexico, Indonesia, Tahiti, and Madagascar (bourbon beans).

turmeric–vanilla

CHOOSE Between beans or the extract.

Beans: These give the true vanilla taste. They should be shiny, slightly oily, supple, slightly wrinkled, but not brittle or dry—with a rich aroma. Length is a good indication of quality: about 6–8 inches is best.

Extract: Check the label and look for "natural/pure vanilla extract," which is the real thing. It has been taken from the beans, which have been soaked and softened in alcohol to give a liquid with a powerfully concentrated vanilla flavor. Cheaper versions that are not labeled "pure" bear little resemblance to the genuine article.

TASTE Sweetly perfumed, rich, and almost creamy.

STORE If kept well sealed in an air-tight container, the beans will keep for at least 2 years.

PREPARE For an intense vanilla flavor, both beans and seeds can be used. Slit the bean lengthwise and open it. Using the tip of a small sharp knife, carefully scrape the bean to remove the tiny, sticky seeds. When added to a dish, these seeds will appear as little black specks and are a sign of authenticity.

VANILLA

TIPS AND TRICKS: VANILLA

■ *If a recipe calls for the seeds only, scrape them from the bean but don't throw the bean away. Tuck it into a jar of sugar to give you vanilla sugar.*

■ *You can recycle a vanilla bean if it hasn't been used too vigorously to start with. Wash it, dry well, and keep tightly wrapped for another occasion—if it has only been soaking in liquid it should still have a lot of flavor left.*

USE FOR

- Steeping in cream or milk for ice cream, custard (for making trifle, *crème brûlée, crème caramel,* and *panna cotta*), and milk shakes.
- Steeping in sugar syrup for fruit salads.
- Flavoring meringues and other sweet things, such as cakes and cookies.
- Adding a subtle, unusual flavor to fish and shellfish sauces.

GOES WITH Mostly sweet things such as ice cream, cream, chocolate, coffee, most fruits, (especially tropical and summer ones).

USE INSTEAD Use vanilla beans and extract interchangeably.

USE FOR

- Mixing into meringues (especially good in a pavlova) and cookie mixes or bread.
- Beating into whipped cream— good with chocolate desserts.
- Flavoring cake frostings.

GOES WITH Chocolate, nuts, cream.

USE INSTEAD Leave it out of your recipe if it is not available, or mix a little finely ground coffee with a little ground allspice.

Wattleseed

An Australian ground spice that is available by mail order over the internet. It is made from the seeds of a certain type of acacia that is gathered by the Aboriginal people, then roasted, and ground to a powder that has a resemblance to roasted coffee.

TASTE Nutty, slightly coffee-like with a hint of hazelnut.

4

Fruit and Veg

FRUIT

FRUITS OFFER AN ABUNDANCE OF HEALTH-GIVING PROPERTIES, BEING HANDY-TO-EAT PACKAGES OF VITAMINS, MINERALS, FIBER, AND DISEASE-FIGHTING PLANT COMPOUNDS. USUALLY LOW IN CALORIES AND SODIUM, BUT CRAMMED WITH ANTIOXIDANTS, THEY PROVIDE AN OPTIMAL WAY TO IMPROVE HEALTH. WHETHER BUYING FRUITS FOR EATING RAW OR FOR MAKING INTO DESSERTS, THIS CHAPTER WILL BE A HANDY ALPHABETICAL GUIDE, WITH LOTS OF EASY SERVING SUGGESTIONS.

BUY IN SEASON

To get the best possible flavor and nutritional value from fruit, buy when it is in season and look at the label to check that it hasn't traveled too far.

FREEZING FRUIT

Fresh is best, but freezing is convenient if you are want to use fruit for cooking. Some fruits suit being frozen whole by open freezing (below), while others are better frozen as a purée, in a compote, or in a sugar syrup.

CHECK LIST Choose fruit in peak condition—for fruit to be good quality after freezing, it must be good quality before it goes into the freezer.

■ For best flavor the fruit should be just ripe (not too hard or too soft).
■ Wash it gently only if necessary and pat dry with paper towels.

Open freezing

This is a technique for freezing certain fruits whole, so they don't stick together in a big lump or get crushed or damaged. When ready to use, just pour or scoop them out of their container.

Fruits to choose: Summer berries and currants, cherries, cranberries.
How to do it: Lay the fruit in a single layer on a cookie sheet lined with waxed paper and "open freeze" (that is, put in the freezer uncovered) for a few hours, or until the fruit goes solid. You can then tip the fruit into freezer bags or containers, seal, label, and return to the freezer; they will keep for up to a year.

Freezing in syrup

Since freezing causes many fruits to discolor or lose their texture, particularly tree fruits such as peaches, plums, and apricots, they benefit from immersion in sugar syrup for freezing.

Fruits to choose: Peaches, pears, nectarines, plums, apricots, apples.

How to do it: Make a syrup by dissolving one part sugar to two parts water (that is ½ cup golden superfine sugar and 1 cup water to 1 pound 2 ounces fruit), then simmer until it is syrupy. Add 1–2 tablespoons lemon juice and let cool. Peel the fruit (see individual fruits, pages 202–249), halve or slice, removing any pits, seeds, or cores, then pack into rigid freezer containers. Pour the cold syrup over the fruit, insuring it is covered. If necessary, pack some crumpled foil on top to keep the fruit immersed in the syrup. Seal, label, freeze—the fruit will keep for about 6 months.

BAKING EN PAPILLOTE

To seal in all the juices of a fruit completely when cooking, try baking in foil. For each serving, cut out a large square of foil. Pile the fruit in the center, enrich with a pat of butter, sweeten with a sprinkling of sugar, or a drizzle of honey or maple syrup, then add a splash of wine or other alcohol. Bring the sides of the foil up and fold over to seal tightly. Place on a cookie sheet and bake at 350ºF (325ºF in fan ovens) for about 15 minutes or until just tender. Alternatively, cook on the barbecue for 5–10 minutes.

INSTANT FREEZER DESSERT

For an instant freezer dessert, sprinkle frozen fruits straight onto serving plates and pour over a warm chocolate sauce made by gently melting 5 ounces white chocolate with ⅔ cup heavy cream. The warm chocolate soon starts to thaw the fruits.

FRUIT A–Z

Apple

Although there are several thousand apple varieties, only a few are available commercially. If you come across a variety that is new to you, why not try it. Apple types are divided into eating and cooking apples. The main difference is that cooking apples are tarter; some eating apples can, however, also be used for cooking (see Use For, opposite).

CHOOSE

■ Available all year around, but often cheaper and at their best in the fall.
■ Firm fruit, with no sign of wrinkles or bruises.
■ Sweet-smelling fruit—apples should smell as well as taste sweet (apart from cooking apples).

STORE Keep apples in a perforated plastic bag in a refrigerator or a cool place. If kept too warm they will lose their crispness.
FREEZE: Stewed or puréed (see opposite), or as applesauce. Or slice and poach for a minute in sugar syrup (see page 201), then freeze.

PREPARE Use a vegetable peeler or sharp knife to peel (a peeler will

remove less flesh than a knife).
To core, cut the apple into fourths, cut out the core with a small, sharp knife, then peel, slice, dice, or chop. To keep the apple whole, remove the core first, using an apple corer; if you want to remove the peel too, do that after coring as the apple is less likely to crack. Grate, with peel on or off, using the coarsest hole on the grater, for adding to granola, cakes, or salads.

COOK

Bake: Core as above with an apple corer, keeping the apple whole, skin on. Score around the middle with a sharp knife, just over halfway up, then put in a shallow ovenproof dish. Stuff with whatever you fancy, such as dried fruits, crushed amaretti or ginger cookies, nuts, chunks of marzipan, or pieces of crystallized ginger, then sprinkle with a little molasses sugar or superfine sugar, dot with butter, and pour about ½ inch water into the dish. Bake at 350°F (325°F in fan ovens) for about 40–45 minutes (depends on the size of the fruit), or until tender when tested with a skewer.
■ Serve with ice cream, cream, crème fraîche, or custard.
Poach: See Pear, page 240.
Pan-fry: Melt some butter—about 2 tablespoons—in a skillet with 3–4 tablespoons golden superfine

apple

sugar until the sugar starts to color. Add the apple, cut into thickish wedges, and cook over a medium heat for a few minutes until starting to turn brown around the edges and soften.

■ Serve over ice cream or with thick cream on their own, or with pancakes or waffles.

Stew: Peel, core, and slice or chop 1 pound 2 ounces apples and put in a pan with a couple of spoonfuls of water, sugar to sweeten, a squeeze of lemon, and a pat of butter. Butter a round of waxed paper and place snugly on top of the apples, then cover with a lid. Cook over a fairly low heat, stirring often, until the apples are soft, about 10–15 minutes. Boil to thicken, add water to thin, or purée to make the mixture smooth.

■ Serve as applesauce, or when cold mix with equal amounts of ready-made thick custard and whipped cream for a quick dessert.

USE FOR

Eating: Crisp, fresh and juicy such as Cox, Braeburn, Pink Lady, Jonagold, Royal Gala, Fuji, Golden Delicious, Egremont Russet, Empire, Red Delicious, Spartan.

Salads: Golden Delicious, Pink Lady, Fuji, Red Delicious.

Baking: Granny Smith, Fuji, McIntosh, Jonathan.

TIPS AND TRICKS: APPLES

To stop apples turning brown when cut, toss them with lemon juice. If you use an eating apple for cooking, you may not need to add so much sugar (as they are sweeter than cooking apples).

MATCHING FRUITS AND ALCOHOL

If you want to add a splash of something alcoholic to your fruits, here's a quick guide:

■ *BRANDY—cherries, apples, pears, oranges, peaches, apricots*
■ *CASSIS—summer currants and berries, plums*
■ *KIRSCH—cherries, summer berries*
■ *PORT—cherries, plums, cranberries, red currants*
■ *RUM—pineapples, mangoes, bananas, mandarins, clementines*
■ *VODKA—pears*
■ *WINE (white or rosé)—grapes, nectarines, peaches, apricots*
■ *WINE (red)—strawberries, plums, pears*

Dessert: Golden Delicious, Braeburn, Empire, Ida Red, Granny Smith, Cox, Discovery, Jonagold, Royal Gala, Pink Lady, Egremont Russet.
Apple sauce: Ida Red.

GOES WITH Pork, cured ham, cheese, blackberries, pear, lemon, nuts, cinnamon, cloves, thyme, hard cider, brandy.

GOOD FOR YOU A source of fiber and vitamin C, although the bulk is found in the skin and core.

USE INSTEAD Pear.

Apricot

This belongs to the family of fruits with pits, along with cherries, plums, peaches, and nectarines. Apricots began their life in China before being introduced into the Middle East. They need a warm climate in which to thrive and today they are grown in Spain, France, Greece, North America, Australia, South Africa, Chile, and some parts of the former Soviet Union.

CHOOSE

■ Best during the summer months.
■ You can't always go by the color, but apricots should feel heavy and be reasonably firm, but with a little tenderness and no brown spots.

■ They should smell deliciously fragrant when ripe.

STORE If they are not ripe when you buy them, leave them to ripen at home at room temperature for several days. When ripe, they will keep in the refrigerator for up to 4–5 days. FREEZE: In sugar syrup (see page 201).

PREPARE No need to peel. To halve, using the dimple as a guide, go around the pit with a sharp knife. Gently twist apart with both hands, then remove the central pit. Brush any cut flesh with lemon juice as it browns quite quickly.

COOK The flavor is highlighted by cooking, so unless they are really fresh and ripe, apricots are often more popular cooked for desserts.
Poach: As for pears, page 240, but poach for 10–15 minutes, using half white wine, half water, or all water.

USE FOR

■ Making compotes, preserves, and chutneys.
■ A fruit crumble.
■ Poaching to use as a topping for cheesecake or sponge cake.
■ Mixing into a stuffing for lamb with nuts and herbs, or adding at the last minute to a Moroccan lamb stew.

apple–banana

GOES WITH Chicken, duck, lamb, almond, orange, chocolate, sweet white wine.

GOOD FOR YOU Contains high levels of the antioxidant beta carotene and vitamin A.

USE INSTEAD Peach or nectarine.

Banana

see also PLANTAIN, *page 243*
Bananas look like fat fingers, which is probably how they got their name, as banana comes from the Arabic word *banan* which means finger. This fruit originated in the Far East, but the biggest exporter is now Ecuador in South America.

CHOOSE The familiar yellow, or the more unusual red or apple banana. Red bananas come from Ecuador, have a red-purple skin, and a drier taste than yellow bananas (otherwise they can be used interchangeably), but are good for baking. Black patches on their skin indicate ripeness. Apple bananas are tiny in size and some-times known as dwarf bananas. They are sweeter than ordinary bananas, but are treated the same. The perfect size for pan-frying (see page 206).
■ They are available all year around.

TIPS AND TRICKS: BANANAS
■ *If bananas get too ripe for eating, peel, mash and freeze them for using in cakes, muffins or smoothies.*

■ Buy when yellow if you want to eat them straight away, slightly green if not (leave them for a few days at room temperature to ripen). Or buy a mix of the two so that you have some for now and some for later.

■ For baking, bananas that are over-ripe and brown-skinned are softer to mash and give the best flavor.

STORE Not in the refrigerator as the skin goes black, although the flesh can still be used for baking. Best kept in a fruit bowl on their own (or they can help ripen other fruits, see Speedy Ripening, page 221).

FREEZE: In their skins. The texture of the flesh will not be the same but it is handy to have them for mashing and using in baking.

PREPARE Just peel and slice or mash with a fork. Use lemon juice to stop them going brown.

COOK

Bake: Peel 2 bananas, halve them lengthwise, and lay them in a shallow ovenproof dish. Squeeze with the juice of half a lemon, dot with a pat of but-ter, sprinkle with 3 tablespoons light or dark soft brown sugar, and drizzle with 1–2 teaspoons rum. Cover and bake at 350°F (325°F in fan ovens) for about 20 minutes until softened.

■ Serve warm with cream, crème fraîche, or yogurt.

Grill: Make a small slit in the skin to stop the banana bursting. Put on a hot barbecue grill and cook for about 10 minutes, turning often, until the skin is completely black. Lift from the grill and slit open lengthwise with a sharp knife.

■ Serve with grilled meats, or sprinkle with cinnamon and light soft brown sugar as a dessert with cream or ice cream.

Pan-fry: Peel and halve lengthwise. Put about 2 tablespoons each butter and superfine sugar into a skillet and heat until melted. Add the banana halves, fry until just softening, then splash in 2–3 tablespoons rum, and let bubble to warm through.

■ Delicious with ice cream.

Broil: Peel and halve lengthwise, lay the pieces on a cookie sheet, brush with lemon juice, and sprinkle with sugar. Broil for a few minutes until soft and caramelized.

■ Serve with chicken or cured ham.

USE FOR

■ Mashing and mixing into baked goods such as banana bread and muffins, or into flapjacks for a softer texture.

■ Puréeing for milkshakes and smoothies.

■ Making a chocolate banana popsicle

—peel and thread on a small wooden skewer, wrap tightly, and freeze. Once it is frozen, unwrap and coat in melted chocolate, which will quickly harden.

GOES WITH Bacon, cured ham, cream, yogurt, honey, maple syrup, lemon, rum, cinnamon.

GOOD FOR YOU A great source of potassium and slow-release carbo-hydrate, plus several vitamins

Berries

There are many members of the berry family, with strong family resem-blances—all are small, juicy, simple to prepare, and bursting with vitamin C.

CHOOSE

Blackberries: Late summer–early fall; try also loganberries (part black-berry, part raspberry) which are longer in shape and sharper in taste, so better cooked with sugar than raw.
Blueberries: All year around, but especially good in the summer.
Gooseberries: Early summer for the green cooking ones, midsummer for dessert varieties.
Raspberries: Have the most flavor in high summer.
Strawberries: Available all year around. Bigger fruit doesn't always

have more flavor. Try also alpine or wood strawberries (*fraises de bois*), both smaller, fragrant, and sweet.

■ If they're sold in a carton, check the lower layers of berries for signs of mold or crushing—any that are past their best will quickly infect the rest.

■ All should look unblemished, plump, and bright.

STORE Best eaten soon—they keep for no more than a couple of days after you buy or pick them, except for gooseberries (they will keep for up to 2 weeks if not fully ripe) and blueberries (4–5 days). Spread softer berries out on a plate to avoid crushing, preferably on paper towels. If you are going to eat them fairly quickly, don't store in the refrigerator. If chilled, bring them out about an hour ahead of eating and serve at room temperature for optimum flavor.
FREEZE: By open freezing (see page 200). Firmer berries, such as gooseberries and blueberries, do not need to be open frozen first, but can go straight into freezer bags. Strawberries go mushy after freezing, so are best frozen as purée.

PREPARE Berries need very little attention apart from the following.
Gooseberries: Trim them—snip off the bits at both ends.

Raspberries: Due to their fragility, they are best not washed. If you really want to, give them a very quick rinse in a strainer or colander.
Strawberries: To prevent the fruit from becoming waterlogged, wash briefly before hulling (see page 28) and dry on paper towels. With ripe or homegrown fruit, you can gently pull out the leaves and core. For imported and unripe strawberries, the center isn't always so loose, so cut around the leaves and stalk with the tip of a small, sharp knife, and ease them out. You can use strawberries whole, in halves, fourths, or slices.

EAT All berries are wonderful eaten raw just as they are, apart from tart-tasting gooseberries. Cook these first with sugar (ripe dessert varieties can be eaten raw). Blueberries also benefit from a little cooking.

COOK
Gooseberries: Use early season green fruit. Put 9 ounces fruit in a pan with ⅔ cup water and ½ cup sugar and cook over a low heat until they soften and half have burst. Add more sugar if needed.
Blueberries: Dissolve 2 tablespoons sugar in a pan with 1–2 tablespoons water. Stir in 2¼ cups blueberries and simmer for a few minutes, until

berries

they brighten in color, start to burst, and turn the syrup a deep purple.

USE FOR

■ Creating a simple dessert. Tip the berries into a large bowl, sprinkle with confectioners' or superfine sugar and an optional splash of red wine or balsamic vinegar for strawberries, cassis for blueberries, blackberries, and raspberries. Leave for half an hour to create a flavorsome juice, then serve with cream or just as they are.

■ Making a milkshake or smoothie. Blend a handful of berries (not gooseberries) with a sliced banana in a food processor or blender until smooth, then whizz in enough milk or apple juice to create the desired thickness.

■ Dropping whole or sliced fruits (raspberries, strawberries, and blueberries) into glasses of chilled sparkling wine as an aperitif.

■ Mixing and matching. Make up your own combination of berries for a summer fruit salad and marinate in lemongrass syrup (see page 147).

■ Stirring a few blueberries or raspberries into a brownie mix, or mixing with peaches after poaching.

■ Stewing blackberries or gooseberries and serving with yogurt on your morning granola.

QUICK BERRY COULIS

To make an uncooked fruit purée or coulis, drop 1 cup strawberries or raspberries, with 1 tablespoon each sugar and water into a food processor or blender, whizz until smooth, then check for sweetness.

■ *Swirl through cream, yogurt, or crème fraîche and use as a filling, spoon into glasses for a dessert, or press through a strainer to make an instant coulis.*

BERRIES ON ICE

For dropping into summer drinks and cocktails, put a few mixed berries in ice-cube trays with strips of lime zest, top off with water, and freeze until solid. Pack into freezer bags and store in the freezer.

GOOD FOR YOU

Blackberries: Rich in both vitamin C and fiber.

Blueberries: Thought to be a real superfood because they contain a high concentration of phytochemicals, which can help protect against many illnesses such as heart disease, some cancers, and type-2 diabetes.

Gooseberries: Excellent source of vitamin C; some fiber.

Raspberries: High in vitamins; the seeds add fiber.

Strawberries: Particularly high in vitamin C; contains fiber.

Cherry

A small pitted fruit belonging to the same family as peaches, plums, apricots, and nectarines.

CHOOSE Either sweet, or sour cherries such as Morello (these are very sour, so are used for cooking).

■ Home-grown are cheaper and sweeter during early to mid summer. Producers include France, Turkey, Spain, United States, Chile, and South Africa.

■ Look for cherries with green fresh stems that are still attached, as they keep longer than those without stems.

■ Go for plumpness and glossiness; avoid split or bruised fruit.

STORE Keep in a bowl on the kitchen counter, or in a perforated plastic bag in the refrigerator for up to 2 days. If the bag has no air holes, the cherries will sweat and go bad quickly. Don't wash until ready to eat. FREEZE: Remove the pits first, then open freeze (see page 200).

PREPARE Rinse, then pluck the fruit from the stems. The easiest way to remove the pit is with a cherry pitter (see opposite). It keeps the cherry whole and you can use it for pitting olives, too. Another way is to score all the way around the cherry with a small, sharp knife, twist each half in opposite directions to separate, and pull out the pit.

COOK

Poach: For every 2 cups cherries, dissolve scant ½ cup golden superfine sugar in 1¼ cups red wine or port in a wide, shallow pan. Throw in a couple of star anise if you like, then add the cherries, pitted or not, and gently simmer for a few minutes until tender.

■ Unbeatable with thick cream or ice cream.

USE FOR
Sweet cherries

■ Serving simply at the end of a meal in a pile, on a platter with big

berries—cranberry

chunks of brie and goat cheese.

■ Dipping in melted chocolate.

■ Stirring into cake mixes: they go especially well with chocolate and almond flavors.

■ Chopping finely or coarsley to mix with lime juice and grated zest, some chopped cilantro, a pinch of dried chili flakes, and some finely chopped shallot for a fresh salsa to serve with roast duck, broiled cured ham, or cold meats.

Sour cherries

■ Making preserves or adding to pies.

■ Adding to fruity red wine based savory sauces.

GOES WITH Duck, chicken, cured ham, cheese, chocolate, almond, Kirsch, port, cream.

GOOD FOR YOU Provides vitamin C and is packed with antioxidants.

USE INSTEAD Canned or in jars if you can't find fresh.

Cranberry

Drop a cranberry and it should bounce if fresh: That's why they are sometimes called "bounce berries." They grow on trailing vines on boggy marshlands in Canada and the United States, and also in northern Europe.

CHERRY PITTING
The easiest way to remove the pit is with a special cherry pitter. Just press the cherry pitter into the indent in the stem end and the pit should pop right out the other end.

FRUIT A–Z

CHOOSE
- A fall/winter fruit.
- Should be dry, plump, and not at all shriveled.
- Look for bright red, about the size of a small grape.

STORE They will keep for at least a month in the refrigerator.
FREEZE: Cranberries freeze beautifully, so best to buy when in season, then open freeze (see page 200) and keep for up to 4–6 months. They can be used straight from frozen.

PREPARE Just cook.

COOK Cranberries are not usually eaten raw as they are so tart—cranberries benefit from being cooked with sugar to get the juices to flow.

USE FOR
- Mixing into stuffings with nuts (especially hazelnuts) and orange zest, to serve with chicken or turkey.
- Making cranberry sauce (see opposite) or mixing into muffins or sticky steamed puddings.
- Folding sweetened, cooked, and cooled fruit into whipped cream to fill a pavlova or orange- or hazelnut-flavored cake.
- Chopping and mixing into dried fruit for Christmas pies and tarts.

GOES WITH Poultry, nuts, dried fruit, orange, cinnamon.

GOOD FOR YOU Contains vitamin C and flavonoids (antioxidants that help fight heart disease and cancer).

Currants
(red, black, and white)

The three types, red, black, and white, grow on low bushes and hang in little clusters on slender stalks. All are tart—black currants have the boldest flavor, and white (red currants with no color pigment) are sweetest.

CHOOSE
- At the height of summer.
- All should look clean and glossy and not squashy. White are rather harder to find in stores and supermarkets than red and black currants.

STORE In the refrigerator, unwashed, for up to 3 days.
FREEZE: Open freeze with their stalks on—they will easily become separated after freezing (see page 200).

PREPARE Wash, then hold each stalk firmly at the top over a bowl. Run a fork down its length so the stalk

cranberry–currants

goes between the tines, allowing the berries to be released easily.

EAT White and red can be eaten raw, sprinkled generously with sugar. Black are rarely eaten raw.

COOK They are usually cooked with sugar to bring out their juiciness.
Poach: Pour 3 tablespoons water into a pan with ⅓ cup superfine sugar. Heat, stirring, to dissolve the sugar, then add scant 4 cups fruit. Simmer briefly until just starting to burst.

USE FOR
- Mixing with soft summer berries for summer pudding (all colors).
- Combining colors for contrast in tarts or pies, or to decorate cheesecakes, pavlovas, and creamy desserts.
- Making fruit coulis and syrups, preserves, cordials, and jellies (red or black).
- Making an instant sauce. Defrost frozen currants, then mash with sugar and a squeeze of lemon juice, and press through a strainer until smooth.
- Creating purées for sherbets, ice cream, and mousses (black).
- Freezing in tiny clusters in ice-cube trays filled with water, for dropping into summer drinks (any color).
- Crushing and adding a few to oil and vinegar dressing (red or black).

QUICK CRANBERRY SAUCE
Tip 2 cups cranberries into a pan with 5 tablespoons water. Bring to a boil, cover with a lid, and cook for 10 minutes until the skins pop. Tip in generous ½ cup superfine sugar, the finely grated zest of 1 orange, and 2 tablespoons red wine or port (optional). Cook, stirring to dissolve the sugar, then simmer for about 5 minutes or until the sauce reaches the thickness you want. Cool. It will keep for several days in the refrigerator, or for up to 3 months in the freezer.

FRUIT A–Z

GOES WITH

Black currants: Duck, game, mint, red wine, cream, yogurt.

Red currants: Lamb, goose, raspberries, strawberries, melon, peaches, rosemary, cream.

White currants: Mix with red and black for summer desserts.

GOOD FOR YOU All contain vitamin C, black currants the most.

Date (fresh)

for DRIED, see page 85

Fresh dates are moister but not so sweet as dried. Dates look dried even if fresh, so it is not always easy to tell which you are buying, but in supermarkets they are likely to be dried.

CHOOSE

■ All year around, but fresher in the winter months.

■ Go for plump, shiny, and a little wrinkly, with dark brown skin.

■ Medjool dates are particularly good.

STORE Will keep in the refrigerator for several days in an airtight container, or at room temperature. FREEZE: Remove pits from fresh dates, pack into freezer bags or containers. and freeze for up to a year.

PREPARE Simply remove the pit by pushing it through the date. For a neater look, slit the date lengthwise, open it, lift out the pit, and close it up again. If you need to remove the skin, pull the stem off, then hold the date by pinching it at one end and pushing the flesh so it squeezes out the other end.

USE FOR

■ Stuffing with cream cheese or farmer's cheese, after slitting lengthwise and mixing the cheese with a little finely grated orange zest.

■ Making chutney.

■ Adding to cakes and desserts to make them moist and sticky.

■ Snipping over your breakfast cereal to sweeten instead of sugar.

■ Putting in sandwiches—just chop and mix with softened cream cheese.

■ Sweetening savory stews, especially Moroccan lamb or chicken ones.

USE INSTEAD Dried figs, prunes, or dried dates.

GOES WITH Lamb, chicken, creamy cheeses, honey, nuts, oats.

GOOD FOR YOU A great source of fiber, vitamin C (more than cranberries and cherries), and chloride.

Fig

Most of the inside of the fig is made up of wine-red edible seeds. Originally from western Asia, figs are now mainly produced in Mediterranean countries. They are delicate, so are often shipped unripe to prevent bruising. Treat gently.

CHOOSE

■ Available at different times depending on the variety and country of origin.
■ Should feel soft, but not excessively so, with no blemishes or bruises, which indicate they have been damaged.
■ Look for plump figs with no signs of shriveling.
■ They range in color from green to almost black, with shades of yellow, brown, red, and purple in between.

STORE At room temperature for ripening, or individually packed in paper towels in the refrigerator. They will only keep for a day or two. FREEZE: Gently wash and remove the stems, pat dry, then open freeze (see page 200).

PREPARE Keep them whole or cut into fourths, so their shapeliness can be admired. For a nice effect, cut through the skin and cut the flesh into four without cutting all the way through; you can then open out the

FRUIT A–Z

fruit like a flower to show off the juicy red flesh (see opposite).

EAT Best eaten at room temperature, so if you've stored the figs in the refrigerator, take them out about an hour before you want to serve them. There's no need to peel them; just tuck in as they are, or split them open first with your fingers.

COOK

Broil: Cut in half lengthwise, drizzle with honey, and broil for a few minutes until lightly caramelized.

Poach: In red wine. Heat 2½ cups red wine with generous ⅔ cup sugar in a medium pan until dissolved. Bring to a boil, then lower the heat to a simmer. Add the figs (there is enough liquid for about 12). Put in as many as will fit in the pan in a single layer: Do in batches if necessary. Cover and poach for 5–8 minutes or until softened. Lift the figs out with a slotted spoon into a serving dish and bubble the wine for another 5–8 minutes until reduced to a thin syrup. Cool, then pour over the figs.

Roast: Sit 6–8 figs in an ovenproof dish so they are upright and fit snugly. Drizzle with 2 tablespoons each honey and orange juice. Roast at 425°F (400°F in fan ovens) for 8–12 minutes or until the skins start to crack.

USE FOR

■ Making kabobs—cut into fourths, wrap with prosciutto, thread on skewers, then serve, or lightly brush with oil and broil for a few minutes.

■ Cut into fourths and adding to salads with goat cheese and arugula, drizzled with an olive oil dressing.

■ Serving raw or roasted as a simple dessert, drizzled with honey, and served with spoonfuls of plain yogurt or farmer's cheese and a sprinkling of toasted nuts.

GOES WITH prosciutto, ricotta, goat cheese, nuts, honey, cinnamon.

GOOD FOR YOU Figs have iron and potassium and are high in fiber; they are also high in calcium—½ cup chopped figs has twice as much as the same quantity of milk.

Gooseberry
see BERRIES, *page 207*

Grape

One of the oldest cultivated fruits in the world, grapes have many uses. They produce wine, vinegar, and verjuice and, when dried, shrivel to become currants and raisins, as well as being a juicy fruit in their own

fig–**g**rape

right. They are grown mostly in Greece, Spain, Italy, United States, India, South Africa, and Chile.

CHOOSE

■ All year around, as varieties from around the world come into season. Choose from black, red, and green (also called white), with or without seeds. Flavors vary—black, such as Ribier and Black Italia, tend to have more depth. Favorite green grapes are Vittoria and Italia, while favorite red-skinned are Flame and Muscat Rosada. Seedless grapes are convenient, but those with seeds are often tastier.
■ Check that they have a fresh bloom, the stalks are fresh, and there are no bruised or small, shriveled grapes.
■ Don't buy in bulk unless you are going to eat them quickly, as grapes are closely packed on the bunch, so they can squash and bruise each other if left sitting around too long.

STORE Pluck off any bad ones from the bunch, wash, then store in a fruit bowl for a day or two if you are going to eat them straight away. Otherwise they will last unwashed in a perforated plastic bag in the vegetable drawer of the refrigerator for up to a week. For the best flavor take them out about an hour before eating.
FREEZE: Not recommended.

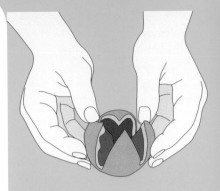

OPENING FIGS
If you want an attractive presentation, cut through the skin and flesh into fourths, without cutting all the way through, and open the fig out like a flower.

FIX IT: FIGS

If your fig lacks juiciness and flavor, drizzle with honey and roast or broil.

PREPARE Wash before use and, unless they are seedless, halve, and pick out the seeds. If a recipe calls for skinning the grapes, prick each end, drop into boiling water for 1 minute, then into cold water, and peel.

COOK Grapes are not used a lot in cooking, but when they are, they should be added toward the end to keep their shape and texture intact.

USE FOR

- A healthy snack or serving in little clusters still on the stalks with cheese.
- Adding to both sweet and savory salads.
- Classic cooked savory dishes such as sole Véronique.
- Decorating desserts by "frosting" the grapes. Brush each grape all over with lightly beaten egg white, then sprinkle with superfine sugar (or dip) to coat evenly, shaking off any excess. Lay on baking parchment to dry.

GOES WITH Chicken, game birds, fish, cheese, white wine, tarragon.

GOOD FOR YOU Low in nutrients, but the red varieties particularly contain a lot of flavonoids (anti-oxidants).

Grapefruit

Grapefruit is a citrus fruit, a descendant of the sweet orange and the larger pomelo (see right). Grapefruit have been cultivated for centuries in hot countries such as Israel, Morocco, South Africa, Cyprus, and Jamaica, and the 1970s saw the sweeter pink grapefruit grown in Florida and parts of the Caribbean. The United States is a huge producer.

CHOOSE

- All year around, although there is more choice and sweeter and juicier fruit in winter and spring.
- Shiny, thin-skinned ones that feel heavy with juice—light ones usually indicate a thick peel and less flesh.
- Between yellow (white) flesh, pink, and ruby red. Pink is much sweeter.

STORE Can be left at room temperature (better served like that too), and will keep for a week or two.

PREPARE To serve at breakfast, see below. Alternatively, segment as you would an orange (see page 234).

EAT Best raw. The pink and red don't need sugar, but you might want to sweeten the yellow-fleshed, tangier ones. To prepare, cut in half width-

grape–grapefruit

wise, then dig out, and discard any
seeds, and loosen the flesh from the
pithy shell with a small, serrated knife
(or a curved grapefruit knife). Then
loosen each fleshy segment from the
membranes that separate them. Serve
in the shell.

COOK

Broil: Prepare each half as above, put
on a small cookie sheet, sprinkle with
1 tablespoon light brown or superfine
sugar and a little ground cinnamon or
ground ginger. Put under the broiler
until the sugar melts and caramelizes.
■ Serve as a refreshing breakfast.

USE FOR

■ Making a tangy marmalade.
■ Combining (segmented) with orange
segments for a lively fruit salad;
sprinkle with toasted chopped hazelnuts or pistachios.
■ A side salad (segmented) with slices
of avocado and crisp salad greens or
with baby spinach leaves, or arugula,
avocado, and orange.
■ Squeezing the juice to use for a
dressing instead of lemon. Sweeten
with a little honey.

GOES WITH Chicken, oily fish
(especially trout and mackerel), shellfish, avocado, spinach, mango, other
citrus fruits, ginger, honey.

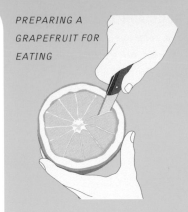

*PREPARING A
GRAPEFRUIT FOR
EATING*

WHAT IS A POMELO?
*This is similar to a grapefruit,
but thicker-skinned and pithier.
It is less juicy, so serve sprinkled
with sugar.*

FRUIT A–Z

GOOD FOR YOU High in vitamin C and potassium. The pink grapefruit varieties are a good source of beta carotene.

USE INSTEAD Pomelo (see page 219).

Guava

A fragrant tropical fruit—it looks like a smooth lemon and smells like an expensive perfume. Inside is a sweet-sharp flesh, varying in color from yellow to salmon pink.

CHOOSE

- Available most of the year.
- Yellow aromatic fruit indicates ripeness, although as they bruise easily, guavas are often sold unripe —green and hard.
- They should feel firm, but give slightly in your hand when squeezed very gently.

STORE If they are unripe when bought, leave them to ripen at room temperature, then keep in the refrigerator in a perforated plastic bag.
FREEZE: Best as a purée.

PREPARE Peel first, if you like, then slice or cut in chunks.

EAT Make sure the guava is ripe first—the perfumed smell (which is often more beguiling than the taste) will tell you; otherwise it tastes sharp. You can eat the whole fruit, with skin and crunchy seeds, although one way to eat it is to cut it in half, then scoop out the flesh and seeds with a spoon.

COOK Cooking lifts the flavor. Try chopping or slicing and mixing with apples or pears for a crumble or compote. Or stew in the same way as apples (page 203) and purée to make a sauce for serving with meats.

USE FOR

- Adding peeled, sliced, or chopped to a fruit salad.
- Squeezing like a lemon to make a drink with the juice.
- Chopping to make a salsa for serving with rich meats.
- Preserves, ice creams, and sherbets.

GOES WITH Rich meats such as duck, pork, and game, pineapple, strawberries.

GOOD FOR YOU Extremely rich in vitamin C, containing much more than an orange, guava are also rich in potassium, niacin, and beta carotene.

Kiwi

This furry, brown-skinned fruit, with bright green flesh and black seeds, is named—and rebranded—after the national bird of New Zealand and is also grown there. Native to China, it used to be called the Chinese gooseberry. The golden variety is less hairy and has yellow-gold flesh that is sweeter than the green, somewhere between mango and melon.

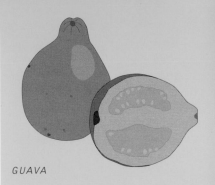

GUAVA

CHOOSE

■ Available all year around.
■ Look for slightly firm fruits which give a little when gently squeezed. Avoid overripe ones.
■ Check there are no bruises, and the skin is tight-fitting, not shriveled.

STORE When ripe they will keep in the refrigerator for about a week. To speed up the ripening process, if not ripe when they are bought, see right.
FREEZE: Not recommended as the flesh becomes mushy on thawing.

PREPARE

With a knife: Peel off the thin, inedible skin with a knife or vegetable peeler, then chop or cut the flesh in thickish slices (thin slices break

SPEEDY RIPENING

Fruit, especially kiwi, is often sold underripe. To ripen quickly at home, put the fruits in a paper bag along with an apple or a banana, giving them plenty of room so they don't get squashed. Leave at room temperature, away from direct sun.

up easily). The central white core is edible too, but if it is tough, just cut it out.

With a spoon: Cut a thin slice off each end of the fruit. Have a plate underneath to catch any juice, then, holding a dessertspoon in one hand and the fruit in the other, rotate the fruit with your hand, keeping the spoon flush with the peel as you go. When you get all the way around, the peeled fruit will plop right out. You can then slice it or cut it in wedges.

EAT Cut in half widthwise and scoop out the flesh with a teaspoon.

COOK Don't cook kiwi—it will destroy all the vitamin C and the color.

USE FOR
■ A filling for pavlovas or tarts.
■ Chopping into salsas.
■ Blending with a banana or other tropical fruits for a smoothie.

GOES WITH Chicken, pork, raspberries, papaya, banana, cream.

GOOD FOR YOU Eat a kiwi and you'll get your daily supply of vitamin C (for adults). It's also an effective natural laxative.

Lemon

Although it is not often eaten on its own, every part of a lemon is a culinary treasure—this citrus fruit is loved around the world for its myriad uses. Its sour, tart taste makes it one of the most invaluable fruits.

CHOOSE
■ Available all year around.
■ Those that are shiny with a real lemon yellow color. The darker, more orangey-yellow are less sour.
■ Heavy, smaller lemons with thin, smooth skins have lots of juice—good for slices or wedges.
■ Large lemons can have more pith and skin—fine if you're making preserves or candied peel.
■ Italian lemons are big with thick, knobby skins, so have plenty of zest.

STORE Lemons will keep for 2 weeks or more in a perforated plastic bag in the refrigerator, or for a week in the fruit bowl. Check regularly for mold. Cut and wrapped in plastic wrap, they will last 3–4 days in the refrigerator. FREEZE: Either whole or sliced. Whole—wash and dry, then pack into freezer bags, seal, and label. Sliced—open freeze (see page 200).

PREPARE Most lemons are waxed to

kiwi–lemon

preserve their skin, so unless they are organic, give them a scrub. If they have been in the refrigerator, let them reach room temperature before squeezing to get more juice.

Zest: This is the yellow outer part that holds the key to the lemon's flavor—if you go too deeply and take off the white pith too, it can make a dish taste bitter. Fine for marmalade, but not for most other things. To release the aromatic oil in the zest, use a grater, or a zester for fine pieces (see pages 62 and 72).

Juice: Halve and twist the juice out with a lemon squeezer or reamer.

COOK Add toward the end of cooking as heat destroys the vitamin C.

USE FOR

■ Stopping peeled or cut fruits and vegetables from going brown (see Acidulated, page 8).

■ Flavoring desserts, cookies, cakes (cuts through richness in heavy fruit cakes), risottos, pasta, couscous, sherbets, ice creams.

■ Adding grated zest to sharpen the taste of mayonnaise, or making a salad dressing by mixing one-third lemon juice to two-thirds olive oil.

■ Garnishing and flavoring. Sprinkle slices with sugar, flash under the broiler, and use to decorate desserts such as cheesecake and lemon tart.

TIPS AND TRICKS: KIWIS

■ *For really tender meat, lay a few slices of kiwi over it about an hour before cooking.*

■ *Don't use kiwis in any recipe involving gelatin, as the same enzyme that tenderizes also inhibits gelatin from setting. The enzyme curdles milk and light cream too.*

- Deglazing a pan. After frying fish, add 1–2 tablespoons juice, let it bubble, add herbs, and pour over the fish.
- Helping jellies and marmalades set (it has a high pectin content).
- Roasting with wedges of potatoes. Coat the potatoes in oil, squeeze the juice from lemon wedges over the potatoes, then tuck in among them, season with pepper, and roast.
- Cooking wedges on an oiled stove top grill pan to serve with fish, chicken, pork.
- Threading wedges onto skewers with wedges of onion and cubes of pork, chicken, or fish.
- Adding fragrance to roast chicken. Halve a lemon and place inside the cavity with a couple of bay leaves.

GOES WITH Any fish, chicken, salad greens, honey, fruits, vegetables.

GOOD FOR YOU Contains lots of vitamin C.

USE INSTEAD Limes—but their flavor is stronger, so use about two-thirds the amount.

Lime

Looks like a small, green lemon but has a refreshing flavor all its own. Another member of the extended citrus fruit family, limes are particularly popular in Southeast Asia, from where they are thought to have come.

CHOOSE
- Available all year around.
- As with lemons, thin-skinned and heavy indicates lots of juice.
- Even, shiny, green skin, or with patches of yellow too.
- Use kaffir limes for Thai cooking, although these are not so readily available—look in Asian specialty stores. They are darker green, more knobby-skinned, and are used for their zest. Use ordinary limes if you can't find them.

STORE Will keep in the refrigerator for up to 2 weeks in a perforated plastic bag, or for about a week at room temperature.
FREEZE: Either whole or sliced. Whole—wash and dry, then pack into freezer bags, seal, and label. Sliced—open freeze the slices (see page 200).

PREPARE The same as for lemons (see page 222), and take care when grating not to include the white pith as lime is thinner than lemon zest.

EAT Like lemons, not usually eaten as a raw fruit.

lemon–lime

COOK Add toward the end of cooking as heat destroys the vitamin C.

USE FOR

■ Making margueritas and daiquiris.

■ "Cooking" raw fish as in ceviche. When the juice is squeezed over raw fish, such as thin slices of salmon, and left to marinate, it has the same effect as cooking it and changes the appearance of the flesh from raw to opaque.

■ Adding to many Thai dishes, especially soups, and Mexican guacamole.

■ Bringing out the flavor of fruits—squeeze over chunks of papaya, blueberries, melon, avocado, or mango.

■ Making salsas—the juice and zest are great with mango, a little oil, and chopped chili to serve with Mexican or Indian food, or fish dishes.

■ Dropping slices into drinks such as gin and tonic, iced tea, fruit punch.

GOES WITH Chicken, fish, blueberries, tropical fruits such as mango and papaya, chili.

GOOD FOR YOU Contains vitamin C, but less than lemons and oranges.

USE INSTEAD Lemons—use a little more because they are milder.

TIPS AND TRICKS: LEMONS

Microwave lemon on medium-high for 20-40 seconds or until just warm (the timing depends on the size of the lemon). This warms it a little so you'll get more juice (1 lemon generally gives about 2–3 tablespoons juice).

If you haven't got a microwave, warm the lemon up by rolling it on a flat surface for a minute or two with your hand.

Lychee

With its brittle, pinky-red, bumpy shell, a lychee can look a hard nut to crack. But it is thin-skinned with a juicy, fleshy, translucent, white fruit that looks a little like a swollen grape and tastes sweet and perfumed. It originated in China (hence its popularity with Chinese food) and now grows in tropical areas such as Madagascar, Mauritius, South Africa, Australia, and Thailand.

CHOOSE

■ Available at different times of the year, especially in the winter.
■ Should look pinky red for freshness (green means not yet ripe, brown means they are past it). If they feel heavy they will be plump and deliciously juicy inside.

STORE At room temperature and try to use them as soon as possible. FREEZE: Not recommended.

PREPARE Make a slit across the tight-fitting, brittle shell, then peel it off, or just use your fingers. To keep the inside fruit whole, make a slit in the juicy, white flesh and pull out the pit. Or make a slit around the fruit's middle after peeling, twist to separate into halves, and discard the pit.

EAT Just peel and eat your way around the shiny, dark pit as you would a plum. Or prepare as above.

USE FOR

■ Adding to fruit salads—goes well with melon, mango, pineapple, grapes in a lemongrass syrup (see page 147), especially after a Chinese or Thai meal.
■ Serving with vanilla ice cream.
■ Creating an instant dessert—put a few, peeled and pitted, in a bowl with a handful of blueberries and a squeeze of lime.

GOES WITH Other tropical fruits, blueberries, lemongrass.

GOOD FOR YOU Contains vitamin C and phosphorus.

USE INSTEAD Canned if you can't find fresh, but they taste less fragrant.

Mango

There are so many varieties of mango, there's no way to describe the perfect one. Not only can the color vary, but also the texture, size, and flavor. Whatever the variety, when ripe a mango is the perfect-tasting fruit.

lychee–mango

CHOOSE

■ Different varieties come into season at different times, from the tropics—mostly Brazil, Mexico, Pakistan, India, Jamaica, South Africa.

■ Don't always go by color—go by feel as well. When ripe a mango yields slightly when held and gently pressed.

■ For an especially tasty mango, try the small, golden Indian Alfonso mango, around only for a few weeks in the stores in late spring. Its soft texture when ripe makes it really easy to mash.

STORE
A week or two in the fruit bowl, depending how ripe they are when bought. If underripe, keep them at room temperature to soften. Eat as soon as they are ripe, or keep for a couple of days in the refrigerator.
FREEZE: Sliced or cubed, in sugar syrup (see page 201).

PREPARE
Using a sharp knife, cut down either side of the pit, feeling where the pit is with the knife and cutting close to it. This gives two mango "cheeks." For cubes, prepare it "porcupine style" (see right).
Or slice off the peel and cut the flesh into slices or chunks. Slice off any flesh left on the pit too.

LYCHEE

PREPARING A MANGO

1 *Score evenly spaced lengthwise lines through the flesh almost to the skin. Score across in the opposite direction to make cubes.*

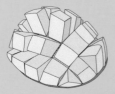

2 *Bend the mango back and the cubes will pop up making them easy to eat with a spoon.*

EAT On their own in slices, chunks, or halves, or "porcupine style" (see page 227).

COOK Mango is mostly enjoyed raw, but if used in cooking, it is usually added at the end (except in chutney).

USE FOR

■ Adding cubes or slices to a turkey or chicken stir-fry at the last minute.

■ Blending, then folding into cream, crème fraîche, or yogurt to use as a filling for pavlova. Or to pile on top of a trifle with tropical fruits.

■ Mixing up into a smoothie with a banana, milk, and yogurt.

■ Combining with lime, chili, and cilantro for a chutney or salsa. Serve with grilled shrimp.

■ Using unripe sour and crunchy mangoes in Asian salads or with chili dips. Use also to marinate meat to tenderize.

■ Making sherbets and ice cream.

GOES WITH Chicken, turkey, shellfish, prosciutto, coconut, chili, orange, passion fruit, peach, cream, yogurt.

GOOD FOR YOU A great supplier of beta carotene and vitamins C and E.

Mangosteen

The thick, leathery skin of the mangosteen protects a delicate-tasting, white flesh which is segmented like an orange. It has a refreshing tang a little like rhubarb and grows in tropical countries such as India, Thailand. and Indonesia. Despite its name, it has nothing to do with a mango.

CHOOSE

■ All year around; best in the summer.

■ The skin should be dark purple, almost the color of an eggplant. When green it is unripe.

■ It should feel heavy. If it's light. the fruit inside has probably dried out.

STORE Will keep for a couple of weeks in the refrigerator, wrapped, but for less at room temperature.

PREPARE Cut through the skin around the middle with a sharp knife, then twist it off in opposite directions to reveal the white segments.

EAT There is more skin than flesh. To get at the edible part, cut it in half, then scoop out the flesh with a teaspoon, avoiding the large seeds. Or remove the skin only, as above, then separate the flesh into segments, and simply eat the flesh off the seeds.

COOK An expensive fruit which is best eaten on its own.

USE FOR

- Mixing with other tropical fruits for a fruit salad.

GOES WITH Other tropical fruit.

GOOD FOR YOU Not especially nutrient rich, but mangosteen is high in phytochemicals.

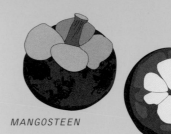

MANGOSTEEN

Melon

A member of the squash family this grows on the ground like a pumpkin. Melons come in many different sizes, colors, shapes, and flavors.

CHOOSE

- All year around, as different varieties are available at different times, but best at the height of summer.

Cantaloupe: Sweet, aromatic, and juicy with a peachy-orange flesh.

Charentais: Small and round, deep orange, juicy, fragrant flesh, and pale green skin.

Honeydew: Mild flavor, yellow or pale greenish-yellow flesh, sweet, and refreshing.

Ogen: Small and round, delicate tasting, pale yellow flesh.

Piel de Sapo: Mild and sweet with

FRUIT A–Z

a pale, yellowy-green flesh. Its name means "toad's skin."

Watermelon: Not a true melon, but used in a similar way. Looks stunning with bright red flesh and black seeds dotted throughout the flesh (seedless are also obtainable). Huge in size compared with other varieties, so often sold in big wedges rather than as a whole. It can lack flavor, but owing to its juiciness, it is refreshing to eat on a hot day.

■ Test for ripeness by smell—melons can give off a lovely fragrance (Canteloupe, Charentais, Ogen).

■ Test for ripeness by feel—the melon should give slightly when pressed with your thumb at the stalk end.

■ Ripe watermelons sound hollow when shaken.

STORE At room temperature until ripe, then use as soon as possible. Once peeled and cut, they will store in the refrigerator (well wrapped or the smell and taste will taint other foods) for up to 2 days.

FREEZE: Sliced or cubed, in sugar syrup (see page 201).

PREPARE Cut in half—it doesn't matter which way—and scoop out the seeds and any stringy, fibrous parts with a spoon. Cut in wedges and peel off the skin, then slice, or chop. Or,

while still in halves, scoop out little balls of melon with a melon baller.

EAT Small melons, like Ogens, can be served in halves with the seeds scooped out. Otherwise serve in wedges —to make it easier to eat, release each wedge from the skin by sliding a knife under the flesh close to the skin. Most refreshing if served chilled.

USE FOR All types can be used for sweet or savory dishes.

■ Serving in a salad—try watermelon and salty feta cheese, Cantaloupe with shrimp and lime, or Charentais with avocado and crab.

■ Combining different colors of melon or making up a vibrant fruit salad or platter.

■ Making a purée for a juice mixed with orange.

■ Wrapping wedges with prosciutto for an appetizer, or serving on a platter with wedges of melon with prosciutto, arugula, and Parmesan shavings.

■ Creating an instant dessert. Tip chunks of melon into a bowl with some grapes. Chill, then pour over some elderflower cordial diluted with sparkling apple juice, and serve sprinkled with freshly torn mint.

GOES WITH Cured ham, shrimp, feta cheese, mint, nectarines.

melon–nectarine

GOOD FOR YOU Melons are a great source of beta carotene—cantaloupe is really high; other melons have vitamin C and niacin.

see also PEACH *page 236*

Nectarine

The rosy-cheeked nectarine bears a strong resemblance to its relative, the peach, but has thinner, smoother skin and firmer, often juicier, sweeter flesh. Mostly grown in America, South Africa, and Mediterranean countries.

CHOOSE
■ At their juiciest in midsummer.
■ When ripe they smell fragrant and should feel fairly firm, just giving a little when pressed.
■ Any bruising or mold is a sign that the fruit is past its best.

STORE Ripen (if necessary) at room temperature for a couple of days. They will then keep for a couple more days, or in the refrigerator for longer.
FREEZE: In sugar syrup (see page 201).

PREPARE No need to peel unless you want to. Cut around the middle, until you reach the pit, and twist both halves in opposite directions to separate them. Dig out and discard the pit,

TIPS AND TRICKS: NECTARINES
Nectarines discolor quickly once cut, so brush cut slices with lemon juice to stop them going brown.

FRUIT A–Z

then keep it in halves, or cut into slices or chunks.

EAT Best eaten raw, just as it is, skin intact.

COOK
Poach: This is a good idea if the fruit is unripe (see Peach, page 238).
Roast: In a shallow dish with ⅔ cup sweet white wine, a sprinkling of sugar, and grated orange zest for 15–20 minutes at 350°F (325°F in fan ovens).

USE FOR
▪ Tossing with fruits such as melon, mango, and raspberries, for a refreshing fruit salad.
▪ Caramelizing (see page 14) to serve with cheesecake and other creamy desserts. Dissolve generous ½ cup superfine sugar with 4 tablespoons water in a heavy skillet. Cook until caramelized, then stir in a pat of butter, and add 3 nectarines cut in wedges. Cook gently until soft, turning to coat in the caramelized sauce.
▪ Adding wedges or chunks to a stir-fry of chicken, turkey, or pork.

GOES WITH Chicken, mascarpone cheese, Chinese flavors, amaretti, rosé and white wine.

GOOD FOR YOU Contains beta

carotene and vitamin C. Nectarine is more nutritious than peach.

USE INSTEAD Peaches.

Orange
Part of the citrus fruit family, oranges are mostly sweet, but you can also get bitter ones for cooking. Oranges come mainly from Israel, Spain, Morocco, the United States, and South Africa.

CHOOSE
▪ All year around; different varieties are available at different times.
▪ You can never be sure how juicy an orange is until you cut it, but select small and heavy fruit over large and light, as heaviness indicates that they have a lot of juice.
▪ The rind should look thin and be tight; if not, it may have excess pith.
▪ Between the sweet eating orange and the bitter variety:
Sweet
Blood—attractive for their wine-red color, available only for a few months at the beginning of the year. Sweet, juicy, and aromatic.
Navel—popular for being seedless and easy to peel, with a lovely flavor.
Valencia—smooth-skinned and sweet with just a few seeds; a great orange to choose for juicing.

nectarine–orange

Bitter

Temple—the rougher-skinned, coarser-fleshed, bitter-tasting oranges used for making marmalade or in cooking, but not for eating raw. You need to look out for them at the beginning of the year, when they are available for just a few weeks.

STORE Up to a week or two at room temperature.
FREEZE: The juice freezes well and keeps for about 4 months. Because of their short season, Temple oranges are worth freezing, which they do well—just wipe them and pack whole into freezer bags. Thaw before using.

PREPARE

Zest: Unless the oranges are organic and unwaxed, give them a scrub. Use a grater or zester to remove the zest only (see pages 62 and 72), not the white pith, which is bitter. Or use a vegetable peeler to remove wider strips of zest. Add these to dishes such as stews or soups for flavoring, or cut with a sharp knife into batons to use as a decoration or for adding to sauces.
Juice: Halve and squeeze out the juice with a lemon squeezer.
Segment: By doing this you eliminate pith and membranes at the same time, so it's an attractive way to prepare an orange and makes it nicer

WHAT'S IN A NAME? SOFT CITRUS FRUITS

These easy eaters, all members of the mandarin family, have loose skins that make them so easy to peel.

■ *MANDARIN AND TANGERINE: These names are often used interchangeably. It is hard to define the difference—they refer to small, loose-skinned citrus fruits.*

■ *CLEMENTINE: A type of tangerine, small, virtually seedless, easy to peel, sweet, and juicy.*

■ *SATSUMA: A variety of tangerine with a mild taste, sometimes a little sharp, very easy to peel.*

to eat. Trim a small slice off both ends of the fruit. Sit the orange upright on a board. Using a small, sharp knife, slice downward through the skin and pith, following the curve of the fruit, but avoiding cutting into the flesh. This leaves a whole rindless, pithless orange. Hold the orange over a small bowl to catch the juice, and cut down both sides of each segment to release it from the membranes (see illustration, opposite). Squeeze what's left of the membranes to get all of the juice.

USE FOR

■ Flavoring cake frostings, whipped cream, mascarpone dessert fillings/toppings (zest or juice).

■ Making a salad with arugula or Belgian endive, crumbled blue cheese, and walnut (segments).

■ Adding unpeeled slices to mulled wine, Pimms, sangría, and other summer or winter punches.

■ Temple orange—making marmalade; adding zest and juice to dressings and marinades with honey, garlic, and oil, or to orange sauces to go with duck and game; adding zest to stews.

GOES WITH Many things, especially cured ham, duck, chicken, pork, game, beef, carrot, Belgian endive, beet, watercress, nuts, peach, apricot, plum, chocolate.

GOOD FOR YOU Contains potassium, vitamin C, folate, and biotin.

Papaya

Also known as paw paw, this tropical fruit is shaped like an overgrown pear and has a subtle but sweet flavor, similar to peach and apricot. It is grown in tropical countries such as Hawaii, Brazil, Jamaica, Malaysia, Ghana, and Peru.

CHOOSE

■ Available at different times of the year—best from spring to early summer, then again in the fall.

■ When ripe a papaya should feel slightly soft all over, like an avocado.

■ The skin should be yellowy-green with orange tinges. Avoid any with pitted skin as they could be bruised.

■ Green papayas (unripe) are used in Thai cooking as a vegetable, or for shredding into salads.

STORE If not ripe when bought, leave at room temperature to ripen. Otherwise ripe papayas can be kept in the refrigerator.
FREEZE: In sugar syrup (see page 201).

PREPARE With the skin still on, slice in half lengthwise. Inside is an

orange-papaya

apricot-orange or deep salmon-pink flesh and clusters of sparkly black seeds. Scoop out the seeds with a spoon and discard. Peel off the skin with a sharp knife (easier if cut into fourths), then slice the flesh, or cut into chunks. The flesh does not discolor, so this can be done ahead. To purée papaya, seed, peel, and chop as above, then whizz in a blender or food processor, with a squeeze of lime or lemon juice.

EAT Once it has been halved and seeded, squeeze each cut half with lime juice (to intensify the flavor), and eat out of the shell with a spoon.

COOK Cooking can spoil its delicate flavor, so papaya is best eaten raw.

USE FOR
- Mixing into salads (goes well tossed with cold chicken, grapes, and a curried mayonnaise or vinaigrette dressing), into leafy salad greens, or with other tropical fruits in a fruit salad.
- Puréeing for sherbets, or for a drink sweeten with sugar, freshen up with lime juice, and thin with apple juice.
- A dessert—halve, seed, then fill each half with blueberries or raspberries, and finish with a squeeze of fresh lime.
- An appetizer or light lunch—cut into wedges and wrap with prosciutto.

SEGMENTING AN ORANGE and eliminating the pith and membranes at the same time, is an attractive way to prepare it, plus it makes it easier to eat.

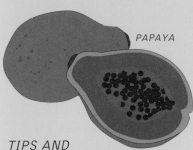

PAPAYA

TIPS AND TRICKS: PAPAYA
- *Papaya contains the enzyme papain that prevents gelatin from setting, so it's best not used for desserts that involve gelatin (unless the papaya has been cooked first as this destroys the enzyme).*
- *When adding papaya to a fruit salad, put in just before serving as it goes soft if added too far ahead and can also soften other fruits.*

■ Marinating and tenderizing meat (see page 31).

GOES WITH Chicken, grapes, blueberries, watermelon, lime, mango, and other tropical fruits.

GOOD FOR YOU Contains even more vitamin C than oranges; also a good source of vitamin A, folate, and fiber.

Passion fruit

A highly aromatic and flavorsome fruit. The wrinkled skin disguises what lies beneath—an intensely perfumed, juicy pulp surrounding lots of seeds.

CHOOSE
■ Available all year around.
■ The skin should be red or purple and not too wrinkly. Smooth skin means the fruit is unripe, so leave it at room temperature until the wrinkles appear.
■ Avoid fruit that are very light in weight, with dark, wrinkly skins, as they are dried out.

STORE Best kept at room temperature, not in the refrigerator.

PREPARE Cut in half and scoop out the seeds and pulp. If you want only the fragrant juice, sit a nylon strainer over a bowl, tip in the pulp and seeds, and press the juice through with a wooden spoon.

EAT Cut in half and scoop out the contents with a spoon—everything (apart from the skin) is edible.

USE FOR
■ Sprinkling over desserts such as pavlovas and ice cream, or into fruit salads for an exotic fragrance.
■ Mixing the strained juice or pulp and seeds with whipped cream to pile into meringues or use as a filling for cakes.
■ Stirring the strained juice into unwhipped cream for a quick sauce, or blending with other fruits for a refreshing drink.

GOES WITH Pineapple, raspberries, mango, lychee, banana, orange, kiwis, papaya, cream, venison, and some game birds.

GOOD FOR YOU A great source of beta carotene, iron, niacin, phosphorus and fiber.

Peach

see also NECTARINE *page 231*
Native to China, but now grown worldwide, peaches have mottled,

papaya–peach

rosy-pink skin and either yellow (more common) or white flesh.

CHOOSE
■ Best and cheapest during the summer.
■ Peaches should smell sweetly fragrant and feel firm but give slightly when pressed gently in your hand. Avoid hard or bruised fruit.
■ If you can, buy them tree-ripened. Underripe peaches will soften at room temperature but will not be so sweet.

STORE Once ripened, they will keep for 1–2 days at room temperature. FREEZE: As a purée or in sugar syrup (see page 201).

PREPARE Cut around the dimple of the peach with a sharp knife, then gently twist in opposite directions to separate into halves. Remove the pit. Slice or chop.
To skin: Try peeling it off with your fingers, but if the skin is too clingy, drop the whole peach into boiling water for about 15 seconds, or a little longer if it is large or less ripe. Remove and immediately put it briefly into cold water. Peel off the skin with your fingers. If it still doesn't work, resoak, and try again, or use a vegetable peeler.

EAT Eat whole as it is. You can eat the skin too—any fuzzy bloom will

PASSION FRUIT

TIPS AND TRICKS: PASSION FRUIT
There is only about 1 tablespoon of pulp in each passion fruit—so you may need to buy quite a lot of them if serving a crowd.

FRUIT A–Z

easily rub off under cold running water. Peel if the skin seems tough.

COOK

Poach: Pour a bottle of rosé or white wine (or half wine, half water) into a wide pan and add scant ¾ cup superfine sugar. Stir over medium heat until the sugar has dissolved. Lower the heat, add about 6 whole or halved pitted peaches (skins on), and flavor with a cinnamon stick, split vanilla bean, or bashed lemongrass stalk. Cover and poach for about 10 minutes for whole peaches, 4–5 minutes for halves, turning them occasionally if they aren't completely covered in the syrup. Lift them out with a slotted spoon and peel off the skins. Bring the syrup to a boil and bubble for 10 minutes or so until it is syrupy. Cool and pour over the peaches.

Roast: Place the halved, pitted fruit cut-side up in an ovenproof dish and pour in 5–6 tablespoons sweet white or rosé wine. Drizzle with honey or a sprinkling of confectioners' sugar and roast for 15–20 minutes or until tender at 350°F (325°F in fan ovens). Serve hot or chilled.

USE FOR

■ Same as nectarines (page 231).
■ Piling wedges into tall glasses with layers of whipped cream or ice cream, raspberries or strawberries, and bought raspberry coulis.
■ Serving simply in slim wedges with plain yogurt drizzled with honey.
■ Making a salad with arugula, crumbled goat cheese and a balsamic dressing.

GOES WITH Cured ham, chicken, goat cheese, raspberries, almonds, ginger, cream, ice cream.

GOOD FOR YOU Contains beta carotene and vitamin C.

USE INSTEAD Nectarine.

Pear

There are thousands of varieties of pears. They grow well in cooler climates, as well as in hotter ones such as those of Chile, Spain, and South Africa. The basic pear shape varies from long and thin to round and bulbous, and colors range from speckly brown through to bright green, yellow, and blushing red.

CHOOSE

■ At their juiciest in the late summer and early fall.
■ As they easily bruise when ripe, buy pears when they are slightly underripe, firm but not hard, then

peach–pear

finish ripening them at home.

■ Don't poke and prod to check if they are ripe. Pears ripen from the inside out, and when ready should give slightly at the base. Avoid those that are too soft and squashy at the base. Some of the varieties available are:

Anjou: Sweet, meltingly soft flesh, mild flavor. Grown a lot in America. Good for eating and cooking.

Bosc: Nice and juicy for eating, good texture for stewing.

Doyenné de Comice: From France, buxom, and remarkably juicy and rich, with a melting texture. Good for eating, especially with cheese; also good for cooking.

Concorde: A mix of Comice and Conference, juicy and sweet. Good for eating and cooking.

Conference: Slim and elegantly British, with a juicy, aromatic, sweet flavor and a firm, slightly gritty flesh. Good all-rounder.

Rocha: Firm, juicy, and very sweet. Good for eating and cooking.

Packham's: Native to Australia and a favorite there; yellow with smooth, musky-tasting flesh. Good for eating.

Bartlett (Williams Bon Chrétien): Very juicy and sweet, with tender flesh. Good for both cooking and eating.

Asian pear: Firm and crunchy (like an apple), very juicy, and fragrant. Better eaten raw, unpeeled, as it

FIX IT: PEACHES
If the only peaches you can get are hard, poach them to bring out their flavor (see opposite).

TIPS AND TRICKS: PEACHES
Toss cut peaches in lemon juice to stop them turning brown.

doesn't soften so much as other varieties when cooked.

STORE If they are bought underripe, keep them in a coolish place until they ripen. Use as soon as possible.
FREEZE: Slice and poach for a minute in sugar syrup first (see page 201). Comice freeze particularly well.

PREPARE

After peeling or cutting, brush with lemon juice to prevent browning.
Whole: Keep the stems on, then peel lengthwise (use a vegetable peeler for the smoothest look).
Halves: Halve lengthwise and scoop out the core with a teaspoon. Use for stuffing, roasting, or broiling.
In pieces: Cut into fourths lengthwise, cut out the core, then peel with a sharp knife. Slice or chop.

COOK Use underripe pears as they keep their shape better.
Roast: Melt 2 tablespoons butter with 2 tablespoons light brown sugar and 1 tablespoon cider vinegar in a skillet. Add 4 pears (halved and cored), coat well, and cook for a minute. Put them in a small roasting pan (or arranged around a roast) and spoon over the pan juices. Roast at 400°F (350°F in fan ovens) for 20–25 minutes.
■ Goes well with roast pork and game.

Broil: Lay wedges on a cookie sheet, brush with lemon juice, and sprinkle with superfine sugar. Cook under a hot broiler for 4–5 minutes, until golden.
■ Serve with cream or ice cream.
Pan-fry: Melt some butter in a skillet, toss in pear wedges, and cook until starting to soften. Sprinkle with a spoonful of sugar and cook, stirring, until golden, about 4–5 minutes.
■ Great with leafy salad greens and cheese.
Poach: Dissolve ½ cup superfine sugar in a small pan with 2½ cups red wine (or half wine, half water, or all water). Add 4–6 peeled pears (stalks on). Cover and gently poach for 15–25 minutes, or until tender, not soft. Remove with a slotted spoon. Thicken the syrup by bubbling for a few more minutes, then strain, and pour over the pears.
■ Good with ice cream.

USE FOR

■ Adding to salads (raw or broiled) with blue cheese such as Roquefort, toasted walnuts or pecans, crisp salad greens, and a dressing flavored with walnut oil—or more simply with arugula and shavings of Parmesan.
■ Chopping or slicing into cakes, teabreads, pies, and crumbles.
■ Cooking in chutneys—or using raw for a salsa mixed with apple, lemon or

lime juice and zest, a drizzle of honey, chopped thyme, and nuts, to go with roast pork.

GOES WITH Prosciutto, pork, cheese (especially blue), crisp salad greens, chocolate, vanilla, ginger, nuts, red wine, spices (see right).

GOOD FOR YOU Pears contain lots of fiber.

USE INSTEAD Apple.

Pineapple

This rather regal-looking fruit, with its crown of leaves, originated in South America. Pineapples are now grown a lot in Costa Rica and the Ivory Coast.

CHOOSE

■ Available all year around.
■ Buy when ripe. It should smell sweet and strongly of pineapple. If you pull on a leaf at the top it should come out easily. The base should be slightly soft.
■ The rind should look fresh, not dry or shriveled, the leaves green and perky.
■ Apart from the standard pineapple, others to try are Golden—ultra-sweet with a smooth flesh—and Queen. Very sweet and juicy, Queen is the perfect

TIPS AND TRICKS: PEARS

To stop pears from toppling over when poaching whole, cut a thin slice from the bottom so that they can stand upright.

LIVEN UP THE POACHING LIQUID

Make your poaching liquid more spicy, fragrant, or downright fruity by adding different flavorings:
■ *NICE AND SPICY: Cinnamon stick, star anise, cloves, slices of fresh ginger root.*
■ *FRAGRANTLY PERFUMED: Sprigs of lavender, rosemary, or mint, bruised lemongrass, slit vanilla bean. (Use with all water poaching syrup only, see left.)*
■ *REALLY FRUITY: Strips of lime, orange, mandarin, or lemon zest, pared off with a vegetable peeler.*

TIPS AND TRICKS: PINEAPPLE

Pineapple is best not used in conjunction with gelatin as it contains an enzyme that prevents the gelatin from setting—unless the pineapple has been cooked first, as heat destroys the enzyme (so canned is fine).

size for one or two people, plus the core is edible, so there is less preparation.

STORE At room temperature for up to 3–4 days, or in an airtight container in the refrigerator, cut into pieces. FREEZE: Sliced or cubed in sugar syrup (see page 201).

PREPARE

Slices: Slice the top off first with a sharp knife, taking the knife down until you reach the fleshy fruit. Don't throw this away if you want to use it as decoration. Cut a slice from the base of the pineapple, then peel (see opposite). Cut into rings and stamp out the cores with an apple corer, or slice the pineapple in fourths lengthwise and, holding each piece peeled side down, cut out the hard cores. Brush with lemon juice to prevent browning. Halves or fourths: Take the whole pineapple, leaves too, and cut through the center lengthwise in halves or fourths. Cut out the core, then the fruit, and use the shells as containers for serving fruit salad.

COOK

Pan-fry: Melt some butter in a skillet, toss in some pineapple slices, and cook for a few minutes until starting to soften. Sprinkle a couple of spoonfuls of sugar over and cook, stirring, until golden. Pour in a spoonful or two of rum and bubble for a few seconds. Broil: As for pears, page 240.

USE FOR

■ Threading chunks onto skewers with pork or chicken for kabobs.
■ Adding chunks to cakes and sponge puddings.
■ Sprinkling with sugar and Kirsch or rum for a speedy dessert.
■ Topping a pavlova along with kiwi and passion fruit.
■ Tenderizing meat in a marinade— pineapple has an enzyme that breaks down protein, but don't leave the meat in it too long or it will go too soft.
■ Tossing into stir-fries near the end of cooking.
■ Chopping for salsa. Mix with chopped roasted red bell pepper and parsley or cilantro, olive oil, and lime juice. Serve with pork, chicken or shrimp.

GOES WITH Cured ham, chicken, cheese, coconut (think piña colada), rum, Kirsch.

GOOD FOR YOU Contains lots of vitamin C—especially the Golden pineapple. The enzyme pineapple contains helps digestion, so it is the perfect end to a meal.

Plantain

see also BANANA *page 205*

A type of banana, but quite unlike it to eat. You wouldn't snack on one raw, as plantains need to be cooked. Although technically a fruit, many parts of the world (particularly Africa, the Caribbean, and Latin America) use it more as an accompanying vegetable, just like potatoes or rice.

CHOOSE

■ Available all year around.

■ Green unripe plantains for making plantain chips (somewhat similar to potato chips).

■ Ripe, soft, black plantains for roasting, frying, or grilling. The softness of the fruit tells you how ripe it is— the softer and blacker it is the better, rather like an overripe banana. But unlike a banana, even when the skin of a plantain is completely black, the flesh is still fine to use.

■ If you can't find it in your supermarket, look in Caribbean or Latin American markets.

■ Allow about one medium plantain per person.

STORE Keep at room temperature if bought unripe—then leave to ripen in a paper bag for several days (see Speedy Ripening, page 221). Once

PEELING PINEAPPLE

Peel pineapple by sitting it upright on its base and slicing off the peel, working from top to bottom. As you go, nick off as many of the little brown "eyes" as you can; any others can be dug out with the tip of the knife or the end of a vegetable peeler.

FRUIT A–Z

they are blackened and softened, you can keep plantains in the refrigerator for a few days.

PREPARE

When green: The skin is too hard to peel, so slice it off with a sharp knife. Cut the flesh into thin slices and make plantain chips (see opposite). **When soft and black:** The skin is much easier to peel—use a knife to remove any fibrous parts. Can be cooked whole, or sliced straight or diagonally (the thickness depends on how you are going to cook them).

EAT Must be cooked first.

COOK Only when soft and black. **Grill:** Keep their skins on and wrap in foil, then grill for 20–25 minutes, turning occasionally until softened. Slit the skin open and serve whole, or peel and cut into 1 inch chunks. Serve with a pat of butter and black pepper. **Roast:** Peel and cut into 1-inch chunks. Toss with a little olive oil then roast at 400°F (350°F in fan ovens) for about 40 minutes, turning every 15 minutes, until golden and tender. Serve sprinkled with salt and pepper. **Fry:** Peel and cut into ¼-inch slices. Heat 2–3 tablespoons olive or sunflower oil in a pan, add the plantains, and fry slowly in a single layer until

golden, turning once, for 4–5 minutes each side. Season with salt and pepper.

USE FOR
- An accompaniment to roast chicken, other roast or grilled meats or fish, or with rice and peas.
- Making plantain chips (see opposite).

GOES WITH Fish, chicken, Caribbean curries, lime, rice, butter, nuts, allspice, cinnamon.

GOOD FOR YOU A good source of beta carotene, folate, and vitamin C.

USE INSTEAD Sweet potato or green, unripe banana (sweeter, softer).

Plum

The juiciest of all fruits with pits. One of the most famous plums is the Victoria, sweet and good for cooking or eating. Plums are grown in Spain, Chile, South Africa, and France. Beach plums grow wild at Cape Cod.

CHOOSE
- All year around; best in late summer to early fall, when in season locally.
- As many of the varieties have different colors, ranging from yellow to dark purple, the color is not a good

plantain–plum

indication of ripeness. Look instead for the chalky-white "bloom" on the outside of the skin which indicates freshness.

■ Pick plump ones—they should give a little when squeezed. Avoid if soft in the dimple near the stem.

STORE Keep at room temperature for 3–4 days once ripe, or in the refrigerator in a perforated plastic bag for 4–5 days.
FREEZE: Stewed or sliced in sugar syrup (see page 201).

PREPARE Cut around the dimple of the plum with a knife, then twist apart, and remove the pit, using the tip of the knife if stubborn. Leave as halves, chop, or slice. They are easier to skin after cooking.

EAT Sweeter varieties, such as Black Amber, Angelino, Victoria.

COOK Most plums are good for use in cooking, especially Czar, Mirabelle, and Quetsch.
Stew: Melt 2 tablespoons butter with 2 tablespoons light brown sugar in a pan. Tip in 1 pound 2 ounces plums, the finely grated zest and juice of an orange, and simmer for about 10 minutes, until soft.
■ Serve with cream or ice cream.

PLANTAIN CHIPS
Serve these instead of potato chips with fish or chicken, or with a spicy dip as a snack.

Peel a couple of green plantains and slice very thinly (like potato chips), either with a sharp knife or a mandoline (see page 70). Heat enough sunflower or vegetable oil to reach about 1½ inches up the sides of a deep skillet. Drop a cube of bread in the oil— if it browns quickly, the oil is ready. Add the plantain slices in batches and fry until golden. Drain on paper towels, then sprinkle with salt and pepper, or a pinch of dried chili flakes.

Poach: As for pears (page 240), but in halves (skin on) for 10–15 minutes.
Roast: As for peaches (see page 238), with red wine.

USE FOR

- Adding to pies, tarts, and crumbles.
- Making a sauce for pork or duck.
- Chutneys, jams, and fruit compotes.
- Tossing (raw) in slices into savory salads with chicken and arugula, or with tropical fruits in sweet salads.

GOES WITH Pork, duck, game, nuts, orange, Chinese spices.

GOOD FOR YOU Contains iron, fiber, beta carotene, niacin, vitamin E.

Pomegranate

Originally from Iran, now grown mostly in the United States, India, Spain, Turkey and the Middle East, this fruit consists of a myriad of edible seeds within a sweet, juicy, ruby-red pulp.

CHOOSE

- Best in the fall and winter.
- Hard, deep-red-blushing (or yellowy) skins that are smooth and shiny.
- Fruit should be heavy and plump.

STORE In the refrigerator in a per-forated plastic bag for a week or two.
FREEZE: Not recommended.

PREPARE

Seeds and flesh: Cut the fruit in half widthwise, hold each half over a bowl, hit the skin hard with a rolling pin, and the seeds just drop out.
Juice: Tip the seeds and flesh into a strainer and press out the juice using the back of a spoon. Try not to crush the bitter membranes and pith.

EAT Best eaten as is. Cut in half or into fourths and eat the seeds and flesh straight from the shell with a teaspoon (or with a toothpick), avoiding the pith and membranes. You can just suck the flesh from the seeds, or crunch through the seeds too.

USE FOR

- Sprinkling over savory salads—refreshing with crab and fennel.
- Sprinkling over grapefruit and orange segments for breakfast.
- Serving the seeds over lemon sherbet, cheesecake, or ice cream.
- Adding the juice to marinades and salad dressings—good with chicken.
- Garnishing Middle Eastern dips, rice, and other savory dishes.

GOES WITH Duck, chicken, pork,

plum–rhubarb

white fish, lobster, other tropical fruits, salad greens.

GOOD FOR YOU High in vitamin C.

Pomelo
see GRAPEFRUIT, *page 218*

Raspberry
see BERRIES, *page 207*

Rhubarb

Although technically a vegetable, with long leaf stems and large, dark green leaves, rhubarb is treated as a fruit. It is especially popular in Britain but eaten elsewhere too.

CHOOSE
■ Between forced (indoor) and outdoor-grown crops. Forced rhubarb is available at the beginning of the year; the main crop is in season from spring to early summer. Forced rhubarb is delicate in flavor and appearance, being slim, pink, and sweet. Outdoor rhubarb has sturdier, green and red stalks.
■ Stalks should not be limp and bendy.

STORE For a week or two in the vegetable drawer of the refrigerator.

FIX IT: PLUMS
Plums have a lot of juice, which can be a problem when making a pie or crumble. To overcome this, toss them in 1–2 tablespoons of all-purpose flour with the sugar required in the recipe. As the juice comes out in cooking, the result is a syrupy sauce.

PLUMS FOR COOKING
■ *DAMSON: Small and oval with a purply-blue skin. It has a very sour taste, so needs to be cooked, not eaten raw. It makes really wonderful preserves.*
■ *GREENGAGE: A variety of green plum. Because of its color, it goes well mixed with purple or red plums in compotes, pies, tarts, preserves, and crumbles.*
■ *SLOE: Another member of the plum family, this fruit grows wild and looks similar to a blueberry. The fruits are pricked and soaked with gin and sugar to make traditional sloe gin.*

TIPS AND TRICKS: POMEGRANATE
Pomegranate juice stains, so watch you don't get splashed when preparing it.

FREEZE: As a purée. Or cut into lengths, blanch in boiling water for 1 minute, cool quickly in cold water, drain, then open freeze (see page 200).

PREPARE

Remove the leaves—they are poisonous. **Forced:** No need to peel. Wash, then trim both ends of the stalks, and cut them into thin or chunky slices. **Outdoor:** Scrape or peel off any tough skin with a small, sharp knife and prepare as above.

COOK Cook to soften and sweeten— outdoor rhubarb takes longer to cook. You can poach and stew rhubarb, but as it falls apart quickly, so it is best to roast it in the oven. Don't add liquid, as rhubarb gives off enough of its own. **Roast:** Heat the oven to 400°F (350°F in fan ovens). Rinse, trim into pieces about 1 inch long and arrange on a cookie tray. Sprinkle with scant ½ cup superfine sugar. Cover with foil and roast for 15 minutes, then remove the foil, and roast for 5 minutes more, until the rhubarb is soft but has kept its shape and the juices are syrupy. (Timings are for outdoor rhubarb). Reduce by a few minutes if you are using the forced variety.
■ Serve warm or cold with thick cream, ice cream, or custard.

USE FOR

■ Making crumbles, pies, tarts, and jam (alone or mixed with straw-berries).
■ Puréeing after roasting, and cooling to fold into bought custard and whipped cream for an instant fool.
■ Piling (after roasting) on top of a pavlova, or to make a base for trifle.
■ Making a sauce to serve with pork (on its own or mixed with apples).

GOES WITH Strawberries, rasp-berries, orange, ginger, nuts.

GOOD FOR YOU Contains calcium and a little vitamin C and iron.

Strawberry
see BERRIES, *page 207*

Watermelon
see MELON, *page 229*

DECORATIVE AND EXOTIC FRUITS

■ **Kumquat** This looks like a baby elongated orange. The whole fruit is edible, so they can be sprinkled over dishes, sliced or halved.

■ **Persimmon:** Also called Sharon fruit, this is grown in Israel and looks like a big orange tomato. Firm and smooth is best; look for fruit with a bright orange glow. An unusual bittersweet taste, astringent if eaten underripe. Eat as an apple, or slice and chop for mixing into a fruit salad, or slice onto cheesecakes or pavlovas.

■ **Physalis** Also called Cape gooseberry, this orange-colored fruit is enclosed in a flamboyant, inedible, papery husk. Peel back the husk so that it frames the fruit, and use as an edible decoration on desserts °or cakes. Tangy but fragrant.

■ **Prickly pear** One of the cactus family, this has a mild taste like watermelon. Trim off the top and bottom, cut in half lengthwise, peel, and slice its brilliant-red flesh to liven up fruit salads.

■ **Rambutan** Similar to a lychee, although its outer coating of soft, curly spines has a bit more flamboyance. Prepare and use rambutan as lychee. Delicious with scoops of vanilla ice cream.

■ **Star fruit** When sliced, this fruit creates pretty star shapes. The flavor is very mild and can sometimes be bitter. Choose those that are yellow, as green will be unripe and rather sharp tasting.

■ **Tamarillo** A very sleek-looking fruit, rather like an incredibly smooth oblong plum. Peel off the bitter skin, then slice it into thin wedges. It can be eaten raw, but tastes quite sharp, so is best poached or stewed. Try adding some to a curry.

VEGETABLES

USING A WIDE VARIETY OF VEGETABLES IN YOUR DIET CAN BRING A NEW DIMENSION TO YOUR COOKING. THEY ARE A TREMENDOUS SOURCE OF NUTRIENTS AND CAN BE SERVED IN MANY DIFFERENT WAYS—A HEALTHY NIBBLE, A DELICIOUS SIDE ORDER, OR AN IMPRESSIVE MAIN EVENT. AT THEIR PEAK, VEGETABLES NEED LITTLE TO LIVEN THEM UP, BUT YOU'LL FIND LOTS OF IDEAS HERE FOR WAYS TO SERVE THEM AND A WEALTH OF HINTS AND TIPS ON CHOOSING, STORING, PREPARING, AND COOKING.

TOP VEGETABLE TIPS

■ To insure maximum freshness, taste, and nutrient content, buy vegetables when in season and from local suppliers where possible, and use them as soon as possible.

■ Check vegetables regularly after storing for signs of deterioration. Once one starts to spoil, it can quickly infect others.

■ Wash vegetables just before preparing, not before storing.

■ Prepare vegetables just before cooking, as they can lose nutrients quickly once they have been cut.

■ Whenever possible, do not remove edible skins as they are an invaluable source of fiber, nutrients, and flavor.

■ Cut vegetables into even-sized pieces to insure even cooking.

■ It is hard to be exact when giving cooking times as there are many variables, such as the age of a vegetable, how it is cut, and personal preference. To avoid overcooking, start checking sooner rather than later, then keep checking until it is cooked to your preference.

■ Preserve as many nutrients as possible when cooking vegetables by cooking quickly with minimum water. Steaming and microwaving are two of the healthiest ways to maintain the nutrients, texture, and flavor of a vegetable, as the juices are not lost into the cooking liquid.

■ When cooking vegetables for salads, blanch them briefly, then plunge them into cold water to keep their color, freshness, and nutrients.

artichoke

VEG A–Z

Artichoke (globe)

A globe artichoke is the edible,
cultivated flower of a plant in the
thistle family. Serve young artichokes
whole and enjoy the tender ends of
each leaf with melted butter, hollandaise, or a dip, along with the heart,
or just serve the hearts in salads.

CHOOSE

■ Available all year around, but at
their best in late spring and early fall.
■ Those that are a perfect green
(or purple) and tightly closed.
■ There should still be some stalk
attached and the leaves should have
a slight bloom to them.
■ Allow 1 artichoke per person.

STORE In the refrigerator in a perforated plastic bag for up to 3–4 days.

PREPARE It helps to know what is
and isn't edible when preparing an artichoke. You can eat the tender bottom
of the leaves and the heart. You can't
eat the tough outer leaves, the furry
choke, or the inner leaves enclosing it.

It's up to you whether you remove
the choke before or after cooking.
If removing before cooking, break off

BABY VEGETABLES

*Baby vegetables are more tender
in texture and more delicate in
taste than mature vegetables.*

*There are many available, such
as artichoke, beet, broccoli, carrot,
cauliflower, corn, eggplant, leek,
and zucchini. They are a more
expensive way of buying vegetables,
but fun for certain occasions.
Because of their smaller size and
youth, they can often be eaten
whole, needing little preparation
and a shorter cooking time.*

QUICK SERVING IDEA

*For a quick way to liven up hot
or cold greens before serving,
simply toss in a couple of spoonfuls
of vinaigrette dressing.*

VEGETABLES A–Z

the stalk at the base along with any tough pieces attached or going into it. Trim off the top third of the artichoke with a sharp knife, about where it starts to taper in, then trim, and discard any tough outer leaves. (If the artichoke is young, trim higher up.) Spread the leaves out a little so you can get at the middle part. Pull the little cone of pale leaves out from the center to reveal the fuzzy choke. Scoop the choke out with a spoon, being careful not to disturb the best part underneath—the heart. As soon as you have prepared each artichoke, drop it into water with a little lemon juice to stop it browning.

If removing the choke after cooking, trim the raw artichoke, discard the tough outer leaves (see opposite), then cook the artichoke as below. Let it cool slightly, then spread the leaves out so you can get at the middle part. Pull out the central cone of pale leaves and scoop out the hairy choke with a spoon, taking care not to disturb the heart.

COOK

Boil: Place the artichokes in a large pan, half-fill with boiling water, add 3 tablespoons lemon juice, bring back to a boil, and simmer for about 25 minutes for medium artichokes or 30–40 minutes for larger ones. When they're ready, a leaf will come away easily from the bottom of the arti-

choke when pulled, and the heart will feel tender when prodded gently with a sharp knife or a skewer. Drain upside down in a colander or strainer. Steam: Follow the same timings as for boiling, adding a few extra minutes if necessary.

EAT After cooking, cool slightly and serve warm or cold. Pull off the outer leaves, one at a time, starting at the bottom. Dip the tender end in melted butter with finely grated lemon zest added, or in mayonnaise, sauce, or the dip of your choice, then pull it through your teeth to remove the tasty flesh. Discard the rest of the leaf. You then get to the best part—the heart, which can be cut into and eaten with the accompanying sauce or dressing.

WAYS TO SERVE

▪ Wrap slices of prosciutto around cooked hearts and drizzle with an herb dressing for an appetizer.
▪ Create a dipping sauce by thinning pesto with olive oil and mixing it with finely chopped tomatoes.

GOES WITH Hollandaise sauce, mayonnaise, tomatoes, butter, lemon, garlic, vinaigrette dressing, chives, thyme.

GOOD FOR YOU Contains vitamin C and folate.

artichoke

Artichoke
(Jerusalem)

First cultivated in North America, this knobby little vegetable (an underground tuber) belongs to the sunflower family and is not related in any way to the globe artichoke. It looks a little like ginger root, and has a nutty, distinctive flavor. It is delicious roasted, boiled, steamed, or pan-fried, cooked in a soup, or served raw, thinly sliced, in a salad.

CHOOSE

■ Available all year around, but at their best in mid-winter.
■ The fewer knobs they have, the better, as the more misshapen they are, the harder they are to peel.
■ They should be firm.
■ Allow 1½ pounds for 4 people.

STORE For about 1 week in a cool, dark place.

PREPARE Fill a bowl with cold water and add lemon juice. Scrub the artichokes under running water, then, if peeling, cut off any of the knobby bits that will make removing the skin difficult. Most of the nutrients are just beneath the skin, so leave it on when possible. Drop immediately into the lemon water to prevent browning.

TRIMMING A GLOBE ARTICHOKE

1 *Trim off the top third of the artichoke (or where it starts to taper in) with a sharp knife.*

2 *Then trim and discard any tough outer leaves*

JERUSALEM ARTICHOKE

VEGETABLES A–Z

COOK Timing depends on size, but Jerusalem artichokes can be cooked like potatoes. Add lemon juice to the cooking water to stop discoloration.

Boil or steam: Cut into chunks and put in a pan. Pour over enough boiling water to cover, bring back to a boil, cover, and cook for 12–15 minutes, or until tender. Drain. Alternatively, steam, allowing a few minutes longer.

Pan-fry: Cut into thickish slices. Heat about ¼ inch sunflower oil in a skillet. Add the slices and fry for 6–10 minutes, tossing occasionally until golden. Drain on paper towels and season to taste with salt and pepper.

Roast: Heat a few tablespoons of olive oil in a roasting pan in a 400°F oven (350°F in fan ovens) for 5 minutes. Add whole, unpeeled artichokes and toss in the oil. Tuck in a couple of bay leaves and roast for 30–40 minutes or until golden and tender.

WAYS TO SERVE

■ Boil or steam and toss with butter or olive oil, salt and pepper.

■ Make a gratin as you would with potatoes, dot with butter, and sprinkle with grated Parmesan cheese.

■ Use half and half with potato to make a silky-smooth mash.

GOES WITH Potato, cream, lemon, mustard, chives, parsley, tarragon.

GOOD FOR YOU Rich in carbohydrate and iron; a good source of vitamin C and potassium.

Asparagus

An elegant, versatile vegetable which can be served as an appetizer, main course, or accompaniment. However you serve it, keep it simple, so that the flavor is not masked.

CHOOSE

■ At its peak and with the best flavor when in season. It is widely grown in Chile, Peru, South Africa, France, and Spain but the United States— California in particular—is the world's largest producer.

■ Between the two main types—green, which is popular in the UK, America, and Italy, or the white asparagus, favored by the French, Germans, and Belgians (the stalks are cut below the ground—hence their lack of color).

■ Very thin, wild asparagus (called "sprue") is also available.

■ Stalks should look strong and firm, with bright and perky tips.

■ Allow 1 pound 2 ounces for 4.

STORE Wrap the stems in damp paper towels, put them in a perforated plastic bag, and store in the refrigerator for no more than 2–3 days.

artichoke–asparagus

PREPARE Small, young tips sold in packets require no preparation. For the bigger, tastier stalks, bend the spear until it snaps and discard the tough, woody ends. No peeling is required. Leave them whole, cut in half widthwise, or slice on the diagonal.

COOK

Boil: Lay the asparagus in a large skillet, pour over boiling water to cover, add some salt, and cook for about 3–5 minutes (depending on size) until the asparagus turns a bright green. If left too long, it will go soft and dull-looking. (Sprue takes about 1 minute.)

Charbroil: Toss in olive oil and cook on a preheated stove top grill pan for about 5 minutes, turning, until tender and marked with ridges from the pan.

Roast: Toss the asparagus in oil and roast at 400°F (350°F in fan ovens) for about 15 minutes.

Steam: Pile the spears into a steamer set over a large pan or skillet of simmering water, and steam for 4–5 minutes, or until they feel tender if you stick a sharp knife into the stem. (Sprue will take 1½–2 minutes.) Season to taste before serving.

Stir-fry: Trim and slice on the diagonal. Heat a little oil in a skillet. Add the asparagus and stir-fry for a few minutes over high heat until tender.

VEGETABLES A–Z

EAT Pick the spears up with your fingers and dip the tips in melted butter, or toss lightly in olive oil and lemon juice with salt and pepper.

WAYS TO SERVE

■ Serve simply with a good extra virgin olive oil, sea salt, and black pepper, or more traditionally with melted butter for dipping, hollandaise sauce, or a soft-boiled egg.

■ Coil strips of prosciutto around the asparagus, drizzle with a little olive oil, then roast as on page 255. Goes well with fish or chicken.

■ In a salad, toss with cooked new potatoes, fava beans, and peas, and drizzle with pesto thinned with olive oil and a squeeze of lemon juice.

GOES WITH Fish (especially salmon), bacon and cured ham, tomatoes, green beans, new potatoes, pesto, roasted bell peppers, Parmesan cheese, eggs.

GOOD FOR YOU

Contains folate and vitamins C, A, and B6.

Avocado

A tropical fruit, native to Central America, that is used as a vegetable. To enjoy at its best, eat it raw, not cooked.

CHOOSE

■ Available all year around.

■ The most popular varieties are Fuerte, with its sleek, smooth, green skin, and the almost black-green Hass with its thicker, more knobby skin. Avocados without pits are also available (see opposite).

■ A ripe avocado should give slightly when pressed gently with your thumb.

STORE At room temperature, not in the refrigerator. If an avocado is still hard when bought, let ripen in a paper bag for a couple of days.

PREPARE Once cut, the flesh goes brown quickly, so prepare an avocado just before it is needed. With a sharp knife, cut through the skin and flesh lengthwise, all the way around, until you meet the hard pit in the middle. Twist the two halves in opposite directions to separate. Either ease the pit out with a teaspoon, or use a knife, as opposite (top). Peel off the skin as opposite (center). Keep the avocado as halves, slice, or chop it into chunky pieces, or mash. Squeeze lemon or lime juice over to it prevent browning.

COOK Not recommended.

EAT One of the nicest ways to eat an avocado is to halve and pit it as

asparagus–bean

above, leaving the skin on, then serving with a drizzle of olive oil, a splash of balsamic vinegar, and a sprinkling of salt and pepper. Allow one half per person and eat with a teaspoon.

WAYS TO SERVE

■ Wrap wedges of avocado with prosciutto, sit them on a bed of arugula, and drizzle with a garlic and herb dressing.

■ To make a guacamole dip for serving with nachos or raw vegetables, mash 2 avocados with the juice of a lime, 1 or 2 finely chopped scallions, chopped cilantro, a pinch of crushed, dried chilies or tabasco, and salt.

GOES WITH Shrimp, bacon, salad greens, tomatoes, Parmesan cheese, grapefruit, lime, basil, balsamic vinegar, mayonnaise, sour cream.

GOOD FOR YOU Full of vitamin E and a source of iron, potassium, and niacin. Unlike other fruits, avocados contain fat, but it's the healthy, mono-unsaturated sort.

Bean sprout

The Chinese discovered the nutritional merits of bean sprouts, so you will find them in many Asian dishes, especially stir-fries. The most widely available

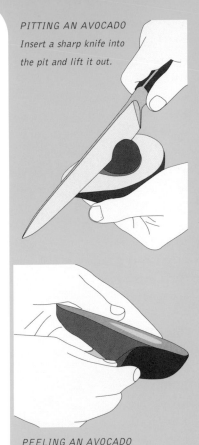

PITTING AN AVOCADO
Insert a sharp knife into
the pit and lift it out.

PEELING AN AVOCADO
Score lengthwise down the center
through the skin without cutting
into the flesh. Peel the skin away
from the flesh in two pieces.

PITLESS AVOCADO
Look for pitless "baby" avocados.
These can be eaten with a teaspoon
and even the thin skin is edible.

type is that of the mung bean.
To sprout your own, see opposite.

CHOOSE

■ Available all year around.

■ They should look fresh and crisp with white roots—avoid those where the sprouting tips are wilting and brown.

■ Buy only as much as your immediate needs as they quickly lose their crunch and fresh taste.

STORE Loosely wrapped in paper towels inside a perforated plastic bag in the vegetable drawer of the refrigerator, for no more than a day or two.

PREPARE Quickly rinse in cold water and pat dry with paper towels.

COOK Mung bean sprouts will easily withstand brief cooking.

Stir-fry: Only for 1–2 minutes; any longer and they will lose their crunch.

WAYS TO SERVE

■ Add raw to salads with Chinese flavors, or in spring rolls.

■ Sprinkle into a chicken or beef sandwich for a touch of crunch.

■ Toss into an omelet with a splash of soy sauce.

GOES WITH Chicken, beef, bell peppers, rice, ginger, chili, cilantro.

GOOD FOR YOU A good source of folate, iron, and some B vitamins.

Beans

The good thing about beans is that you can eat the whole thing—pods and all. Like peas, beans belong to the legume family. Most are long and slender and hang elegantly from thin stalks as they grow.

CHOOSE

■ The pods of all beans should be firm and crisp. Avoid fava beans when they feel flabby as they contain pockets of air instead of plump beans. The most widely available types are:

Fava: A plump bean that is available in summer, at its best early on. The pod containing the beans can be eaten only when very young and tender. Allow 1 pound 2 ounces in their pods for 2 people. Buy 3–4 pounds beans in their pods for every 1 pound 2 ounces of podded beans that you need.

Flat (helda): Similar to a string bean, but flatter and smoother.

Green: Also called *haricot vert*, this is a dwarf green bean variety that originally came from America. Available all year around. Allow about 9 ounces for 3 people.

String: A popular homegrown vegetable, native to Central America.

bean sprout–beans

Larger, flatter, and longer than a green bean. At their best in mid to late summer—the small, younger beans are the most tender and sweet; later in the season they can become a little tough and stringy. Allow about 1½ pounds for 4 people.

Yellow wax: A yellow variety of the green bean. Allow about 9 ounces for 3 people.

STORE Beans will keep in a perforated plastic bag in the refrigerator for up to 2–5 days. To check if they are still fresh, do the snap test. If a pod snaps in half easily when you bend it, it is still fresh.

PREPARE

Fava: Begin by podding the beans, as shown right. You can then skin them, which may seem fiddly, but it is worth it if you have the time, as the skins can sometimes be tough. Then cook the beans in boiling water (see page 260). Drain, tip them into cold water, then slit open the skin of each one with your fingernail, and pop out the shiny green bean inside.

Green and yellow wax: Slice off the stalk ends, as on page 261.

String: Trim, then remove any strings from both sides by pulling along the length of the bean with a small, sharp knife. Slice into long, slim, diagonal

GET SPROUTING

To grow your own bean sprouts using mung or garbanzo beans, or Puy lentil sprouts, follow these steps. The beans will expand, so 3 tablespoons dried beans will give you about 1 cup of sprouted beans.

- *Soak the beans in plenty of cold water overnight. Drain and rinse.*
- *Tip them into a large jar and cover with lukewarm water. Lay a piece of fabric or cheesecloth over the top, secure with an elastic band, and drain off the water. Put the jar on a tray in a warm, dark place.*
- *Rinse with cold water and drain twice daily. The beans should start sprouting after 2–3 days and be ready to eat after 5–6. If you want a little green on the sprouts, expose them to the light for the last day.*

PODDING FAVA BEANS
Press the pod all the way along one of its seams, then open it out with your fingers. Push your thumb along the furry inside to release the beans.

lengths, to show off the pretty mottled pink seeds inside.

COOK Beans are best cooked quickly and briefly so they keep their bright color. Test with a skewer or sharp knife—either should go in easily.

Boil: Put the beans in a pan, just cover with boiling water, and return to a boil. Cook fava in their skins for 3–5 minutes (depending on their size), yellow for 4–5 minutes, green for 4–6 minutes, string for 3–5 minutes. Drain and season (see Tips and Tricks, opposite). When using in a salad, blanch first by cooking for about 2–3 minutes, then tip into a colander or strainer, and hold under cold running water so they cool quickly and keep their crispness and color. Drain well.

Steam: For 4–10 minutes, depending on the bean.

WAYS TO SERVE

- Toss boiled or steamed green or string beans in butter or olive oil, salt, and pepper.
- Top boiled or steamed green or string beans with an herb butter (see Herbs and Spices, page 133).
- Toss boiled or steamed green or string beans while hot with olive oil and lemon juice, coarsely chopped parsley, and chopped scallions.

- When fava beans are very young and tender, serve them between courses Italian-style, raw in their pods with a wedge of tasty romano cheese and chunk of bread.
- Briefly fry 3–4 chopped anchovies and some chopped garlic in olive oil, then toss with cooked, skinned fava beans.

GOES WITH Prosciutto, pancetta, and bacon, chicken, tomatoes, legumes, herbs, anchovies.

GOOD FOR YOU Packed with protein, all beans are also blessed with fiber, potassium, calcium, niacin, beta carotene, and some iron—so they are good in a vegetarian diet.

Beet

A root vegetable loved for its earthy flavor, silky-smooth texture, and vibrant red-purple color. (Golden-colored varieties are also available.) Beet is closely related to spinach and chard. Beet greens can be eaten when they are cooked.

CHOOSE

- Available all year around.
- When raw, the roots should be firm and evenly shaped, and the greens fresh and not wilting.
- Also available ready-cooked.

beans–beet

STORE

Raw: In a cool, dark place for about 3–4 days.

Cooked: They will keep in the refrigerator for about 5–7 days. Precooked, vacuum-packed beet from the supermarket will last much longer—check the "best before" date. Also check they're "natural," not pickled.

PREPARE
For raw beet, twist or trim off the stalks, leaving about 1 inch. Leave the whiskery parts at the bottom. If you trim too close to the flesh, the beet will "bleed" into the cooking water and lose its bright color. Wash but don't peel (if you peel the beet before cooking, it will bleed).

COOK

Boil: Place in a large pan, cover with boiling water, then bring back to a boil, and cook for 1–1¼ hours, or until tender. If undercooked they can taste bitter. To tell if they're done, don't pierce them with a knife but lift them out with a slotted spoon and gently rub the skin—it should start to come away. Drain and plunge the beets into cold water, then the skin will be easy to peel off. The peeled beet can be sliced, chopped, or grated.

Roast: Gently pat dry after washing, then lay them whole in a roasting pan with ⅔ cup water. Cover with foil and

TRIMMING BEANS
The quickest way is to line the beans up on a cutting board, with the stalk ends all pointing the same way, then slice down the line in one movement.

TIPS AND TRICKS: BEANS
Adding salt to beans while they cook toughens the skins, so it's best added later.

MORE UNUSUAL BEANS
Yard-long beans (or Chinese or snake beans): These originated in Asia and can be used in the same way as green beans.
Borlotti beans: One of the prettiest beans, with creamy-colored pods splashed with pink. These need to be podded like fava beans. Popular in Italy for soups and stews, or served simply with olive oil and garlic.

FIX IT: BEET
Beet bleeds, so staining other foods is almost inevitable. To reduce the amount of staining in salads, add beet at the last minute when everything else has been tossed together.

roast at 400°F (350°F in fan ovens) for 45 minutes–1 hour. Peel before serving.

WAYS TO SERVE

■ Cut roasted beet into fourths and serve tossed with olive or a nut oil and snipped chives.

■ Toss arugula leaves and crumbled feta cheese in a honey-mustard dressing. Arrange wedges of cooked beet on top, sprinkle with toasted walnuts, and drizzle with a little more dressing.

■ Arrange cooked beet wedges or slices with batons of cooked carrot. Drizzle with some olive oil, lemon juice, chopped garlic, chopped cilantro, and toasted cumin seeds.

GOES WITH Smoked fish, horseradish, feta/goat cheese, carrots, nuts, oranges, cream/sour cream, mint.

GOOD FOR YOU A fantastic source of folate, beet also contains fiber, potassium, and phosphorus.

Belgian endive

The tightly packed, crunchy leaves form the shape of a small torpedo. They can be eaten raw or cooked.

CHOOSE

■ All year around, although they're at their best in winter.

■ Between the white with yellow tips (also called Witloof chicory) or red-leaved (see radicchio, opposite).

■ If choosing white Belgian endive, make sure the tips are yellow—if green they can taste too bitter.

■ Allow 1 head per person.

STORE In a perforated plastic bag in the refrigerator for up to 4–5 days.

PREPARE Just trim the ends if necessary and discard any limp outer leaves. The inside leaves can then be separated for a salad, or the whole head can be cut lengthwise into halves or fourths. If you cut the Belgian endive, brush the cut sides with lemon juice to stop them going brown.

COOK

Pan-fry: Cut into fourths. Heat some olive oil in a skillet and fry a little chopped garlic or shallot. Lay the Belgian endive in the pan, cut-side down, and fry for 3 minutes. Turn and fry for 2–3 minutes more, until tender and golden. Season with salt, pepper, and a splash of balsamic vinegar.

Roast: Lay halves in an oiled ovenproof dish or a roasting pan. Sprinkle with a few bay leaves and garlic cloves, drizzle with olive oil, cover with foil and roast at 400°F (350°F in fan ovens) for 30 minutes. Remove the foil and roast for 15–25 minutes more until golden and tender.

WAYS TO SERVE

■ Toss raw leaves with crisp slices of apple and pear, a few salad greens, and toasted pecans or hazelnuts with a lemon and nut oil dressing.

■ Serve pan-fried Belgian endive sprinkled with grated or crumbled cheese and fresh thyme leaves.

■ Use the raw leaves as containers for canapés. Fill with salad such as ham and cheese or chicken Caesar.

GOES WITH Chicken, bacon, cheese (especially blue cheeses, Swiss, and crumbly cheeses), nuts, apples, pears, mustard.

GOOD FOR YOU Belgian endive can contribute to potassium intake.

USE INSTEAD Radicchio (see right).

Bell pepper

Related to chili peppers, bell peppers have a much milder and sweeter taste. Most bell peppers start off green (although some are purple), then, as they ripen, the color changes to red, orange, or yellow, depending on the particular variety.

BELGIAN ENDIVE

RADICCHIO

The most common type of radicchio is Rossa di Chioggia. With its white leaves streaked with deep pink, this radicchio is similar in shape to a small cabbage. Its color adds drama to salads and mixing it with other leaves will tone down its strong, bitter and peppery flavor. Use in Italian-style salads with other strong flavors such as anchovies, capers, and red wine dressings. As it is quite sturdy, it can be cut into wedges and griddled. It is also delicious shredded and used with cream and garlic as a pasta sauce. Just wilt in the cream with some chopped garlic, then toss with cooked pasta. Other types of Italian radicchio include Radicchio Rossa di Treviso, which is grown in a similar way to Belgian endive.

CHOOSE

- All year around, but especially good in the summer and fall.
- Those that are shiny and firm, not wrinkled or soft.
- Between different colors, red, green, orange, and yellow being the most common. Red, yellow, and orange bell peppers tend to be sweeter than green, which have a less developed flavor but are good for long, slow cooking. Red, yellow, and orange are better for eating raw or cooking quickly in stir-fries.

STORE In a perforated plastic bag in the refrigerator for 3–4 days. Roasted and skinned, seeded, and covered with olive oil, they keep in the refrigerator for up to a week.

PREPARE First you need to remove the core, pith, and seeds.

For halving: Slice off the stalk end, then cut in half lengthwise. Scoop out the seeds and white pith (see illustration, opposite). Usually done for stuffing or roasting.

For chopping or slicing: The easiest way is to sit the bell pepper upright on a board. Then, holding it by its stem end, slice the four sides away down its length, so you are left with the core and seeds in the center. Cut each piece of bell pepper length-wise into thin, even strips for slices, and cut across the slices for small cubes. Start with bigger slices for bigger chunks.

- **To skin:** see opposite.

COOK

Roast: Halve, core, and remove the seeds, then drizzle with olive oil and put in the oven at 350°F (325°F in fan ovens), for 35–40 minutes. For more flavor, drop some sliced garlic and sprigs of thyme or oregano into the halves, then drizzle with oil and roast.

Stir-fry: Cut into even, thin strips, heat a little oil in a skillet or wok, then add the bell peppers, and cook over a high heat, tossing often, for 3–4 minutes until slightly blackened around the edges.

WAYS TO SERVE

- Stir-fry bell pepper strips until softened. Add a splash of balsamic vinegar, some torn basil, chopped flat leaf parsley, and finely chopped garlic. Serve with fish or roast chicken.
- Skin the bell peppers, then tear into bite-size pieces, lay them on a plate, and sprinkle with slices of anchovy, torn oregano or basil, sliced raw garlic, toasted pine nuts, and a drizzle of olive oil. Serve at room temperature with French bread or ciabatta.

GOES WITH Chicken and fish (especially anchovies), olives, capers, cheese, rice, pasta, tomatoes, basil, cilantro, garlic, balsamic vinegar, olive oil.

GOOD FOR YOU Contain lots of vitamin C and beta carotene. Raw, red bell peppers have about 10 times more beta carotene than raw or cooked green bell peppers.

More in the pepper family

Peppadew: This is a sweet and mildly spicy pepper from South Africa, available preserved and tightly packed whole in jars. Adds a spicy kick to salads, pizza toppings, stir-fries.

Romano: Perfect for roasting or stuffing, this long, narrow, red pepper is both sweet and tender. Prepare and use them as regular bell peppers.

Bok choy
(also called pak choi)

A member of the cabbage family, this Chinese vegetable has bright white, chunky stems and dark green leaves, both of which are delicious to eat.

CHOOSE

- Available all year around.
- The smallest are the most tender.
- Avoid any with yellowing leaves.

HALVING AND SEEDING A BELL PEPPER

Cut in half lengthwise, then scrape out the seeds and pith with a sharp knife.

HOW TO SKIN A BELL PEPPER

Removing the skin gives smooth bell peppers, that are softer and sweeter with a slightly smoky flavor and that are more digestible.

Lay whole bell peppers on a foil-lined broiler pan. Put under a hot broiler and turn once the skin starts to blacken. Keep turning until blackened all over—about 20 minutes. Place in a bowl and cover with plastic wrap, or in a plastic bag and seal. The steam helps loosen the skin. When cool, peel off the skin with your fingers. Remove any stubborn pieces with a sharp knife. QUICK FIX: If you only need to skin one or two bell peppers, spear one onto a long handled fork. Hold it over a gas flame, turning until the skin is blackened all over.

VEGETABLES A–Z

STORE In a perforated plastic bag in the refrigerator for up to 4 days.

PREPARE Both leaves and stems are used, each having a slightly different texture and flavor. Wash, then steam them whole, or cut in halves or fourths lengthwise, or separate the leaves and stems and slice across finely or chunkily.

COOK They are best cooked briefly to preserve taste and texture, either by stir-frying or steaming.

Stir-fry: Heat 1 tablespoon peanut or vegetable oil in a wok. With the heat on high, add the stems and toss in the pan for 1–2 minutes, then add the leaves. If you want to cook leaves and stems together, slice the leaves into wide strips and the stems more finely.

Steam: Lay whole or halved bok choy in the steamer and cook for about 4–8 minutes, or until the stems feel tender-crisp when pierced with a sharp knife. Or coarsely slice the leaves and thinly slice the stalks so that both cook at the same time, and steam for about 2–3 minutes.

WAYS TO SERVE

■ Serve drizzled with hoisin, oyster, or soy sauce or sesame oil.

■ Use the leaves to line a steamer when cooking fish. They offer protection and flavor.

■ When stir-frying, add chopped garlic and fresh ginger root and finish with a splash of sesame oil.

GOES WITH Fish, chicken, hoisin/ oyster/soy sauce, Chinese five spice.

GOOD FOR YOU Bok choy contains vitamins C and K, and beta carotene.

USE INSTEAD Spinach or cabbage.

Broccoli

A member of the cabbage family. A popular variety is calabrese, from the Calabria region of Italy. This has tightly packed, dark green flowerets shaped a little like cauliflower. Sprouting broccoli (see page 269) has purple-green flowerets on longer, more slender stalks.

CHOOSE

■ Available all year around.

■ Heads should be firm and bright green (avoid any that are turning yellow), with firm stalks, not at all limp.

■ Allow about 4 ounces per person.

STORE In the vegetable drawer of the refrigerator for up to 3 days.

PREPARE If the broccoli is bought already trimmed, just freshen up the ends of the stalks by taking off a slim

bok choy–**b**roccoli

slice. For non-trimmed pieces, neaten up stalks by trimming any tough outer parts with a vegetable peeler or sharp knife. Any tough leaves attached to the stalk should be discarded, but the tender ones can be used. Divide the broccoli and cut it into small flowerets with a little stem attached. The rest of the thicker part of the stem can be sliced diagonally (peel it first if the outside is dirty, discolored, or tough). Wash. If using in stir-fries or tossing with pasta, cut the flowerets and stems into ½-inch pieces.

BOK CHOY

COOK Don't overcook broccoli— cook until tender, but not soft. Test by pushing a sharp knife into the stem— the knife should go in easily, but the stem should still feel firm.

Blanch: If you are using broccoli for a salad, follow the instructions for boiling. Otherwise, cook sliced broccoli for 2–3 minutes, whole flowerets (depending on size) for 4–6 minutes, until tender-crisp. Drain in a colander or strainer and hold under cold running water to stop cooking. Drain well.

Boil: Divide into individual flowerets with a little stalk attached, then cut lengthwise in half or leave whole. Put the broccoli in a pan, just cover with boiling water, bring back to a boil, then cover, and cook for 4–6 minutes for small flowerets, 3–4 minutes for very small pieces. Drain well and season with salt and pepper to serve.

Steam: Small flowerets for about 4–6 minutes, smaller cut pieces steam for 3–4 minutes, until tender.

Stir-fry: Heat 2–3 tablespoons sunflower or peanut oil in a skillet until very hot. Add the broccoli (cut into ½-inch pieces) and stir-fry with the heat on high for a few minutes until the broccoli is turning golden and tender. Add a chopped clove of garlic and cook for about 30 seconds. Remove from the heat. For extra flavor, splash in some soy sauce and sprinkle with toasted, sliced almonds, cashew nuts, or sesame seeds.

WAYS TO SERVE

■ After cooking, drizzle with a little olive oil or melted butter, or add any or all of the following: a squeeze of lemon, a sprinkling of grated Swiss or Parmesan cheese, and a sprinkling of toasted almonds or pine nuts.

■ For a broccoli and pasta supper for 2, chop 8 ounces broccoli into ¾-inch pieces. Put 7 ounces pasta on to boil and drop the broccoli into the pan 4–5 minutes before the end of the pasta's cooking time. Meanwhile, fry some finely chopped garlic in olive oil with a seeded, finely chopped red chili. Add some lemon juice and grated zest and toss with the drained pasta and broccoli, plus a 7-ounce can tuna, drained and flaked, and seasoning.

GOES WITH Tuna and other fish, chicken, cheese, eggs, bell peppers, mushrooms, tomatoes, lemon, almonds and other nuts, garlic, ginger, soy sauce.

GOOD FOR YOU Broccoli is wonderfully nutritious—a good source of vitamin C (a 4-ounce portion gives you your daily requirement), plus folate and other B vitamins, vitamin K, calcium, iron, and beta carotene. Also packed with antioxidants called flavonoids. A true superfood.

Brussels sprout

Belonging to the cabbage family, Brussels sprouts look like miniature cabbages and grow clinging in rows to long, thick stems.

CHOOSE

■ Best in winter (after frost), but they are also available in the fall and spring.

■ Look for a bright green color, avoiding any that are going yellow around the bottom.

■ Choose plump, crisp sprouts with tightly packed leaves. They are sometimes sold on the stalk, which keeps them fresh for longer.

broccoli–brussels

■ For sweetness, go for small sprouts.

■ Allow about 4–6 ounces per person.

STORE Keep in a cool place or in the refrigerator for up to 3 days.

PREPARE If they are still on the stalk, twist them off. Trim off any outer leaves that look old or are coming off of their own accord, then wash, and trim off the bases. Cutting a cross in the base of sprouts will help them cook evenly—but there's really no need, especially when they're small, and it can make the insides go soggy.

COOK Timing is crucial, as under- or overcooking spoils their taste. They can overcook very quickly, so test often by piercing with the tip of a sharp knife or skewer. The tip should go in easily but the sprout will feel slightly crunchy and still have its bright green color.

Boil: The classic cooking method for sprouts is to drop them (whole or halved) into a pan with a little salt, pour in enough boiling water to cover, bring back to a boil, cover the pan, and cook for 5–9 minutes, depending on size, or until just tender. Drain well.

Steam: For 5–10 minutes (depending on size) over simmering water. Season.

Stir-fry: Either halve or thinly slice, then heat a little olive oil in a skillet or wok with a little chopped garlic and

SPROUTING BROCCOLI

Also called purple sprouting broccoli, this has slimmer stalks and heads tinged with dark purple. It is sweeter and more tender than ordinary broccoli.

TO PREPARE, leave the broccoli whole and just trim the stalk ends to freshen it up.

TO COOK, steam or boil whole pieces (stalks and heads) for about 5–8 minutes or until tender. If stir-frying, parboil first for 2 minutes, then stir-fry for 4–5 minutes. For extra flavor, add chopped garlic and chili to the oil in the pan.

shallot. Add the sprouts and cook for 8–12 minutes. Top with a pat of butter and season to serve. If cooking a lot, add a splash of water or stock.

WAYS TO SERVE

■ Top cooked sprouts with butter and black pepper, or a sprinkling of grated nutmeg. As an optional extra, toss with crispy fried bacon pieces or lardons and toasted pine or pecan nuts, or almonds (or with cooked chestnuts).

■ Try them Italian style as a pre-meal snack. Boil whole until tender-crisp, then cool quickly in a strainer under cold running water, drain, and serve seasoned and tossed with olive oil.

■ Add frozen peas to the pan a couple of minutes before the end of cooking, then drain, and toss them with butter mixed with grated orange zest.

GOES WITH Poultry (especially turkey), game, bacon, chestnuts and other nuts, water chestnuts, oranges.

GOOD FOR YOU Has lots of vitamin C and fiber, plus beta carotene, vitamins E and K, folate, and potassium.

Cabbage

The many varieties of cabbage range from the basic round red, white, or green cabbage with tightly packed leaves, to the more sophisticated loose-leaved Italian *cavolo nero* and the slender Chinese cabbage.

CHOOSE

■ Different varieties are available at different times of year.

■ The leaves of all varieties should look crisp and bright. The core should not be split or dry. Red, green, and white cabbages with tightly packed leaves should feel heavy.

■ Avoid cabbages that have holes in the leaves—a sign of intruders. Or those whose outer leaves have been removed—a sign of not being fresh.

■ Choose between loose-leaved (usually pointed in shape) or tightly packed (round).

■ 1 small to medium cabbage is plenty for 4 people.

TIGHTLY PACKED

Green: Round with very firm hearts, these are a later variety than collard greens (see right), which has much looser leaves.

Savoy: Has bright, dark green crinkly leaves that are mild and tender when cooked. It makes a colorful accompaniment to roasts, stews, casseroles, and other wintry dishes. The leaves are also perfect for stuffing.

Red: Unique in the cabbage world for the wonderful color it gives a dish. Its crisp, tightly packed leaves are finely shredded raw for salads, or chopped roughly and braised with spices and fruity flavors.

White: Round with pale, greenish-white leaves on the outside that get progressively whiter toward the center. Crisp and crunchy, it is good shredded raw in salads, especially coleslaw, or boiled or steamed, then tossed in a little butter and freshly ground black pepper. It is famous for being pickled to make sauerkraut.

LOOSE-LEAVED

Cavolo nero: A dark green cabbage from Tuscany, with a pleasantly bitter taste. Sometimes referred to as kale and also known as Tuscan cabbage. Use shredded in soups or stir-fried. If you can't find it, use Savoy or kale.

Collard greens: Bright green leaves, the first of the season. Shred, steam, and toss with butter to accompany winter comfort food. Or toss into stir-fries.

Chinese cabbage: Also called Peking cabbage, it has elegantly long, pale green leaves with a crisp texture and milder cabbage flavor and less of a cabbage odor. It is popular shredded for stir-fries or for dropping into soups during the last few minutes of cooking as it takes on other stronger flavors well.

Kale: See page 288.

SHREDDING CABBAGE

FIX IT: RED CABBAGE

Red cabbage can lose its natural color once cut. To keep it red, pour 3–4 tablespoons hot red wine vinegar over the shredded cabbage (this is enough for half a medium-sized cabbage), mix, and leave for 5–10 minutes. Drain and serve raw with a dressing, or add to cooked dishes.

Pointed: As its name implies, this is recognizable by its pointed head. The green leaves are softer and sweeter than tight-packed green cabbage.

STORE In a cool place, or the vegetable drawer of the refrigerator. Tight-leaved cabbages, such as white and red, keep for up to a week or so, while looser-leaved ones keep for 2–3 days.

PREPARE

Tight-leaved: Take off and discard loose or damaged outer leaves. Wash the cabbage and slice it lengthwise into fourths, then cut out, and discard the hard core from each fourth. Chop fairly coarsely, or shred quite finely.
■ To shred by hand—lay one of the cut sides of each wedge on a board and cut across to make even-sized strips (see illustration, page 271).
■ To shred by machine—Use the shredding disk on your food processor. With the machine running, feed each cabbage fourth into the feed tube.
Loose-leaved: Take off and discard loose or damaged outer leaves. Separate the leaves from the tighter central part and cut out the tough central stalks with a sharp knife, then chop or slice the leaves. A quick way is to pile several leaves on top of each other, roll them up loosely, then shred

across with a sharp knife. Shred the tight central part too.

COOK Cabbage should be cooked very quickly with only a little water to keep its crunch and vibrancy. The only exception to this is red cabbage, which is cooked for a long time when it is braised with liquid and spices. The timings below vary depending on the type of cabbage and how you have cut it. To test when it is done, check that it is tender with a little crunch, and that the color is still bright.
Boil: Shred thickly and press into a large pan with a little salt. Add enough boiling water to almost cover it, bring back to a boil, cover the pan, and cook for 4–6 minutes, stirring half way through. Tip into a large strainer or colander and press out the excess water with the back of a spoon.
Steam: For 4–8 minutes until wilted, depending how it is cut.
Stir-fry: Softer-leaved cabbages, such as Chinese cabbage, are best. Shred finely, heat vegetable or peanut oil in a wok, add the cabbage, and stir-fry on a high heat for 2–4 minutes or until tender.

WAYS TO SERVE
■ Stir-fry Savoy cabbage or Chinese cabbage with chopped garlic and ginger, then splash in some soy sauce.

cabbage–carrot

■ Use different colors of tight-leaved cabbages. Mix finely shredded raw white, green, and red cabbage with a little oil and lemon juice, some toasted sesame seeds, raw peanuts (unskinned), golden raisins, and a splash of sesame oil, and serve as a colorful salad.

GOES WITH Bacon, tomatoes, apples, mustard, sesame, garlic, ginger.

GOOD FOR YOU Cabbage contains lots of fiber as well as vitamins C, B, and K, beta carotene, and folate.

Carrot

A versatile root vegetable that is as good roasted in the oven for lunch as it is grated into a cake for dessert.

CHOOSE
■ Available all year around, but in the spring look for tender young carrots in bunches, still with their feathery leaves. Later in the year carrots become bigger and tougher.
■ All carrots should be bright in color, and feel hard. If they have leaves, these should be fresh and perky.
■ Allow 1 pound carrots for 4 people.

STORE Will keep in a cool, dark place, or in a perforated plastic bag in the refrigerator, for a week or so.

PREPARE No peeling is needed for young carrots—just rinse, then trim off the stalks and the wispy bits from the narrower end. Older carrots should be trimmed and peeled with a vegetable peeler. Young, small carrots are usually cooked whole, but older ones can be cut in any of the following ways:

■ Across into thin rounds or thicker chunks, or sliced diagonally.

■ Down the length of the carrot in slim strips, then chopped across into dice or batons.

■ Into ribbons—with a vegetable peeler, shave off thin strips down the length of the carrot. Use in salads.

■ Grate for salads or baking (helps keep a cake mixture moist, such as carrot cake and rich fruit cake).

COOK To test when done, insert the tip of a sharp knife into the carrot. It should go in easily, but the carrot should still be firm in the middle.

Boil: For small, young carrots, put them whole into a pan with a little salt, add enough boiling water to just cover, bring back to a boil, and simmer until tender, about 5–7 minutes. Boil sliced carrots the same way, allowing 4–5 minutes. Drain.

Roast: Heat a few tablespoons of olive oil in a roasting pan in a 400°F oven (350°F in fan ovens) for 5 minutes. Add large chunks of carrot and toss in

the oil with some salt and pepper. Add a sprinkling of ground cumin and coriander. Roast for 30–35 minutes.

Steam: Small whole young carrots for 6–8 minutes, sliced for 5–6 minutes.

WAYS TO SERVE

■ Toss boiled or steamed carrots in a little butter or olive oil, salt, pepper, and chopped herbs such as chives, tarragon, or parsley.

■ Fry some chopped garlic, fresh ginger root, and mustard seeds in a little oil. Add some cooked young whole carrots and stir to coat.

■ Melt a pat of butter with a spoonful of maple syrup and a scoop of wholegrain mustard. Pour over boiled or steamed carrot slices.

■ Boil the carrots and drain, or steam them, then place them in a food processor with a pat of butter, black pepper, and a little ground coriander and whizz to a chunky purée, or mash them for a "carrot crush."

■ Tuck some grated raw carrot into a pita pocket filled with shredded lettuce and hummus.

GOES WITH Oranges, beet, mustard, cumin, parsley, cilantro, chives.

GOOD FOR YOU Carrots are very high in beta carotene and also contain vitamin C, calcium, and fiber.

carrot—cauliflower

Cauliflower

A member of the cabbage family, cauliflower is known for its creamy-white flowerets.

CHOOSE

■ Available all year around.

■ Those with pure white, densely packed heads and crisp, green leaves.

■ Do not buy those where the white part is starting to discolor, or if you can see that the discolored parts have been sliced off.

■ Look at the base. The whiter it is, the more recently it has been picked.

■ For an alternative, look out for small varieties with bright green heads (see Romanesco cauliflower, right).

■ 1 medium cauliflower serves 4.

STORE In a perforated plastic bag in the vegetable drawer of the refrigerator for several days.

PREPARE Slice across the base, to release some of the outer leaves. Trim away all the outer leaves, discarding any you don't want (if fresh and green they can be cooked too). Leave the head whole or cut off the individual flowerets from the main stem, and slice again if large. Aim to have similar-size pieces so that they will cook at the same speed. Wash before use.

TIPS AND TRICKS: CAULIFLOWER

Squeeze a little lemon juice over cauliflower flowerets to keep them snowy white.

PERK UP CAULIFLOWER CHEESE

■ *Add some snipped chives or a spoonful of grainy mustard to the sauce.*

■ *Cook the cauliflower with some frozen peas or broccoli flowerets.*

■ *Give it a crunchy top—sprinkle with buttery fried bread crumbs mixed with finely chopped anchovies or crispy pieces of bacon just before serving.*

■ *Lay slices of fresh tomato, roasted bell pepper, or sun-dried tomatoes over the top, sprinkle with grated Parmesan cheese, and broil until bubbly and golden.*

ROMANESCO CAULIFLOWER

This has a pointy shape and is bright lime green in color. Smaller in size than the white cauliflower, it is also milder and sweeter in taste. Use as for regular cauliflower, raw or cooked. If you are looking for something to liven up a vegetable platter with dips, flowerets of romanesco do the job well.

COOK The flowerets are cooked when you can push the tip of a sharp knife or skewer into the stalk. Take care not to overcook or they will disintegrate.

Boil: Put the flowerets in a pan with a little salt, cover with boiling water, and bring back to a boil. Simmer, covered, over medium heat for 5–10 minutes depending on the size of the flowerets. Drain well. If you are cooking whole, start testing after 10 minutes.

Steam: Flowerets keep their shape best when steamed. Put them into the steamer (with any leaves), with the heads facing up, for 5–10 minutes, depending on size.

WAYS TO SERVE

- Top with a pat of butter, black pepper, some grated cheese, and a pinch of grated nutmeg.
- Heat 2 tablespoons vegetable oil in a skillet. Add a chopped garlic clove and 1 teaspoon each mustard and cumin seeds and cook briefly until the seeds start to pop. Stir in ½ teaspoon ground turmeric, then tip in lightly boiled or steamed flowerets and stir for about a minute until well coated. Serve sprinkled with chopped parsley.

GOES WITH Cured ham, bacon, cheese (especially firm cheeses like Cheddar), potatoes, anchovies.

GOOD FOR YOU Contains vitamins C and B6, folate, and biotin.

Celery

A good backdrop vegetable when added to soups and stews, celery also has many merits in its own right, providing flavor as well as crunch. Bunches of celery range in color from white to green. The darker in color, the stronger the flavor.

CHOOSE

- All year around.
- The stalks should look fresh, firm, and evenly shaped with no bruising.
- Select stalks with lively-looking leaves.

STORE In its plastic bag in the vegetable drawer of the refrigerator for 2–3 weeks.

PREPARE Remove any large, stringy outer stalks as they are often tough. You can add them chopped with onion and carrots to give flavor to stocks, stews, or soups—peel off any tough strings with a vegetable peeler first. The slimmer inner stalks are tender, so are good for eating raw or stir-frying. Snap off the stalks as needed, and wash. Trim the ends, then leave the stalks whole or cut into slices. The leaves can be used in salads, or as a garnish for soups.

cauliflower–celery

COOK Celery is mostly eaten raw, traditionally accompanied by cheese, but it can also be cooked.

Braise: Fry whole stalks in a little butter for a few minutes, pour in enough water to cover, and simmer for 10–15 minutes or until tender. Sprinkle with chopped parsley and serve with roast meats or chicken.

Stir-fry: Heat 1 tablespoon oil in a wok or skillet. Tip in diagonally sliced celery and stir-fry for 4–6 minutes until tender-crisp. Season.

WAYS TO SERVE

■ Slice for a salad and toss with Belgian endive leaves and thin shavings of fennel and Parmesan cheese.

■ Add chopped celery to a stuffing for chicken or turkey, or use as a flavoring for stocks.

■ Lightly fry some celery stalks, then put into an ovenproof dish, cover with cheese sauce (see page 461) and a sprinkling of grated cheese, and bake at 375°F (340°F in fan ovens) for about 15–20 minutes until golden and bubbling.

■ Use the chopped leaves as an herb.

GOES WITH Cheese, beet, apples, mayonnaise, nuts, nut oils.

GOOD FOR YOU Celery contains potassium and some fiber.

FIX IT: CELERY
If celery has gone rather limp, bring it back to life by standing it in a tall jar of water in the refrigerator.

TIPS AND TRICKS: CELERY
When fresh, celery should snap in two easily.

Celery root

Beneath the uninspiring exterior of the celery root, lurk flavor, creamy texture, and great potential. A member of the parsley family, this large, ungainly, bulbous winter root vegetable has a hint of celery in its taste and can be turned into mash, grated raw into salads, roasted, or used to liven up the flavor of winter stews. It is traditionally cut into very thin sticks or grated for the French salad *rémoulade*.

CHOOSE

■ Available from early fall through to spring.

■ Celery root varies in size, and the outside skin can be rough and knobby. It should feel firm and heavy. The smoother it is, the easier it will be to prepare and the less you will waste.

■ If you have a choice, go for small–medium size: about 1½ pounds.

■ Allow about 2 pounds celery root (unpeeled weight) for 4 people.

STORE It will keep in a cool, dry place for up to a couple of weeks.

PREPARE Slice off the top and bottom, then trim off any really knobby parts. As the outside is quite tough, lay the celery root cut-side down on a board and peel quite thickly down its length to reveal the creamy flesh, going all the way around with a sharp knife. Cut out any blemishes, then cut into whatever shape you like—chunks, slices, small dice, fine strips—or grate for using raw. Celery root quickly discolors once peeled and cut, so unless you are using it straight away, drop the prepared pieces into water with a squeeze of lemon juice or a little white wine vinegar.

COOK

Boil: Put the prepared celery root into a pan with some salt, just cover with boiling water, and add a squeeze of lemon juice. Bring back to a boil and cook for about 10–15 minutes, depending on size.

Steam: For about 15 minutes.

Roast: Heat a few tablespoons of olive oil in a roasting pan in a 400ºF oven (350ºF in fan ovens) for about 5 minutes. Add chunks of peeled celery root (like roast potatoes) and toss in the oil. Season with salt and pepper and roast for 40–55 minutes, turning occasionally or until golden. They taste good but don't go crisp like potatoes.

WAYS TO SERVE

■ Boil and mix with equal amounts of potatoes for a different type of mash.

■ For spicy roast celery root, instead of tossing in oil as above, toss it in melted butter mixed with some curry powder and mustard seeds.

GOES WITH Salmon, roast meats (especially pork), mustard, mayonnaise.

GOOD FOR YOU Celery root contains minerals such as calcium and potassium, as well as some vitamin C.

USE INSTEAD Parsnip or potato, but flavor and texture are different.

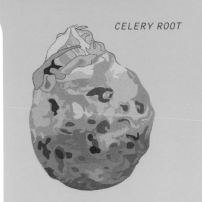

CELERY ROOT

Chard (also called Swiss chard, ruby chard)

This leafy vegetable is a stunning version of spinach. Its stems are either vivid ruby red or pure white, and the crinkly leaves are dark green.

CHARD

CHOOSE
■ Available most of the year, although best in summer and fall.
■ Go for crisp, fresh-colored leaves, with no brown marks on the stems.
■ Small leaves don't necessarily mean tenderness. Big ones can be as tender.
■ Allow about 2 pounds chard for 4 people.

STORE In a perforated plastic bag in the refrigerator for 3–4 days.

PREPARE The stalks (or ribs) and leaves are best cooked and served separately. The leaves can be steamed, boiled, or pan-fried, like spinach. The stalks are good chopped, then steamed or boiled, and added to a sauce or soup, or fried.

■ Chop the stalks from the bottom of the leaves (on older, bigger leaves you may also need to cut the stalks out of the leaves). Stalks can be left whole or chopped.

■ Give the leaves a quick rinse and drain well; leave them whole, tear into pieces, or shred thinly.

COOK

Boil: Pack the leaves into a large pan with a little salt. Add just enough boiling water to cover, bring back to a boil, and simmer for 1–2 minutes or until wilted. Drain thoroughly in a colander or strainer and press out any excess moisture with the back of a spoon.

Stir-fry: Heat a little oil in a large wok or pan. Add the chopped stems and stir-fry for 2 minutes. Add the shredded leaves and toss for another 2–3 minutes until wilted. Season and squeeze over a little lemon juice.

Steam: For 3–4 minutes or until just wilted. Press out the excess moisture with the back of a spoon. Serve with melted butter.

WAYS TO SERVE

■ Stir-fry the leaves with a little chopped garlic and crushed dried chilies, then sprinkle in some chopped tomatoes and parsley.

GOES WITH Tomatoes, lemon, cream, garlic, nutmeg, chili.

GOOD FOR YOU Chard is high in fiber, plus vitamin C.

USE INSTEAD Spinach.

Chili
see SPICES, *page 169*

Chinese cabbage
see CABBAGE, *page 271*

Collard greens
see CABBAGE, *page 271*

Corn

Also called corn-on-the-cob, this is actually a grain which is used as a vegetable. It is native to the Americas, where it is very popular. In Mexico the husks are used as a wrapping to make spicy *tamales*. A real summery vegetable. For canned corn see Pantry Staples, page 81.

CHOOSE
■ Through the summer into the early part of fall.
■ Corn preferably still in its husk.
■ The corn kernels should look plump, shiny, and pale golden yellow, and the outside leaves (husk) a healthy green. You'll know just how fresh the raw corn is when you cut into it, as the kernels should release a milky-looking liquid.
■ Allow 1 head (cob) of corn per person.

STORE In the refrigerator (best unhusked and wrapped in damp paper towels) for no more than a couple of days, less if possible as the natural sugars in corn quickly start to change into starch after picking, making the kernels less tender and far less sweet.

PREPARE Holding the cob at its base, pull the outer leaves down from the top to expose the kernels, leaving them still attached, or remove them, depending how you plan to cook it. Pull away any of the wispy threads (silks) clinging to the cob. Trim off the cob ends with a sharp knife, then give the whole thing a wash. You can serve corn whole or cut into chunks. If you want

CUTTING OFF THE KERNELS
Instead of eating corn whole, you can cut off the kernels and eat them as a side dish, or add them to dishes such as chowders, salads, and stews.

HOW TO DO IT: After removing the green husks and wispy silks as described left, stand the whole cob stalk-end down on a board. Cut down the stalk in smooth strokes to release the kernels, going all the way around. Keep the knife as close to the hard center as you can so that you keep the kernels whole.

to serve corn chunks, it's best to cook it whole first, then cut it up—corn is hard to cut through raw. To cut off the kernels, see page 281.

COOK It's best to cook corn as soon as possible (see above). To test if the kernels are done, they should be tender, but still have some bite.

Grill: There are three ways:

■ Husks off in foil: This gives the least barbecue taste but is the most convenient. Remove the husks and silks. Toss the cobs with a little oil or butter and wrap them in foil. Place on the grill rack for 8–15 minutes, turning occasionally, until tender.

■ Husks on without foil: Peel the husks back (don't remove) and pull out the silks. Cover the corn with the husks again. If you have time, soak the corn in cold water for an hour or two—this creates steam during cooking, making the corn juicier, and helps stop them from burning, but reduces the barbecue taste. Lay each cob straight onto the grill and cook for 8–15 minutes depending on size and heat, turning with tongs, until brown and tender.

■ No husks, no foil: This gives the most intense barbecue flavor. Remove the husks and silks as described, then put the cobs on the grill rack, turning frequently for even browning, for 5–7 minutes.

Serve with butter, salt and freshly ground black pepper.

Roast: prepare and time as for grilling, but cook in a 425°F oven (400°F in fan ovens).

Boil: Whole in boiling water for about 3–6 minutes, depending on the age of the corn. Never add salt to the cooking water as this will toughen the corn. Start testing after 3 minutes. (Kernels will take no more than a couple of minutes.) Drain well.

EAT If serving whole, pick up and hold both ends, and nibble your way along the cob. It's easier to hold if you use corn-on-the-cob "handles" or you can stick a small fork into each end; or cut the cob into pieces after cooking and hold it in your fingers.

WAYS TO SERVE

■ Serve Cajun-style, cooked whole (by boiling or grilling) and topped with butter mixed with crushed dried chilies and some fresh or dried thyme.

■ Make a salsa by mixing cooked corn kernels with chopped scallion, red bell pepper, some lime juice and grated zest, and a drizzle of olive oil. Great with fish and shellfish.

GOES WITH Chicken, fish and shellfish, cured ham, bell peppers, chilies, tomatoes, thyme, basil.

GOOD FOR YOU Corn is rich in fiber with small amounts of B vitamins and vitamin C.

USE INSTEAD Frozen or canned corn, when the fresh is not in season.

Cress
see page 293

Cucumber

Linked to the squash family, cucumber is a cooling vegetable, good at the height of summer when it is at its best.

CHOOSE
- Available all year around.
- Best if it is plump and firm with a bright color and no dents or bruises.
- Between the long, slender glasshouse cucumber and the shorter, thicker ridge cucumber which has more seeds.

STORE In the vegetable drawer of the refrigerator for up to 4–5 days if uncut; about 3 days if cut.

PREPARE Peeling isn't necessary with fine-skinned glasshouse cucumbers, and the color and texture of the peel contrasts well with the flesh. Smaller ridge cucumbers have quite tough, bumpy skins, which are better

SIMPLE GREEK SALAD
Mix chunks of cucumber with chunks of red bell pepper, tomato, and a little chopped red onion. Crumble over some feta cheese, sprinkle with oregano, then drizzle with olive oil, a squeeze of lemon juice, or a splash of wine vinegar, and season with plenty of freshly ground black pepper and a dash of salt.

TIPS AND TRICKS: CUCUMBER
To stop cucumber sandwiches from going soggy you can salt the cucumber like an eggplant. Just slice the cucumber, sprinkle with salt, and leave for 20–30 minutes. This draws out the moisture. Pat dry with paper towels, removing the salt as you do so, and you will have crisp, less watery slices.

removed with a vegetable peeler. Trim both ends, wash the cucumber, then slice, dice, or cut in chunks or sticks. For a ridged effect, score down the length of the cucumber with the prongs of a fork.

COOK Usually eaten raw.

WAYS TO SERVE
■ Cook slices of ridge cucumber briefly in melted butter, to warm them through. Season and serve with fish.
■ Grate coarsely and mix with yogurt, garlic, and a little chopped mint to make a refreshing Indian raita.
■ Chop and mix with chopped avocado and scallion, and toss with olive oil, lime or lemon juice to make a salsa for serving with salmon.

GOES WITH Fish (especially salmon), yogurt, dill, mint, fennel, chives, and garlic. Cools down curries.

GOOD FOR YOU Cucumber is about 96% water.

Eggplant

Like the tomato, the eggplant is really a fruit that is used as a vegetable. Native to Southeast Asia, it is used in many cuisines, including Indian, Thai, Mediterranean, and Middle Eastern.

CHOOSE
■ Available all year.
■ The slightly bulbous, pear-shaped eggplant is the most common. It should be shiny, deep purple, smooth, and plump. You can also find white eggplants, small, round, green pea eggplants the size of grapes and long, thin, purple ones (sometimes striped with white) the shape of a cucumber.
■ The stalk end, with its hood-like calyx, should be bright green and the vegetable should feel heavy.

STORE In a perforated plastic bag in the refrigerator for up to 3–4 days.

PREPARE To avoid discoloration, prepare just before cooking. No peeling is required: just trim off the green calyx and stalk at the narrower end, then cut into slices or chunks. Some traditional recipes advise salting eggplants to draw out any bitterness (see opposite), but modern varieties are less bitter, so there's no real need. If you are going to fry the eggplant, however, salting will reduce the amount of oil needed.

COOK Eggplants soak up oil like a sponge when they are fried, so it is best to broil or roast them.
Charbroil: For ridge marks, cook on a stove top grill pan. Brush the egg-

cucumber–eggplant

plant slices with oil, heat the pan until very hot, then lay the slices on the pan, cooking a few at a time in a single layer. As they start to brown, turn them over, and cook the other side.

Broil: Lay slices in a single layer on a foil-lined broiler pan, brush with oil, and sprinkle on herbs such as thyme or rosemary, then broil until starting to turn golden. Turn over and broil the other side (brush and sprinkle again).

Stir-fry: Heat a little oil in a non-stick wok or skillet, add some small, chopped eggplant pieces, and stir-fry, turning often, for 4–5 minutes until golden and tender, adding more oil if needed.

Roast: Place eggplant slices or chunks on a cookie sheet in a single layer. Drizzle and toss with olive oil, sprinkle with herbs as before, and roast at 400°F (350°F in fan ovens), for 20–25 minutes, or until tender.

WAYS TO SERVE

■ Sprinkle roast eggplant slices with grated Cheddar or Swiss cheese and broil until golden and bubbly.

■ Fry chunks in oil with garlic and ground cumin until golden. Add a can each of tomatoes and drained garbanzo beans, simmer for 10 minutes, add a handful of spinach leaves. and cook until the leaves wilt. Serve with rice.

■ For "chips," slice the eggplant thinly, then salt and pat dry (see right). Heat

TIPS AND TRICKS:
SALTING EGGPLANTS
Lay the prepared eggplant on a board or tray and sprinkle evenly with salt. Leave for about 30–45 minutes, by which time little beads of moisture will appear on the cut surfaces. Pat them off with paper towels.

about ½ inch oil in a skillet and fry in batches until golden. Drain on paper towels. Sprinkle with salt and serve with fish or chicken, or as a snack.

GOES WITH Garlic, onions, tomatoes, bell peppers, cheese, lentils, warm spices such as cumin, yogurt.

GOOD FOR YOU Fairly low in vitamins and minerals but has a good amount of fiber.

Endive
see BELGIAN ENDIVE,
page 262

Fennel

Although it looks like portly celery, fennel's wonderful aniseed flavor sets it apart. It's loved by Italians and used in many Italian recipes. Whether it's cooked in attractive wedges or thinly shaved and served as crisp raw slices, its taste is distinctive. The herb fennel (see page 140) is a close relation but not to be confused with the vegetable.

CHOOSE

■ Available all year around, but it's at its best in the summer months.
■ Smaller bulbs are more tender and should be white and feel heavy.
■ Any feathery fronds should look fresh, bright, and green, not yellow and floppy.
■ Allow 1 small or ½ large fennel per person.

STORE Will keep in a perforated plastic bag in the vegetable drawer of the refrigerator for up to 3–4 days.

PREPARE Remove any feathery green fronds at the top and, if they are fresh, keep for garnishing. Trim off the top shoots and the root of the fennel, then peel off any damaged or brown-looking outer layers. To cook and serve whole, cut out the tough inside core in a cone shape from the bottom end with a small, sharp knife. Slices can be cut across or down the bulb. Alternatively, cut the whole bulb into wedges by slicing in half lengthwise, then in fourths, then cut out the core from each wedge (take care not to remove all of it or the wedges will fall apart).

For a salad: Keep the slices really thin. A mandoline gives very thin shavings, although a very sharp knife can also be used. Hold the fennel by its root end to slice, so it doesn't fall apart. To keep the raw slices crisp and white, soak them in ice water with a little lemon juice.

eggplant–fennel

COOK This brings out the sweetness of fennel.

Boil: Place the whole fennel or wedges in a pan with a little salt. Add boiling water to cover, and a squeeze of lemon juice. Bring back to a boil, cover, and cook whole fennel for about 15–20 minutes, wedges for about 8–10 minutes. Drain well to get rid of any water trapped between the layers.

Pan-fry/griddle: Boil or steam wedges until tender, then heat a little oil in a skillet or on a stove top grill pan, add the fennel, and cook until golden, turning occasionally.

Roast: Toss wedges or thick slices in olive oil with sprigs of rosemary in a roasting pan and roast at 400°F (350°F in fan ovens) for about 40–50 minutes.

Steam: Whole fennel for about 20 minutes, wedges for 10–12 minutes.

WAYS TO SERVE

■ Lay steamed or boiled wedges on a buttered cookie sheet, dot with butter, sprinkle well with grated Parmesan cheese, and broil until golden.

■ Toss very thinly sliced raw fennel with olive oil, grated lemon zest and juice, salt, and pepper.

■ Simmer fennel slices in a simple tomato sauce (see page 121), covered, for about 15 minutes, or until tender. Good with chicken or fish.

TIPS AND TRICKS: FENNEL
When boiling fennel, increase its flavor by dropping a star anise into the water.

GOES WITH Chicken, white fish, salmon, smoked fish, tomatoes, Parmesan cheese, dill.

GOOD FOR YOU Fennel contains some beta carotene and B vitamins.

Garlic

see page 302

Kale

Hardy members of the cabbage family, both kale and curly kale are available. Curly kale is the most familiar, with its robust, frilly leaves and strong, distinctive flavor.

CHOOSE

■ When in season—it is at its sweetest and best in winter and early spring.

■ Look for crisp leaves with a bright color.

■ Curly kale—the leaves should be tightly curled.

■ Kale—this has smooth leaves, good for pan-frying when the leaves are young and tender.

■ Allow about 1½ pounds kale for 4 servings.

STORE In the refrigerator for up to ays—the longer it is kept, the more the leaves become.

PREPARE Cut the leaves from the stalks. Cut out and discard any tough-looking rib parts of the stalks from the leaves. Wash, then chop, or shred.

COOK

Boil: Don't cook kale in lots of water. Pour about ½ inch water into a large pan. Add some salt, bring to a boil, and add the washed, chopped or shredded leaves. Cover and cook over medium heat, shaking the pan occasionally, for 4–5 minutes, or until wilted and just cooked. Drain and press out any excess water with a spoon. Serve tossed in butter, and salt and pepper.

Pan fry: Heat 2–3 tablespoons olive oil in a large pan. Rinse 1 pound 2 ounces kale, shred it and add enough to make a thin layer in the pan, then let it wilt before adding more. Keep adding in this way, then cover, and cook for 5–10 minutes depending on the tenderness and size of the leaves.

WAYS TO SERVE

■ When pan-frying, add some chopped garlic to the last of the leaves, and serve sprinkled with chopped crispy bacon and a drizzle of extra-virgin olive oil.

GOES WITH Chicken, bacon, sausages, garlic.

GOOD FOR YOU Kale is full of vitamins C, B, E, and K and is a good source of fiber, beta carotene, folate, calcium, and iron.

Kohlrabi

Although it belongs to a branch of the cabbage family, kohlrabi has no resemblance to cabbage. Instead of having layers of leaves, it looks a little like a turnip and is sometimes called "cabbage turnip". It can be pale green or purple, stir-fries beautifully, and has a delicate, sweet flavor and a crisp and crunchy texture.

CHOOSE

■ All year around, although it's best from summer to early winter.
■ A small–medium size is best, about the size of a tennis ball, as some of the larger ones can be tough.
■ The bulb should feel firm and heavy, and the leaves should be crisp-looking.
■ Allow 1 small kohlrabi per person.

STORE In a perforated plastic bag in the refrigerator (leaf stems trimmed off) for up to 2 weeks.

PREPARE Trim off any leaf stems or leaves (these can be washed and used in salads and stir-fries if tender or cooked like cabbage). Trim off both

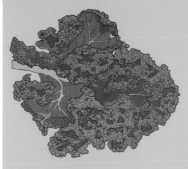

CURLY KALE

KOHLRABI

KOHLRABI CRUNCH
Young kohlrabi can be used raw as a dipping vegetable, or you can nibble on wedges of it like an apple. It also makes a great salad: Toss thin strips in a vinaigrette or mustardy dressing, or use it grated with finely shredded carrot and thin slices of apple.

ends, then peel it like an apple with a potato peeler or a small, sharp knife. Cut into chunks, wedges, or thin slices. Slice into thin strips if using in a stir-fry or in a salad. (Blanch briefly for a salad.)

COOK

Roast: Steam wedges for 5 minutes, then toss in a roasting pan with oil, salt, and pepper, and roast at 375°F (340°F in fan ovens) for 40–50 minutes, turning occasionally, until golden.

Steam: For 8–12 minutes, or until tender-crisp.

Stir-fry: Cut into strips. Heat some oil in a skillet, add the kohlrabi, and stir-fry for 2–3 minutes. Toss in some thin slices of fresh ginger root and garlic, and fry for 2–3 minutes more, or until tender-crisp. For extra flavor, finish off with a splash of soy sauce and sesame oil.

WAYS TO SERVE

■ Steam chunks or slices and toss with butter, lemon juice, and dill or parsley.
■ Roast chunks with other root vegetables, such as carrots and parsnips.
■ Add strips to stir-fries, or cook chunks or slices in soups and stews.

GOES WITH Chicken, fish, bacon, cheese, carrots, leeks, peas and

cream, and herbs like parsley, dill, chives, and chervil.

GOOD FOR YOU Kohlrabi is a good source of vitamin C and potassium.

USE INSTEAD Turnip.

Leek

Related to the garlic and onion family, leeks taste similar to mild onion, but are more subtle and slightly sweet.

CHOOSE

■ All year, but best from the end of summer through to the end of spring.
■ Scrubbed, trimmed, and ready to use for convenience, or loose and unwashed for more taste.
■ For tenderness and sweetness, choose small to medium leeks.
■ The lower white part should be firm, the top green part, crisp and bright.
■ About 1¼ pounds untrimmed leeks will serve 4 people.

STORE Wrap well in a plastic bag so that their smell doesn't overpower other foods. They will keep for up to a week in the vegetable drawer of the refrigerator.

PREPARE Pre-packed leeks are already trimmed, so just trim the ends.

kohlrabi–leek

For loose leeks, slice off most or all of the green part. Slice off the roots, then peel off any damaged outer leaves. Dirt can collect inside the furled leaves, so insert a knife where the white part meets the green part and slice lengthwise (going about half way into the leek), almost down to the root end. Open it out and rinse the layers of leaves under cold running water. Leave whole, slice into rounds (thick or thin), or lengthwise into strips.

COOK Leeks can turn mushy if over-cooked or cooked with too much water, so it's better to steam or pan-fry them. To test when done, prod with the tip of a sharp knife. The leek should feel tender but still be firm.
Steam: 4–8 minutes for sliced, 10–18 for whole, depending on size.
Pan-fry: Melt a large pat of butter in a skillet. Tip in sliced leeks and seasoning and simmer on a low heat for about 5–8 minutes, uncovered, stirring occasionally.

WAYS TO SERVE
■ Crumble goat cheese over steamed leeks, sprinkle with chopped fresh oregano or thyme, and serve drizzled with olive oil.
■ Blanch sliced leeks for a couple of minutes, drain well, then stir-fry with bacon lardons (see page 353).

■ Toss hot steamed leeks with a mustard or herb dressing and chopped sun-dried tomatoes for a warm salad.
■ Coat with cheese sauce (see page 461), top with grated cheese, and broil until golden.

GOES WITH Bacon, chicken, fish, potatoes and other root vegetables, tomatoes, eggs, cheese, mustard.

GOOD FOR YOU Leeks have plenty of fiber, plus some vitamin C and folate.

Lettuce

Lettuce may be crisp or floppy, different shades of green, or green with red highlights. Flavorsome dressings and sturdy ingredients bring out the best in crisp leaves, while floppy ones respond well to more delicate accompaniments.

CHOOSE

■ Available all year around.
■ Leaves should be perky-looking, not limp or with signs of discoloration. Crisp lettuce may have fading leaves on the outside which can be removed.
Bibb: Small in size, with tight, crisp leaves, it tastes slightly bitter and is less tender than other lettuces. Good shredded or cut in wedges and served with something sweet or fruity such as apple slices, or a creamy dressing to temper its bitterness. The leaves are also good as "containers."
Butterhead: Also called round; the soft, buttery leaves are vibrant green with a mild taste. Good with a simple herb vinaigrette as well as a stronger, Thai-flavored or creamy dressing.
Escarole (broad-leaved endive): Pale green, floppy, soft leaves, which are curly, but less so than those of frisée. Escarole goes well with mild-flavored dressings.
Frisée (curly endive): A member of the chicory family, it looks like a curly mop of hair. Its frilly, green leaves get progressively paler toward the center, where they are pale yellow or white. The outer leaves are slightly bitter. Good mixed with milder salad greens and blue cheese dressing.
Iceberg (crisphead): What this lacks in flavor it gains in crispness. It is round with pale green, tightly packed leaves. Its mild taste is best in mixed salads with flavorsome dressings.
Lollo rosso and oak leaf: Both have soft and floppy, green leaves with splashes of plum red, but they don't have much flavor, so are better mixed with other leaves. They go well with oil and vinegar dressings with herbs to sharpen up their taste.
Quattro Stagioni: Similar to escarole but has leaves with purple-red edges. It is best with a mild dressing.

leek–lettuce

Romaine: The crisp texture of its long thin leaves goes well with thick creamy dressings, bacon, avocado, and Parmesan. A classic choice for Caesar salad, it is also good stir-fried.
Webb's Wonder: Another in the crisphead category, tight-packed in the center like Iceberg, but a darker green color.

STORE Don't wash before storing. Soft-leaved lettuces will keep in a perforated plastic bag in the vegetable drawer of the refrigerator for about 1–2 days, crisp lettuce for 3–4 days.

PREPARE For optimum crispness, prepare just before serving. Separate individual leaves, wash briefly, drain, and shake well (or use a salad spinner). Treat gently as the leaves bruise easily. The leaves can be used whole, torn, or shredded, but are best torn rather than cut as this can cause the edges to turn brown. If cutting wedges from crisp lettuce (such as Bibb), brush them with lemon juice immediately.

COOK Lettuce is usually eaten raw, but can be shredded into soups at the last minute or braised with peas.

GOES WITH Other salad greens, nuts, avocado, cheese, eggs, peas, fruit, herbs.

A FEW MORE GREENS
Salad greens can be used alone or mixed and matched to give a variety of looks, textures, colors, and tastes. Add some herbs too and you have the makings of a great salad.
■ CORN SALAD (also known as mâche): Comes in attractive bunches of long, oval leaves and mixes well with beet and arugula. Will take a slightly spicy dressing, or a mild one that doesn't detract from its flavor.
■ MIZUNA: Looks a little like arugula, only more feathery and delicate. A Japanese leaf with a mild mustardy taste, it goes well with a sesame oil dressing.
■ SALAD CRESS: This has tiny, spicy leaves. Usually sold growing on fragile, thin white stems in cartons. Snip into sandwiches or over salads, or mix with other salad greens. (See also Spicy Salad Greens, page 295.)

TIPS AND TRICKS: LETTUCE
Add dressing to lettuce leaves just before serving, or the leaves will wilt and lose their crispness. If you want to prepare ahead, make the dressing in the salad bowl, lay the salad servers over it and pile the leaves on top. When ready to serve just toss everything together.

GOOD FOR YOU Lettuce contains beta carotene, some B vitamins, and vitamin K.

Marrow

A marrow looks like a giant zucchini (a close relation). It is not widely available in the US. It can grow huge, but the bigger it gets, the more water it contains and the less flavor it has. It is also sometimes called vegetable marrow, and can be used in similar ways to zucchini (see page 323), but its flavor is blander and it is much more watery. You can add flavor to it by slicing and baking it, then piling a savory stuffing on top (see right).

CHOOSE

■ Available in the summer months.
■ If it is more than 12 inches long, don't buy it as the flesh will be watery.

STORE In a cool place for several weeks.

PREPARE

For chunks: Cut the marrow in half lengthwise, scoop out and discard the seedy center, then peel, and chop it into chunks.

For slices: Cut crosswise into slices about 1 inch thick, then remove the center seeds and trim off the peel.

COOK Because marrow contains so much water, it is best to bake or pan-fry it rather than boil.

Bake: Cut into slices as above. Place them in a shallow dish with a spoonful of water. Bake at 375ºF (340ºF in fan ovens) for 15 minutes, or until tender. Drain off any liquid. Serve seasoned and sprinkled with cheese.
Alternatively, top with chopped onion fried with garlic and diced tomatoes, then arrange slices of mozzarella cheese on top of that, and broil until melted and golden.

Pan-fry: Heat a little butter and oil in a skillet. Add chunks of marrow and cook briefly, stirring occasionally, until it is softened but not going mushy. Season with salt and pepper.

WAYS TO SERVE

■ Fry some chopped onion and garlic in a little butter and oil. Pan-fry marrow chunks as above, then season, and stir in some freshly chopped parsley.

GOES WITH Ground beef, pork, or lamb, tomatoes, parsley, ginger (good for flavoring marrow jam).

GOOD FOR YOU Contains plenty of fiber, plus some beta carotene.

USE INSTEAD Large zucchini or other summer squash.

Mushroom

for DRIED, *see* PANTRY
STAPLES, *page 95*

The white mushroom is the best
known, but many edible fungi are now
cultivated that were once available
only in the wild, such as shiitake and
oyster, so it's easier to mix different
types together to liven up your meals.

CHOOSE

■ Cultivated are available all year
around. True wild are seasonal, and
are in the shops mostly in the fall.
■ Caps should be fresh and firm, stalks
fleshy, not shriveled.
■ Select from the many varieties, both
cultivated and wild. The most common
is the white mushroom which starts
life very small and, if left unpicked,
doubles in size every 24 hours. As it
grows it changes from a a closed-cup
to an open-cup mushroom, and finally,
after 5 days, a large, flat mushroom.

WHITE

"Baby": Small, white and very mild in
flavor. Use raw or lightly cooked in
sauces and salads, or increase the flavor
by marinating in spicy dressings.
Closed-cup: A large version of the
same mushroom with a similar taste.
Use for slicing into stir-fries, onto
pizzas or cooking whole.

SPICY SALAD GREENS

■ *ARUGULA: For the true peppery
flavor of arugula, choose organic
wild arugula—it has smaller, more
ragged leaves than regular arugula
and a livelier taste. Toss into salads,
wilt on top of pizzas or tarts as
they come out of the oven, or into
pasta at the end of cooking.
It is also delicious tossed with a
little olive oil, a splash of balsamic
vinegar, and a few shavings of
Parmesan cheese.*

Open-cup: The radiating, pinkish gills are starting to show as the white mushroom finally opens up.

Flat/open: More developed still, with more flavor.

BROWN

Closed-cup/portabellini/crimini: These brown capped mushrooms have more flavor and a meatier texture than the white cap. Use sliced raw in salads, or cooked in pasta and other sauces, or chopped in stuffings.

Flat/portabello: A mature version of the crimini mushroom. Completely open with dark gills, a gutsy flavor, and meaty texture. Use for broiling or stuffing whole (remove the stalk first), slicing and stir-frying, flavoring stews and casseroles.

STORE Keep mushrooms unwashed in a carton or paper bag—if in a plastic bag they will sweat and quickly rot. Store in the vegetable drawer of the refrigerator for up to 3 days.

PREPARE Waste nothing—every bit is edible. There is no need to peel mushrooms: just rinse them briefly in a colander and pat dry with paper towels. (Never soak mushrooms in water as they absorb liquid like a sponge and go soggy.) The ends of the stalks can then be trimmed and the

mushrooms left whole, halved, cut into fourths, sliced, or chopped.

COOK Small, whole mushrooms can be added to dishes such as sauces and casseroles 5–10 minutes before the end of cooking. Otherwise they are best stir-fried or broiled.

Stir-fry: Slice or chop any that are large; leave small ones whole. To bring out their flavor, brown mushrooms first. Pour some oil into a skillet (preferably nonstick) and get it hot before adding the mushrooms, or they will steam rather than fry. Keeping the heat high, stir-fry for 3–4 minutes until golden, tossing occasionally.

Broil: Brush with oil and cook whole under a preheated broiler for 3 minutes. Turn and broil for another 2–3 minutes. Broil the larger, flat mushrooms for about 5 minutes on each side.

WAYS TO SERVE

■ When frying mushrooms, cook some finely chopped garlic and red chili in the oil briefly before adding them to the pan. Add and stir-fry the mushrooms, season, and finish with chopped parsley and a squeeze of lemon juice. Good with a mixture of different mushrooms.

■ Fry whole small white mushrooms with chopped scallions, then stir in

mushroom

crème fraîche or sour cream, and sprinkle with paprika. Great with steak or chicken.

■ Thinly slice small white mushrooms and serve raw as a salad tossed with sliced radish, arugula, crumbled crispy bacon and a full-flavored dressing such as mustard, garlic, or blue cheese.

■ Fry the mushrooms for 2 minutes, then add chopped shallot and garlic, and fry for another couple of minutes. Stir in a few spoonfuls of heavy cream and heat. Season with salt and pepper and serve on toast sprinkled with chopped parsley.

GOES WITH Many things, especially beef, chicken, fish, tomatoes, bacon, pasta, cream, crème fraîche, sour cream, cheese, onions, scallions, soy sauce, garlic, lemon, thyme, parsley.

GOOD FOR YOU Mushrooms have plenty of fiber and B vitamins and more vegetable protein per ounce than many other vegetables, so they are especially good for vegetarians and vegans.

Exotic and wild mushrooms
EXOTIC (CULTIVATED WILD)
A lot of the exotic-looking mushrooms available in the stores are actually cultivated and not truly wild.

FIX IT: MUSHROOMS
To give a wild mushroom flavor to fresh cultivated mushrooms, use 14 ounces cultivated (a mix is good) tossed with ½ ounce of soaked dried porcini. (Soak the dried mushrooms in ⅔ cup warm water for about 1 hour, and use the resulting flavored liquid too.)

VEGETABLES A–Z

Blewit: This has a purple-blue, tinted stem. It should be sliced and cooked thoroughly to bring out its distinctive taste. Delicious stir-fried with bacon.

Enoki: A tiny, creamy-white, mild-flavored Japanese mushroom with a long, slender stem. Eat in salads, or stir-fry, or sprinkle into soups at the last minute—it cooks instantly. Separate the joined-up stalks before you use them.

Horse: When young and tender, these little, subtle-flavored mushrooms with sturdy, long stems and helmet-like caps can be used interchangeably with white mushrooms.

Oyster: These delicate-flavored mushrooms require minimum cooking and are best flash-fried to prevent wilting. Pretty and shaped like fans, they can be pink and yellow as well as gray, although the color disappears when they are cooked.

Shiitake: Used a lot in Chinese and Japanese cooking, these are enjoyed for their subtle flavor and unique texture. Tougher than most mushrooms, they need longer cooking to soften them. Good in stews, or roasted with Asian flavors. Trim off the tough stalks before using.

TRUE WILD

These are less easy to buy than cultivated mushrooms, as they are picked in the wild and are available only when they are in season.

Chanterelle: A pretty, apricot-colored mushroom with a slightly frilly cap and pleasant flavor. The small ones are called *girolle* in France. They go well with other varieties in a stir-fry, or on their own with scrambled eggs for breakfast. They may need a brief wash before using. Dry with paper towels.

Morel: Highly prized and expensive, this has a wrinkly, dark brown, dome-shaped cap. It is more likely to be found dried than fresh and goes well with creamy sauces.

Cep, porcini (in Italy), cèpes (in France): Full of flavor with a meaty texture, these are difficult to find fresh, but are readily available dried (see Pantry Staples, page 95). To prepare fresh ceps, brush them briefly under cold running water, but don't peel as all the flavor is in the skin. Dry with paper towels, then trim the end off the bulbous stalk. To get the benefit of the shape, slice them length-wise. Delicious quickly fried in butter.

Okra (bhindi)

Also known as ladies' fingers because of the elegant way it tapers to a point at one end, okra has a slightly furry, green-ridged skin and

mushroom–okra

a creamy, seedy flesh with a pungent taste. Popular in Indian and Middle Eastern cooking, and for making Cajun gumbos.

CHOOSE

- Available all year around.
- Should be firm and small, no longer than 3–4 inches—the bigger and older the okra, the tougher it is.
- Avoid those with brown markings on the skin—this indicates that the okra is not fresh.
- Allow 12 ounces for 4 people.

STORE In a perforated plastic bag in the refrigerator for up to 3 days.

PREPARE Wash, pat dry, then trim both ends. You can then leave the okra whole, cut lengthwise in half, or slice into pieces about ¾ inch long.

COOK Okra is best fried or cooked with other ingredients.
Stir-fry: Heat a little oil or ghee in a wok or skillet. Add the okra and fry for 6–12 minutes, depending on how it has been cut, until starting to brown.

WAYS TO SERVE

- Fry some sliced onion for a few minutes before adding okra (as above). When both are brown, stir in a pinch of turmeric and crushed dried chilies

OKRA

FIX IT: OKRA

Okra can be glutinous and sticky when cooked for long—so it will thicken soups and stews, but it is less appetising when served like this as a vegetable. To avoid this sticky texture you have two choices:
1 Use small, very fresh okra and cook very briefly.
2 Cook them whole, trimming around the stalks in a cone shape, so that the pod isn't pierced and therefore does not release its sticky juices.

and cook for a few more minutes. Serve sprinkled with chopped cilantro.

GOES WITH Serve as a vegetable accompaniment to curries, or as part of a curry. Goes well with potatoes, tomatoes, and coconut.

GOOD FOR YOU A great source of calcium, magnesium, iron, niacin, folate, and vitamin C.

Onion

This has to be the most versatile vegetable in the world as it brings flavor to many dishes and can be used as a vegetable in its own right.

CHOOSE

- Available all year around.
- Those that are firm with no soft spots or shoots.
- From the following types:

Bermuda: This has a similar brown skin to the common brown/yellow onion, but tastes milder and sweeter. It is also bigger. The mild flavor makes it good for salads, omelets, salsas, and stir-fries.

Brown/yellow: The most common type and a good all-rounder. It has golden-brown skin and white flesh.

Red: Mild and sweet-tasting, the pink-tinged flesh looks attractive and

tastes good raw in salads and salsas. A good choice for roasting.

White: Strong in flavor, with white skin and flesh. Use raw in salads when you want the onion taste to dominate.

STORE Keep loose in a cool, dry place, where the air can move around them—they will keep for several weeks. Best stored on their own, as they are quick to take on moisture from other vegetables such as potatoes. Discard them once they start sprouting. Don't store cut onion in the refrigerator or it will flavor your milk, unless wrapped well in plastic wrap.

PREPARE Onion is best prepared just before using. Cut a thin slice off the top of the onion, then peel by removing the papery outer skin and any soft or brown outer layers.

Chop: Keep the root end on so the onion doesn't fall apart as you chop it. Put the onion on its side on a cutting board and cut in half lengthwise. Place the cut side down and make a series of horizontal cuts stopping just short of the root end each time. Next, make a series of equally spaced vertical cuts down through the onion, again stopping short of the root end (see opposite, above). To do this, hold the onion firmly with your fingers, then cut down and across, so it falls away in small pieces (see right, center). If you want smaller pieces still, carry on chopping or start with cuts very close together. Discard the root end.

Slice: Trim the root end. Hold the onion on its side on a board with your fingers across the center. Slice down the onion into thick or thin slices, then separate each slice into rings or keep the slices whole (see page 303).

Cut into wedges: Slice off the top and root end and cut in half lengthwise. Lay the cut side down and make lengthwise cuts into fourths or eighths.

COOK Fry an onion well and it will bring lots of flavor to a dish—not only does the onion brown, it also creates sticky bits in the bottom of the pan which will flavor any added liquid. It's important to get the pan and fat hot before you start.

Pan-fry: Heat olive or sunflower oil in a skillet, then add chopped or sliced onion. The oil should be so hot that it sizzles when the onion goes in, otherwise the onion will stew rather than fry. Cook on medium heat for 7–10 minutes, stirring occasionally. Aim to get it golden all over for the best flavor. The longer it cooks, the sweeter it will be.

Caramelize: This involves long, slow cooking until the onions reduce right down and become meltingly tender, so

CHOPPING AN ONION

After making horizontal cuts through the onion, stopping just short of the root, make a series of evenly spaced vertical cuts, again stopping short of the root.

Cut down across the vertical cuts so that the onion falls into small pieces.

FIX IT: CHOPPING ONIONS

If cutting onions makes you cry, try the following:

■ *Chill the onions for 30 minutes (well wrapped), then keep the root end on while chopping (it contains a substance called allicin that makes your eyes water).*

■ *Put the onions in a bowl of cold water while peeling, and keep the water running while you chop them.*

start with lots of them. Melt 2 tablespoons butter with 3 tablespoons vegetable oil in a very large pan. Add about 2½ pounds (8–9) onions, sliced. With the heat very low, cook for 40–50 minutes, stirring occasionally, until they are completely softened. Sprinkle in 1–2 teaspoons superfine sugar, turn the heat up slightly, and cook for 10–15 minutes, until golden.

Roast: Lay wedges in a roasting pan, sprinkle with thyme sprigs and a couple of bay leaves, then drizzle with olive oil. Season and roast at 400°F (350°F in fan ovens) for 40–50 minutes, turning occasionally.

WAYS TO SERVE

■ Fry onion slices as above and toss with cooked new potatoes.

■ Mix chopped, raw red onion with sliced cherry tomatoes and chopped cilantro. Add a squeeze of lemon juice and serve as a salad with curries.

GOES WITH Most savory ingredients, but especially meat, sausages, and vegetables.

GOOD FOR YOU Contains niacin but is not particularly nutrient-rich.

USE INSTEAD All onions can be used interchangeably, but use only the red when you want a sweet taste.

More in the onion family

Garlic: Choose plump, firm bulbs with no green sprouts. Divide the whole bulb into separate cloves and peel off the skin (not necessary if the garlic is to be crushed). If the garlic has a tiny, green shoot in the center, take it out before chopping as it may have a bitter taste.

CRUSH: Leaving the skin on, lay the flat side of a large chef's knife on top of the garlic clove and give it a heavy blow with your fist, then remove the skin. If you want the garlic more than just bruised, sprinkle a little salt on it and crush again. Alternatively, peel it first and then use a garlic press.

CHOP: Peel and slice the garlic, then move the knife back and forth in a rocking motion (like chopping herbs).

COOK: Garlic can become bitter if cooked too long over too high heat, so when frying, do so briefly and gently— don't let it get too brown. Or add it toward the end of cooking when combining with other ingredients, so it doesn't burn. To roast, toss whole bulbs in olive oil and roast at 375°F (340°F in fan ovens) for 20–25 minutes or until they feel soft. A few unpeeled, separate cloves can be thrown in with other vegetables for the last 20 minutes of their roasting time. To eat, separate the cloves and squeeze out the soft purée. Great with roasts and fish.

onion

Pearl onion: This small sweet onion is perfect for dropping whole into slow-cooked dishes. Its thin skin makes it hard to peel, so soak it first for a few minutes in boiling water to make it easier. Drain, rinse under cold water, then peel using a small, sharp knife. Keep the stem end on so that the center doesn't pop out.

Pickling onion: This is a regular onion picked when small, so is quite strong in flavor, and slightly smaller than a pearl onion. Besides pickling, it is used for adding whole to stews. Soak as for pearl onion (see above) to make peeling easier.

Shallot: Closely related to the onion, the shallot is smaller, softer, and sweeter in taste. Use when a hint of onion flavor is wanted. The longer banana shallot and the pinkish Thai shallot are also available. Trim off both ends, peel, and if there is more than one bulb inside, separate them. To aid peeling, soak shallots in boiling water for a minute or two after trimming. Slice or finely chop. Like garlic, shallots need softening rather than browning as they can turn slightly bitter, so fry gently over low heat, stirring often. They tend to cook more quickly than onions.

Scallion: Also called green onion, this is mild in flavor and popular raw or in stir-fries. Trim off the root at the

SLICING AN ONION

TIPS AND TRICKS: ONIONS

■ *If you want to reduce the strong flavor of raw onion, slice and soak it in ice-cold water for a few hours.*

■ *To get rid of an oniony smell from your hands, rub them with lemon juice or vinegar.*

■ *If you are going to fry onions, chop them with a knife, rather than in a food processor. Using a machine can make them watery, causing them to steam rather than fry.*

bottom, and any ragged green ends, then slice into rounds, or shred by trimming off the top darker green part (this can be used separately), and cutting the lighter part lengthwise in half, then in half again into thin strips. Use in salads or for sprinkling over fish and chicken dishes, rice, and noodles as a garnish. To make the shreds go curly, put into ice cold water for about 30 minutes. For a mild onion taste, use them like shallots by frying gently in a little oil or butter for 1–2 minutes.

Pak choi

see BOK CHOY, *page 265*

Parsnip

A root vegetable that resembles a plump, cream carrot. It brings a delicate sweetness to winter soups, stews, and roasts.

CHOOSE

■ Available all year—but at their best in mid-winter. After a frost, the starch is converted into sugar which highlights their sweetness.

■ Small and firm—large parsnips can be rather woody.

■ Do not buy parsnips with brown patches on the skin—this is a sign that they may be rotten inside.

■ Allow 1 pound parsnips for 4.

STORE In a perforated plastic bag in the vegetable drawer of the refrigerator for up to a week.

PREPARE Trim off both ends. Peel thinly with a vegetable peeler or sharp knife. Cut into even-size chunks. If the parsnip is older and larger, you may need to cut out the central core if it is woody. Small ones can be left whole, or cut into lengths or chunks.

COOK Roast to bring out the natural sweetness, or boil and transform them into a creamy mash.

Boil: Cut into chunks and put in a pan with a little salt. Cover with boiling water, bring back to a boil, then cook, covered, for 15–20 minutes until tender. Drain.

Roast: Heat a few tablespoons of olive oil in a roasting pan in a 400°F oven (350°F in fan ovens) for 5 minutes. Peel the parsnips, cut them into thickish, long sticks and toss in the oil. Roast for about 40–55 minutes, shaking the pan occasionally, until tender and golden. Season.

WAYS TO SERVE

■ Boil and serve with butter, salt, pepper, a pinch of grated nutmeg, and a sprinkling of grated Parmesan cheese.

onion–peas

■ Make a creamy mash using equal amounts of boiled parsnip and ruta-baga. After draining, coarsely mash the vegetables, leaving some texture. Season and flavor with a little cream or sour cream, horseradish sauce, and fresh thyme.

■ Cut into chunks and roast with squash and wedges of onion, sprinkled with rosemary, bay, or thyme.

GOES WITH Roast meats, sausages, and chops, most other root vegetables, cream, rosemary, thyme, curry spices.

GOOD FOR YOU Parsnip has folate, niacin, vitamin E, and potassium.

Peas

Belonging to the legume family, peas (also called garden peas) are a summer vegetable with a very short season. They start converting sugar into starch as soon as they're picked, so freshness is crucial. Commercially frozen peas are frozen within 2½ hours of being picked, so are sometimes fresher-tasting than fresh peas bought from the store.

CHOOSE

■ Available all year (in their pods and ready shelled, homegrown and from different parts of the world).

ONION GRAVY
Quick and easy to make. Add broiled sausages and you have an instant supper.

Fry 2 peeled and sliced onions in 1 tablespoon oil and a large pat of butter until softened and golden. Stir in 2 teaspoons flour and cook for 1–2 minutes to give a golden color. Gradually pour in about 1 cup stock, stirring all the time, then add a pinch of dried rosemary and a good teaspoonful of red currant jelly. Bring to a boil, stirring, then simmer for a few minutes until it has reached the thickness you prefer.

MINTED PEAS
For extra flavor, drop a couple of sprigs of mint into the water when boiling fresh peas.

■ The pods should be bright green, firm, and plump.

■ There should be some air between each pea in their pod. If they feel too full and bloated, the peas may be hard and tough.

■ Allow about 8 ounces peas in the pod per person.

■ From 2 pounds pods you should get 1–1½ pounds—about 4–6 cups—shelled peas.

STORE Use fresh peas as soon as possible after buying or picking as they lose their sweet taste very quickly.

PREPARE Snap the pod open with your fingers at the top, then push the peas out along the pod with your thumb.

COOK The best way to tell if peas are cooked is to bite into one—the inside should be bright green in color and not too soft.

Boil: Place peas in a pan and cover with boiling water. Cook in the minimum of water needed, so that nutrients aren't lost. Don't add salt as this can toughen the skins, but a pinch of sugar helps intensify their sweetness. Bring the water back to a boil, cover, and simmer for about 2–3 minutes. Drain and season with salt and pepper.

Steam: For 1–2 minutes when young and in season, 3–5 minutes if older.

WAYS TO SERVE

■ Melt some butter in a pan, add chopped scallions, and cook briefly to soften. Add some steamed or boiled peas and stir to warm them through adding some salt, pepper, and a handful of chopped mint.

■ When cooking new potatoes, drop some peas into the cooking water for the last 3–4 minutes. Drain and toss with butter and chives.

■ Cook in stock with some chopped shallot and a handful of soft lettuce leaves to make the classic *petits pois à la française.*

GOES WITH Salmon, bacon and cured ham, duck, risotto, scallions, garlic, mint, chives, basil, parsley.

GOOD FOR YOU Contain protein, fiber, B vitamins, vitamin C, iron.

USE INSTEAD Use fresh and frozen peas interchangeably.

More in the pea family

Baby peas: The same variety as garden peas—but picked earlier so they are smaller and sweeter.

Snow peas: This type of pea is picked while flat and immature. It has a tender pod and tiny peas inside. You eat the whole thing like a bean. Break off the stalk end and pull along the length of the pod to remove the "string" that runs underneath it. Trim off the other end. To preserve their crispness, boil in the minimum of water for about 2–3 minutes, or steam, or stir-fry for 3–4 minutes. If used in a salad they taste better when blanched briefly first.

Sugar snap: A more mature version of the snow pea so plumper, but not quite so plump as a garden pea. Both pod and pea are eaten together, raw or cooked. No preparation is needed, apart from trimming (see right). Boil or steam for about 3–4 minutes so they still have some crunch left. Or slice very thinly lengthwise and eat raw in a salad.

Plantain
see FRUIT, *page 243*

Potato
A favorite world staple, this native of South America is one of the most versatile of vegetables. Always served cooked, each variety has many differ-ent characteristics—whether light and mealy for making the perfect mash or fries, or waxy for using in salads. Potatoes are also divided into early-growing varieties (new) and larger, older maincrop varieties.

TRIM
This means to trim off both ends of vegetables or fruits, where only minimal trimming is required, as with beans, peas, or currants.

TIPS AND TRICKS: POTATOES
■ *If you are not sure whether your potatoes are the mealy or waxy type, drop one into a pitcher with a mix of 11 parts water to one part salt. If the potato sinks, it is almost certainly a mealy one, if it floats it's waxy.*

■ *The thicker you cut potatoes for French fries, the less fat they will absorb during cooking.*

GREAT MASH
Boil a quantity of potatoes (see page 308), drain them, return them to the pan and pour over hot milk—allow ⅔ cup per 2¼ pounds potatoes. Mash with a large pat of butter and some salt and pepper until smooth and creamy, using a potato masher or electric hand mixer. For a smoother finish, use a potato ricer.

CHOOSE

- Available all year around, except for early-season new, which have a short season in late spring and early summer (check for true early potatoes by rubbing the skins—you should be able to rub them off easily with your finger).
- Potatoes should be firm.
- Allow about 6–7 ounces raw unpeeled potatoes per person.
- Select the type of potato that suits the way you want to cook it:

Waxy: Firm, keep their shape when cooked, but not good for mashing. Use them for salads, boiling, steaming, baking (for cheese-layered gratins), e.g. Cara, Carlingford New, Charlotte, Marfona, Nicola, Pink Fir Apple, Wilja.

Mealy: Have a soft, dry texture when cooked. Use them when you want the cooked potato to have a fluffy texture as in baked potatoes, mash, roast, and French fries, but not for boiling (they will fall apart), e.g. King Edward, Maris Piper, Desirée (red skins).

Good all-rounder: Can be used when a recipe calls for no specific variety, e.g.: Red Pontiac, Maris Piper, Desirée, Nicola, Romano.

Salad: Choose a firm, flavorsome variety such as Jersey Royal, Pink Fir Apple, Nicola New, Charlotte.

STORE In a cool, dark, well-ventilated place. Clear plastic bags let in the light so that the potatoes can turn green and sprout, and plastic can make them go moldy. Store them in a nontransparent paper bag. Maincrop potatoes will keep for a few weeks; new potatoes for a few days.

PREPARE

Maincrop: Give them a scrub and dig out any "eyes." When possible, leave the skin on (it is full of nutrients), or peel them very thinly with a vegetable peeler. Then wash them thoroughly.

New: No need to peel, just give them a wash and scrub.

COOK Use similar-size whole potatoes, or cut into equal-size pieces, to insure even cooking.

Bake: Whole in their skins. Wash, then pat dry with paper towels. Prick all over with a fork, or lightly score around the middle of the potato. Place on a cookie sheet or directly on an oven rack in a preheated oven at 400ºF (350ºF in fan ovens) for 50 minutes to 1¼ hours, depending on size. To bake in the microwave, stand one potato on paper towels and microwave on high for 6 minutes, turning once, then let stand for 2 minutes. Allow 8–10 minutes for 2 potatoes. When ready, the sides of the potato should feel soft when pinched.

Boil: Peel, cut into even pieces (not too small or they will go watery), put in a

potato

pan with a little salt, and pour over boiling water to cover. Return to a boil, cover the pan, and boil gently for 15–20 minutes. Drain as soon as they are cooked. Cook new potatoes as above for about 12 minutes, with a sprig of mint in the water for extra flavor. When ready, the potato should feel tender when tested with a skewer or the point of a sharp knife.

Roast: Potatoes take on the flavor of the oil used for roasting—choose either light olive oil or sunflower oil (for a mild flavor), or goose or duck fat (for a rich flavor).

■ Maincrop: Peel and cut the potatoes into big, even chunks. Put them in a pan, cover with boiling water, bring back to a boil, then simmer for 3 minutes. Drain in a colander and shake it to roughen them slightly—this gives a crisper potato. Heat the oil or fat of your choice (allow about 2 tablespoons per pound of potatoes) in a roasting pan in a 400°F oven (350°F in fan ovens) for 5 minutes. Tip in the potatoes, toss to coat them in the oil, and roast for 45–60 minutes, turning once or twice. Season with salt at the end of cooking— they can go soggy if salted at the beginning. When ready, they should be golden and crisp on the outside and fluffy inside.

■ New: Keep whole, tip into a roasting pan (tuck in some unpeeled garlic

CRUSH—THE NEW MASH

Boil some whole new potatoes in their skins for 12–15 minutes or until tender. Drain well, tip back into the pan, and crush coarsely by pressing down with the back of a fork. Generously drizzle in some olive oil, season with salt and pepper, and toss with one or more of the following herbs: chives, thyme, oregano, rosemary, or parsley.

SAFE TO EAT?

Green patches can appear on potatoes caused by exposure to light— if these are small, they can be cut away before cooking, but if they are extensive, the potatoes should be thrown away as they could make you ill. If the potatoes have sprouted, they are perfectly safe to cook and eat, but need using up quickly as they won't keep so well. Just slice off the sprouted parts before using.

FIX IT: POTATOES

■ *Potatoes can discolor once peeled, so if you are not going to use them immediately, put in a bowl and cover with cold water.*
■ *If you tip too much salt into a soup, curry, or stew, add a chopped potato to soak up the salty taste.*

cloves and thyme sprigs if you like), drizzle with oil, season, and roast at 400°F (350°F in fan ovens) for about 30–40 minutes or until golden, turning a couple of times.

WAYS TO SERVE

- Maincrop: Stir a spoonful or two of creamed horseradish or grainy mustard into mashed potatoes.
- New: When cooked, toss with pesto, a pat of butter, or a splash of extra-virgin olive oil and a generous handful of chives or mint. For a spicy kick, add a pinch of crushed dried chilies or a little harissa.

GOES WITH Many things, including roast meats, fish, bacon, cheese, eggs, onions, mayonnaise, and herbs.

GOOD FOR YOU Full of vitamin C, carbohydrate, and fiber, as well as potassium. They are at their most nutritious when eaten with the skin left on as this increases the iron content.

Pumpkin

see SQUASH, *page 315*

Radicchio

see BELGIAN ENDIVE, *page 262*

Radish

A root vegetable related to the mustard plant. Varieties include the common red-skinned radish (including the more elongated French Breakfast variety), which is eaten for its color and crisp, peppery white flesh. Strongly flavored black radishes are popular in eastern Europe and are usually peeled; white radishes are also available (see opposite).

CHOOSE

- Available all year around.
- The leaves (if still attached) should be lively and bright green, the red part firm and not at all soft.
- Smaller radishes are better—if they are too big, the white flesh goes spongy.

STORE In the refrigerator for 3–4 days, preferably without the leaves as they take the moisture from the root.

PREPARE Begin preparing them just before you intend to serve, as radishes lose their bite after slicing. Trim off any leaves (unless you want to serve them with leaves on as part of a salad) and the root at the bottom. Leave them whole, or chop or slice.

COOK Red and black are usually eaten raw. For white, see opposite.

potato–rutabaga

WAYS TO SERVE

■ Slice thinly on the diagonal, mix with slender strips of cucumber, scallion, and seeded red chili, and toss in a dressing of lime juice, olive oil, and a splash of soy. Serve Asian-style with broiled or roasted salmon or chicken.

GOES WITH Arugula, cucumber, lime juice, feta cheese.

GOOD FOR YOU Contains vitamin C, some iron, and potassium.

Rutabaga

This root-like vegetable, a member of the cabbage family, answers to several different names—swede, yellow turnip, Swedish turnip, Russian turnip. In America it is called rutabaga and in Scotland, where it is a traditional accompaniment to haggis on Burns Night, it is known as "neeps." It looks like a colorful version of a large turnip except the flesh is more yellowy-orange and the skin purple.

CHOOSE

■ Best in late fall to early spring.
■ Larger radishes can be quite tough, so pick out the smallest ones with smooth, undamaged skins.
■ Allow about 1½ pounds, unpeeled, for 4 people.

WHITE RADISH

Popular in Asia, these are bigger and milder in flavor than red-skinned radishes and look like a white carrot. They are also known as mooli, mouli, or daikon in Japan. Use them as an ordinary radish by slicing into salads. They can also be stir-fried, diced, and added to soups or stews, or grated to serve with sushi.

RADISH SALSA

Make a colorful salsa—finely chop some radishes and mix them with chopped cherry tomatoes and a little red onion, and toss with some lemon juice, olive oil, and a little chopped garlic and mint to taste. Serve with cold meats.

STORE In a perforated plastic bag in the refrigerator for up to a week.

PREPARE Cut off the root end, then prepare like a potato: remove the peel with a peeler and cut into chunks.

COOK

Roast: Heat a few tablespoons of olive oil in a roasting pan at 400°F (350°F in fan ovens) for 5 minutes. Add chunks of peeled rutabaga and toss them in the oil. Roast for 40–55 minutes until golden around the edges. Or roast rutabaga chunks around a cut of meat.
Boil: Cut in chunks like potatoes and put into a pan with a little salt. Pour boiling water over to cover, bring back to a boil, and cook, covered, for about 12–15 minutes or until tender. Drain.
Steam: In small chunks for about 10 minutes, larger ones for about 15 minutes.

WAYS TO SERVE

■ After boiling or steaming, mash with butter and a spoonful of horseradish sauce. Good with beef.
■ Make up a mixed crush. Boil equal quantities of rutabaga and carrot, drain well, then crush coarsely with a fork or potato masher. Season and add a splash of olive oil, or butter if you prefer. Then, if you wish, whizz to a chunky or smooth purée in a food processor.

■ Add chunks to soups, stews, and winter casseroles—rutabaga takes on other flavors well.

GOES WITH Beef, poultry, sausages, haggis, other root vegetables such as carrot, potato.

GOOD FOR YOU Rutabaga contains vitamins B and C, and fiber.

USE INSTEAD Turnip—but this is smaller and not so sweet tasting.

Samphire

A true wild food, rock samphire is a small shrub that is found growing on coastal rocks and cliffs. Marsh samphire, also known as glasswort, is an unrelated European plant that grows wild on coastal salt marshes and is used in the same way. It is crisp, juicy, and salty.

CHOOSE

■ In mid-summer.
■ It should look fresh and perky—avoid any that looks slimy.

STORE Best used on the day of purchase.

PREPARE Wash it well, then trim any tough parts from the stalks.

COOK

Boil: Put into a pan, cover with boiling water (no salt required—it's salty enough), and bring back to a boil. Cook for a minute, then drain in a strainer or colander.

Steam: For a couple of minutes.

WAYS TO SERVE

■ Boil or steam, then toss in butter, lime juice, chopped parsley, and fresh black pepper, to serve with fish.

■ Raw in a salad with shellfish, such as crab or shrimp, and a little light vinaigrette.

■ Toss into a fish stew toward the end of cooking.

GOES WITH Fish and shellfish, especially crab, asparagus, Parmesan cheese, lime.

Spinach

With its dark green leaves, spinach just seems to ooze goodness. It is one of the fastest-cooking vegetables. Very young leaves are good eaten raw in a salad (see right).

CHOOSE

■ Available all year around, but at its best from late spring to early fall.

■ The leaves should be bright green, avoid any that are turning yellow.

SAMPHIRE

BABY LEAF SPINACH

These are the tenderest of spinach leaves, so are the best choice for serving raw in a salad.

They are also good sprinkled on top of a pizza just as it comes out the oven, so that they wilt slightly in the heat of the pizza.

■ The stalks should look tender and crisp.

■ Spinach contains a lot of water and reduces considerably in volume when cooked—you'll be surprised how much you need. Allow about 7–8 ounces per person for serving as a vegetable accompaniment.

STORE Keep spinach in a perforated plastic bag in the refrigerator for up to 2–3 days. Don't wash until it is ready to use.

PREPARE Pre-washed, bagged spinach will probably need only a quick rinse. Loose spinach, however, can have a lot of grit, and needs washing well. Remove any wilting leaves, then tip the spinach into a large bowl of cold water, and swish it around, changing the water a few times, until all the grit has gone. Tip it into a colander and give it a good shake to drain. Don't leave it standing in the water. If using raw or in a stir-fry, pat it dry with paper towels. If the spinach is young and tender, it may not need any more attention, but if the leaves are large and old, trim off any tough-looking stalks. If these are very thick in the leaf, fold each leaf lengthwise along the central rib with the rib facing outward, then tear the rib away from the leaf.

COOK Spinach cooks very fast and you don't need to cook it in water, it is naturally moist. After washing, just shake off any excess water and the amount left on the leaves is all you need. As soon as the leaves have wilted, they are cooked.

In a pan: Melt a pat of butter in a large pan. Pack in the leaves, cover the pan, and cook over a medium heat for just under a minute. Stir the spinach to get any uncooked leaves to the bottom of the pan, cover, and cook for another 30 seconds or so, shaking the pan occasionally, until it has all wilted. Drain into a colander, then put a small plate on top (or use a large spoon), and press down firmly to squeeze out all the moisture.

In a bowl: With young, tender leaves you can simply tip the spinach into a large bowl, pour boiling water over it, and leave for about 30 seconds until wilted, then drain, and press out the excess moisture as above.

Steam: Pack the leaves into a steamer and cook for 1–3 minutes, depending on the amount, until the leaves have just wilted. Press out the excess moisture as above.

WAYS TO SERVE

■ After cooking and draining, toss with caramelized onions, or stir in cream or crème fraîche, and a

spinach–squash

sprinkling of grated nutmeg and chopped parsley, chives, or basil.

■ Fry some finely chopped garlic, toss in a handful of pine nuts, and cook until toasty brown, then mix in cooked spinach with a handful of raisins.

■ Add raw to a salad with crispy fried bacon, pancetta, or prosciutto, croûtons, mushrooms, and some crumbled blue cheese.

GOES WITH Fish (especially smoked haddock), chicken, bacon, cured ham, pasta, beans, mushrooms, potatoes, cheese (especially Swiss, Emmental, and Italian cheeses such as Parmesan and ricotta), eggs, nutmeg, garlic, chives, lemon, curry spices.

GOOD FOR YOU Contains lots of iron and calcium; vitamins C and A.

Squash
(including pumpkin)

There is a huge variety available— summer squash (thin-skinned with soft, moist flesh), such as zucchini (see page 322), pattypan, and crookneck, and the thick-skinned and firm, sweet-fleshed winter squash. Winter squash, such as butternut, spaghetti, and kabocha, come in many different shapes, and color combinations include orange, green and yellow.

SEEDING BUTTERNUT SQUASH

Once you have cut your squash in half, remove the seeds and any stringy parts with a spoon.

SPICED SQUASH

Serves 4

Fry an onion in 2–3 tablespoons vegetable oil in a skillet, until golden. Add 3½ cups peeled, cubed squash and fry for 5 minutes. Season with a sprinkling of ground cinnamon, add a handful of raisins, cover, and cook for another 10 minutes or so until tender, turning every now and then. Season and serve sprinkled with toasted almonds.

CHOOSE

■ Some squash are available all year; pumpkins usually only in the fall.

■ They should feel firm, not hollow, and be heavy for their size.

■ Allow about 8–12 ounces unpeeled squash per person.

■ The following varieties are the most common:

Acorn: A ridged, small, dark green-(sometimes orange-) skinned squash with a vibrant orange flesh that has a sweet flavor of chestnuts.

Butternut: Has a slim neck and curved base, which contains the seeds and fibrous parts; tan-colored skin with an orange flesh and a nutty taste.

Crown prince: Bluey-gray in color. Firm flesh, so good for roasting, cutting into chunks and threading on kabob skewers with lemon and red onion wedges, or in stews or curries.

Gem: Has dark green skin and is small and round, about the size of a large onion, perfect for stuffing. Leave whole to cook—no need to peel.

Kabocha: Dark green with pale markings and deep orange, sweet flesh.

Onion: A large, orange squash, so named because of its onion-like shape.

Pumpkin: As well as being useful for Halloween decorations, pumpkin is great roasted, puréed for a soup, stuffed into pasta, or in a traditional pumpkin pie where it gives a silky-smooth texture and the flavor is enhanced with spices. Smaller ones are sweeter and easier to prepare than large ones, which can be extremely hard to cut into as the skin is so tough.

Spaghetti: This is a one-off in the world of squash. When you open it up after cooking, the flesh pulls out like strands of spaghetti, hence its name.

STORE In a cool, dark, well-ventilated place for a few weeks. Once cut, pumpkin keeps for up to a week in the refrigerator, as long as it is well wrapped.

PREPARE Some squash, especially pumpkins, have very tough skins, so you need brute force to get into them. Put the squash on a towel to keep it steady, then use a strong, heavy knife to cut it in half. For a pumpkin, you may need to use a rolling pin or hammer to hit the knife into the skin. Pull the knife out and work down in sections until you get to the bottom. Start again on the other side so you can cut it in half. Scoop out the seeds and any fibrous, stringy parts. Take a small, sharp knife and cut off the skin. You may find it easier to do this if you cut the squash into smaller pieces first. (If you are going to roast the squash, you can leave the skin on.) Cut the flesh into wedges or chunks.

squash

COOK

Boil: Peel and cut into even chunks, put into a pan with a little salt, and cover with boiling water. Bring back to a boil, cover, and cook for about 10–15 minutes, depending on size, or until tender. Serve broiled, sprinkled with grated cheese, or mash with butter, salt, and pepper. For Gem squash, prick all over with a skewer, then boil whole for about 25 minutes or until tender. Halve, scoop out the seeds, and serve with a pat of butter, salt, and pepper. For spaghetti squash, cut in half lengthwise and scrape out the seeds. Put in a large pan and cover with boiling water. Boil for about 20 minutes or until tender. Scrape the flesh out with a fork. It will look like fine strands of spaghetti.

Roast/bake: Roasting is one of the best ways to cook winter squash. Have the skin on or off (it's easier to leave it on), then cut in wedges or chunks, toss in olive oil, and season with salt and pepper. Roast at 400ºF (350ºF in fan ovens) for 30–40 minutes or until tender and brown at the edges. For spaghetti squash, cut in half lengthwise and scrape out the seeds. Put in a roasting pan, drizzle with olive oil and season with salt and pepper. Roast at 375ºF (340ºF in fan ovens) for 40–45 minutes, or until tender. Scrape out the strands with a fork.

WAYS TO SERVE

■ Roast wedges or chunks of your favorite winter squash. Heat some olive oil in a small pan, briefly fry some chopped garlic, then throw in some dried sage leaves (or rosemary or thyme). As soon as they sizzle and go crisp, pour the hot dressing over the squash and season.

■ Boil or roast spaghetti squash as above and serve like spaghetti with a drizzle of oil or a pat of butter, grated Parmesan cheese, salt, and pepper.

GOES WITH Roast meats and poultry, bacon, pancetta, pasta, garbanzo beans, orange, cream, sage, thyme, curry spices, nuts.

GOOD FOR YOU Squash contains lots of fiber, vitamins, and minerals.

USE INSTEAD Use different squashes interchangeably, except for spaghetti squash.

Sweet potato

Not a true potato, this looks like an elongated maincrop potato. It can have a thin yellow or white skin, but the most commonly available is the thicker-skinned, dark orange type. Prepare just as a regular potato,

see page 307, but thanks to its softer flesh it will cook a little more quickly. The flesh is also sweeter-tasting, more like squash than potato, so it goes well with spicy flavorings such as garlic, cinnamon and chili.

COOK

Roast: Cut into wedges, keeping the peel on (scrubbed first), and lay them in a roasting pan. Drizzle with oil, season, toss together, and spread out into a single layer. Roast at 400°F (350°F in fan ovens) for about 25–30 minutes, turning half way through, until tender (the skin can be eaten as well as the flesh).

Bake: Peel the whole sweet potato and cut into thickish slices, keeping the potato in its whole shape. Lay it on a large square of foil, drizzle all the slices with olive oil, sprinkle with crushed dried chilies, salt, pepper, and thyme, and rub them all in, then reshape. Wrap the foil around to make a packet and bake at 375°F (340°F in fan ovens) for about 40 minutes or until tender.

GOES WITH Chicken, turkey, pork, nuts, chili, cinnamon.

GOOD FOR YOU The orange-fleshed variety of sweet potato is packed with beta carotene.

Swiss chard

see CHARD, *page 279*

Tomato

There are many varieties to choose
from, with colors ranging from red to
orange, yellow, green, and even white,
and shapes ranging from tiny and
round to big and beefy. A tomato is
technically a fruit, but is used and
eaten as a vegetable.

CHOOSE

■ Different varieties are available
all year around. The best flavor is
during the summer months.

■ Look for smooth, firm tomatoes with
healthy-looking, wrinkle-free skin and
a strong tomato smell.

■ When using tomatoes out of season,
cherry or good-quality canned will
give you the best flavor.

■ The type of tomato you need depends
what you want to do with it:

Beefsteak: The biggest tomato with
the meatiest texture. Great for stuffing, broiling, or slicing for salads. To
prepare for stuffing, take a thin slice
off the stalk end, then scoop out the
center with a teaspoon.

Cherry: Small and sweet. Serve whole
or halved in salads. Also good for
pasta sauces and roasting on the vine.

*SWEET
POTATOES*

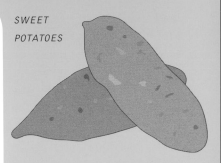

YAM

*A tropical vegetable that is similar
in texture to a potato, but starchier
and much bigger in size. In the
Caribbean, South America, and
Africa it is a staple food, just like
potatoes are in other parts of the
world. In the United States the
orange-fleshed sweet potato is often
referred to as a yam, but it is not
the same thing, although it can be
cooked in much the same way with
similar flavoring partners such as
spices, and nuts. (See sweet potato,
opposite.)*

Green: Green tomatoes can be simply unripe, but there is also a variety which, although green, are ripe and tangy-tasting. They are firm, so are good for slicing and frying, tossed in polenta, to give a crunchy coating. Unripe green tomatoes are too sharp to eat raw, but make great chutney and are good fried for breakfast.

Plum: Oval in shape, its firmness and flavor, plus the fact it has fewer seeds, make it popular for cooking in sauces and stews. You can buy baby plum tomatoes too.

Salad tomato (round): The traditional tomato, this varies in size. A good all-rounder—use in salads and cooking.

Yellow: Subtle in taste, it looks pretty when mixed with other colors in salads, and is good for chutney too.

STORE Best kept at room temperature, as the refrigerator spoils their flavor. If you want to keep ripe tomatoes in the refrigerator, put them in a perforated plastic bag in the vegetable drawer and they will last for up to a week, but take them out of the refrigerator half an hour before serving to bring them to room temperature.

PREPARE Wash them, then remove the stalks. They may be left whole, or may be halved, cut into fourths, sliced, chopped, and seeded and/or skinned.

How to seed: If there is a risk that the seeds and juice could make a dish watery and dilute its flavor—such as in fresh tomato salsa—they need to be removed. The seeds can also add a bitter taste to a dish. To remove them, halve the tomato widthwise if round, lengthwise if oval. If you want to chop the flesh, hold each half cut side down over a bowl and squeeze out the seeds and juice. To keep the shape of the tomato, scoop out the seeds with a teaspoon.

How to skin: Pieces of skin floating around in tomato sauces and other cooked tomato dishes can look unsightly and are not to everybody's taste. To remove the skins, score a cross in the base of the tomato with a sharp knife. Put it into a bowl and pour over enough boiling water to cover it completely. Leave for about 15 seconds for smallish tomatoes, and 30–40 seconds for larger ones, just until the crosses start to peel back and the skin splits. Don't leave them any longer or the tomatoes will start to soften. Lift them out of the hot water with a slotted spoon and plunge into ice water, then drain, and peel back the loosened skins with the tip of a small, sharp knife. Sauces can also be strained after cooking.

tomato

COOK

Broil: Cut in half, drizzle with olive oil, season with salt and pepper, then cook under a hot broiler until they start to soften and brown around the edges. There's no need to turn them over.

Pan-fry: Heat a little oil or butter (or use half oil, half butter) in a skillet. Add thick slices of tomato, season, and fry for a minute or two until starting to brown around the edges. Turn and repeat.

Roast: Drizzle with olive oil and a splash of balsamic vinegar and roast at 400°F (350°F in fan ovens) for about 15 minutes for cherry tomatoes, 15–20 minutes for round, or until they start to burst and soften. Season with salt and pepper.

WAYS TO SERVE

■ Add 2 teaspoons grainy mustard and a handful of snipped chives to an oil and vinegar dressing. Pour over thickly sliced tomatoes and serve as is, or sprinkled with crisply fried bacon.

■ Chop some tomatoes with garlic and pile onto slices of toast. Sprinkle with some torn basil and freshly ground black pepper, and drizzle with olive oil.

■ Arrange halved cherry tomatoes on a large plate, sprinkle with a little finely grated lemon zest and chopped garlic, and drizzle with oil.

MAKE YOUR OWN SUNBLUSH TOMATOES

Roast tomatoes long and slow in the oven and it will be almost as if they had been dried in the Italian sun. If you store them in a jar covered in olive oil, they will keep in the refrigerator for a couple of weeks.

■ *USE FOR: Tossing into pasta and salads, serving with pan-fried chicken or fish, adding one or two to tomato sauces to concentrate the flavor.*

■ *HOW TO DO IT: Use medium-size plum or round tomatoes, cut them in half (cut plum ones lengthwise), then seed. Toss with olive oil, salt and freshly ground pepper, and a pinch of sugar, then lay them cut-side up on a cookie sheet. Bake at 230°F (200°F in fan ovens)—or the lowest setting you have for 4½–5 hours—until chewy but not tough.*

■ Heat 1–2 tablespoons olive oil in a skillet, add some chopped garlic and several chopped tomatoes. Cook for a few minutes until the tomatoes have softened. Add a good handful of basil, then toss with freshly cooked pasta and a spoonful or two of the pasta water to moisten. Sprinkle with toasted pine nuts and drizzle with oil.

GOES WITH Chicken, fish, bacon, cheese, avocado, bell peppers, olive oil, balsamic vinegar, basil, oregano, chives, thyme, garlic, olives.

GOOD FOR YOU Tomatoes are super-healthy, having lots of lycopene which is thought to fight certain cancers and heart disease. Lycopene is even more effective after cooking, so canned tomatoes are excellent too. They also contain lots of vitamins C and A, plus E when eaten raw, and plenty of fiber and beta carotene.

Turnip

Turnips were a major staple food in the West before potatoes became popular. Their skin is creamy white, tinged either purple or pale green, and they have a nutty taste.

CHOOSE

■ Available all year around.

■ The skin should be smooth and without blemishes, and the turnip should feel heavy for its size.

■ Small turnips, about the size of a small apple, have a more delicate flavor than large, which can develop a very strong taste and woody texture.

STORE In a perforated plastic bag in the vegetable drawer of the refrigerator for up to a week.

PREPARE Older turnips need trimming and peeling. Young tiny ones with tender skins need only scrubbing and trimming and can be left whole. Both young and old turnips can be chopped, sliced, diced, or cut into thin batons.

COOK To test when they are done, pierce with a skewer or sharp knife—the tip should go in easily with no resistance.

Boil: Chop into chunks (small turnips into fourths), then put in a pan with a little salt and cover with boiling water. Bring back to a boil and cook for 8–10 minutes or until tender. Drain and serve, or mash or purée with butter and milk or cream.

Roast: Small turnips can be roasted whole, large are best roasted in wedges. Toss with olive oil and pepper, then roast at 400°F (350°F in fan ovens) for 35–45 minutes or until tender. Roasting makes turnips taste sweeter.

Steam: Cubes of turnip should be steamed for 8–12 minutes; young, small, whole turnips take around 30–35 minutes.

WAYS TO SERVE
■ Caramelize drained, boiled turnips by frying with a pat of butter and a little sugar for several minutes.
■ Eat young turnips raw in salads in very thin slices, or grated with a soy-based dressing, or cut in sticks and serve with a dip.

GOES WITH Most roast meats and root vegetables, bacon, cheese, nutmeg, parsley, garlic.

GOOD FOR YOU Turnips have vitamin C, potassium, and calcium.

USE INSTEAD Rutabaga— although this is larger and sweeter and takes longer to cook.

Zucchini

One of the smaller-sized members of the squash family. Zucchini don't have a lot of flavor of their own, but take on other flavors really well—try frying them with olive oil, onion, and garlic, or simmering with tomatoes and other sauce ingredients.

Their vibrant yellow flowers are very popular in Italy where they are served stuffed or deep-fried in a light batter. They are rarely available in supermarkets or grocery stores.

CHOOSE

■ All year around—they tend to be cheaper during the summer.

■ Both green and yellow varieties are available.

■ Look for those that aren't too big (they will be less watery), with shiny, bright, smooth, and firm skin. (Any sign of softness or hollowness in the middle means they will be fibrous.)

■ Allow 1 pound 2 ounces to serve 4 people.

STORE They will keep in the refrigerator for several days, but are best used as soon as possible.

PREPARE Wash, then trim both ends. There is no need to peel them. Choose how you want to cut them:

■ Into round or diagonal slices.

■ Down the length of the zucchini in slim lengthwise strips, then chopped into dice or thin batons.

■ Into ribbons—with a vegetable peeler, shave off thin strips down the length of the zucchini to use in

salads, or drop into boiling water with pasta at the end of cooking. For salads, ribbons taste better when blanched briefly first (see page 11), then plunged into cold water, and drained.

■ Grated for a salad or for use in baking (zucchini helps keep some cake batters moist during cooking).

■ Halve lengthwise through the middle, scoop out the seedy center, then stuff, and bake.

COOK Because zucchini contain a lot of water, steaming, frying, or roasting in the oven are the best ways to cook them. Boiling just makes them more watery. Test they are ready by piercing with a sharp knife—they should be tender-crisp, the color still vibrant.

Stir-fry: Heat a little olive oil in a skillet or wok (or use a mix of butter and oil). Add the sliced zucchini, but don't crowd the skillet—you may need to cook them in batches. Stir-fry, turning occasionally, until golden on both sides.

Roast: Cut the zucchini into chunky pieces, put them in a roasting pan, drizzle with oil, and sprinkle with pepper and herbs. Roast at 400°F (350°F in fan ovens) for 25–35 minutes, or until golden and tender, turning half way through the cooking time.

Steam: For 3–5 minutes depending on their size.

zucchini

WAYS TO SERVE

■ Steam, then toss with olive oil and basil or oregano, or fry and serve with grated Parmesan cheese and freshly ground black pepper.

■ For a salad, toss blanched zucchini ribbons (see left), with an oil and vinegar dressing, some chopped garlic, herbs, and halved cherry tomatoes.

GOES WITH Mozzarella and Parmesan cheeses, eggplant, tomatoes, onions, garlic, herbs such as basil, oregano, parsley.

GOOD FOR YOU Zucchini are mostly made of water, but the seeds give fiber; they also contain some iron and vitamin C, potassium, and beta carotene.

FIX IT: ZUCCHINI

If you have stir-fried zucchini and they are still watery and insipid, toss a handful of dried bread crumbs into the pan. Turn up the heat and they will crisp up the zucchini and remove the sogginess.

FIVE A DAY

Fruit and vegetables are loaded with vitamins, minerals, and fiber and can help reduce the risk of heart disease and some cancers. So if you aim to eat at least five portions a day, it can help keep you healthy.

■ **What is one portion?** The following count as a portion: 2¾ ounces of fresh fruit or vegetables (such as 1 medium apple or banana, 2 satsumas, 3 heaped tablespoons cooked peas, corn, or carrots, 1 cereal size bowl of salad), 3 dried fruits such as apricots, ⅔ cup of pure fruit juice (can only be counted as one of your "five a day" portions, however much you drink). Potatoes cannot be counted as a portion at all, but sweet potatoes can. Beans and other legumes such as garbanzo beans and kidney beans can only be counted as one portion, however much of them you eat.

■ **How can I eat them?** If you include one or two portions of fruit or vegetables in your main meal of the day, a glass of juice between meals, and the occasional piece of fruit or vegetable to snack on during the day, you'll make the five.

The fruits and vegetables can be fresh, frozen, canned, or dried.

■ **Go by color.** It is important to eat a good variety of fruit and vegetables, and choosing ones of different colors will bachieve this. Think of a rainbow of colors to help you—green (e.g. kiwi fruits, broccoli, arugula, and leafy greens), red (e.g. tomatoes, strawberries, bell peppers), blue and purple (e.g. blueberries, grapes, plums, eggplants), orange (e.g. citrus fruits, carrots, bell peppers), yellow (e.g. bananas, pineapple).

■ **What about fruit and vegetables in ready-made meals?** They count, but this type of meal is best served in moderation as the foods themselves can contain a lot of added salt, fat, and sugar.

5

Meat, Poultry, and Game

MEAT

AN IMPORTANT SOURCE OF PROTEIN FOR MOST OF US, MEAT
IS THE MAIN INGREDIENT IN MANY OF THE DISHES WE COOK—
BOTH FOR EVERYDAY MEALS AND SPECIAL OCCASIONS. USING
THE RIGHT CUT FOR A RECIPE OR COOKING METHOD IS ESSEN-
TIAL FOR TENDER, JUICY RESULTS, AND TO ACHIEVE THIS,
TODAY'S LEANER MEATS REQUIRE EXTRA CARE.

CHOOSE

Always buy meat from a reputable
source—a good supermarket, butcher,
farm store, or market, or a tried-and-
tested website that has been recommended to you. It pays to shop around
until you find an outlet you can trust.

Traceability

If you buy from butchers, farm stores,
and markets, they can usually tell you
everything you want to know about
their meat—where it comes from (and
perhaps even what breed it is), the way
it was reared, fed, and slaughtered,
and whether it has been matured and
for how long. Labels on packaged
meat in supermarkets are governed by
law. They will tell you some, but not
all, of these things, so take care to
read them before you buy. To feel reas-
sured about the traceability, quality,
and safety of the meat you are buying,
the more information you get the better. One thing is certain—animals
that have been allowed to feed and
grow as naturally as possible, and
that have been slaughtered without
the stress of a long journey, will provide the best quality meat in terms
of flavor and tenderness.

Buy the best

Cooking meat can be tricky, especially
if you are new to it. Buy good quality
to help insure successful results.

■ Organic meat is expensive, so too
is meat from special breeds. The
quality and flavor will be good, but
they come at a price.

■ Most important is the length of time
that meat has been allowed to mature
after slaughter, as this develops its
flavor and makes it more tender. Meat
bought from a reputable source will
have been matured for the requisite
amount of time for optimum flavor and
tenderness—10–14 days for beef,
8 days for lamb, 4 days for pork.

What to look for

■ Flesh that is moist and a tiny bit sticky, not dry, wet, or slimy.

■ Beef and lamb should be dark red—the color of Bordeaux wine—not bright red. A dark red color indicates that it has been matured, and it will be tender and flavorful. Veal should be a creamy pale pink, pork should be a darker pink.

■ Light marbling (thin streaks of fat) throughout the meat is a good sign. During cooking, these will melt and give the meat succulence and flavor. Meat that is totally lean can be the opposite of this—dry and tasteless.

■ Any fat on the outside of the meat should be firm and creamy white, not yellow. White fat indicates freshness, yellow fat may be rancid or "off."

■ Do not buy meat that looks gray, or that has a greenish tinge—it will be past its best. If you see this in packaged meat, it is a sign that the meat is nearing its use-by date or that there is air inside the wrapping.

SAFE HANDLING

Common sense prevails.

■ Always wash hands, boards, and utensils in hot, soapy water, before and after handling meat.

GOOD FOR YOU

Meat, especially red meat and variety meats, is packed with nutrients:

■ *PROTEIN—essential for growth, good health, and well-being.*

■ *VITAMINS A, D, and B—for healthy eyes, skin, bones, teeth, nerves, and blood cells.*

■ *MINERALS, especially iron and zinc. Iron for healthy red blood cells, zinc for growth, healthy immune and reproductive systems, and skin.*

Many of the important nutrients are found in the lean part of meat, so you can reduce fat content by buying lean cuts or trimming off excess fat without losing nutritional benefits.

■ Never deal with raw and cooked meats together. Ideally, keep a separate board for each.

■ Meat cooks best when it is at room temperature, not taken straight from the refrigerator to the pan or oven. To safeguard against bacteria, especially in summer, remove it from the refrigerator 30–60 minutes before cooking, and keep it covered in a cool place.

■ Leftovers of meat, or dishes containing meat, should be cooled as quickly as possible, then stored, well covered, in the refrigerator for up to 2 days maximum, or they can be frozen. To serve, reheat thoroughly until piping hot in the center (any liquid should be bubbling) and eat straightaway. Frozen leftovers should be thawed slowly—in the refrigerator—before reheating. Do not reheat meat leftovers more than once.

STORE

Always keep meat in the refrigerator.

■ Remove all wrappings and, before throwing them away, check for any use-by dates. The exception to this is vacuum-packed meat, which should be kept in its original wrapping—the storage time should be given on the label, or ask the butcher.

■ Place unwrapped meat in a sealed container in the bottom of the refrigerator, so that it cannot touch or drip onto other foods, and keep raw meat away from cooked meat.

■ Fresh meat will keep for up to 2 days, unless it is ground meat or variety meats, which are best cooked within 24 hours.

■ Do not eat meat that smells high or "off."

Freezing

Meat freezes well, provided it is very fresh when it goes in the freezer.

■ To prevent ice crystals from forming in the meat, which will spoil its texture, freeze small amounts at a time, and prepare the freezer by switching it to fast-freeze or super-freeze beforehand (consult the manufacturer's handbook for timings and amounts).

■ Wrap tightly, excluding all air. If not properly wrapped, meat will get freezer burn (see page 26).

■ Double wrap bones before freezing, to stop them piercing the packaging.

■ Wrap chops, steaks, and scallops individually, or separate them with film or foil, so that they do not freeze together and you can take them out singly as required.

■ Store ground meat in the freezer for up to 3 months, small cuts up to 6 months, and roasts and large cuts up to 9 months.

store–prepare

■ Always thaw frozen meat before cooking, either slowly (in its wrappings on a plate in the bottom of the refrigerator) or quickly in the microwave, and cook it as soon as possible after thawing.

■ Never refreeze raw meat after it has thawed, but if you cook it after thawing, it is safe to refreeze.

PREPARE

Sometimes meat needs a little help before cooking, to improve both its flavor and texture. The simpler the technique, the better.

MARINATING

Flavor and juiciness are given to meat by marinating (see also Terms and Techniques, page 31), which can help tenderize it too. It is ideal for lean, boneless meat like steaks and scallops, for cubes that are to be cooked by dry heat such as broiling or grilling, and for tough cuts on or off the bone that will be pot roasted, braised, or stewed.

■ To marinate meat, coat or steep it in olive oil or plain yogurt with lemon juice or wine vinegar, herbs and/or spices and other flavorings. Fresh pineapple and papaya contain enzymes that help tenderize, so for tough cuts, mix in the juice from these into the marinade (see pages 31 and 242).

FRESH VERSUS FROZEN

There is nothing wrong with commercially frozen meat, but its texture when cooked is never so good as that of fresh meat. This is because there are so many factors that can affect it—its original quality (which you have no control over), how it was frozen and stored, and how you thaw it. Getting this combination right is tricky, so it is easy to see why frozen meat is not always on a par with fresh. If you freeze meat yourself at home (see opposite), you will have more control over the process.

POUNDING

This tenderizes meat by breaking down tough connective tissue, and it also makes the meat thinner so it will cook more quickly. It is good for lean, boneless meat like steaks, scallops, and tenderloin.

■ To pound meat, cover with plastic wrap and bash with a meat bat or rolling pin (or the base of a heavy pan). Don't be too heavy-handed or you will tear the meat, and try to keep it the same thickness throughout so that it will cook evenly.

Roasting times for meat

It is impossible to be entirely accurate with roasting times because individual ovens vary, and no two pieces of meat are exactly the same. Also bear in mind that bones are good conductors of heat, so cuts on the bone cook slightly more quickly than boneless cuts.

Whether the cut is on or off the bone, preheat the oven, and start by roasting at 400°F (350°F in fan ovens) for the first 15 minutes, then continue at 350°F (325°F in fan ovens) for the remainder of the time given below.

Beef	RARE	15 minutes per 1 pound + 15 minutes
	MEDIUM	20 minutes per 1 pound + 20 minutes
	WELL-DONE	25 minutes per 1 pound + 25 minutes
Veal	MEDIUM	20 minutes per 1 pound + 20 minutes
Lamb	RARE	15 minutes per 1 pound + 15 minutes
	MEDIUM	20 minutes per 1 pound + 20 minutes
	WELL-DONE	25 minutes per 1 pound + 25 minutes
Pork	MEDIUM	20 minutes per 1 pound + 20 minutes
	WELL-DONE	25 minutes per 1 pound + 25 minutes

roasting

How to roast a cut of meat

When buying a roast on the bone, allow 8–12 ounces per person, raw weight; for boneless cuts, allow 6–8 ounces per person, raw weight. Cuts of meat do not always come with cooking instructions, but roasting is one of the easiest of cooking techniques, so you do not have to consult a recipe. Check the weight of the roast and calculate the cooking time according to the chart (see opposite). If you are going to stuff the meat, weigh it after stuffing.

■ Meat should be at room temperature when it goes into the oven, so take it out of the refrigerator some 30–60 minutes before cooking.

■ Just before roasting, massage the roast with vegetable oil or olive oil, sea salt, and freshly ground black pepper, plus any other spices, rubs, or seasonings you like.

■ Baste frequently during roasting, unless it is a pork roast with cracklings (see page 347).

■ After taking the meat out of the oven, cover it loosely with foil and let it rest for 15–20 minutes. This will make carving easier and allow you time to make gravy and cook the vegetables.

TIPS AND TRICKS: SEASONING MEAT

Do not season meat until just before cooking. Salt draws out moisture, so if you sprinkle salt over meat and leave it for a while before cooking, the juices will be drawn out and the cooked meat will be dry.

HOW DO YOU KNOW THE ROAST IS COOKED?

Pierce the meat in its thickest part (away from any bones) with a metal skewer, and leave it there for about 30 seconds. When you take the skewer out, the tip should feel warm for rare meat, fairly hot for medium, and very hot for well-done.

For greater accuracy, use a meat thermometer (see page 58) to check the internal temperature of the meat. Beef and lamb can be cooked rare, but veal and pork should be either medium or well-done.

TEMPERATURES SHOULD BE:

■ *RARE*   *140°F*

■ *MEDIUM*   *160°F*

■ *WELL-DONE*   *175°F*

BEEF

American beef has long been renowned, and some states like Texas are almost synonymous with cattle rearing. Most cuts come ready-prepared for cooking. The only thing you may need to do is trim off excess fat, but be careful not to trim off too much—fat is good for basting and keeping the meat moist.

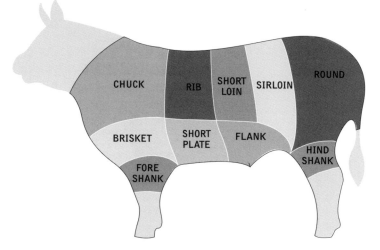

CUTS FOR ROASTING

Top-quality, tender meat is best for roasting. For temperatures and times, see the roasting chart on page 332.

Rib, on the bone

■ The classic cut for a roast, this looks like huge chops joined together. There are two types, wing rib and fore rib. The wing rib contains the sirloin, has three bones, and will serve 6–8 people. The fore rib has four bones and will serve 8–10 people, but is often halved to give two roasts, each serving 4–6.

■ For easy carving, rib joints must be chined (see page 16).

■ Rib is tender and full of flavor, but expensive. The natural layer of fat and the marbling in the meat make it extremely succulent.

Rib, boned and rolled

■ Fore rib that has been boned, rolled, and tied with a layer of fat on top makes an easy-carve roast.

■ This is the same quality meat as rib on the bone (left), but more expensive. Don't overcook or it may be dry.

Rump roast

■ A boneless, good-quality, good-value roast of lean meat. Usually sold tied with a layer of fat to prevent dryness.
■ Has good flavor and succulence, and very little waste. Best served rare or medium, as well-done can be dry.

Sirloin

■ A rolled and tied boneless roast from the wing rib, with a light marbling of fat through the meat. It has a natural layer of fat on top that bastes the meat during roasting and helps keep it moist.
■ Easy-to-carve, lean meat with lots of flavor and little waste. Dearer than rib.

Tenderloin

■ The thick end cut from a whole tenderloin makes a neat, easy-to-carve, plump cut. For 4–6 people buy a piece weighing 3–4 pounds. A château-briand serves 2 people (see page 15).
■ Tenderloin is very expensive, lean meat with a good flavor. The best is deep red with a marbling of fat. It is meltingly tender, especially when served rare, with little or no waste.

BEEF STOCK

Makes 10–12½ cups and keeps in the refrigerator for up to 3 days, or in the freezer for up to 3 months.

3 pounds beef bones, chopped into pieces by the butcher
2 onions, cut into fourths
2 carrots, cut into fourths
2 celery stalks, cut into large pieces
1 large bouquet garni (see page 129)
10 peppercorns
4¼ quarts water

Preheat the oven to 425°F (400°F in fan ovens). Place the bones in a roasting pan and roast for 30 minutes. Add the vegetables and roast for 20 minutes more. Transfer everything to a stockpot or large pan. Skim the fat from the juices in the roasting pan, then stir 1 cup boiling water into the juices that are left and pour into the stockpot. Add the rest of the ingredients and bring to a boil. Half cover and simmer very gently for 4–5 hours, skimming occasionally and topping up with water as necessary. Strain and cool, then refrigerate or freeze.

CUTS FOR
POT ROASTING

Less tender cuts that are not suitable for roasting can be pot roasted—boned, rolled, and tied cuts are best. Pat the meat dry with paper towels and season, then sear in hot oil until browned. Put in a pan with 1 pound browned, chopped onions, celery, and root vegetables and 1¼ cups liquid (stock, wine, or beer). Cover and cook slowly on the stove, or in the oven at 325°F (275°F in fan ovens). A 3-pound pot roast takes about 2½ hours and serves 6 people.

Brisket

■ Quite fatty, but with a good flavor.
■ The fat melts during cooking to give tasty meat that is easy to carve.

Pot roast

■ A similar cut to top round, but very slightly tougher.
■ Needs slow cooking to become tender.

Top round

■ Very lean meat with no marbling. Usually tied with an additional layer of fat.
■ Good flavor with little waste. Cook gently and slowly to avoid dryness.

CUTS FOR STEWS
AND CASSEROLES

For a casserole or stew to serve 4–6 people, you will require about 1½–2 pounds meat. Brown it in hot oil, then cook gently in a covered pan, with 1 pound browned, chopped onions, celery, and root vegetables and 1¼ cups liquid—stock or water, with added beer or wine according to taste. Cooking can be done on the stove top, or in the oven at 325°F (275°F in fan ovens), and the usual timing is 2–3 hours.

Braising steak

■ Boneless meat, usually slices of chuck, although top round can also be used. The ideal thickness for slices is ¾ inch, or you can cut the meat into 2-inch cubes.
■ Tender and full of flavor when cooked slowly.

Stewing steak

■ This boneless beef may be shank from the foreleg or from the hindquarter, cut into 1–2-inch cubes.
■ Connective tissue that is visible in the raw meat breaks down during cooking to produce tender meat and rich gravy.

STEAKS FOR QUICK COOKING

All steaks (except for braising, stewing, and ground steak) can be charbroiled, broiled, grilled, or pan-fried (see right). Steak is also good cut against the grain into strips or cubes for sautés and stir-fries. Cooking time for these is about 2–4 minutes, from rare to medium.

Fillet steak

■ A round slice from the tenderloin, usually 1–2 inches thick. Expensive, prime-quality meat.
■ Very lean and very tender, with no waste. Best served rare.

Sirloin steak

■ Boneless cut from above the fillet. About 1 inch thick, with a thin border of fat. If part of the tenderloin is included and it is left on the bone, this is a T-bone steak. A porterhouse is on the bone from the rib end of the sirloin, and rib steaks or entrecôte are sirloin steaks cut from between the ribs. The New York strip, sometimes called shell steak is taken from the porterhouse area of the sirloin.
■ Lean, tender and flavorsome, with little waste. Good cooked any way, from rare to well-done.

HOW DO YOU LIKE YOUR STEAK COOKED?

For charbroiling, broiling, or grilling, insure the pan, broiler, or grill is very hot first. Lightly oil the steak and season with salt and pepper. For pan-frying, heat 1–2 table-spoons oil in a heavy skillet and sea-son the meat just before cooking.

Cook the steak according to the times given below, turning once. Timings are approximate, for a steak cut about 1–2 inches thick. Fillet steak takes the least time, round steak the most. For success when pan-frying, don't overcrowd the pan. Keep the steak flat by gently pressing down on it with a metal spatula.

After cooking, let the steak rest for a few minutes before serving so that it is juicier and easier to cut.

■ *BLUE (bleu) or very rare: 1–1½ minutes each side*
■ *RARE (saignant): 1½–2 minutes each side*
■ *MEDIUM RARE: 2–2½ minutes each side*
■ *MEDIUM (à point): 2½–3 minutes each side*
■ *WELL DONE (bien cuit): 3–3½ minutes each side (to prevent charring, turn the heat down after the initial searing on each side)*

MEAT:BEEF | VEAL

Rib eye steak

- The "eye" of the meat from the fore rib, about 1–1½ inches thick.
- Cheaper than sirloin and fillet. Marbled with fat, so tender and juicy with lots of flavor.

Round steak

- Large, boneless slices of quality meat, with a thick border of fat. Usually about 1 inch thick.
- Not quite so tender as other steaks, but has a good "beefy" flavor and firm texture.
- Can be fatty, so trim before or after cooking.

VEAL

The meat from calves that are no more then a year old, veal is lean and tender and requires careful cooking. Highly prized, white veal—actually very pale pink— is from milk-fed animals under three months old. Pink veal, comes from grass-fed animals aged about four or five months old. The most commonly available and cheapest veal, sometimes called gray veal, is from older animals that may have been more intensively reared, but not invariably.

THE BEST CUT FOR ROASTING

For temperatures and times, see the roasting chart on page 332.

Loin

Other cuts can be roasted, but this is the most readily available and will give good results.

- Prime-quality meat with a thin layer of fat sold boned, rolled, and tied.
- Very lean meat, so the roast is best stuffed and wrapped in bacon, or smothered in butter (seasoned with herbs, spices, or mustard), to give flavor and succulence.

CUTS FOR QUICK COOKING

Loin chops

- Lean, tender meat on the bone, with a border of fat. They look rather like pork loin chops, only larger and thicker.
- Pan-fry or broil, 6–7 minutes on each side.

Scallops

- Slices of lean meat, usually cut from the leg or rump, pounded very thin.

■ Pan-fry in hot oil (or oil and butter) for 2–3 minutes each side, coated in egg and bread crumbs to make schnitzels. Scallops are also good cut into strips for sautées and stir-fries—the cooking time will be 3–4 minutes in total.

CUTS FOR SLOW COOKING

Cubes

■ Sometimes called "pie veal," these are boneless pieces cut from the shoulder, leg, or neck that require long, gentle cooking to become tender. They can be quite fatty, but this is good as the fat breaks down during cooking and helps make the meat moist. Use in casseroles (especially goulash), for braising and stews, and in pies.

Osso bucco

■ Thick slices of shank, with a round bone in the middle. Most often used for the braised Italian dish of the same name.

■ With long, gentle cooking in liquid, osso bucco becomes the most tender and succulent of all the veal cuts, and the marrow in the center of the bone (see right) is a delicacy.

MARROW

The marrow in the center of osso buco bones melts during long, slow cooking. In Italy it is highly prized in the stew of the same name, with diners traditionally saving it until last and eating it with a spoon. You can buy beef marrowbones from the butcher (they may have to be ordered) and extract the marrow to serve as a garnish for broiled meat, or to eat on garlic toast with salt. Ask the butcher for pieces of marrowbone cut about 3 inches thick, and dig out the marrow from the center with a teaspoon or small, sharp knife. Poach in lightly salted water for 2 minutes, then drain, and serve.

LAMB

Good-quality lamb is available all year around. The season for lamb starts around Easter, and continues into fall and early winter. Chilled fresh imported lamb may then take over in the winter months. Bear in mind that the size of the cuts varies according to the time of year—small in spring, getting larger until fall. Welsh and French salt marsh lamb are especially prized for their flavor. They are expensive, but worth it.

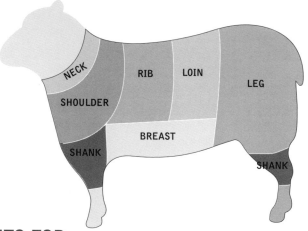

CUTS FOR ROASTING

There is a good choice of different cuts for roasting, but they can be quite fatty. Trim well before cooking and remove any skin. For temperatures and times, see the roasting chart on page 332.

Breast

■ Inexpensive, thin cut from the breast, sold boned, rolled, and tied. There is a high proportion of fat, so check that the meat has been well trimmed before buying.
■ Excellent flavor and succulence. To make the meat go further and counteract fattiness, slow roast or pot roast with a fruity stuffing.

Leg

■ A favorite for roasting, although expensive. A whole, bone-in leg weighing about 5 pounds will feed 6 and a 6–7½-pound leg will feed 8. Often the leg is halved into two smaller roasts—

the fillet end (top of the leg) and shank end (the bottom), each of which serves 4 people. Legs are also sold part-boned or boned, rolled, and tied. A "butter-flied" leg has been boned and opened out. It can be rolled and tied for roasting (with or without a stuffing).

■ Prime-quality, lean meat that is tender and flavorful with little waste. The fillet end is more tender, although the shank end has a very good flavor.

■ When buying a leg, ask the butcher to loosen or remove the aitchbone to make carving easier, and to saw through the shank bone and fold it under so the roast will fit in the oven.

GUARD OF HONOR

Loin

■ Sold on the bone (chined), or boned, rolled, and tied. Boneless roasts are good for stuffing and easy carving. A whole loin will serve 2–3 people.

■ Good-quality meat with a layer of fat, that is succulent and full of flavor, with little waste. A good compromise between lean leg and fattier shoulder, for quality and price.

CROWN ROAST

Rib

■ Also called rack of lamb. This consists of six to nine rib chops joined together. One rack serves 2–3 people. When the bones are scraped clean, it may be described as a French rack, or French-trimmed. Two racks with bones interlocked to form an arch shape are called a guard of honor (see page 341) and a crown roast is when two racks are tied in a ring (see page 341).

■ Prime-quality, juicy nuggets of meat form the "eye" of each chop.

■ Expensive, but easy to cook and carve if the backbone has been chined (see page 16)—just slice between the bones.

Rump

■ A small roast for 1–2 people, from between the loin and the leg. Often sold boned and tied.

■ Good value, with little waste. Tender, flavorsome meat that is easy to carve.

Saddle

■ Two loins joined by the backbone. Best bought boned so that it can be stuffed and rolled for easy carving.

■ A large, expensive roast for a special occasion—a whole saddle will serve 8–10 people. Remove excess fat before stuffing and rolling to get juicy, tender, flavorsome meat with no waste.

Shoulder

■ A whole shoulder should serve about 5–6 people. It is often halved and sold

as two roasts (the blade and the shank end) each of which will serve 3–4. A boned, rolled, and stuffed shoulder will serve 6–8.

■ Has quite a lot of fat, which gives it succulence and flavor. A well-trimmed boned roast is best for stuffing and easy carving with little waste. Some boned roasts are sold rolled, others are tied into pillow-shaped roasts.

CUTS FOR QUICK COOKING

Prime-quality chops and boneless meat can be broiled, pan-fried, charbroiled, or grilled. Cooking instructions are the same as for steaks (see page 337).

Butterflied leg

■ A whole boneless leg, cut so that it has flaps on either side like butterfly wings. It will serve 5–6 people.

■ Flavorsome meat with little fat. Juicy and tender if not overcooked—broil or grill for 30 minutes maximum, turning once, then let rest for 10–15 minutes. Cut across into thick slices to serve—there will be no waste.

Leg chops

■ Meaty slices, cut about ¾ inch thick, from the loin end of the leg. They are

rib–loin chops

available both on and off the bone. Boneless chops sometimes have quite a thick border of fat along the top.
■ Good flavor, but the meat can sometimes be chewy and there is quite a lot of fat. Cook for 3–4 minutes each side or, better still if time allows, braise (see page 12).

Leg steaks
■ Large slices cut from the top of the leg, sometimes with a piece of bone left in, surrounded by a thin layer of fat. A good thickness is 1–1½ inches; if they are any thinner than this they will be dry.
■ Lean meat with a good flavor, firm texture and no waste. Undercook for succulence, allowing about 3 minutes each side. Can also be cut into strips for sautéing or stir-frying.

Loin chops
■ A large nugget of meat on the bone, with a flap of meat and fat attached. Double loin chops are cut across the saddle, so they have a central bone (they are also called butterfly chops because of their shape). Noisettes and medallions are made from boneless loin that is rolled and surrounded with fat, tied neatly with string, and then cut into rounds.

TIPS AND TRICKS: KABOBS
When threading cubes of meat onto skewers for kabobs, push the cubes as close together as possible. This helps prevent them from overcooking and drying out.

■ Lean, tender meat that has just enough fat to be self-basting, which helps make the chops juicy. As they are usually quite thick, 1½–2 inches, they take 5 minutes each side to cook.
■ Medallions and noisettes are very easy to eat and have hardly any waste.

Rib chops

■ An "eye" of meat attached to a long, curved bone surrounded with fat. Usually cut quite thin. Look best when they are French-trimmed.
■ Juicy, tender and flavorsome, especially when rare—cook for just 2–3 minutes each side. Allow 2–3 rib chops per person.

Tenderloin

■ Expensive, lean meat sold in long, thin pieces; each one weighs about 10 ounces and will serve 2 people. It is the "eye" of the loin.
■ Can be cooked whole, or cut length-wise and opened out (butterflied). It can also be cubed for kabobs, or sliced and pounded for scallops, sautés, or stir-fry strips.
■ Juicy and tender, with little waste. A whole or butterflied tenderloin takes 10–15 minutes to cook, kabobs take 6–8 minutes, scallops and strips 2–3 minutes each side.

CUTS FOR SLOW COOKING

Gentle braising or stewing suits lamb well. Prime, lean cuts benefit from the extra moisture that slow cooking brings, and fattier, tougher cuts become meltingly tender. For 4–6 people, you will need 1½–2 pounds meat. Brown the meat in hot oil first, then cook with around 1 pound browned, chopped onions, celery, and root vegetables, and 1¼ cups liquid. Cook on the stove top or in the oven at 325°F (275°F in fan ovens) for 2–3 hours, or until tender.

Leg

■ Whole or half legs, or boneless cubes. Can be braised as a piece on the bone, or boned and cubed for casseroles, stews, curries, hotch-potch, navarins, and tagines.
■ Lean meat with very little fat, can be dry and chewy—so it is important not to overcook.

Leg chops

■ Slices on or off the bone are good for braising.
■ Meat has enough fat to make it tasty and tender. With long, slow cooking, the fat melts off, leaving little waste.

Neck

■ Neck slices tend to be quite thick, fatty chunks on the bone. Slices from the middle of the neck are less fatty and may be sold on or off the bone. Boneless middle neck comes either as one long piece, or cut into cubes.

■ Fatty slices need trimming before cooking, so there is some waste. They make good stews, which should be chilled and degreased (see page 20) before serving. Middle neck slices are juicy and tender—use on the bone for hotch-potch, or as boneless cubes for curries, casseroles, and tagines.

Shank

■ The lower part from the foreleg, on the bone. Allow 1 shank per person.

■ Very tender, gelatinous meat that literally falls off the bone when slow cooked in liquid. Full of flavor, with little waste. Cubes can be stewed.

Shoulder

■ Whole or half cuts on the bone, or boned and rolled. Also diced meat. Needs excess fat trimmed off before cooking, so some wastage.

■ Has enough marbled fat to make it juicy and tender. Cuts are good for pot roasts, cubes for casseroles and curries.

MUTTON

Meat from sheep that are over 2 years old is usually described as mutton. You can order it from your butcher or mail order over the web.

■ *If it has been properly matured, mutton has an excellent flavor, and is worth seeking out. The cuts are similar to those of lamb, but they must be cooked slowly to become tender.*

■ *Cuts, chops, and meat on the bone can be pot roasted, chops and boneless cubes can be used in casseroles and stews—they are especially good in curries.*

PORK

Most pigs are bred leaner than they used to be, which is good from a health point of view, but traditional breeds often have a good amount of fat. They also take longer to fatten and so tend to acquire more flavor. Both are equally good, but for succulence and flavor, lean meat needs careful cooking.

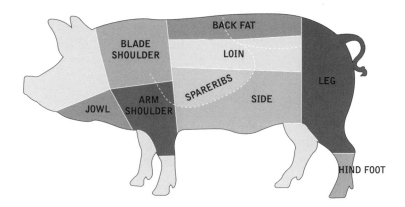

CUTS FOR ROASTING

Roast pork should not be served rare or underdone—for temperatures and times, see the chart on page 332. Check that the juices run clear, not pink, from the middle of the roast. If using a meat thermometer, the internal temperature should be at least 160°F.

Leg

■ Expensive prime-quality meat with rind, best bought boned and rolled, or tied into shape with string. Whole legs are huge and rarely cooked at home,

so legs are usually cut into 3–3½-pound roasts to serve 4–6.
■ Lean and tender, easy-carve meat with good flavor and little waste. Do not overcook.

Leg—loin end

■ From the rump, between the loin and the leg. Sold on the bone, or boned and rolled. Good amount of marbling and fat under the rind, and moderately priced.
■ The meat is quite succulent with little wastage, although slightly difficult to carve into neat slices.

leg–shoulder

Loin

■ Prime-quality meat, with little waste. Sold on the bone as a rack like a row of chops (sometimes French trimmed), or boned and rolled, with or without rind.

■ Lean, tender and flavorsome, with just enough fat to be self-basting. Racks on the bone should be chined (see page 16) and any rind scored so you can slice easily between the chops. Rolled roasts carve easily with minimal waste, but have little room for stuffing.

Ribs

■ Country-style rib bones, also called spare ribs (not to be confused with sparerib chops and steaks, see page 349). Usually sold cut into ribs, but can be joined in a sheet.

■ Inexpensive. If necessary, separate bones by chopping between them. Tasty meat that becomes tender-sweet and crisp when simmered in stock, and then roasted.

Shoulder

■ Huge piece of meat that can serve 15–20 people, but usually cut into three pieces—spare rib, blade, and hand. All can be bought on the bone, with rind, but are difficult to carve,

HOW TO GET CRISP CRACKLINGS

Crisping the rind on pork during roasting can be rather hit-and-miss. A lot depends on the animal itself, but there are a few things you can do to increase your chances of success.

■ *Score the rind at about ¼-inch intervals. Ask your butcher to do the scoring, or do it yourself with a very sharp knife or a scalpel. Work from the middle of the roast out to one side, then from the middle out to the other side—you will find this much easier than trying to score in a continuous line.*

■ *Make sure the rind is absolutely dry before cooking by wiping and patting it with paper towels or a dish towel.*

■ *Rub the rind with a little vegetable oil, then with salt.*

■ *Roast according to the chart on page 332, but do not baste at all during roasting. The drier the rind during roasting, the better.*

■ *If the cracklings are not crisp at the end of the cooking time, turn the oven up to its hottest temperature for about 10 minutes.*

■ *If this doesn't work, you can try crisping up the crackling with a blowtorch, or lifting it off the meat and popping it under a hot broiler.*

so boned, or boned, rolled, and tied roasts are better. Spare rib is the most useful size to serve 6–8 people, while blade is rather smaller and will serve 4–6. Hand is the cheapest of the three. It is a very large cut, best slow-cooked. Some butchers use it for sausage links and ground meat.

■ Price-wise, shoulder is good value compared to leg and loin and, as the meat is fattier, it tends to be juicier and sweeter.

Side

■ The cheapest cut. Comes as a large rectangle of fatty, streaky meat containing rib bones and topped with rind. Best bought boned as a whole piece or in slices, or boned, rolled, and tied.
■ Well trimmed of fat and slow roasted, side is sweet and tasty, with melt-in-the-mouth succulence.

Tenderloin

■ Very lean, boneless, prime-quality pork without fat or rind. Looks like a thick sausage. Weighs between 12 ounces and 1 pound, enough to serve 2–3 people. It is expensive, but needs little trimming, so there is virtually no waste.
■ Tender, but can be dry and bland. Best wrapped in bacon or prosciutto

to protect and moisten during roasting, or butterflied and stuffed, then wrapped or tied. Do not overcook.

CUTS FOR QUICK COOKING

Prime, tender pork such as chops, scallops, and steaks can be broiled, pan-fried, charbroiled or grilled. Cooking instructions are the same as for steaks (see page 337).

Leg chops/ steaks

■ From the rump end of the leg. Usually boneless and rindless. Best cut 1–1½ inches thick.
■ Lean, flavorsome, and moderately priced. Trim off any fat for healthy cooking and cook for 6–8 minutes each side. Do not overcook.

Loin chops/ steaks

■ The most familiar looking of the pork chops, with a large eye of meat on the bone, usually bordered by a layer of fat and rind. Occasionally the kidney is included. Loin steaks are simply the chop with the bone and rind removed.

■ Lean meat that needs careful cooking or it can be dry. Trim off any fat and rind for healthy cooking and cook no longer than 6–8 minutes each side. Steak meat can be drier than chop meat as the bone helps keep the meat moist. It can be cut into strips against the grain for stir-frying—cooking time is 4–5 minutes.

Sparerib chops/steaks

■ Sometimes called shoulder chops/steaks, because this is the part of the animal they come from. Untidy-looking, with seams of fat running through. The chops have a bone along one side, the steaks are boneless.

■ Inexpensive, juicy, and full of flavor. Cook for 6–8 minutes each side.

Tenderloin

■ Boneless meat is cut crosswise into round slices to make medallions and noisettes. When these are pounded flat, they are called scallops.

■ Very lean and tender meat with no rind and no fat, so no waste. Cook for 2–4 minutes each side. Can be cut into strips for sautés and stir-fries, which will cook even more rapidly.

SUCKLING PIG

You can buy a whole suckling pig by mail order or from the butcher —it makes an unusual roast (and a good talking point) for a special occasion. Suckling pigs, correctly called sucking pigs, are piglets that have been fed on nothing more than their mother's milk. The meat is pale and sweet-tasting, and very tender. The usual weight is about 7½–10 pounds, which is enough to feed 12 people and will just about fit in a standard oven (you may need to lay it diagonally in the roasting pan), or it can be grilled on a spit. Look in Spanish, Portuguese, and Italian cookbooks for recipes.

CUTS FOR SLOW COOKING

Pork is a lean meat with no marbling of fat in the way that you find with beef and lamb. Marinating and cooking with vegetables and liquid help make it moist—use the slow cooking instructions for lamb on page 344.

Leg

■ Boned meat is sold diced for casseroles, curries, and stews.

■ Good and lean. Keep the heat low and do not overcook or the meat can be dry.

Leg chops/ steaks

■ From the rump end of the animal, a lean meat with enough fat to make it moist and flavorsome.

■ Trim off the rind and excess fat before cooking. Chops are good braised, steaks can be cut into cubes for casseroles and curries.

Loin

■ Boned and rolled loin, chops on the bone, and boneless steaks.

■ Very lean. To counteract any dryness, look for a good covering of fat between the rind and the meat. Braising with vegetables and liquid is a good way to make sure the loin is moist and tender.

Shoulder

■ On the bone, or boned and rolled cuts (either the spare rib or hand).

■ Meat becomes sweet and succulent when pot roasted or braised. Skim off excess fat or degrease (see page 20) before serving.

Side

■ Comes as a slab of the belly, or boned, rolled, and tied as a roast. Also sold as thick slices, cut crosswise from a boned slab.

■ A fatty cut that is tender, moist, and full of flavor. It is at its best when slow-roasted.

■ Trim off the rind and excess fat before cooking.

Sparerib

■ Chops and steaks (not to be confused with country-style ribs).

■ Fatty meat is the best pork for braising on or off the bone, and for casseroles, curries, and stews when boned and cubed. Degrease the dish (see page 20) before serving.

spare ribs

BACON

Bacon is pork that has been cured, with either a wet or a dry cure.

■ When pork is wet cured it is steeped in brine—a mixture of salt and water.

■ Dry-cured pork is rubbed with a mixture of salt and sugar.

■ After curing, bacon can be left as it is, in which case it is called unsmoked, or it can be smoked. Unsmoked bacon is paler in color and milder in flavor than smoked, which can often taste quite salty.

CHOOSE

There are many different cures, and it is a matter of personal taste which you choose to buy.

■ Dry-cured bacon gives less shrinkage and wastage than wet-cured, and slices will be more crispy.

■ It is easy to see when bacon is fresh—it looks bright pink, and damp, not dark, discolored, or dry. When checking for freshness, look at the fat as well as the meat—it should be white or creamy white, not yellow, greasy, or curling at the edges.

■ Wet, sticky, smelly, or slimy bacon is not good, so do not buy it.

STORE

All bacon must be kept in the refrigerator, and storage times on any

CAUL

If you see this at the butchers, you may wonder what it is—it looks like lacy fabric. In fact, it is the membrane that surrounds a hog's stomach, used in cooking for wrapping meat to help keep it together and make it moist.

■ *Two sheets of caul are enough to wrap most cuts of meat, or up to 8 burgers, sausages, or patties (crépinettes in French).*

■ *Soak for a few minutes in cold water, then lift out gently, and lay flat on a board.*

■ *Wrap meat in one piece of caul, then double wrap with the second piece to cover any tears or holes.*

■ *Roast, fry, broil, or grill in the usual way—the caul will melt and disappear.*

packaging should not be exceeded. If bacon slices are bought loose, keep them in an airtight container or wrapped in foil—unsmoked will keep for up to 7 days, smoked for up to 10 days. Large pieces of bacon, raw or cooked, will keep fresh for up to 3 days. Vacuum-packed bacon freezes well, for up to 2 months.

PREPARE

Mild-cured and unsmoked pieces of bacon need no preparation, but if you buy smoked bacon it will need soaking before cooking to remove excess salt (if in doubt, soak it anyway).

■ To soak a piece of bacon, put it in a large bowl or pan and cover with fresh cold water. Leave overnight in a cold place (the refrigerator is best). Drain, then cover with fresh water if the bacon is to be boiled, or dry it thoroughly with paper towels if it is to be baked or roasted.

■ Bacon slices can be trimmed of any rind and excess fat with scissors, either before or after cooking, if you prefer them without.

COOK
Large pieces

These can be boiled and/or roasted, according to individual cuts and recipes. Boiling times are calculated at 20 minutes per pound, plus 20 minutes, roasting is best at 350°F (325°F in fan ovens), allowing 30 minutes per pound, plus 30 minutes. Let all pieces rest for about 15–20 minutes before serving.

■ **Arm shoulder**, is an economical cut that is usually divided in two and sold boned and rolled. Prime shoulder is a large cut, while end of shoulder is about half the size. Both are good for boiling and braising.

■ **Hock** comes in various sizes, including the knuckle end, all cut from the front leg of the pig. This is the best cut for soups (especially split pea and ham), when the meat is stripped from the bone and diced or shredded. It is also good in casseroles and stews.

■ **Cured ham**, from the hind leg of the pig, comes in three sizes. The largest, prime-quality cut is the hock (knuckle end), the one for boiling and baking, and serving as ham on the bone, traditional at celebrations. Middle ham, from the top end of the leg, is a lean and meaty cut that is sold on the bone or boned and rolled. It is good, lean meat that can be boiled and baked, braised, or roasted (it is also cut into steaks and slices—the one for "ham and eggs"). Corner ham is a small boneless cut from the top of the leg that is corner-shaped, hence its name. Its lean meat is good boiled or roasted and served hot or cold.

cuts–slices

Slices

There are three different types, all of which are sold with or without rind. They come from the middle (the back and the side) of the hog, and are suitable for broiling or frying. Cooking time is 2–3 minutes per side, longer if you like it crispy.

■ **Bacon** from the loin—the leanest, meatiest, and most expensive cut. It comes with varying degrees of fat— look for the leanest—and is the one for big cooked breakfasts and bacon, lettuce, and tomato sandwiches.

■ **Middle cut bacon** is two in one— back and side together—and is a useful cut as you can divide it into back and side, according to your needs. It is sold as long slices or slices from a rolled cut. Rolled slices look good on the breakfast plate.

■ **Bacon** from the side is the fattiest cut, but also often the tastiest. It is an inexpensive alternative to bacon from the back for breakfast, and is good for making BLTs. You can also use it for wrapping around lean meat and delicate fish (pork tenderloin, turkey, chicken, and monkfish) to flavor and moisten. Bacon cut from the side is also used to line pans and to make lardons (see right).

TIPS AND TRICKS: CURED HAM STEAKS

To prevent curling during cooking, snip the edge of ham steaks and slices at right angles with scissors.

TIPS AND TRICKS: BACON

■ *Use rindless fatty bacon to line pans and molds for pâtés and terrines. Before lining, stretch the slices by pressing them with the flat side of a large knife blade. This makes a little bacon go a long way.*

PANCETTA AND LARDONS

Pancetta is Italian for cured pork side. You can buy it in straight or round slices, or diced. Lardon is the French word for diced bacon.

■ *Pancetta slices can be used in place of fatty bacon—you may prefer their milder, sweeter flavor. They come both smoked and unsmoked, and can be quite fatty.*

■ *Diced pancetta and lardons are interchangeable in recipes. Sold in packets, they are quite expensive. It's cheaper to dice slices yourself, although the meat will not be as thick. Use for flavoring and adding protein to soups, stews, stuffings, casseroles, quiches, risottos, pasta sauces, salads, pizzas, and omelets.*

SAUSAGES

Size, shape, flavor—there is such a bewildering array of sausages for sale. Personal taste will dictate which ones you buy.

CHOOSE

Pork, beef, and lamb are the main meats used in sausages. Ingredients and flavorings vary enormously, and many sausages are high in fat, but there is an increasing number of specialty sausages being made with other meats such as venison, buffalo, and ostrich that are lower in fat. Always check labels for meat, fat, cereal, and salt content, or ask the butcher what is in the sausages if they are made on the premises. Sausages with at least 75–90% meat, with no artificial ingredients and additive-free, are the healthiest choice.

Chef's choice

Ap yeung cheung: A Chinese sausage made from pork and pre-served duck liver, flavored with garlic and rice wine. Traditionally they are steamed over rice, but they can also be grilled.

Blood sausage: Is made from hog's blood and cereal, with varying amounts of fat. The French *boudin noir* is generally good quality, if you can get it. Slice and broil or fry, or crumble or chop and use in stuffings.

Chorizo: An orangy-red, spicy sausage originally from Spain but now also from Mexico. Fresh and dried are both available—it is the fresh one you need for broiling and pan-frying. Chorizo is used in paella, and it is also good with eggs, and in risotto, pasta sauces, and stuffings.

Cumberland: A traditional British sausage, often sold in a long coil. A good breakfast choice, or when you want to cook sausages and mash with onion gravy. Good brands will have a high meat content. Broil, fry, grill, or roast (see opposite).

Italian sausage: Fresh from the deli, these are generally very meaty sausages with punchy flavorings (fennel and garlic are particular favorites). Good halved lengthwise and broiled, fried, or grilled, but also excellent chopped in stuffings and pasta sauces.

Loukanika: A good, meaty pork sausage from Greece, flavored with herbs, spices, garlic, and orange rind. Good broiled, fried, or grilled.

Merguez: A spicy, hot, thin sausage from North Africa, made with lamb. Good broiled or fried, or chopped in pasta sauces, risotto, and couscous.

Toulouse: The classic cassoulet sausage, also good for frying and broiling. Very meaty and garlicky, also excellent grilled.

STORE

Sausages are highly perishable. Always store well wrapped in the refrigerator and do not eat after the use-by date on the packaging. Freshly made sausages from the butcher should be eaten within 2 days. Cooked sausages should be stored in the refrigerator and eaten within 24 hours of cooking. Sausages can be stored in the freezer for up to 3 months, and should be thawed in the refrigerator before cooking.

PREPARE AND COOK

- If sausages are in links, snip them apart with scissors.
- Broil or fry in a little hot vegetable oil in a nonstick pan. Slow cooking for 15–20 minutes is recommended, turning frequently. Check they are cooked through by cutting one in half lengthwise.
- Sausages are also good cooked in the oven at 350°F (325°F in fan ovens) for 20–25 minutes, turning them once.
- If you are grilling sausages it is a good idea to start them off in the oven for 10 minutes (temperature as above), then finish cooking on the barbecue grill. This insures that they cook through without overcharring.

TO PRICK OR NOT TO PRICK?

If you prick sausages with a fork or toothpick before cooking, this will make the fat run out.

- *THE UPSIDE—it will prevent the casings from bursting, and give you less fatty sausages, especially if you drain them well before serving.*
- *THE DOWNSIDE—the sausages will be less moist and less juicy.*

GROUND MEAT

Versatile, inexpensive, and quick to cook, ground meat is an invaluable ingredient for the busy cook. For dishes like Bolognese, shepherd's pie, keema curry, and moussaka, first brown the meat in a little hot oil (or dry-fry in a nonstick pan) for 4–6 minutes, then cook according to your recipe for 20–30 minutes. Burgers, meatballs, and patties should be cooked for 4–6 minutes on each side. All ground meat can be kept in the refrigerator for up to 24 hours, or frozen for up to 3 months. Defrost before using.

Beef

■ Tough cuts such as flank are often used to make ground beef, but it won't say this on the supermarket label. If it is described as "ground steak," it is likely to be made from better quality meat than ordinary ground beef, and will be good for burgers, meatballs, Bolognese, and stuffing vegetables.
■ Ground beef can be coarsely or finely ground, with varying amounts of fat—check the label. Regular ground beef may have 10–20% fat, lean or extra-lean 5–7%. Lean meat is more

healthy, but it can be dry. Steak is very finely ground, and is usually the least fatty.
■ To be sure of what you are getting, ask your butcher to grind lean meat for you when buying.

Lamb

■ Usually made from breast or shoulder, richly flavored cuts with a fair amount of fat (ground lamb can contain up to 25% fat). Good for burgers and meatballs, as the fat helps to keep them moist.
■ Dishes like shepherd's pie, keema curry, and moussaka are traditionally made with ground lamb, but they can be fatty. Ideally, skim off the fat during cooking.

Pork

■ Ground pork may have up to 30% fat, making it a good choice for burgers and meatballs. To make them less fatty, mix with lean ground beef.

Veal

■ Rump roast or pie veal may be used for ground veal, which makes good lean burgers and meatballs.
■ For extra flavor, mix it with another meat such as beef or pork.

VARIETY MEATS

Delicious when properly cooked, variety meats deserve to be eaten more often. You will find more choice at butchers than at the supermarket, and a good supplier will advise you on cooking methods if you are keen to try out different kinds. Traditional dishes made with kidneys, liver, and oxtail are quintessential comfort food. They are also cheap and nutritious, and easy to prepare and cook.

CHOOSE

Three types of variety meats are readily available.

- **Kidneys**: Veal, ox, lamb's, and pig's.
- **Liver**: Pig's, lamb's and calf's.
- **Oxtail**

When buying kidneys and liver, look for a fresh and glossy sheen, and absolutely no smell. Lamb's and veal kidneys from the butcher may have thick fat (suet) around them—it should be off-white and crumbly, not yellow or greasy. Oxtail should look freshly cut, with plenty of deep red meat surrounded by white fat.

STORE

Variety meats are best eaten fresh, on the day of purchase if possible, but can be kept in a covered container in the refrigerator for up to 24 hours. They don't freeze particularly well.

PREPARE

Very little preparation is needed.

Kidneys: If you have bought kidneys encased in suet, pull it away carefully. The kidneys themselves are covered in a thin membrane. Nick it with scissors or the tip of a small, sharp knife, then peel off with your fingers. Now cut out the white cores, halving the kidneys or cutting them into pieces according to the type of kidney and the way you are going to cook them.

Liver: Pull away any covering membrane, taking care not to tear the liver itself. With a very sharp knife, slice the liver as thinly as possible—¼ inch is the best thickness for quick cooking and tenderness. If you see any ducts or blood vessels while you are slicing, cut them neatly away.

Oxtail: Comes cut into pieces ready for cooking. You can buy them individually (a tail usually cuts into 4 pieces), or tied together as a crown roast. Trim away excess fat from the outside of each piece, if this has not been done by the butcher.

COOK

All variety meat is richly flavored, so portion sizes are generally small.

Kidneys

■ Veal and ox kidneys come joined together as lots of "lobes," sometimes surrounded by suet. A whole veal kidney usually weighs about 1 pound and will feed 3–4 people. Tender and sweet, it is the chefs' favorite for sautéing. Cut it into bite-size pieces and cook for 3 minutes maximum. Ox kidney is the traditional one for steak and kidney pudding. Strong and tough, it needs braising or stewing for a long time to become tender.

■ Lamb's kidneys are the smallest and mildest, and the most readily available—the best ones to try if you have not eaten kidneys before. They weigh 2–3 ounces each, so allow 2–3 per person. Broil whole or halved on skewers (to keep them flat) for around 2–3 minutes each side. Or pan-fry them in butter, then coat in a Dijon-style sauce made with white wine, cream, and mustard. They can also be used in steak and kidney pie or pudding if you do not like the rather strong flavor of pig's or ox kidney.

■ Pig's kidneys are larger and stronger in taste than lamb's, and they can be tough. They are best soaked in lightly salted water for a few hours to make them milder, then halved or sliced, and used in pies and steak and kidney pudding.

Liver

- Calf's liver is the most expensive, and the most tender. Its delicate flavor is almost sweet. For 2 people allow 8 ounces. Thin slices are best seasoned and pan-fried over high heat in olive oil (or oil and butter for extra flavor) for only 60 seconds on each side. Lemon, lime, and sage are good flavors with calf's liver, so too is balsamic vinegar.
- Lamb's liver is good fried, as long as it is thinly sliced and not over-cooked—3–4 minutes each side is the recommended time. Allow 1–2 slices per person. It is stronger in flavor than calf's liver, but not too strong. Fried onions are the classic accompaniment—their flavors complement each other perfectly.
- Pig's liver is strong and robust, and dark in color. To make it milder, soak it in milk for an hour or two, then drain and dry. The best use for pig's liver is chopped or ground in pâtés and terrines.

Oxtail

- This needs to be browned in hot oil, then braised very gently in liquid for at least 2 hours, during which time it becomes so tender that the meat literally falls off the bones. Allow 2 pieces per person (there is a lot of waste) and cook with wine and/or tomatoes to help cut the fat. Cook the day before serving so you can chill in the refrigerator overnight and then lift off the solidified fat before reheating.

OTHER VARIETY MEATS

Heart

■ Size varies according to the animal the heart comes from. Lamb's heart has a good flavor and texture, and 1 small heart per person is the usual portion size. They can be sliced and pan-fried, but one of the best ways to enjoy them is stuffed and braised—they need long, slow cooking for 2–3 hours. When sliced, the stuffing gives them an appealing shape and the meat is juicy, tender, and sweet.

Pig's feet

■ Pig's feet are prized for their jelly, and are sold split down the middle. Pop one in a long-cooking casserole or stew and you will notice how it enriches the gravy.

Sweetbreads

■ Lamb's sweetbreads are a real delicacy, with their melt-in-your-mouth texture and mild flavor. They need to be soaked in cold water and blanched to remove impurities, then skinned, and poached in milk or stock for 8–10 minutes until tender. After this initial cooking, they are good swiftly pan-fried to give them color, and are often served in a cream and white wine sauce with chopped fresh herbs. Always cook and eat sweetbreads on the day you buy them as they are highly perishable.

Tongue

■ Whole ox tongue is sold salted or cured in brine. It needs poaching in liquid for 3–4 hours, then peeling, and pressing (you can buy special presses at kitchenware stores, or use a cake pan). Home-pressed tongue is very good served well chilled and thinly sliced.

Tripe

■ The white, spongy stomach of cows and pigs is a great delicacy in Europe, where it is often slow-cooked with tomatoes and pungent garlic and onions—look for recipes in French and Italian cookbooks. It is sold blanched or "dressed" ready for cooking, and you will need 6 ounces per person.

SPECIALTY MEATS

Farmers' markets, farm stores, and specialist butchers sell some unusual meats that are worth buying, and you can also order them fresh or frozen over the web. When you buy the meat, ask the supplier for cooking instructions—he or she will know all about the meat they are selling.

■ **Buffalo:** The same as bison and also sold under this name, buffalo is a red meat that is like beef, but contains about a third less fat. It can be used in any recipe for beef—the cuts are similar. Steaks can be broiled, charbroiled, or pan-fried like beef steaks, but because they are so lean and low in fat, they benefit from being marinated before cooking, and they should not be overcooked. Buffalo burgers, broils, and sausages are tasty.

■ **Ostrich:** Fillet, rump roasts and steaks are the most popular cuts, but burgers, sausages, and meatballs are also made from this rich meat. Like all red meats, ostrich is a good source of protein and iron, but it is worth noting that it is lower in saturated fat than beef, lamb, or pork. As they are so lean, steaks are best cooked rare or they can be dry.

■ **Wild boar:** Increasingly available, boneless roasts are popular, together with steaks, sausages, bacon, and burgers. Marinating and long, slow roasting are essential to make this mature, gamy meat tender and juicy. Roasting time is 35–40 minutes per pound, and the oven temperature should be no more than 325°F (275°F in fan ovens).

POULTRY

CHOOSE

The majority of chickens and turkeys on sale in supermarkets have been intensively reared indoors. This information won't appear on the label, but the price will be a good indicator— indoor-reared birds are generally the cheapest, with organic the most expensive, and barnyard somewhere in between the two.

Organic birds are allowed to roam outside in the daytime. Most (but not always all) of their feed is organic. The flesh will be tender yet firm, with a tasty, satisfying flavor, because these birds are allowed to mature slowly. Chickens are reared for up to 14 weeks (indoor-reared birds are matured for up to 6 weeks). The name of the farm or producer may be given on the label, which may give you extra reassurance. Don't be put off if organic chickens look scrawny compared to those reared indoors. Slower-growing breeds are less plump than indoor-reared birds. The amount of exercise they have can also make them leaner and longer in the body.

Barnyard—these birds have had some access to the open air. They are less expensive than organic free-range birds.

Corn-fed birds—these golden yellow chickens are fed on a diet containing corn. The color makes them look appetizing, but the feed makes very little difference to the flavor.

What's in a name?

Organic and barnyard poultry with the name of the breed on the label is generally more expensive than ordinary kinds, but these top-quality birds are well worth paying extra for.

Chicken: Look for slower-growing, specialist breeds. These will have firm flesh with plenty of good old-fashioned taste. The French *poulet de bresse* has

choose

an AOC like wine. It is reared under strict conditions, and is highly prized for its succulence and gamy-flavored flesh. You may also see *poulet d'or*, *poulet noir*, and *poulet anglais*, three other excellent French breeds. However, these may be difficult to find outside France.

Turkey: Traditional breeds are barn-yard raised, slow-maturing birds with densely textured meat that has more flavor and succulence than indoor-reared turkeys. Traditional "farm fresh" birds have been dry hand-plucked and hung for 2 weeks. These turkeys will have a good, gamy flavor. So, too, does wild turkey which is also sometimes available and makes a special treat for Thanksgiving.

Duck: There are a number of traditional breeds descended from the northern hemisphere's wild mallard. They are renowned for their distinctive flavor, which is similar to wild duck. They have crisp skin and moist flesh, and a good meat-to-fat ratio. Last but not least, Barbary and Nantais ducks are two French breeds worth seeking out for their tasty meat. Barbary ducks are descended from wild Muscovy ducks from Central and South America. Wild duck (page 390) is also popular. It has a stronger flavor and oilier flesh than domesticated breeds.

GOOD FOR YOU

Poultry contains similar nutrients to red meat:

- *PROTEIN, essential for growth, good health, and well-being.*
- *B VITAMINS, especially niacin, B6 and B12, for healthy blood cells and nervous system.*
- *ESSENTIAL MINERALS, especially iron (for healthy red blood cells), zinc (for growth, healthy immune and reproductive systems, and skin), and selenium (an antioxidant essential for a healthy immune system, fertility, and thyroid metabolism).*

Chicken and turkey are low in fat; their livers are rich in iron, and in vitamin A (good for eyes, vision, skin, and growth).

Buying frozen poultry

■ It is always best to buy fresh rather than commercially frozen poultry. Fresh poultry has a better texture, and you can be more sure of what you are buying, but it is handy to keep a pack or two of your favorite pieces in the freezer, especially if they are wrapped individually so you can use them as you need. Whole birds take up a lot of room and need a long time to defrost, so are hardly worth the freezer space, but pieces defrost rapidly in the microwave, or in about 4 hours in the refrigerator.

■ If you buy a frozen bird, take care to defrost it properly before cooking. Defrosting instructions and times are given on page 379.

SAFE HANDLING

All of the safe handling criteria for meat on page 329 apply, but with poultry (especially chicken) there is some risk of salmonella contamination. As long as you have bought from a reputable source, the risk is minimal, but in any case you should always follow these guidelines.

■ Refrigerate poultry in the as soon as you can (see right) and eat within the recommended guidelines.

■ Wash the kitchen counter, cutting boards, hands, and utensils with hot, soapy water before and after dealing with raw or cooked poultry, and do not deal with the two together.

■ Keep a separate cutting board for raw poultry if you can, and wash it well in hot soapy water straight after use. When preparing raw poultry do not let it come into contact with other foods, especially foods that will not be cooked or reheated before being eaten.

■ Bacteria are easily killed by cooking, as long as you make sure poultry is properly cooked through before eating. This is especially important with whole birds (see page 366).

■ Refrigerate leftovers as soon as they have cooled, and eat within 2 days.

■ Leftovers should not be reheated more than once.

■ If you are dealing with frozen poultry, or freezing it yourself, see the guidelines below, above left and right.

STORE

Fresh poultry is highly perishable, especially in warm weather, so you should keep it in the refrigerator.

■ Remove all wrappings, then wipe the poultry all over with paper towels (including inside any cavities). If there are any giblets, remove them and keep in a covered bowl in the refrigerator.

choose–store

■ Place the poultry on a tray or a large, deep plate and cover loosely with foil before storing in the bottom of the refrigerator (this will prevent any blood dripping onto other foods).

■ Birds and pieces will keep fresh for up to 2 days; livers and ground poultry should be cooked within 24 hours.

Freezing

Small amounts of poultry can be successfully frozen at home, provided it is very fresh when it goes in the freezer. General guidelines are the same as for freezing meat (page 330).

■ All poultry can be stored in the freezer for up to 6 months, apart from ground poultry, which should be stored for a maximum of 2 months. Nothing bad will happen after this time, but the texture of the meat will not be so good.

■ The best poultry for home freezing is portion-sized pieces such as breasts, legs, drumsticks, and thighs, and packs of cubes or strips. Wrap pieces individually in plastic wrap, then overwrap them with foil or in an airtight plastic bag—poultry is delicate and susceptible to freezer burn (page 26).

■ Whole birds are an awkward shape to store, and take a long time to defrost, so they are generally not really worth the bother.

GRAVY
Makes enough for 6–8 people

When roasting a bird, thickening the juices from the roasting pan is a good way to make a delicious gravy.

Remove the bird from the pan and pour off all but 1 tablespoon fat. Put the pan over a low heat, add 1 tablespoon all-purpose flour, and stir well.

Slowly whisk in 2 cups hot water or stock, turn up the heat and bring to a boil. Simmer, whisking, for 1–2 minutes, then season with salt and pepper to taste, and serve.

CHICKEN

Versatile, quick, and easy to cook, chicken is lower in fat than most meats (especially without the skin)—it is small wonder that chicken is so popular. Choosing, preparing, and cooking the different cuts is simple when you know how.

Whole birds
CHOOSE

■ Oven-ready chickens weigh from 3–5 pounds. A good, average weight for a bird to serve 4–6 people is 3½–4 pounds.

■ Very small birds, called poussins or spring chickens, are baby chickens no more than 4 weeks old. They weigh about 14 ounces each, enough for 1 per person.

■ Large "roasters", weighing from 6–10 pounds, are usually available to order from the butcher throughout the year, and at Christmas you may see them in the supermarket —they have replaced capons (castrated roosters) that were a traditional alternative to turkey. Prepare and roast as for turkey (see page 380).

■ Boiling fowl are old laying hens, good for making stocks and soups—they require long, gentle simmering to become tender. They are hard to come by—ask your butcher whether he can get one for you.

PREPARE

Whole chickens and poussins can be poached with liquid and vegetables, but they are more usually roasted. They can also be grilled (page 368). They are sometimes trussed (tied into a neat shape) with string, or just have their legs tied.

■ Take the bird out of the refrigerator and bring it to room temperature before cooking. Allow 1 hour for this.

■ Remove any trussing strings that are tied around the body of the bird. These keep the chicken in a neat, compact shape, but they slow down the cooking and prevent the bird from cooking evenly.

■ Wipe the bird inside and out with paper towels, removing the bag of giblets if there is one. The giblets are the neck, gizzard, heart, and liver. They can be used to make stock (page 371), although the liver is best left out as it can give a bitter taste.

■ For easy carving, remove the wishbone before cooking. Pull back the skin from the neck cavity to expose it, then cut around it with the tip of a small, sharp knife, and cut it free at the bottom.

■ To add flavor and make the chicken more succulent, push onion or lemon

whole birds

wedges, or a few chunks of garlic, into the body cavity. During cooking, the juices of these ingredients will flow, flavoring and basting the chicken from within.

■ Sprigs of herbs such as tarragon, rosemary, thyme, and sage, can also be pushed into the cavity.

■ Stuffing can be pushed in the neck end (see right), but do not stuff the body cavity. If the cavity is stuffed, the heat may not penetrate right through to the center of the bird and this will prevent it cooking all the way through.

■ To make the breast meat moist, lift up the skin at the neck end and insert your fingers between the skin and the flesh of the breast to create a pocket, then push in flavored softened butter or soft cheese to cover the breast. Grated citrus zest, chopped fresh herbs, ground spices, or crushed garlic make good flavorings for the butter or cheese.

■ Turn the bird upside down and pull the neck skin over the neck cavity (and any stuffing). Cut off any excess skin with scissors. Twist the wings around so that the tips secure the neck skin in place, then tie the legs together with string, if this has not already been done (see illustration, below right). Weigh the bird and calculate the cooking time, allowing 25 minutes per pound, plus an extra 25 minutes. The bird is now ready for roasting.

STUFFING A CHICKEN

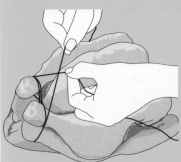

TYING THE LEGS WITH STRING

TESTING FOR DONENESS

Do this simple test at the end of the recommended roasting time—do not go by the time alone.

■ *Ease one of the legs away from the body and pierce the thigh at its thickest point with a knife—the juices that run out should be clear. The juices between the thigh and the body should be this color too. If any of the juices are pink or red, return the bird to the oven and test again after 20 minutes.*

ROASTING A CHICKEN

■ To help the bird cook more quickly, make two or three deep diagonal slashes across the tops of the thighs and into the back of the bird before roasting. This will allow the heat to penetrate right from the start.

■ Rub the bird liberally all over with softened butter or olive oil, then season with sea salt and freshly ground black pepper. This will make crisp, flavorsome skin.

■ A rub of paprika will give the skin a good color, or you can use dried herbs for a different flavor.

■ Roast in a preheated oven at 375°F (340°F in fan ovens) for the cooking time calculated (page 367).

■ For succulent, golden-brown flesh, lay the bird on its side in the roasting pan and cook for 10–20 minutes, then turn it onto its other side for the next 10–20 minutes. Turn it breast-side down for another 10–20 minutes, then sit it breast-side up for the remainder of the cooking time to crisp and color the skin. If you nestle the bird in a cradle-style rack in the pan, it will be easier to manage and stay in position more securely, but if you don't have one, use scrunched-up foil instead.

■ Make sure the bird is thoroughly cooked—see page 367.

■ Leave the bird, covered with foil, in a warm place for 10–15 minutes after roasting. This resting time is essential for the juices to settle in the meat and make it easy to carve. Carve as for turkey (page 381).

GRILLING A CHICKEN

If you have a kettle barbecue, you can cook a whole bird on it with the lid down, but it will cook more quickly and evenly if it is butterflied or spatchcocked (split open along its back and splayed flat, see page 46). You can buy butterflied chickens and poussins, or butterfly the bird yourself (see page 387)—cut along either side of the backbone and remove it, then press down hard on the breast to flatten it. For ease of handling and to keep the bird flat during cooking, insert skewers through the wings and legs before cooking.

Breast portions
CHOOSE

■ Available boneless (with skin or skinless), part-boned/on the bone (called "suprêmes" when part of the wing bone is attached), or cut into cubes or strips.

■ Allow 1 breast portion, on or off the bone, per person. The usual weight is 4–6 ounces.

■ The meat is lean and tender, but can be dry. Portions with bone cook better than boneless portions, and are juicier.

whole birds—breast

PREPARE

- Strip off any skin, if you prefer (see Cutting the Fat, below right).
- Pull away the tender strip of fillet from underneath, and set aside.
- With the tip of a small, sharp knife, cut out the silvery-white tendon from underneath, as this can be chewy.
- Marinate to make the lean meat more moist, slashing the flesh to allow the marinade to penetrate better. Leave in the refrigerator for at least 4 hours, or overnight.

COOK

- Whole breast portions can be pan-fried, broiled, charbroiled, or grilled. Cook on a high heat for 7–10 minutes, turning once. They can also be roasted for 15 minutes in a preheated oven at 375°F (340°F in fan ovens).
- Cubes or strips are good for stir-frying, sautéing, broiling, and grilling on skewers. They are also good in Mexican fajitas and Japanese teriyaki and yakitori. Cook for 5–7 minutes, tossing them often.
- Tender fillet strips (detached from underneath the breast) cook much more quickly than the rest of the breast, so add them at the end of the cooking time—they need about 3 minutes.
- Cubes and strips can be used in curries and casseroles, but if the cooking is longer than 20 minutes, use thighs.

TIPS AND TRICKS: COOKING CHICKEN

- *PAN-FRYING and CHARBROILING: To make boneless skinless breast portions cook more quickly, and to help tenderize them, cut horizontally in half through the thickness of the meat, cover with plastic wrap, and pound with a meat bat or rolling pin until thin. Pounded halves will cook in 5–6 minutes.*
- *BROILING: To keep meat moist, keep the skin on during cooking (the fat underneath will melt and baste the meat). Rub the skin with melted butter or oil, dried herbs or spices, and seasoning, or make three diagonal slashes in the skin on each portion and insert flavored butter or herbs. Remove the skin before serving if you like.*
- *ROASTING: Do the same as for broiling (above), or wrap skinless portions in thin slices of prosciutto or bacon, tucking herbs such as sage, tarragon, or basil in between. For portions with skin, push flavored butter or soft cheese between the skin and the flesh.*

CUTTING THE FAT

- *Chicken breast meat with the skin on contains 10% more fat than skinless chicken breast, so remove the skin for a more healthy option.*

Drumsticks

CHOOSE

■ Drumsticks are the lower part of the leg, with the bone in, covered with skin.

■ Allow 2 per person.

■ The meat is dark and is more succulent than white because it contains more fat.

PREPARE

■ Chop off the bottom joint, to neaten the knuckle.

■ Make several slashes through the skin, deep into the flesh.

■ Marinate to make more succulent and tasty, if you have the time (at least 4 hours or overnight).

■ Rub with oil, then with dried herbs and/or spices and seasoning.

COOK

■ Broil or grill for 25–30 minutes, turning a few times. Or roast at 375°F (340°F in fan ovens) for 35 minutes, turning two or three times. Eat with your hands, wrapping the knuckle end in a napkin or foil.

Quarters/pieces

CHOOSE

■ These may be the leg quarter (the thigh and drumstick), or the wing quarter (the wing with part of the breast attached). The skin is always intact.

■ Allow 1 per person.

■ Legs are all dark meat, while wings have some white breast meat, so check what you are buying, especially if they are sold in packs rather than as individual pieces.

PREPARE

■ To reduce the fat content, carefully pull the skin away from the flesh with your hands.

■ Slash and marinate for 4–24 hours for extra flavor and succulence.

COOK

■ Rub with oil and seasonings, and grill or roast at 375°F (340°F in fan ovens) for 40 minutes, turning two or three times.

■ Season and brown in hot oil before using in casseroles and stews.

Thighs

CHOOSE

■ There are three types—on the bone with skin, boneless and skinless, and boneless skinless "mini" fillets.

■ Allow 2 thighs or 4 fillets per person.

■ The dark meat of thighs is more succulent and tastier than white. Thighs are more tender than drumsticks.

drumsticks–**w**ings

PREPARE

- Pull off skin if necessary, and trim off visible fat.
- Slash and marinate for 4–24 hours for extra flavor and succulence.
- Boneless thighs can be stuffed.

COOK

- Brown in hot oil, then use in casseroles and curries. Whole thighs take 40–60 minutes, fillets take 25–30 minutes.
- Boneless, skinless meat is good grilled on skewers. Allow about 25–30 minutes, turning often.
- Roast stuffed thighs for 40 minutes at 375°F (340°F in fan ovens).

Wings

CHOOSE

- These are the bony wing joints (with skin) that are sold in packs or loose.
- Allow 4 per person.
- Inexpensive, tasty, dark meat with crisp skin.

PREPARE

- Marinate for 4–24 hours, for extra flavor and succulence.

COOK

- Grill or roast for 40 minutes at 375°F (340°F in fan ovens). Best eaten with your hands.

CHICKEN STOCK
Makes about 6¼ cups

about 1½ pounds chicken bones
  and carcass
chicken giblets, without the liver
  (optional)
¾ cup mixed coarsely chopped
  onion, celery, and carrot
1 bouquet garni
6 peppercorns

Blanch the chicken bones, carcass, and giblets in boiling water for 2 minutes, drain, and rinse. Place in a pan with the remaining ingredients and cover generously with water. Bring to a boil, then simmer for 2–3 hours, skimming often and topping up with water as necessary. Strain the stock and let cool, then store in the refrigerator for up to 3 days or freeze for up to 3 months.

CHICKEN LIVERS
These are sold in tubs, often frozen. They are rich in iron and vitamin A and have a very mild flavor.
Use in pâtés and terrines, or pan-fry in oil and/or butter with herbs and seasonings for 5–7 minutes and toss with salad greens and fresh herbs for a warm salad.

DUCK

Weight for weight, there is less meat on duck than on chicken or turkey. This is because duck has a higher bone-to-meat ratio, and more fat underneath the skin. On the plus side, duck meat is rich and tasty, so portion size can be smaller.

Whole birds

Ducks and ducklings weigh from 3½ to 7 pounds. A duckling is a bird under 6 months old. Roasting is the best cooking method for a whole bird, and you should allow 1½ pounds raw weight per serving.

A duck or duckling weighing 3½–4 pounds will serve 2 people, a 5–6-pound bird will serve 4 people.

ROASTING A WHOLE DUCK

■ Take out of the refrigerator and bring to room temperature for 1 hour.
■ Cut away all visible fat from inside and around the body cavity and neck.
■ Stuff the neck end if you like, and secure in place with a skewer. A sharp-flavored, citrussy stuffing will counteract fattiness and help the meat go further.
■ Preheat the oven to 400°F (350°F in fan ovens) before you put the duck in. Placing the bird in an oven that is already hot will help crisp the skin.

■ Just before roasting, prick the skin all over with a fork and rub liberally with salt—this will allow the fat to run out and make the skin crisp.
■ Sit the duck breast-side down on a rack in the roasting pan. This will help the fat drain off quickly, and keep the duck out of the fat that melts off.
■ Roast for 25 minutes, then pour off the melted fat from the bottom of the pan and turn the bird breast-side up. Roast for another 20 minutes.
■ Pour off the fat again, baste the duck, and reduce the oven temperature to 350°F (325°F in fan ovens).
■ Continue roasting for 1½ hours for a duck weighing 3½–4 pounds, or for 2 hours for a duck weighing 5–6 pounds.
■ Pour off the duck fat from the bottom of the pan several times during the final roasting time to prevent smoking and help keep the skin crisp.

SERVING

After roasting, lift the duck onto a carving board and let it rest for 15–20 minutes. Don't try to carve a duck—it is far easier simply to cut it into serving portions.

■ For 2 people: cut the duck in half lengthwise, then cut each half diagonally across the breast so that each

person has a leg and a wing portion
with breast meat attached.
■ For 4 people: cut off the legs, then
cut away the breast meat in two
pieces, one on either side of the
breastbone. Cut the breast meat into
slices on the diagonal. Serve each
person some breast meat together
with either a leg or a wing.

Breasts

Without the skin and fat, duck breast
meat is actually quite lean, containing
5% fat. Marinating before cooking
will help make it moist and juicy, so
too will not overcooking it—duck
breast is best served quite pink in the
middle.

CHOOSE

■ Boneless breasts with the skin on are
sold individually. The French *magrets*
are excellent for flavor, and are often
sold in vacuum packs for long keeping.
■ The average-sized duck breast
weighs 4–6 ounces, and is a generous
portion for one person. Larger duck
breasts can serve 2 people, depending
on appetite and what other ingredients
are served with them. For a stir-fry
to serve 4 people, you will need only
2 duck breasts.
■ The meat is richly flavored, so a
little goes a long way.

GOOD FOR YOU

*Duck meat contains more B12
vitamin than chicken, and almost
as much iron as beef.*
■ *Eaten together, cooked duck
meat, fat, and skin contain 29%
fat, but you can reduce this considerably if you remove the fat and
skin before cooking.*
■ *If you cook duck with the skin on,
drain it well before serving and pour
the fat off into a small container.
It will keep for up to a month in
the refrigerator, and is excellent
for frying and roasting, especially
for potatoes and parsnips.*

FLAVORS TO GO WITH DUCK

*Many Chinese and Thai recipes
use duck with spices and sweet-
and-sour flavors, while in Western
cooking duck is often cooked with
fruits to offset its richness. The
following fruits go especially well
with duck:*
■ *BLUEBERRIES*
■ *CHERRIES*
■ *CRANBERRIES*
■ *ORANGES*
■ *RASPBERRIES*

PREPARE

- Leave breasts whole for pan-frying, broiling, or roasting. If the skin is left on, score it through to the fat in a diamond pattern.
- For sautéing or stir-frying, remove the skin and fat and cut the meat into strips, working diagonally against the grain.

COOK

- Season and dry-fry or charbroil whole breasts skin-side down for 3 minutes, pressing hard with a spatula to keep them flat and to squeeze out the fat. Turn and cook for 3–4 minutes.
- Season and broil whole breasts skin- side up for 3 minutes, turn over, and broil for another 3–4 minutes.
- Roast seasoned whole breasts in a preheated oven at 400°F (350°F in fan ovens) for 30 minutes.
- Leave whole breasts to rest for 10 minutes before serving.
- Stir-fry strips for 5–7 minutes.

Legs
CHOOSE

- Duck leg portions are sold singly, on the bone, with the skin on.
- Allow 1 leg per person.
- Dark meat needs a long cooking time to make it tender.

PREPARE

- Prick the skin all over with a fork.

COOK

- Dry-fry until the fat runs and the skin is browned. Drain and use in casseroles and stews with vegetables and liquid. The cooking time is 1–1¼ hours at 350°F (325°F in fan ovens).

Smoked duck breast

- Cured and oak-smoked duck breast is sold sliced and ready to eat in the deli chiller cabinet in supermarkets.
- The lean meat edged with fat is tender and full of flavor. The fat is easy to remove before serving.
- Use slices for antipasti platters or sandwiches, or snip into salads.

Confit

Duck legs that have been cooked and preserved in their own fat are called *confit de canard*. You can make confit yourself, or buy it in cans and jars at supermarkets and delis.

- All it needs is reheating, and the quality is excellent—juicy, tender leg meat on the bone. Serve with creamed potatoes or French bread.
- It is traditionally added to cassoulet.

GOOSE

Rarely available other than at Christmas time, goose is a real treat and a welcome change from turkey for the festive meal, especially if you are hosting a small gathering. The meat is rich, tasty, and succulent, but the bird is fattier and bonier than turkey, so weight for weight it will not feed so many people.

CHOOSE

Go for a barnyard, traditionally reared bird from a reputable farm (there are many to choose from by mail order and on the web), or order from your farmers' market or butcher. Some good supermarkets and food halls also sell geese, so check availability with these too, in plenty of time for Christmas—geese are in limited supply from Michaelmas (September 29) until New Year.
■ For 6–8 people, the ideal weight is 10 pounds. This size will have the best meat-to-bone ratio.

PREPARE

■ Take the goose out of its wrapping and remove the giblets, keeping all trussing strings intact as they will keep the goose in shape while cooking.
■ Store the giblets in a covered bowl in the refrigerator until you are ready

to use them for stock or gravy (they will keep for 24 hours).

■ The liver comes as part of the giblets, but it should not be used for making stock or gravy because it may make them taste bitter, so separate it and either fry it on its own as you would chicken livers, or use in the stuffing for the goose.

■ If there is any white fat with the giblets, save this separately (see opposite).

■ Put the goose on a tray, cover loosely with foil, and keep at the bottom of the refrigerator (or in a cool place at no more than 56°F, until 1 hour before you are ready to roast. It will keep for 2 days.

ROAST

This tasty bird can be roasted just as it is, but a fruity stuffing suits it particularly well because it cuts the richness of the meat and helps it go further. There are plenty of ready-made fresh stuffings available from supermarkets at Christmas time—those with dried fruit, such as apricots or prunes, and fresh apples flavored with orange or lemon go especially well with goose.

■ Bring the goose to room temperature for 1 hour before roasting, during which time you can wipe inside the body cavity with paper towels and push the stuffing inside (you can do this with the legs still tied).

■ Weigh the bird after stuffing. The timing given below is for a 10-pound bird with stuffing in the cavity. If your bird is a different weight from this, allow 15 minutes per pound, plus 30 minutes.

■ Preheat the oven to 375°F (340°F in fan ovens).

■ Prick all over the breast with a fork and sprinkle with coarse sea salt.

■ Place the goose on a rack in a roasting pan and cover with a large, loose tent of foil, scrunching and tucking it tightly around the edges of the pan.

■ Roast for 1½ hours.

■ Carefully take the pan out of the oven and slowly pour off the fat. Use some to baste the goose, then cover with foil again, and return to the oven for another hour.

■ Repeat the draining and basting with the fat and put the pan back in the oven for another 30 minutes, with the breast uncovered so the skin becomes crisp and golden.

■ Remove the goose from the rack and hold it with the legs facing downward so that the fat drains off.

■ Leave the goose to rest, covered loosely with a tent of fresh foil, for about 30 minutes before carving and serving.

roasting–fat

SERVING

Carving is best done in the kitchen, but you may like to show off the whole bird on a platter first.

■ Cut the breasts away from either side of the breast bone and set aside.

■ Cut off the legs. Holding them one at a time by the knuckle end, thinly slice off the meat down to the bone.

■ Cut off the wings.

■ Cut away the two oyster fillets from the underside where the legs meet the body.

■ Carve the breast on the diagonal and serve alongside the other meat.

WHAT TO DO WITH THE FAT

There is a lot of fat on a goose. Although it is predominantly the monounsaturated kind, at least one-third is saturated fat, so it is best not to eat too much of it. On the plus side, goose fat is a good source of niacin and vitamin B6.

■ Before stuffing and roasting the bird, cut away any excess fat you find inside, particularly around the openings, and add to any white fat that was supplied with the giblets. This can then be rendered (melted very slowly) in a pan over low heat, strained through cheesecloth into a bowl or jar, and kept in the refrigerator or freezer for up to 6 months. Use it for roasting and frying at high temperatures (it has a high smoke point), or for sealing the tops of pâtés and terrines.

■ Do not throw away the fat that melts out of the goose during roasting. It will not be as pure as the rendered white fat, but it is still excellent for frying and roasting, especially for potatoes, and it will keep in the refrigerator for up to a month.

■ If you like goose fat, you can buy it in jars and cans, and in chilled packs, at most good supermarkets and delis. A lot of goose fat is imported from France (look for *graisse d'oie* on the label).

Foie gras

■ The liver of ducks or geese that has been artificially fattened by force feeding the bird—*foie gras* means "fatty liver." Its texture is melt-in-the-mouth soft, and its flavor mild and delicate, unlike that of any other liver.

■ In France, pan-fried thin slices of foie gras are a delicacy, eaten hot at the start of a meal, and accompanied by Monbazillac or Sauternes wine, or a sweet Sauternes jelly. The raw liver is also used chopped in stuffings, and to enrich classic sauces.

■ Foie gras is available at good delis and food halls, and over the web—a lot of it comes from southwest France,

and it is very expensive. Look for *foie gras de canard* (duck) and *foie gras d'oie* (goose).

■ For the ultimate luxury burger, add a little chopped raw foie gras to ground beef. It may seem extravagant, but it will melt into the meat during cooking to give a juicy result.

TURKEY

Available all year round in many different forms other than the festive bird at Thanksgiving and Easter, turkey is an inexpensive, healthy choice for everyday meals. Slightly lower in fat than chicken, it has all the other nutritional attributes (see Good for You, page 363), and is just as versatile, quick, and easy to cook.

Whole birds
CHOOSE

■ Fresh and frozen birds are normally available in stores from fall until Christmas, and appear again at other vacation times, especially at Easter.

DEFROSTING A FROZEN TURKEY

■ Whole birds must be completely defrosted before cooking or they will not cook through. Defrosting takes

foie gras–defrost

longer than you think, especially for large birds, so it is important to allow plenty of time, calculating backward from the time you are planning to put the bird in the oven.

■ Once the bird is totally defrosted, it can be kept in the refrigerator for up to 2 days before cooking, so it is always best to start defrosting earlier than necessary, to be sure the bird is completely defrosted.

■ Remove all wrappings, place the turkey on a tray or a large, deep plate, and cover loosely with foil.

■ Leave to defrost in a cool place (no warmer than 56°F).

■ Remove any giblets once loose.

■ Check there are no ice crystals in the cavity before cooking, and pat dry inside and out with paper towels.

MINIMUM DEFROSTING TIMES

If your bird is a different weight from the ones listed here, calculate the defrosting time by allowing 1 hour 48 minutes per pound. Refrigerate the bird immediately after defrosting if you are not cooking it straightaway.

5 pounds	10 hours
8 pounds	16 hours
10–12 pounds	21 hours
15 pounds	30 hours
20 pounds	39 hours

SHORT OF TIME TO DEFROST THE TURKEY?

All is not lost—there is a short cut. It is perfectly safe to use the following defrosting method, as long as you stick to the guidelines.

■ *Calculate the defrosting time at 44 minutes per pound.*

■ *Unwrap the frozen bird and immerse in cold water. Leave in a cool place (no more than 56°F) for the calculated time, changing the water regularly.*

■ *At the end of the time, check inside the body cavity that no ice crystals remain. If there are still some there, hold the bird under cold running water and rinse it thoroughly, letting the water run through the bird, then immerse in fresh cold water again until all the ice crystals have gone.*

■ *Drain and dry thoroughly, inside and out, before cooking.*

WHAT SIZE OF TURKEY?

These quantities are generous, allowing for plenty of leftovers.

5 pounds	serves 4–6
8 pounds	serves 6–8
10-12 pounds	serves 8–10
15 pounds	serves 10–12
20 pounds	serves 12–15

ROAST

■ Take out of the refrigerator and bring to room temperature for 1 hour.
■ Put any stuffing in the neck end.
■ Secure the neck skin (and any stuffing) with the wing tips and a skewer.
■ Season inside the body cavity and push in a few orange and/or lemon wedges and sprigs of herbs (thyme, parsley, and bay are good).
■ Tie the legs with string.
■ Weigh the bird (you may need to use bathroom scales) and work out the cooking time, allowing 18 minutes per pound. Calculate the time you need to put it in the oven by working backward from the time you want to serve the bird, building in extra time for preheating the oven and the resting time at the end.
■ Preheat the oven to 375° (340°F in fan ovens).
■ Sit the bird on a rack in a roasting pan (or on a bed of red onions, cut into fourths, to give flavor to both the turkey and the gravy).
■ Rub plenty of softened butter or olive oil all over the breast and legs.
■ Season well and cover loosely with foil.
■ Roast for the calculated time, basting the bird with the pan juices every 30 minutes and removing the foil for the last 30 minutes to brown the breast.

■ When the turkey is done (see Testing for Doneness, page 367), transfer it to a carving board, cover with a loose tent of foil, and let rest in a warm place for 30 minutes. This allows plenty of time to make the gravy with the pan juices and cook any vegetables. To carve, see opposite.
■ Roast turkey can be kept, covered, in the refrigerator, for up to 3 days.

Turkey roasts

Oven-ready breast roasts (on the bone, and boned and rolled) are available all year round, and come in a wide variety of different shapes and sizes. They are a convenient and quick alternative to a whole turkey, especially if you are catering for a small number of people, or if you are not used to carving a whole bird. The quality of these roasts is generally high, and the meat is usually succulent, but read the label carefully—not only for cooking instructions but also for the ingredients. Some butter-basted turkeys and roasts contain unhealthy mono-unsaturated hydrogenated oil.

Crown roast: This is the most popular turkey roast, it is simply the bird without its legs and wings. Legs take longer to cook than breast, which is why the breast is often overcooked

whole birds–breast

and dry on a whole bird. This problem is solved with a crown, and since most people prefer white meat to dark, there is less waste.

CHOOSE
■ Crowns weigh from 7¾–10 pounds, and provide 4–10 portions.

PREPARE
As for a whole turkey (see left).

COOK
As for a whole turkey (see left), allowing the same amount of roasting time—18 minutes per pound.

Breast steaks
CHOOSE
■ Skinless, boneless slices of breast, 1–1½ inches thick.
■ Allow 1 slice per person.
■ Lean, tender, white meat.

PREPARE
■ Use whole, or in cubes or strips.
■ Marinate if time allows, to increase succulence and flavor (see right). A minimum of 4 hours is required.

COOK
■ Season the slices, then pan-fry in hot oil (or oil and butter), or brush with melted butter or oil, and broil.

*HOW TO CARVE
A TURKEY*

You need a very sharp knife for slicing, and a carving fork to steady the bird on the board.

■ *Cut off the legs. Stand each leg on the board with the knuckle end facing up and cut between the thigh and the drumstick.*
■ *Holding the knuckle end of each drumstick, slice downward to remove the meat until you reach the bone, working all the way round. Slice the thigh meat.*
■ *Cut off the wings, then cut them in two at the joint.*
■ *Slice the breast meat neatly on either side of the breastbone, using the fork to steady the bird underneath.*

POULTRY:TURKEY

The cooking time for pan-frying or broiling is 6–8 minutes, turning once.
■ Grill whole slices, or cubes or strips on skewers. The cooking time is 20 minutes for whole slices, 10 minutes for cubes or strips.
■ Use cubes in sautés, casseroles, and curries, strips in sautés, stir-fries, and fajitas. The cooking time is 5–6 minutes.

Cubes
CHOOSE
■ Boneless thigh or breast meat is sold ready-cubed.
■ Allow 4–6 ounces per person.
■ Dark thigh meat is more succulent than breast, but it contains more fat and takes longer to cook.

PREPARE
■ Use cubes straight from the packet, or marinate (see pages 31 and 331) for 4–24 hours.

COOK
■ Brown in hot oil before using in casseroles, stews, and pies.
■ Or thread on skewers and broil or grill. The cooking time is 15 minutes for thigh meat, 10 minutes for breast.
■ Use cubes of breast in stir-fries and fajitas—they will cook in about 7–10 minutes.

Drumsticks
CHOOSE
■ This is the bottom part of the leg, the same as a chicken drumstick only much larger.
■ The cheapest cut, but not always available all year around.
■ Each drumstick weighs about 1¼ pounds and serves 2 people.
■ The dark meat of drumsticks is more succulent than breast, although higher in fat.

PREPARE
■ Slash and marinate (see pages 31 and 331) for 4–24 hours, for extra flavor and succulence.

COOK
■ Brush with oil or marinade, season and roast; or braise with vegetables and liquid. The cooking time is 1¼ hours at 375°F (340°F in fan ovens), turning once.

Ground turkey
■ Low-fat, as long as it is 100% lean breast meat without skin and fat. You can be sure of this by grinding it yourself in a food processor.
■ Use as a substitute for ground beef, veal, pork, or lamb, or mix half-and-half to lower the fat content.

breast–scallops

Scallops

CHOOSE

- Very thin slices of breast meat (sometimes called quick-cook steaks), also sold as strips.
- Allow 1 scallop, or 4–6 ounces, per person.

Lean and tender, white meat.

PREPARE

- Use straight from the packet.

COOK

- Pan-fry in hot oil and/or butter for 3–4 minutes each side
- Sauté or stir-fry strips for about 5 minutes.
- Good with Mexican spices in fajitas.

TIPS AND TRICKS: TURKEY MARINADES

Turkey pieces are low in fat, but they can be bland and dry, especially the white breast meat. Marinating before cooking is one of the best ways to inject flavor and moisture.

- *A good marinade base is 3 parts olive or sunflower oil to 1 part lemon, lime, or orange juice, wine, or balsamic vinegar.*
- *To the base, add fiery ingredients like chili, ginger, pepper, paprika, and mustard seeds—they will quickly pep up any blandness, so too will pungent Indian spices such as cumin, coriander, and cardamom, perfumed Moroccan flavorings like cloves and cinnamon, and spice blends such as Chinese five spice powder.*
- *Mexican flavors go especially well with turkey, as in the famous "mole" made with onions, garlic, cloves, tomatoes, chilies, and chocolate.*
- *Mix the marinade and meat until the meat is well coated and keep in a covered glass or ceramic bowl in the refrigerator. The marinating time should be at least 4 hours for the marinade to have a good effect. However, overnight or 24-hour marinating is ideal, and often more convenient.*

GAME

READY-TO-COOK GAME IS AVAILABLE FRESH IN SEASON AND FROZEN ALL YEAR AROUND AT MANY SUPERMARKETS, BUTCHERS, FARM STORES, AND FARMERS' MARKETS, AS WELL AS BY MAIL ORDER AND ON THE WEB. GENUINE GAME IS HUNTED IN THE WILD FOR SPORT AND IS AVAILABLE ONLY IN THE HUNTING SEASON, BUT MANY BIRDS AND ANIMALS ARE BRED FOR THE TABLE, SOMETIMES RELEASED "INTO THE WILD" FOR THE SEASON.

STORE

Game is traditionally matured or "hung" for several days before selling, although young farmed game is often eaten fresh. Check with your supplier, as this will affect the storage time.

■ Keep game wrapped in the refrigerator until about 1 hour before cooking.

■ Immersing cuts and pieces of game in a marinade (see opposite) will preserve the meat, tenderize it, and give it flavor. Store for 2–3 days in a covered container in the refrigerator, or up to 6 months in the freezer.

Grouse

Grouse is a small bird with dark red meat and a pronounced gamy flavor. There are numerous North American species, including ruffed and blue.

CHOOSE Available only as whole birds. Allow 1 bird per person.

PREPARE

■ Remove the wishbone (page 366), and cut the legs and wings at the second joint to neaten them.

■ Wipe the bird with paper towels inside and out.

■ Season inside, and insert slices of orange, lemon, or apple, and a few sprigs of fresh sage and/or thyme.

■ Tie the legs together with string.

■ Season the bird all over and brush liberally with softened butter or oil.

■ To prevent the breast meat from drying out, cover with fatty bacon, pancetta, prosciutto, or grape leaves.

COOK

Roast at 375°F (340°F in fan ovens) for 30 minutes. Let rest for about 10–15 minutes.

Guinea fowl

Originally a wild game bird, most birds are now farm-reared all year around, and are classed as poultry. The meat has more flavor than chicken, which it most resembles (some say it tastes like ruffed grouse), and it is slightly darker. There is more leg meat than breast.

CHOOSE
Available as whole birds, usually weighing about 2½ pounds, perfect for 2.

PREPARE
■ As for chicken (page 366).
■ Guinea fowl is drier than chicken, and benefits from being covered with fatty bacon or pancetta slices before roasting to help make it moist.

COOK
■ Roast at 375°F (340°F in fan ovens) for 15 minutes per pound, plus 15 minutes. Let rest for about 10–15 minutes before carving.
■ Serve carved like chicken, or butterflied (page 387), so that each person gets half a bird.

Jack rabbit
Larger than rabbit (page 388) and with darker, stronger-tasting meat, this is the equivalent of the European hare. It needs to be young (it's best from about August to February) and well-hung to be tender, so check with your supplier.

GOOD FOR YOU
Lower in fat than most red meats, game is an excellent, healthy source of protein, vitamins, and minerals. Because it is richly flavored, portion sizes need not be large.

MARINATING
Game is lean and can be dry. The best way to avoid this is to marinate the meat in the refrigerator for 2–3 days before cooking. The marinade should contain an acid such as lemon juice, wine, or wine vinegar to help break down tough fibers, oil to moisten, and herbs and/or spices for flavor (see page 31).

MEAT:GAME

CHOOSE

- A dressed (skinned and cleaned) whole jack rabbit will serve 6–8 people, and is best bought cut up into serving portions.
- You can buy specific cuts such as bone-in legs and shoulders.
- Saddle is a prime cut, sold on the bone for roasting, or as fillets.

PREPARE

- Marinate cuts before cooking for up to 2 days, to make them more moist.

COOK

- Sear cuts, then braise with vegetables and liquid at 350°F (325°F in fan ovens) for 1½–2 hours. Traditional European recipes thicken and enrich the gravy with the animal's blood.
- Roast the saddle at 400° (350°F in fan ovens) for 30 minutes. Let rest for 10–15 minutes before carving.
- Fillets are best pan-fried—allow 3–5 minutes per side.

Partridge

Available from the fall to late winter, this bird is paler, smaller, and less gamy than pheasant. American partridges have been introduced to France where they are highly prized, sometimes even more than the native red-legged partridge.

CHOOSE

- A whole bird serves 1 person.
- Boneless partridge breasts can be bought in packs. Allow 2 per person.

PREPARE

- Prepare whole birds for roasting as for grouse (page 384), or butterfly (see right, and pages 46 and 368) for broiling or grilling, in which case the skin is best left on.
- Breasts are very lean and can be dry—marinating for 4–24 hours before cooking will help to counteract this tendency to dryness.
- Breasts can be skinned, although skin protects the meat and keeps it moist.

COOK

- Roast whole birds at 375°F (340°F in fan ovens) for 25–30 minutes. Let rest for 10–15 minutes before serving.
- Brush butterflied birds with butter or oil, season, and broil or grill for 15 minutes, turning several times.
- Pan-fry breasts in hot oil and butter for 5–7 minutes, turning them once.

Pheasant

This is the largest and one of the most widely available of the game birds as it is farmed in such large numbers. Pheasants are traditionally sold in pairs, but can be bought individually.

jack rabbit–pheasant

CHOOSE

- A whole bird serves 2 people.
- Boned and tied birds are available at some specialty butchers—they look good and are easy to carve with no waste.
- Boneless breasts can be bought in packs. Allow 1–2 breasts per person.
- Bone-in thighs and whole legs are available. Allow 2 pieces per person.

PREPARE

- Prepare young whole birds for roasting as for grouse (page 384). If you don't know the bird's age, pot roast it or the meat may be dry and tough. You can pot roast it whole, or cut up.
- Breasts, thighs, and legs benefit from being marinated for 4–24 hours before cooking to prevent dryness.
- Breasts are best cooked with skin on, to protect the meat and keep it moist. It can then be removed before serving.

COOK

- Roast whole young birds as for grouse at 375°F (340°F in fan ovens), but allow about 40–50 minutes. Let them rest for 10–15 minutes before serving.
- Pot roast whole birds with red wine and vegetables after browning all over. For 4 people, allow 2 birds, and cook in a covered casserole at 325°F (275°F in fan ovens) for about 1¼–1½ hours.
- Pan-fry breasts in hot oil and butter

A ONE-OFF

Kangaroo is available by mail order and on the web. It is a lean, low-fat red meat that can taste quite gamy if it has come from a mature animal.

- *Cuts from virtually the whole animal are available, and you can use them in any recipe for chicken or rabbit.*
- *Do not overcook or the meat will be dry.*

BUTTERFLYING A BIRD
Cut out the backbone (top), then flatten the bird and push two skewers through the wings and legs (above). The skewers will keep the bird flat when cooking, and make it easier to handle.

MEAT:GAME

for about 7 minutes, turning once.
■ Thighs and legs are good casseroled—cook for 40 minutes. They can also be grilled (most successful after marinating). Cook for about 30 minutes.

Quail

This tiny bird is bred for eating, and is available all year. It tastes delicate and is best bought boned and stuffed.

CHOOSE

Served whole—you will need 2 each. A boned, stuffed bird will serve 1.

PREPARE

Wipe and season inside and out. Tie the legs and wrap the whole bird in fatty bacon, pancetta, or grape leaves.

COOK

Roast at 350°F (325°F in fan ovens) for 20 minutes. Let rest for 10 minutes before serving.

Rabbit

Farmed rabbit is pale in color and tastes rather like chicken. Wild rabbit is darker, tastier, and a little tougher. Both are available all year around. The North American cottontail rabbit, a fairly distant cousin of the common rabbit is also edible.

CHOOSE

■ A dressed (skinned and cleaned) whole rabbit will serve 3–4 people if it is stuffed.
■ Whole rabbits cut into portions are available, or individual portions such as bone-in legs, shoulders, and saddle.
■ Boneless rabbit meat is sold by the pound, cubed ready for cooking.

PREPARE

■ Soak wild rabbits in lightly salted or acidulated water for 2–3 hours to whiten the flesh and reduce strong flavors, then drain, rinse, and pat dry.
■ A lean, dry meat, rabbit benefits from being marinated for 4–24 hours.

COOK

■ Whole rabbit can be roasted, but it needs to be boned, stuffed, and barded (covered with strips of fat)—best left to the professional cook.
■ Braising is the best option for cooking rabbit at home. Sear bone-in cuts on all sides, then braise with vegetables and liquid on the stove top or in the oven at 350°F (325°F in fan ovens) for 1¼–1½ hours.
■ Boneless diced rabbit is good in casseroles and stews—it takes about 50–60 minutes when cooked over gentle heat, or in the oven at 325°F (275°F in fan ovens). Also good in pâtés, terrines and pies.

Squab

Most oven-ready squab are bred for the table and are available all year around. Rarer wild wood birds are at their best during the summer.

CHOOSE

- A whole bird is enough for 1 person.
- Boneless squab breasts are sold in packs, or slice them off the whole bird yourself. Allow 2 breasts per person.

PREPARE

As for pheasant (page 387).

COOK

- Pot roasting is preferred for whole birds. Follow instructions for pheasant (page 387), allowing 45–60 minutes.
- Pan-fry breasts as for pheasant (page 387), for 4–6 minutes.

Venison

Farmed venison is available all year around, and offers flavor and tenderness. Wild venison is seasonal and its quality variable. The animal's age, and whether the carcass has been matured, will affect its quality.

CHOOSE

Several different types of deer provide venison. Allow 8–12 ounces meat on

ROASTING A JOINT OF VENISON

For perfectly cooked, juicy roast venison, undercook it and then let it rest in a warm place to finish cooking. Sear the joint in hot oil, then roast at 425°F (400°F in fan ovens) for 10 minutes per 1 pound. Use a meat thermometer for best results, as follows:

- *For rare venison, remove the meat from the oven when the internal temperature is 95–122°F and let it rest until it has risen to 140°F.*
- *For medium venison, remove it when the internal temperature is 120–131°F and let it rest until it has risen to 149°F.*

LEAN AND LOW-FAT

- *Venison is super-rich in iron and has less fat than conventional red meats.*
- *Ground venison is really lean; use it to replace beef in sauces and for children's meals. It makes tasty burgers and sausages, too, but check the label as pork and beef fat may be added.*

MEAT:GAME

the bone, or 6 ounces boneless per person.

■ For roasting, use saddle (bone-in), loin (boneless saddle), haunch (back leg, on the bone, or boned and rolled), whole tenderloin, or shoulder (boned and rolled from young venison).

■ For pan-frying, broiling, or grilling —haunch steaks: top round and rump roast, 4–10 ounces each; loin steaks: medallions, (2–5 ounces); *filet mignon* 8 ounces–1 pound 4 ounces; shoulder steaks (5 ounces maximum; stroganoff/ stir-fry strips (from any of the above); sliced liver.

■ For pot roasting and braising— shoulder (on the bone/boned and rolled); shank; haunch (on the bone/boned and rolled).

■ For casseroling and stewing—diced boneless shoulder; diced shank; osso buco (shank with marrow bone).

PREPARE

Cuts are sold ready for cooking.

COOK

Venison is lean, with no marbling of fat, so needs careful cooking. Serve roasts and steaks rare or pink—overcooked venison is dry and tough. Cooking times depend on thickness rather than weight; use the following as a guide.

■ To roast a joint of venison, see page 389.

■ To pan-fry, broil, or grill, sear steaks quickly in hot oil/butter, then cook for 1 minute on each side. Let rest for a few minutes before serving.

■ Sauté or stir-fry stroganoff strips.

■ Shanks can be pot roasted, as lamb.

■ Diced shoulder can be used in stews.

■ Liver is tender and sweet, excellent sautéed, and good in pâtés and terrines.

Wild duck

Most wild duck is mallard, although sometimes widgeon and teal are available during the fall and winter months.

CHOOSE

■ Whole duck—most will serve 2, although smaller teal will serve only 1.

■ Boneless breasts—1–2 per person.

PREPARE

■ Whole ducks are oven-ready.

■ Breasts can be dry, and benefit from marinating for 4–24 hours.

COOK

■ Roast whole birds at 400°F (350°F in fan ovens) for 40–45 minutes. Let rest for 10–15 minutes before serving.

■ Pan-fry breasts for 3–4 minutes on each side.

6

Fish and Shellfish

FISH

SUPERMARKETS WITH FISH COUNTERS AND INDEPENDENT FISH STORES SELL A WIDE VARIETY OF FRESH AND FROZEN FISH ALL YEAR AROUND. MAIL ORDER AND WEB-BASED COMPANIES ALSO OFFER AN INCREASINGLY LARGE SELECTION OF DIFFERENT FISH —FRESHNESS AND QUALITY ARE HIGH, AND YOU WILL OFTEN FIND MORE CHOICE THAN IN THE STORES. THERE IS ALSO THE ADDED ADVANTAGE OF HAVING IT DELIVERED DIRECT TO YOUR DOOR.

CHOOSE

When buying fish, it is important to know where it has come from, and how it was caught. Over-fishing and the resulting decline in fish stocks are major issues, as are badly managed fisheries and fish farms, and irresponsible fishing methods. Read labels carefully and look for suppliers who support sustainable fishing and environmentally responsible methods, and source their fish from well-managed stocks. For up-to-date information and advice on choosing fish, visit the Marine Conservation Society's website, www.fishonline.org.

What to look for

All fish should have a clean, fresh smell of the sea and seaweed (or river weed in the case of freshwater fish). A strong fishy smell is a sign of staleness. These are the other pointers for optimum freshness and quality:

Whole fish
- Clear, bright eyes that are slightly bulging.
- Gills that are red or rosy pink.
- Shiny, moist, and slippery skin with no missing scales.
- Firm-looking body and stiff tail.

Fillets and steaks
- A firm, springy, translucent flesh with no discoloration.
- Neat and trim, with no untidy edges.

Buying frozen fish

If fish is commercially frozen straight after it is caught, the quality is usually good. Frozen fish is convenient too, and available all year. To be sure of the best quality when buying, check the following:
- The fish is frozen solid, with no sign of thawing.
- The packaging is undamaged.
- There is no sign of freezer burn (see page 26), or dark discoloration.

choose–store

SAFE HANDLING

Fresh fish is highly perishable and should be handled quickly and carefully. Oily fish keep less well than white fish, and whole fish keep longer once they have been gutted.

■ When you have bought fish, take it home as quickly as possible. Do not leave it for prolonged periods in the trunk of the car, especially on very hot summer days.

■ Always wash your hands, boards, and utensils in hot, soapy water, both before and after handling fish.

■ Don't prepare raw fish on the same board as cooked or preserved fish.

■ Cool cooked leftovers quickly and place in the refrigerator as soon as possible. Store for no longer than 24 hours.

STORE

Fresh fish: Remove packaging or wrappings and wipe the fish dry with paper towels, then lay it on a plate, and cover with plastic wrap. Place in the bottom of the refrigerator and store for no more than 24 hours.

Frozen fish: White fish will keep for up to 3 months. Oily and smoked fish, and cooked fish dishes will keep for up to 2 months.

GOOD FOR YOU

Nutritionists recommend eating fish and/or shellfish two to three times a week, including at least one portion of oily varieties such as herring, mackerel, salmon, and sardines.

■ *All fish contain protein (they contain all of the essential amino acids that the body requires but cannot make), but with less fat than meat. Protein is essential for good health and well-being.*

■ *White fish is a good source of B vitamins, especially B12, essential for healthy growth.*

■ *Oily fish is an excellent source of omega-3 fatty acids, which help lower cholesterol and prevent heart disease and strokes, and which play a large part in the healthy development of the brain (which is why fish is sometimes called brain food).*

■ *All fish provide a healthy supply of minerals, especially phosphorus and calcium that are good for your bones and teeth—eating the bones of small fish like sardines and whitebait will give you an instant dose. Fish is also a good source of iodine (which controls thyroid hormones) and the antioxidant selenium (which guards against harmful free radicals).*

FISH

Freezing fish at home

Fish is delicate and best frozen commercially, but there are times when it is convenient and useful to freeze a small quantity at home.

■ Check with your supplier whether the fish is genuinely fresh, or whether it is thawed frozen fish (you will not be able to tell the difference just by looking at it).

■ If it has been frozen and thawed, don't refreeze it while it is raw, but you can freeze it after it has been cooked and cooled—say in a soup, stew, lasagne, or pie, or in fish cakes.

■ Fish can be frozen whole (gutted and cleaned), or as fillets or steaks.

■ First get the freezer as cold as possible by switching to "fast freeze" or "super freeze" according to the manufacturer's instructions.

■ Freeze the fish in individual packages so you will be able to take out as few or as many portions as you need. Double wrap in plastic wrap and foil, then pack in an airtight freezer bag.

■ Store in the freezer for up to 3 months (oily fish are best eaten within 2 months).

■ To thaw frozen fish, unwrap and place on a plate, then cover loosely with plastic wrap or foil. Put it in the bottom of the refrigerator and leave for at least 4 hours, or overnight, until no ice crystals remain (for more rapid defrosting, use the microwave). Before cooking, pat dry thoroughly with paper towels.

PREPARE

Your fish supplier will scale, gut, and clean fish for you. He will also fillet it, or cut it into steaks, if you require, at no extra charge. This is better than buying ready-cut fillets or steaks because the fish will be fresher: It also leaves very little for you to do.

Whole round fish

Not everyone likes the look of a whole fish on their plate, so the neater and tidier it is the better. Prepare along the following guidelines, no matter which cooking method you choose.

Trim: Cut off the fins along the stomach and back with scissors, as close to the body as possible. To make the tail look more attractive, cut it into a V shape. This is called van-dycking after the pointed shape of the painter Van Dyck's beard. Leave the head on for cooking, as it helps to keep the fish in good shape and gives it flavor, but cut it off before serving if you prefer, or cover the eyes with a garnish such as sprigs of parsley.

Scale: This is something the fish supplier should do, but it is useful to know how to do it yourself. Scaling is particularly necessary with mullet, porgy, and seabass, as these are very scaly fish. Grasp the fish by the tail on a board and scrape a fish scaler or the back of a large knife blade from the tail to the head (see right).

SCALING

Wash and dry: Hold the fish under cold running water and rinse it well, inside and out, rubbing off any scales. Pat dry with paper towels.

Score: Optional, but it makes the fish cook more quickly and look more attractive, and if you are using a marinade, it will penetrate the fish faster. Make three or four diagonal slashes in each side, cutting right down to the bone, as shown in Terms and Techniques, page 41 .

Fillets and steaks

These are usually ready for cooking, but advice on scaling and skinning follows just in case. It is best not to wash fillets and steaks before cooking as this can make them waterlogged. Simply pat them dry with paper towels.

Scale: Use the same technique as for whole round fish (see above), working from the narrow tail end to the head end with fillets, against the direction of the scales with steaks.

FISH

Skin: If you leave the skin on, it will hold the fish together during cooking, but many recipes call for skinless fillets. You can ask your fish supplier to remove the skin, but packaged fish from the supermarket is often sold with it on. To skin a fillet, lay it skin-side down on a board and dip your fingertips in salt to give you a good grip. Grasp the tail end or corner of the fillet with your salted fingers and insert the blade of a sharp knife between the skin and the flesh. Work the knife away from you, using a sawing action, until you reach the end of the fillet, gripping the tail end tightly as you go (see illustration, opposite).

Remove pin bones: Run your fingers over the fleshy side of the fish to feel for any tiny bones sticking up. If you find any, pull them out with tweezers or your fingertips.

Trim: Cut into serving portions if necessary (it is easier to control the cooking time of small pieces of fish than one large fillet), and square off any untidy edges so that the fillets look as neat as possible.

Score: If fillets and steaks are to be cooked with their skin on, scoring helps them cook faster. It is very effective if the fish is thick and/or is being marinated. Make two or three diagonal slashes, cutting deep into the flesh (see Terms and Techniques, page 41).

COOK

There are many ways to cook fish, but they should all have two things in common—simplicity and speed. Fish is naturally tender and delicately flavored, so almost without exception it needs the briefest of cooking and the minimum of fuss to be enjoyed at its best. This is good news when you are in a hurry.

How to tell when fish is cooked

Undercooking is better than overcooking (the exception to this is monkfish, which needs slightly longer than most other fish). Overcooked fish will be dry, and may be tough and chewy. The timings given with the following cooking methods are approximate—it is impossible to be exact, because much depends on the freshness and thickness of the fish, the type of pan, and the degree of heat used.

■ A whole fish is done when the eyes turn white and opaque.

■ Fillets and steaks are done when the flesh turns from translucent to opaque.

■ As an extra test, tease a section of the flesh apart with a fork. If cooked, it will separate easily into flakes (see Terms and Techniques, page 24).

Bake

An oven method suitable for whole fish, fillets, and steaks, which are wrapped in a packet (*en papillote*, see Terms and Techniques, page 33) made of foil, waxed paper, or baking parchment, or grape, plantain, or banana leaves. Pastry also makes a good wrapping, but it is a little less healthy because of its fat content. During baking, fish cooks in its own juices that moisten the flesh, so very little extra fat is required. The packet also protects delicate fish from the heat, and locks in the flavor of the ingredients that are baked with it. Leaves used as a packet will scent the dish with their perfume.

Whole fish on the bone: Score (see Terms and Techniques, page 41), then brush with a little olive oil, and season lightly inside and out. Push any flavorings, such as lemon or lime slices, sprigs of herbs, lemongrass and fresh ginger slices, inside the body cavity and any slashes (see illustration, right). With whole, boned fish, the body cavity can be filled with a stuffing.

Fillets or steaks (with or without skin): Score (see Terms and Techniques, page 41) and insert the flavoring ingredients as for whole fish, above. Then brush with a little olive oil and season lightly.

REMOVING THE SKIN FROM A FISH FILLET

ADDING FLAVOR TO FISH

FISH:COOK

To cook: Lightly brush the inside of the wrapping with olive oil to prevent sticking and sit the fish in the center on a bed of herbs or vegetables for extra flavor. Wrap loosely, place on a cookie sheet, and bake at 375°F (340°F in fan ovens) for the following amount of time:

Large whole fish   30–35 minutes
Medium whole fish   20–25 minutes
Small whole fish   15–20 minutes
Fillets and steaks   10–15 minutes

Braise

This is a method for cooking fish in a covered dish in the oven—a cross between baking and steaming (see Terms and Techniques, page 12). It is suitable for whole fish, fillets, or steaks.
■ Score any skin (see pages 41 and 396).
■ Thin skinless fillets are best coiled or folded over, to prevent the flesh from drying out (see illustration, opposite).
■ Put the fish in an ovenproof dish on a bed of thinly cut or shredded vegetables and either sprinkle with liquid, such as wine or stock, or coat with a layer of sauce.
■ Cover the dish with oiled or buttered foil, or waxed paper, and braise at 350°F (325°F in fan ovens).
■ Braising times are 20–30 minutes for whole fish, 10–15 minutes for fillets or steaks.

Broil

A fuss-free, ultra-healthy method using either no added fat, or a bare minimum. Ideal for small to medium, whole fish and for fillets and steaks, with or without skin.
■ Oily fish such as herring, mackerel, sardines, salmon, and trout only need seasoning before broiling. Other fish, especially skinless white fish fillets, should be lightly oiled and seasoned, or coated with a crust or rub (see page 401) to protect their delicate flesh.
■ Whole fish, fillets, and steaks with skin on should be scored (see pages 41, 395, and 396). If time allows, marinating for 1–2 hours before cooking will help moisten and flavor the flesh (see Marinades for Fish, page 417).
■ Preheat the broiler to very hot before cooking, and put the broiler rack about 3 inches away from the heat.
■ Broil thin fillets on one side only, with the skin or skinned side facing upward. Turn whole fish and thick steaks once during broiling. (Thread small fish like sardines and smelts onto skewers first to make turning them easier.) Keep the flesh moist by brushing or basting once or twice with oil or cooking juices.
■ Broiling times are 4–5 minutes for fillets, 5–7 minutes for steaks, and 8–10 minutes for whole fish.

Charbroil/ Griddle

An indoor "barbecue" method, suitable for firm-fleshed fillets and steaks, especially salmon, cod loin, monkfish, seabass, shark, swordfish, and tuna. The fish sits on the ridges of the stove top charbroil pan (see Kitchen Kit, page 54), above any fat, and becomes imprinted with charred lines.

- Keeping the skin on during cooking will help hold the flesh together, but you can cook skinless fish this way too.
- Put the empty (unoiled) pan over a medium to high heat and leave it until very hot—you should feel the heat rising when you hold your hand about 3 inches above it.
- Brush the fish with olive oil and season lightly. Do this just before cooking or the salt will draw moisture out of the fish and make it dry.
- Put the fish on the pan with its skin or skinned side facing up. Leave it undisturbed for 2–3 minutes, pressing down firmly on the fish with a metal spatula (this helps make the charred lines more distinct—moving the fish too soon will cause it to stick). Turn over and repeat on the other side.
- For criss-crossed charred lines, give the fish a quarter turn once it has become charred.

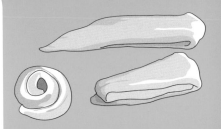

FOLD THIN SKINLESS FILLETS OF FISH BEFORE BRAISING

FISH:COOK

Deep-fry

Deep-frying is an excellent way to cook fish—the fast speed and intense heat insure moist, juicy flesh, while the coating protects the delicate fish and gives a crisp contrast.

To deep-fry, heat peanut or sunflower oil to 375°F: drop in a cube of stale bread—it should turn golden brown in 30 seconds. Fry in small batches, or the oil temperature will drop and the coating and fish will be soggy. Lift it out with a slotted spoon and drain on paper towels before serving. Here are two of the most successful ways to deep-fry fish.

Goujons: Strips of white fish, best for delicate and thin fillets like sole or flounder. Dredge the strips in seasoned flour, dip in beaten egg, and coat with fresh bread crumbs. Spread in a single layer on a plate or tray, and chill uncovered in the refrigerator for 1–4 hours to crisp up the coating. Deep-fry as above for 2–3 minutes until golden.

Tempura: Instant tempura batter mix is available in Japanese stores and Asian sections of some supermarkets. It is crisp and light, perfect for thick fillets of white fish such as cod, haddock, hake, and tope. Dip the fish into the batter, then deep-fry for 3–4 minutes until crisp and golden.

Grill

Hot and fast, grilling is one of the very best ways to cook fish, and is suitable for whole fish, fillets, and steaks. Oily fish like sardines, mackerel, and trout are especially good, as their natural oils make them self-basting. Thick, meaty fish fillets and steaks, such as monkfish, tuna, swordfish, and shark, cook the best this way as their firm flesh holds together well.

■ Marinating before grilling is beneficial, to add flavor and moistness (the fierce heat of the barbecue can make fish dry). The maximum marinating time should be 4 hours (see Marinades for Fish, page 417).

■ To prevent sticking, get the coals and grill really hot before cooking.

■ For easy lifting and turning, use a fish cage, or wrap the fish *en papillote* in foil (see Bake, page 397).

■ For cooking straight on the grill, fillets and steaks are best with their skin on, to help hold the flesh together, and they are also good cut into chunks and threaded onto oiled skewers.

■ If fish is not marinated, brush it with a little olive oil and season lightly just before cooking.

■ Don't overcook or the fish will be dry. Small whole fish take 5–7 minutes, medium whole fish 7–10 minutes, chunky fillets and steaks 7–10 minutes.

Microwave

This is one of the healthiest and best ways to cook fish—it retains juices and nutrients, without added fat.

■ It is best suited to fillets and steaks.

■ Small, whole fish can be micro-waved, but the skin must be scored or it will burst.

■ For even cooking, make sure the pieces are of a similar size and thick-ness. A turntable will help cook the fish evenly, so use one if you have one.

■ Place the fish on a plate, season, and sprinkle with a little citrus juice, light fish stock, white wine, or water, plus a sprinkling of chopped fresh herbs if you wish. Cover with plastic wrap and microwave on High, turning the fish over halfway. For fish that is about 1–1½ inches thick, the usual cooking time is 2–3 minutes, plus 1–2 minutes standing time, but ovens vary so you should consult your handbook for exact timings.

Pan-fry

A no-fuss, quick, and easy method for whole fish, fillets, and steaks. Thick, meaty monkfish, tuna, swordfish, and shark are good cooked this way, but so too are fish with less firm flesh such as cod, haddock, red snapper, seabass, and salmon, and even delicate flat fish

CRUSTS AND RUBS

Before pan-frying or broiling fish fillets, coat them with a flavor-packed crust or rub. It will look and taste good, and protect the flesh from the heat. When pan-frying, cook with the coated side down first; when broiling, start with the coated side facing up.

■ *FOR FISH WITHOUT SKIN—mix chopped fresh herbs such as dill, fennel, parsley, and mint with grated lemon, lime, or orange zest, and season to taste. Press a thick layer of the herb mixture onto the skinned side of the fish, after brush-ing it lightly with oil.*

■ *FOR FISH WITH SKIN—mix spices such as chili, cayenne, or paprika with dried thyme, salt, and coarsely ground black pepper. Rub over the skin and cook until crisp.*

such as sole and flounder, as long as they are cooked with care.

■ Whole fish can be pan-fried as they are, or lightly dusted with seasoned flour. It is best to protect fillets and steaks with a light dusting of seasoned flour or a coating of bread, matzo crumbs, or cornmeal, especially if they are skinless. A crust or rub (see page 401) is an even tastier option.

■ Season and/or coat the fish, then heat 1 2 tablespoons oil in a nonstick or heavy skillet until very hot. The temperature of the oil is important— if the oil is not hot enough, the fish will absorb it and become soggy and greasy. Peanut, sunflower, and olive oils are all good for pan-frying, and you can add a pat of sweet or clarified butter for color and flavor if you like (not too much butter or it may smoke and burn).

■ Once you see bubbles breaking gently over the surface of the oil (any butter will start to foam at this stage), lower the fish into the pan with its skin or skinned side facing up (unless you want crispy skin—see opposite). Don't overcrowd the pan—leave plenty of space between each piece— or the temperature of the oil will drop and the fish will stew rather than fry.

■ Cook over a medium to high heat without moving the fish, apart from turning it just once. It is ready to turn

when it has changed color up to the halfway mark. Don't be tempted to turn it more often or the flesh may fall apart. Total cooking time for thin fillets is 2–4 minutes, thick fillets and steaks 5–7 minutes, small to medium whole fish 8–10 minutes.

■ Lift the fish out with a metal spatula (see Kitchen Kit, page 65) and drain well before serving.

Poach

A moist and gentle, fat-free method for whole fish and fillets, poaching can be done on the stove or in the oven, and is especially suited to salmon and delicate white fish. Once the fish is cooked and lifted out with a perforated spatula, the liquid can be strained and used to make a sauce.

■ Poaching time is 5–7 minutes for fillets, 7–10 minutes for steaks. Small to medium whole fish take about 15–20 minutes.

On the stove: Pour enough liquid to just cover the fish—water, cold fish stock (see page 409), court bouillon (see page 411), or milk into a wide, shallow pan and bring to a gentle simmer. Lay the fish, skin or skinned side down, in a single layer in the liquid, cover the pan, and poach over low heat.

In the oven: Lay the fish, skin or

pan-fry–roast

skinned side up, in a shallow oven-proof dish or roasting pan and just cover with cold liquid (as described for poaching on the stove, opposite). Cover with foil or waxed paper and poach at 350°F (325°F in fan ovens).

In a kettle: Large fish such as a whole salmon or seabass are best poached in a fish kettle. You can then serve the fish hot or cold.

Measure the thickest part of the fish and calculate the cooking time, allowing 10 minutes for each inch, then lay the fish on the rack in the kettle. Pour in enough cold court bouillon (see page 411) to just cover the fish and bring to a boil over medium heat. Lower the heat, cover, and simmer gently for the calculated time.

If the fish is to be served cold, let it cool down in the kettle.

Roast

A quick and easy method, best suited to whole fish like red snapper, seabass, and salmon, and to fillets with the skin. Also good for robust fish without skin, such as monkfish tails, tuna steaks, and thick cod loin. The technique is the same as for roasting meat, but extra care must be taken or the delicate flesh of the fish may dry out.
■ Preheat the oven to 375°F (340°F in fan ovens).

CRISPY FISH FILLETS

Chefs like to serve fish fillets with their crisp skin facing up, often on a bed of mash or seasonal vegetables:

■ *Score the skin on the diagonal (see page 41) and lightly dust it with seasoned flour.*

■ *Heat 1–2 tablespoons oil in a skillet over a medium to high heat until very hot.*

■ *Put in the fish skin-side down.*

■ *Leave undisturbed for 6 minutes, until the skin is crisp.*

■ *Turn the fish over, switch off the heat, and leave for 3 minutes.*

■ *Drain well and serve.*

FISH:COOK

- If the fish still has its skin, score it (see page 41, 395, and 396).
- Brush olive oil all over the fish and season lightly, or coat with a crust or rub (see page 401).
- Place the fish on a lightly oiled cookie sheet and roast uncovered.
- Roast whole fish for 25–35 minutes, 10–20 minutes for fillets and steaks.

Steam

One of the healthiest cooking methods for fish as no fat is used and the maximum nutrients are retained. Suitable for all types of fish—whole, fillets, and steaks—but especially good for those with delicate flesh like flounder and sole.

- Put the fish in a single layer in the steamer basket. For more flavor, lay it on herbs or leaves, such as bok choy or spinach, or on thinly cut vegetables.
- Season lightly (salt takes moisture out of the fish).
- Place the basket over simmering court bouillon (see page 411) or fish stock (see page 409), to give flavor to the fish. Plain water can also be used if neither of these is available.
- Cover and steam for 3–7 minutes for fillets and steaks, 8–10 minutes for whole fish weighing up to 12 ounces, 15–20 minutes for fish weighing up to 2 pounds.

- You can steam fish *en papillote* (in a packet of waxed paper or baking parchment, see page 33). Put herbs or thinly cut vegetables inside the packet with the fish, and allow 5 minutes extra cooking time.
- Bamboo steamers are good for Asian recipes—over time the bamboo becomes scented with the ingredients used, which adds extra flavor to the fish. Scallions, lemongrass, fresh ginger, cilantro, star anise, soy, and sesame are some of the flavors that go well. Add them to the water, and sprinkle them over the fish.

Stew

Fish is good in stews, soups, and curries because it absorbs other flavors so readily. French *bouillabaisse* and *bourride*, American chowder, Spanish *zarzuela*, Thai and Goan curries, Moroccan tagine, Malaysian *laksa*, and Mongolian hotpot all illustrate this point very well.

- Choose fish that is thick and firm, so it does not fall apart. Monkfish is the most obvious choice, and swordfish, tuna, and cod loin also hold their shape well. More delicate fish can be used, but they should be saved until last and dropped in toward the end of cooking so there is less chance of them breaking up.

roast–stir-fry

Stir-fry

This method is healthy for two reasons—quick cooking over high heat retains nutrients, and very little fat is used. The downside is that the fish tends to break up during stirring and turning. Very firm fish such as monkfish, shark, and tuna are best, but you can use softer fish like salmon or cod loin if you are careful.

■ Cut skinless, boneless fish into strips or cubes.

■ Marinate for 1–2 hours, see Marinades for Fish, page 417.

■ Heat 1–2 tablespoons vegetable oil in a wok over medium to high heat until very hot.

■ Toss the fish in small batches into the pan and stir-fry for 2–4 minutes. Lift them out and repeat with more batches. It is essential not to overcrowd the pan or the temperature will drop and the fish will become soggy.

HOW TO SERVE A WHOLE ROUND FISH

Use this technique for any round fish, such as mackerel, salmon, or trout, no matter how it is cooked.

■ *Cut off the head and tail.*

■ *Run the point of a knife along the backbone.*

■ *Peel the skin off the top fillet.*

■ *Ease the top fillet from the bones.*

■ *Flip the top fillet over and set aside.*

■ *Pull the bones away from the bottom fillet.*

■ *Replace the top fillet.*

FISH A–Z

FRESH FISH A–Z

The following fish are commonly available at fish stores and supermarkets, as well as by mail order and over the web for home delivery. Wild fish is seasonal and more expensive than farmed fish, which is usually available all year around. Allow 4–6 ounces filleted fish or 8–9 ounces fish on the bone per person. For general preparation, see pages 394–6. For cooking instructions and times, see pages 396–405.

Cod

A round, white, juicy fish that falls into large, moist flakes when cooked. The bones are large, and easily removed.

CHOOSE

■ Small cod weighing about 1½ pounds are sometimes available, but most cod is large and sold as fillets or steaks, cut crosswise into cutlets with a central bone.
■ You may also see cod loin, which is cut from the thickest part of the fillet.

COOK

■ Small whole cod can be braised, poached, or roasted.

■ Fillets and steaks can be baked, braised, broiled, microwaved, pan-fried, poached, roasted, or steamed.
■ The flavor of cod holds its own when cooked with strong herbs and spices, and with pungent Mediterranean-style tomato sauces.
■ It is also good in fish cakes, lasagne, and pies, and deep-fried in batter. Cod loin is good cut into chunks for soups, stews, and curries.

USE INSTEAD Haddock, hake, or pollock.

Conger eel

A very large sea fish, which is usually sold as steaks on the bone.

CHOOSE

■ Steaks from the tail end are bony, so ask for middle-cut steaks from near the top (head) end.
■ The white flesh is firm, meaty, and rich.

COOK

■ Steaks are good for braising and broiling.
■ Cut into cubes, conger eel is also excellent in soups and stews because it retains its shape during cooking.

USE INSTEAD Cod or haddock.

Flounder

A flat fish with very fine, moist, white flesh and a delicate flavor. Both "sea" and "bay" flounders are available. They are sometimes known as flukes.

CHOOSE Sold as a whole fish (which you can fillet yourself or ask to be filleted) and as fillets. The winter flounder or blackback weighs 1–2 pounds, while the larger summer flounder weighs 1–5 pounds.

COOK Fillets can be baked, broiled, microwaved, pan-fried, poached, or steamed. Also good deep-fried in bread crumbs or batter.

USE INSTEAD Sole.

Haddock

A round, white fish similar to cod but smaller, thinner, and softer, and with a delicate shellfish flavor. The large bones are easy to see and remove.

CHOOSE Small, whole fish are available and are especially delicious, but haddock is mostly available as fillets.

COOK As for cod, preferably with the skin on to prevent the flesh falling apart. Especially good in fish cakes,

FLAT FISH

ROUND FISH

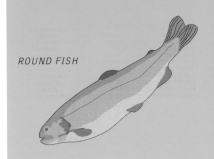

FISH A–Z

lasagne, and pies—partnered with strong flavors such as cheese, capers, and mustard—and deep-fried in batter.

USE INSTEAD   Cod, hake, or pollock.

Hake

A round fish with white flesh. An expensive member of the cod family that is not always easy to find, but worth looking for. The texture is soft and flaky, the flavor delicate, and the bones are easy to remove.

CHOOSE   Hake can be bought as fillets, but steaks on the bone are better because the delicate flesh is less likely to fall apart during cooking.

COOK   It can be baked, braised, broiled, microwaved, pan-fried, poached, roasted, or steamed. Good with Mediterranean flavors.

USE INSTEAD   Cod or haddock.

Halibut

A flat fish with meaty, white flesh and a distinctive flavor. They can grow to a huge size—up to 12 feet long.

CHOOSE

- Large fish are cut into steaks and have a central bone—the best steaks are the thick ones from the middle of the fish.
- Smaller fish, weighing 2–5 pounds, may be sold whole. Small "Greenland halibut", which are not true halibut, are sold filleted—they are cheaper than the real thing.

COOK

- It can be baked, braised, broiled, pan-fried, microwaved, poached, roasted, or steamed. It is especially good with wine-based sauces.
- To help prevent drying out, cooking on the bone is best.

USE INSTEAD   Flounder.

Herring

A small, oily fish with a rich-tasting flesh and many fine bones. See also Whitebait (page 418).

CHOOSE   Available whole (the plumpest are best), or they can be filleted.

COOK

- Good broiled, charbroiled, grilled, or pan-fried.
- Vitamin-packed herring roes are

delicious pan-fried and served on hot toast.

USE INSTEAD Mackerel or sardines.

Hoki

A member of the hake family that comes from Australia and New Zealand. The flavor is bland, but the flesh is white and nicely flaky, with very few bones. It is marketed as a sustainable alternative to some threatened fish stocks, such as cod.

CHOOSE Most often sold as fillets, which are usually frozen.

COOK It is best pan-fried with flavorsome sauces, especially tomato-based ones.

USE INSTEAD Cod, haddock, or hake.

Lingcod

This Pacific fish is not a member of the cod family, but it has a similar flavor and texture. The bones are also easily removed.

CHOOSE This huge fish—up to 60 pounds—is rarely sold whole, but it is widely available as fillets and steaks.

FISH STOCK

Makes about 4 cups, and keeps in the refrigerator for up to 3 days, or in the freezer for up to 2 months.

1 pound fish bones and trimmings, chopped and well rinsed
1 onion, peeled and cut into fourths
1 carrot, peeled and cut into fourths
1 celery stalk, roughly chopped
juice ½ lemon
splash dry white wine (optional)
12 peppercorns

Put all the ingredients into a large pan or stock pot and cover generously with water. Boil, and simmer for 20 minutes. Skim the surface often as the stock simmers, then strain, let cool, and use as the recipe requires.

To freeze, reduce the stock to half its volume by boiling vigorously, then cool. Pour into ice-cube trays and freeze. Put the frozen cubes into a freezer bag, so you can take them out individually— simply drop them into hot liquids or dissolve in boiling water.

COOK

■ Both fillets and steaks can be baked, braised, broiled, microwaved, pan-fried, poached, and steamed.
■ Lingcod can also be used in pies and fishcakes and goes well with strong flavors such as curry spices.

USE INSTEAD Cod or haddock.

Mackerel

An oily fish with a rich flavor and a stunning, iridescent skin. The bones are easily removed.

CHOOSE Sold as whole fish and fillets. Mackerel is at its best when very fresh.

COOK It can be baked, braised, pan-fried, broiled, grilled or microwaved. It goes well with strong flavours like horseradish and mustard, and is traditionally served with gooseberry sauce.

USE INSTEAD Herring or sardines.

Mahi-mahi

Also known as dolphin fish, this silvery fish has quite a flat body and flavorsome fine flesh. It is popular in the Mediterranean, as well as on both coasts of the United States.

CHOOSE Mahi-mahi is sold whole or in fillets.

COOK It is excellent pan-fried or broiled, especially if coated in oatmeal or bread crumbs. It is good in pies and goes well with strong flavors like chili and ginger. When very fresh it can be used raw for Japanese-style sashimi, or salted like *gravad lax*.

USE INSTEAD Pompano, tuna.

Monkfish

Also known as anglerfish, this large fish has a very ugly head. Only the tail section is eaten. The flesh is white, dense, and meaty, with a mild, sweet flavor. It contains just one central bone, so it is a perfect choice for serving to children.

CHOOSE Sold as whole tails or long fillets from either side of the central bone, it is almost always displayed skinned. However, insure that the purple-gray, transparent membrane that covers it has been removed or the fish will shrink and be chewy. To remove the membrane, nick it with the tip of a sharp knife and pull it away with your fingers.

COOK

■ Whole tails are good braised or roasted (and especially tasty when wrapped in prosciutto or bacon).

■ When the fillets are cut into cubes or strips, monkfish is excellent for skewering and grilling, and for cooking in soups, stews, lasagne, and stir-fries, because it holds its shape so well.

■ It is also good sliced into medallions or scallops and broiled, pan-fried, or charbroiled.

USE INSTEAD Lobster, conger eel, cod loin.

Mullet

There are two main types —goatfish and striped mullet. Goatfish is the smaller of the two, with delicately flavored, firm, white flesh and skin that crisps well. Striped mullet is coarser and cheaper, and can taste a bit muddy.

CHOOSE Buy goatfish for preference, either as small whole fish or fillets.

COOK Whole fish and fillets can be baked, braised, broiled, grilled, pan-fried, or roasted. Mullet goes particularly well with Mediterranean flavors.

COURT BOUILLON

Makes about 5 cups and keeps in the refrigerator for up to 5 days.

5 cups water
splash of dry white wine
2 carrots, chopped
2 onions, chopped
1 large bouquet garni
1½ teaspoons rock or sea salt
2 teaspoons black peppercorns
generous ½ cup white wine vinegar

Combine all the ingredients, except the vinegar, in a large pan. Bring to a boil, then simmer, uncovered, for 15–20 minutes, adding the vinegar for the last 5 minutes. Cool before use.

USE INSTEAD seabass, porgy, or red snapper.

Pollock

A round, white fish similar to cod, but blander and cheaper, and not so white.

CHOOSE Best bought as fillets, which may have a few bones. Rub with lemon juice and a pinch of salt to whiten.

COOK As for cod, especially in tomato sauces where the color of the fish is disguised, although the flesh does get whiter when it is cooked. Pollock makes good fish cakes, and mixes well with other fish in soups, stews, and pies—if you use it as a base, you will need a smaller quantity of other, more expensive, fish.

USE INSTEAD Cod or haddock.

Pompano

This slightly oily, sweet, meaty fish is very popular in Florida, Louisiana, and the Caribbean. Its close relative, the amberjack, is also available.

CHOOSE It is available whole, weighing about 1½–3 pounds, or as fillets with the skin on.

COOK
■ It is best broiled and can also be braised. As it can easily dry out, it is well suited to cooking in a packet.
■ Pompano fillets in a paper bag is a classic delicacy from New Orleans. It goes well with tomatoes and garlic.

USE INSTEAD Salmon.

Porgy

There are many types of this white fish, but the sheepshead bream and the scup are the ones to look for. They have juicy, white and tender flesh, and the best flavor. American red porgy is also popular. Check that the fish has been properly scaled when buying.

CHOOSE Buy whole fish, or ask for it to be filleted.

COOK
■ Whole fish are good roasted, or braised with Mediterranean vegetables and flavorings.
■ Fillets can be baked, broiled, pan-fried, poached, steamed, or microwaved.
■ They are also good in fish stews, when added toward the end of cooking.

USE INSTEAD Seabass, goatfish, or red snapper.

mullet–sardine

Salmon

An oily fish with orange-pink, meaty flesh and a good flavor. The bones are few and are easily removed.

CHOOSE Available whole, as fillets, and as steaks with a central bone.

COOK Salmon can be baked, braised, broiled, charbroiled, grilled, microwaved, pan-fried, poached, roasted, or steamed. It can also be made into *gravad lax* (see page 421), and used in fish cakes, kedgeree, lasagne, and pies. Also goes well with Asian flavors, especially ginger, lime, and soy.

USE INSTEAD Trout.

Sardine

A small, oily fish with a good flavor, but many bones. Pilchards are the same fish, only larger. A popular European fish, they are widely exported both frozen and in cans.

CHOOSE Available whole, sardines can be filleted. They are best with the head and backbone removed, so they can be cooked opened out flat (butterflied).

WILD VERSUS FARMED

Wild Atlantic salmon are considered by gourmets and chefs to be the finest fish. Unfortunately, overfishing has severely depleted stocks in both North America and Europe. To some extent fish farming is overcoming this problem, but it is also creating new environmental concerns. Organic farms situated at sea, rather than near the coast, are not only less damaging but also produce the best-tasting fish. Wild Pacific salmon, such as chinook, coho, and sockeye, have not suffered the same decline in numbers. However, neither the flavor nor texture of the flesh is so fine as that of the Atlantic salmon.

FISH A–Z

COOK Great grilled in summer, but also good charbroiled, broiled, or pan-fried. They are also good with pasta.

USE INSTEAD Herring or mackerel.

Seabass

A round fish with fine, white flesh that is moist, delicate, and sweet-tasting. It holds its shape during cooking, and the shiny, silver skin crisps up well. The bones are few and easily removed.

CHOOSE

■ Whole fish vary from 12 ounces–1 pound for 1 serving, up to 7 pounds that will feed 6–8 people. Large sea-bass are expensive.
■ You can also buy fillets, which are sold with the skin on.

COOK

■ Whole fish are best baked, braised, poached, roasted, or steamed.
■ Fillets are good broiled, pan-fried, steamed, microwaved, or stir-fried.
■ Good with Mediterranean and Asian vegetables and flavorings.

USE INSTEAD Porgy, goatfish, or red snapper.

Sea robin

An inexpensive, round, white fish with an extraordinary-looking head and spiky fins. There are several types, all of which are quite bony. The red sea robin is said to have the best flavor, although the gray and yellow are eaten.

CHOOSE Although you may see whole fish at fish stores, there is a lot of waste, so it is best to ask for fillets.

COOK Sea robin goes well with Mediterranean ingredients for baking, braising, microwaving, pan-frying, poaching, or steaming. Also good in soups and stews when added toward the end of the cooking time.

USE INSTEAD Goatfish.

Shark

There are many members of the shark family, but shark sold in the store is unlikely to be named. Mako is the most common, but blacktip and tiger sharks are also eaten. They are all boneless, meaty, and thick, with a dense texture.

CHOOSE Available as steaks, loin, and fillets.

COOK

■ Shark can be braised, broiled, pan-fried, charbroiled, grilled, or preferably marinated beforehand to make the flesh juicier.

■ It is also good grilled in chunks on skewers, or used in curries, stir-fries, soups, and stews.

USE INSTEAD Swordfish or tuna.

Skate

The kite-shaped wings are the only parts of this fish that are eaten. They yield tender, sweet, white flesh between the cartilage (there are no bones).

CHOOSE

■ Wings or parts of wings are sold ready-skinned—for each person allow 1 small wing or a third of a large wing. The thick piece cut from the center of a large wing is best and is called the "middle cut"—this is the meatiest part and is up to 2 inches thick.

■ Skate knobs are chunks of solid white fish that look similar to scallops. You will need about 4 per person.

COOK

■ Best poached, pan-fried, or roasted.
■ Skate knobs can be used in stews.

WHAT'S IN A NAME?

Tope, rock salmon, rock eel, huss, flake, rigg, and dogfish are all one and the same fish—a small member of the shark family—given different names, depending on which country you're in and where you buy it. It is always sold in fillets and has no pin bones. It goes well with strong flavors such as curry spices and sweet-and-sour sauce and can be baked, braised, broiled, deep-fried, or grilled. It is ideal for fish soups.

FISH A–Z

USE INSTEAD Ray (very similar to skate) or sole fillets.

Snapper

There are many kinds, but red snapper is the most common. The flesh is white, with a sweet, slightly nutty flavor. The bones are easy to see and remove.

CHOOSE Available as whole fish, fillets, and steaks.

COOK Whole fish can be baked, braised, grilled, poached, roasted, or steamed. Fillets are good baked, broiled, grilled, microwaved, or pan-fried. Always cook with the skin on to help prevent the flesh from breaking up. Especially good with herbs and chilies, and in Cajun, Caribbean, Mexican and Asian recipes.

USE INSTEAD Goatfish or seabass.

Sole

A flat, white fish with a delicate flavor and a firm, juicy texture. There are several types, and some flounders are also known as sole.

CHOOSE Available whole and as fillets.

COOK

■ Whole fish can be baked, broiled, charbroiled, grilled, or pan-fried.
■ Fillets can be broiled, microwaved, pan-fried, poached, or steamed.
■ Strips can be deep-fried or pan-fried.

USE INSTEAD Flounder.

Swordfish

Firm, compact, and meaty, swordfish flesh is white with a pinkish tinge. It is low in fat, so it can be dry if not cooked carefully. There are no bones.

CHOOSE Available as loins or steaks, or buy a piece of loin and cut it into steaks. Steaks should be cut thickly to prevent overcooking and dryness.

COOK

■ It can be braised, broiled, charbroiled, grilled, pan-fried, or roasted, preferably marinated beforehand to make it juicier.
■ Also good cut into chunks and grilled on skewers.

USE INSTEAD Tuna or shark.

Trout

An oily freshwater fish, the most common are the rainbow trout, which

skate–tuna

is farmed on a large scale, and the sea trout, that sometimes migrates into the sea like salmon, and is often called salmon trout.

CHOOSE Available whole and as fillets.

COOK Trout can be baked, braised, broiled, grilled, microwaved, poached, pan-fried, or roasted.

USE INSTEAD Salmon.

Tuna

A huge fish with dense, meaty flesh that varies from pink to red. There are many types—bluefin, bonito, and yellowfin are three good ones, but most tuna is not be sold by name.

CHOOSE Available as steaks, with no bones.

COOK
■ It can be braised, broiled, grilled, pan-fried, or roasted.
■ At its best as a thick steak that it has been marinated and is served slightly undercooked, or it can be dry.
■ Good with Mediterranean and Asian flavors.

USE INSTEAD Swordfish.

MARINADES FOR FISH

Most fish is lean with little natural fat, so marinating before cooking is a great way to inject moisture and flavor and to prevent dryness. It is especially effective for fish that is to be cooked by dry heat such as broiling, grilling, charbroiling, and roasting.

■ Marinades for fish are very often based on a combination of olive or sunflower oil and an acidic ingredient such as citrus juice, wine vinegar, or wine (the usual ratio is 3 parts oil to 1 part acidic). Plain yogurt can also be used as part of a marinade base, and it works especially well with lemon juice and tandoori or other Indian spices.

■ Fresh herbs and garlic go well with fish—add some for extra flavor.

■ Fish absorbs marinades rapidly, and 1–2 hours marinating is enough, especially if you turn the fish over halfway through the marinating time. Don't marinate for longer than 4 hours, especially when citrus juice is included. The acid in citrus juice "cooks" the fish so that it turns opaque, as in the Mexican ceviche, where lime juice is deliberately used for this effect.

Whitebait

These tiny, silver fish are baby herring or sprats.

CHOOSE Whitebait is almost always sold frozen.

COOK Coat whole fish in spiced or seasoned flour and deep-fry in hot oil for a few minutes until crisp. They are eaten whole (including skin and bones), which makes them an excellent source of calcium.

USE INSTEAD There is no substitute.

Whiting

Round, white fish similar to haddock, but with less flavor.

CHOOSE Available whole and as fillets. It must be very fresh or the texture will not be good.

COOK It can be baked, braised, pan-fried, broiled, poached, or roasted, and is good in soups, stews, fish cakes, or pies.

USE INSTEAD Haddock.

PRESERVED FISH

Fish is preserved in many different ways—smoked, salted, dried, pickled, or canned. All keep well, are on a par with fresh fish nutritionally, and most need no preparation or cooking.

Dried and salted

As you would expect, fish that are preserved by salting and drying have an intense flavor.

Dried salt cod is popular in Scandinavia, the Caribbean, and Africa, but especially around the Mediterranean—in Italy it is called *baccalà*, in Spain *bacalao*, and in Portugal *bacalhau*. To soften and remove excess salt, traditional salt cod needs soaking in cold water for days before use. Modern light cures are softer and less salty and need only 24 hours soaking. Look in Mediterranean cookbooks for salt cod recipes and in French cookbooks for the famous *brandade de morue*.

Mojama is dried salted tuna. It is shaved or sliced wafer-thin and served with olive oil, lemon juice, and black pepper, on its own or on bread. For an appetizer, it makes an unusual alternative to smoked salmon.

Roes are often salted and dried (see page 423).

Smoked

There are two types of smoked fish— "hot smoked" and "cold smoked." Hot smoking cooks the fish at the same time as smoking; with cold smoking, the fish does not cook.

STORE Packaged tightly in plastic wrap, smoked fish will keep in the refrigerator for up to 10 days.

CHOOSE
Eel

■ Available as fillets.

■ Rich and dense, and expensive compared to other smoked fish, but a little goes a long way. A 2–3-ounce serving is ample for 1 person.

■ No need for cooking. Use as a first course or in salads and fish pâtés.

Haddock

■ Available as fillets, and sometimes as whole, split fish on the bone.

■ Buy the pale, naturally cured fish, rather than the artificially dyed, bright yellow kind (which is sometimes cod or pollock rather than haddock).

■ Haddock needs cooking—poach in milk or milk and water, or broil with a pat of butter. It is also very good in kedgeree, fish cakes, and pies.

SOMETHING DIFFERENT

Many unusual and exotic fish are available by mail order and over the web, and occasionally at the fish store and supermarket. Supplies vary, as they come from different parts of the world at different times of the year, so you cannot count on a particular one being in stock when you want it. Ask your supplier for preparation and cooking instructions—anyone selling these kinds of fish will know what to do with them. The following are some of the best that are most widely available:

■ *AMBER JACK*

■ *BARRACUDA*

■ *CARP*

■ *DENTON*

■ *EMPEROR FISH*

■ *ESCOLAR*

■ *KINGFISH*

■ *LING*

■ *MARLIN*

■ *MILKFISH*

■ *OCEAN PERCH*

■ *ORANGE ROUGHY*

■ *POLLACK*

■ *RED DRUM*

■ *RED GROUPER*

■ *SCABBARD*

■ *STURGEON*

■ *TILAPIA*

■ *TILEFISH*

FISH:PRESERVED

■ Arbroath smokies are small, hot-smoked haddock, on the bone and without heads. They are usually sold in pairs, tied together with string. Split them open, remove the bone and they are ready to eat as they are, and also good warmed under the broiler for a few minutes. The flavor is milder than that of other smoked haddock.

Herring

■ The most common type is split-open whole fish that have been brined and oak-smoked, traditionally sold in pairs. The undyed kind are best, especially the famous Manx and Loch Fyne kippers from Britain, where they are known as kippers.

■ Strong-flavored flesh with many tiny bones. If these bother you, buy smoked herring fillets.

■ Needs cooking. Broiling is traditional, although microwaving and poaching are also good (if you add a pinch of sugar to the poaching liquid, the fish are more easily digested). Cooked fillets are good in pâtés.

■ Ungutted, cold-smoked herrings with rich-tasting flesh are also available, but may be difficult to find. They are whole, and need to be gutted before broiling or pan-frying.

■ Brisling, buckling, sild, and sprats are hot-smoked herrings that are normally eaten cold, but they can also be broiled and served hot.

Mackerel

■ Available whole and as fillets.

■ Plump, juicy flesh that is tasty, and less bony than that of smoked herring.

■ Needs no cooking, although can be broiled. The flavor is good in pâtés.

Salmon

■ Cold-smoked salmon is available both as a whole side (usually sliced and interleaved), and as thin slices. You can also buy trimmings, which are cheaper than slices.

■ Lox is a Jewish specialty, a cold-smoked salmon that varies in color and flavor according to the cure. It is usually cheaper than other types of smoked salmon.

■ Hot-smoked salmon looks and tastes like a cross between smoked, poached, and roasted fresh salmon. It is available as thick fillets and flaked pieces.

■ Both cold- and hot-smoked are ready to eat as they are, and are also good diced or flaked in salads, scrambled eggs, omelets, quiches, pasta sauces, and risotto. Hot-smoked salmon fillets are good broiled and served hot. Cold-smoked salmon is good pan-fried very briefly. Sliced lox can be used like smoked salmon, and is traditionally served with bagels and cream cheese.

Trout

■ Hot-smoked trout is available as whole fish and fillets. Cold-smoked

smoked–marinated

trout is sold thinly sliced in the same way as smoked salmon.

■ The delicate, moist flesh of hot-smoked trout is plump and pale pink, and less bony than that of smoked herring and mackerel. Cold-smoked trout looks and tastes very like smoked salmon, but is cheaper.

■ Use as for smoked salmon.

Marinated and pickled fish

Oily fish are preserved in either brine or vinegar and flavors vary, from sharp and vinegary to mild and sweet. They can usually be kept unopened in the refrigerator for up to 10 days, though you should check the "use-by" date on the packaging.

Boquerones: Marinated anchovies with white flesh and silver skin. Mild and sweet, they are nothing like canned or bottled anchovies (page 74). Use as an appetizer or in salads, or fry.

Gravad lax: Raw salmon cured with dill, salt, and peppercorns. Serve thinly sliced as an appetizer.

Herrings: There are numerous varieties of pickled, soused, and marinated herrings. Good ones are the Dutch Maatjes, sweetcure herring fillets, and rollmops. Serve them as an appetizer, or use in salads.

RING THE CHANGES
Thinly sliced smoked salmon is one of the easiest and most popular appetizers, but there are other smoked fish, also sold thinly sliced, that can be served in the same way. If you find them a little on the expensive side, cut the cost by mixing them with smoked salmon —the different colors make an interesting presentation and the flavors also complement one another well.

■ *SMOKED HALIBUT—pale, delicate flesh tinged with a golden-orange border.*

■ *SMOKED STURGEON—fine-grained flesh that is very pale pink and delicately flavored.*

■ *SMOKED TUNA—deep red with an open texture and an intense flavor.*

FISH:PRESERVED | RAW

Canned fish

Canned fish provides protein, vitamins, and minerals just like fresh fish. If you keep a few cans in your pantry, you can whip up a nutritious meal quickly, without cooking.

CHOOSE

Anchovies: Tiny, slim fish packed in oil or salt, sold in jars or cans. See also Pantry Staples, page 74.

Salmon: Pink is cheapest, red the most expensive, and it will say on the label whether it is wild or farmed. Eat the bones (which are soft) because they are a good source of calcium.

Sardines: The ones in good-quality olive oil are best for flavor, but those in tomato sauce provide a nutritional double whammy because the tomatoes contain lycopene, a valuable antioxidant. Pilchards are large sardines that are usually packed in tomato sauce. Both sardines and pilchards are a good source of calcium when the bones are eaten.

Tuna: The pale-colored albacore fillets are very good, sold either in olive oil or spring water (often in jars rather than cans). Look for *ventresca de bonito*, oil-rich belly fillets canned in olive oil. See also Pantry Staples, page 121.

RAW FISH

In Japanese sashimi, sushi, and maki, very fresh raw fish is sliced wafer-thin and eaten uncooked. You can make these dishes easily and safely at home, as long as you are sure of the provenance and freshness of the fish you are using. Buy from a reputable source, letting your supplier know what it is intended for.

■ Fish that are suitable include halibut, goatfish, salmon, seabass, porgy, and tuna.

■ Buy the freshest fish possible and use it on the same day, keeping it in the refrigerator from the moment you get home.

■ When you take the fish out of the refrigerator to prepare it, work speedily in a cool kitchen with cool hands, then return it to the refrigerator immediately, until just before serving. Use within 4 hours.

canned–roe

KNOW YOUR ROE

Roes are fish eggs, which are preserved and used in many different ways. The flavor is very strong, so they are used in small quantities.

■ **Bottarga** is the salted, dried and pressed roe of gray mullet (similar to striped mullet) or tuna, and is regarded as a great delicacy all around the Mediterranean. In Italy they soften it in olive oil and serve it thinly sliced on bread with lemon juice and black pepper. It is also grated over pasta that has been tossed in olive oil to make the classic pasta dish *spaghetti alla bottarga*.

■ **Caviar** is salted sturgeon's roe. The best and most expensive is the black Beluga. Second best is Oscietra, while Sevruga is the least expensive.

■ **Keta** is salted salmon roe, sometimes called salmon caviar. Larger than real caviar, it is orange-red, soft, and moist. It can be used in the same ways as real caviar, at a fraction of the cost.

■ **Lumpfish roe** is salted and dyed black to look like caviar, so it is also known as mock caviar. Another name for it is Danish caviar, and it is sometimes dyed orange or red.

■ **Smoked cod's roe** is normally used for taramasalata, although traditionally gray mullet roe is also used. Before use, soak the roe in boiling water for 1–2 minutes, to take the edge off its strong flavor, then drain and dry, and peel off the skin.

SHELLFISH

SUPERMARKETS AND FISH STORES OFFER A GOOD CHOICE OF SHELLFISH ALL YEAR ROUND, AND SO TOO DO MAIL ORDER COMPANIES AND WEBSITES, WHERE YOU CAN OFTEN FIND MORE UNUSUAL VARIETIES. SHELLFISH DIVIDES INTO TWO GROUPS— CRUSTACEANS AND MOLLUSKS. BOTH HAVE SHELLS, BUT CRUSTACEANS HAVE LEGS AND MOLLUSKS DON'T.

CHOOSE

Shellfish is highly perishable, so always buy it from a reputable source with a quick turnover.

- All shellfish should have a clean, fresh smell.
- The shells should be in perfect condition, not broken or cracked.
- Live clams, mussels, and oysters should have their shells closed. If you can see a lot of open ones, don't buy.

Buying frozen shellfish

A lot of shellfish is frozen at sea, and sold either frozen or defrosted— "fresh" shrimp, for example, are often defrosted frozen shrimp. There is nothing wrong with this (in fact, it insures freshness), but you shouldn't refreeze them when you get home. Check with the supplier, to be absolutely sure. When buying frozen shellfish, also check the following:

- The packaging is unopened and undamaged, and the shellfish inside is frozen solid, with no sign of thawing.
- There is no sign of freezer burn (dry, white patches) or dark discoloration.

STORE

Shellfish should be handled quickly and carefully.

- Keep well wrapped in the refrigerator and eat on the day of purchase, or within 24 hours of buying.
- Frozen shellfish should be well wrapped and stored in the freezer for up to 6 months.
- To thaw, unwrap and place on a plate lined with a thick layer of paper towels, then cover loosely with plastic wrap or foil. Alternatively, place in a colander set over a bowl and cover. Put in the bottom of the refrigerator and leave for at least 4 hours, or overnight, until no ice crystals remain (for more rapid defrosting, use the microwave). Before cooking, pat thoroughly dry with paper towels.

crab

CRUSTACEANS

This group of shellfish has shells and legs. It ranges from expensive lobsters for special occasions to shrimp that are good value for money and are suitable for everyday meals.

Crab

From ocean-front stores to the super-market, crab is on offer all year around, but it is especially good in the summer months. The sand crab and red crab are the most widely avail-able, but you may also see snow crabs on sale if you are on the coast. Whole and dressed crabs are usually sold fresh; white and brown crab meat and claws are often sold frozen.

CHOOSE

Whole live crab: This is the freshest option, but it is time-consuming and awkward to boil a crab and remove the edible meat from the shell and claws, so you may prefer to buy a **whole cooked crab**, the next best thing, and ask the fish store to do the job for you. Whole crabs should feel heavy for their size—weight indicates there is plenty of meat. A crab that weighs 2 pounds will feed 2–3 people; for 4 people you will need one that weighs at least 3 pounds. Small crabs

GOOD FOR YOU
Nutritionists recommend we eat fish, including shellfish, two or three times a week.
■ *Low in fat, shellfish provides protein and valuable vitamins and minerals (especially potassium, iodine, iron, and zinc).*

SHELLFISH:CRUSTACEANS

are difficult to deal with, so the bigger, the better.

Dressed crab: This is a more practical choice than a whole crab because the white and brown meat have already been extracted and piled back into the shell. Dressed crab must look fresh and lively, and have a visible amount of good white meat and decent-sized claws.

Crabmeat: If you need lots of white meat for a recipe, it is best to buy this on its own—it is unlikely you will get enough from a whole or dressed crab. The best white meat comes from the claws, and you can buy cooked claws separately, but if you don't have the time to extract the meat yourself, buy packets of white meat. Check where it has come from if you can—the best is claw meat only; other types may be a mixture of claw and body meat. Allow 4 ounces per person.

If you want **brown meat**, you can buy this separately, although it often comes packed with white meat. Allow 2–3 ounces per person.

Another option is **canned crab**, an all white meat that is excellent quality and handy for fish cakes, salads, soups, and pasta sauces.

PREPARE

■ Frozen crab should be defrosted before use—leave it in its packaging in the refrigerator overnight.

■ Crack open crab claws with a claw cracker or hammer (see opposite) and extract the meat with a skewer.

■ Pick over all crab meat and remove any pieces of shell.

■ Canned crab can be watery, so drain it well in a strainer before flaking with a fork.

COOK

■ The meal from a boiled crab can be eaten cold just as it comes, or tossed over the heat for a minute or two and served hot.

■ Dressed crab can be served straight from the shell, or you can take out the white and dark meats and use them in recipes.

SERVE

■ Flaky white crab meat has a mild, sweet flavor that goes equally well with creamy or fiery sauces. It makes an excellent crab cocktail, is good in salads, soups, and pasta sauces, or as a filling for filled pasta shapes such as ravioli. It marries well with Asian ingredients like lime, ginger, chili, and cilantro, and is good in stir-fries, curries, and fish cakes.

■ Dark crab meat is rich and filling, and is good mixed with white meat to intensify the flavor. It also gives body and flavor to sauces and soups.

crab–lobster

Lobster

The ultimate luxury, lobster is usually expensive but worth every cent—its firm white meat is incomparably succulent and sweet, especially in the summer months. A live lobster has a dark green shell that turns orange-red when cooked.

CRACKING CRAB CLAWS

CHOOSE

■ A whole live lobster is the freshest choice, but then you will have to kill it, split it in half, and remove the inedible parts from the shell—not a job for the faint-hearted. A freshly cooked lobster is a more practical option, which you can buy split in half, cleaned, and ready to eat. Allow half a 1½-pound lobster per person.

■ Spiny lobster and shovel-nosed tails come from clawless lobsters. All the meat is in the tail, which is sold on its own and is usually raw. Preparation is easy, with little waste. Allow 1 tail per person.

PREPARE

■ If you have bought a ready-to-eat, halved lobster, there should be nothing to do, unless the claws are still intact. If they are, crack them open with lobster crackers or a hammer and extract the meat—or leave this to be done at the table if you prefer.

SOFT-SHELL CRABS

These are blue crabs caught after shedding their hard shells and before growing new ones (they shed their shells several times before they reach maturity). Allow 2 per person—the whole thing is eaten, soft shell and all. The flesh is creamy and very tender, with a sweet taste.

■ *If they are frozen, they should be defrosted in the refrigerator before cooking. Allow a minimum of 4 hours, or leave overnight.*

■ *For an appetizer or light lunch, lightly coat soft-shell crabs in seasoned flour and pan-fry in hot oil or butter (or both) for 2–3 minutes each side, until golden. Remove and deglaze the pan with lemon juice, then add chopped parsley and Worcestershire sauce. Pour over the crabs and serve hot.*

SHELLFISH:CRUSTACEANS

■ Some recipes call for tail meat only. Remove and discard the dark intestinal "vein" from the top of the tail meat, then lift the meat out of each shell. For medallions, slice crosswise along the length of the tail (see illustration, opposite).

■ To prepare a whole, raw, spiny lobster tail, put it hard-shell-side down on a board and cut around the flat shell with scissors. Lift this away to reveal the flesh, and snip off any fins.

COOK

■ When you buy a cooked lobster that has been split in half, you can eat it as it comes—the simpler, the better. It is good cold with mayonnaise, as a lobster cocktail, or in a salad. To serve hot, broil flesh-side up in the half shell for 5 minutes, brushing the exposed meat with melted butter before and during cooking.

■ Medallions can be pan-fried in olive oil and/or butter, or used in stir-fries. They are also good in curries. Allow 2–3 minutes' cooking time—just enough to heat the lobster through.

■ Marinate raw spiny lobster tails in the refrigerator in olive oil, citrus juice, and herbs or spices for 4 hours or overnight, then run a skewer through the flesh from the wide to the narrow end,, and cook with the flesh-side facing the heat for 6–7 minutes.

Turn the tail over, and cook the shell side until it turns red—this will take about 4–5 minutes.

■ Another way to cook the tail meat of spiny lobsters is to remove it from the shell in one piece, then slice it crosswise into medallions, as for American lobsters (see opposite). These can then be pan-fried or stir-fried, or poached in stock. Allow 3–4 minutes, or until the flesh is opaque.

■ Asian ingredients like fresh ginger, cilantro, chili, garlic, scallions, and lime suit the flavor of lobster well, and so too do rich ingredients like cream, cheese, wine, and brandy.

■ Lobster and pasta make a good team—either in a tomato or creamy sauce, or as a filling for pasta such as ravioli.

Shrimp

There is a huge variety of shrimp on offer, both raw and cooked, cheap and expensive. All are quick and easy to prepare and cook, and you can use them in many ways.

CHOOSE

Raw shrimp: There are many different types of shrimp available, although most are sold simply described as small, medium, large, or jumbo. Gulf white shrimp is especially

lobster–shrimp

full of flavor and royal red shrimp—
red in color even when alive—look
spectacular. Pacific shrimp include
pink and side-stripe shrimp. You can
buy jumbo shrimp whole in their
shells, or with their heads off. When
the heads are off, they are called
shrimp tails and are also sold peeled.
North Atlantic shrimp are the smallest of the raw shrimp, usually sold
whole. As a compensation for their
small size, cold water shrimp are
more succulent than tropical ones.

Cooked shrimp: These are pink.
The largest, jumbo shrimp, are available whole, or without their heads.
When sold without their heads, their
shells have often been removed too
(but not their tails). Medium and small
shrimp may be sold whole or headless.
When sold without their heads, they
are often also peeled, but they may
still have their tails intact.

■ Depending on size, buy 3–4 jumbo
shrimp per person for an appetizer,
5–6 for a main course. Allow about
3–4 ounces (1 cup) peeled small or
medium shrimp per person as an appetizer, 6 ounces (1½ cups) as a main
course. If the shrimp are in their shells,
buy double this weight.

PREPARE

Peel: This means to remove the shells,
which you can do before or after cook-

CUTTING A LOBSTER TAIL

TIPS AND TRICKS: SHRIMP

*Raw shrimp are good dipped in
tempura batter (buy an instant
mix from a Japanese store or the
supermarket), then deep-fried in hot
sunflower oil for 3 minutes. Serve
them with a soy or chili dip for a
quick and easy canapé—the tails
make perfect handles. They can be
butterflied or straight.*

*■ For butterflied shrimp—peel
and devein, leaving the tail on (see
page 431). Cut a deep slit along
the underside of the shrimp and
open it out, then press it flat.*

*■ For straight shrimp—peel and
devein, leaving the tail on. Insert
a wooden satay stick along the
length of the shrimp.*

ing, but the shrimp will be juicier and tastier if they are peeled after. Pinch and twist off the head, then split the shell open along the underside with your fingertips, and prize it apart until you can pull the shrimp free of its shell, working downward from the head end. You may remove the tail shell or leave it intact, whichever you prefer (see illustration, opposite above).

Devein: After removing the shell, check to see if there is a black line (the intestinal tract) running along the back of the shrimp. This can be eaten, but it looks unsightly and may be gritty, so is best removed. With the tip of a small, sharp knife, make a shallow cut along the length of the black vein (see illustration, opposite center), then lift out the vein with the tip of the knife (see illustration, opposite below).

COOK

■ Shrimp should be cooked as briefly as possible or they will be tough and chewy. Keeping the shells on helps guard against this.

■ Raw shrimp take 3–4 minutes maximum, and are cooked when they turn pink all over.

■ Cooked shrimp can be eaten cold as they are. If you want them hot, heat for 1–2 minutes at the most.

■ Shrimp are good in stir-fries, and dropped into soups, sauces, curries,

and stews toward the end of cooking.

■ To broil or grill, toss in olive oil with herbs or spices and seasonings, and thread on skewers.

■ To charbroil or pan-fry, toss them in olive oil with herbs or spices and seasonings and cook over a medium to high heat, tossing them often.

MOLLUSKS

This group of shellfish has shells but no legs. Mussels are the best-known and most frequently eaten; clams come a close second. Scallops and oysters are more expensive, and are usually reserved for special occasions. Squid and octopus are special kinds of mollusks called cephalopods.

Clams

Clams have always been an American favorite. The clambake is a unique East Coast tradition and clam chowder has become world famous. They are sold live in their shells like mussels, and the two can be used interchangeably in recipes.

CHOOSE

■ Size varies from very large and meaty quahogs to large surf clams, medium steamers, and small sunray Venus. Cherrystones and littlenecks

shrimp–clams

are small clams—in fact they are small quahogs. Then there is the long and narrow razor shell, which looks totally different from the others, resembling an old-fashioned razor. All are sold in their shells.

■ Canned or bottled clams in brine are cooked and ready to use. They are sweet and tender, and worth buying when you can't get fresh ones.

PREPARE

■ Clams can be sandy and gritty. Soaking them before cooking helps get them clean. Put them in a bowl of cold water with a handful of salt and leave for an hour, then drain, and scrub the shells with a stiff brush under cold running water. Discard any with cracked shells, or with shells that are open or don't close when tapped hard on the counter.

COOK

■ Small clams and razor shells can be eaten raw like oysters, but they are usually served cooked like mussels.

■ To serve them raw, prize open their shells with a small, sturdy knife or an oyster shucker, sever the hinge muscle, and discard the top shell, then loosen the clam from the bottom shell by digging underneath with a sharp-edged teaspoon. Serve on the half shell like oysters (see page 435).

PEELING AND DEVEINING SHRIMP

1 *Peel off the shell.*

2 *Cut down the length of the black vein with a small, sharp knife.*

3 *Lift out the vein with the tip of the knife.*

■ The easiest way to get the shells open is to steam them like mussels (see opposite) for about 5 minutes. Discard any that remain closed. After steaming, you can eat them as they are, like mussels, or remove them from their shells and drop them into soups (especially chowders), sauces, and stews, just before serving.

■ Another way to cook clams is to drop them raw into soups, sauces, and stews in their shells, or to put them on top of a paella or risotto. To avoid overcooking them (when they become rubbery), do this at the last minute, cover tightly with a lid or foil, and serve as soon as the shells open.

■ Large clams need to be cooked. They can be steamed and served like small clams (see above), but they are also good if they are steamed, taken out of their shells, and then baked or broiled. Put them back in the half shell and top with a spoonful of pesto or a pat of herb butter (see page 133), then bake in the oven at 375°F (340°F in fan ovens) for 5–7 minutes, or put under a hot broiler for 3–4 minutes.

■ Large steamed and shelled clams can also be dropped into soups, sauces, and stews. Cut them into smaller pieces first if you prefer, and cook only briefly until just heated through. They are also good deep-fried. Coat in seasoned flour, egg, and bread crumbs and drop into hot sunflower oil for 2–3 minutes until golden and crisp.

Mussels

Although they are available all year around, mussels are best eaten from September to April.

CHOOSE Mussels are usually sold live in their shells. You can buy them loose by weight, or in nets or bags. Allow 8 ounces per person for an appetizer, 1 pound per person for a main course.

Blue mussels: These are the familiar-looking mussels with blue-black shells. Their size varies, and the smallest take the most time to prepare, but they are usually the sweetest-tasting because they are the youngest, and so are well worth the extra effort.

New Zealand greenlip mussels: These are larger and meatier than blue mussels, but their flavor is not quite so good. They take their name from the green edging on their shells.

Shelled mussels are available frozen. They are cooked and ready to eat, and are useful for dropping into sauces, soups, and stews.

clams–mussels

PREPARE

- Scrape any barnacles off the shells with a small, sharp knife.
- Scrub the shells clean with a stiff brush under cold running water and pull off the hairy beards from between the shell hinges, grasping them between your finger and thumb with the help of a small knife (see illustration, right).
- Discard any mussels that have broken, cracked, or open shells, or that do not close when tapped sharply on the counter.
- If you are not cooking the mussels at once, keep them in a bowl of salted cold water in the refrigerator for up to 2 hours. If you want to leave them longer than this, leave the debearding until just before cooking. They should be cooked and eaten the same day.

COOK

- Steam mussels in a covered pan with just enough liquid to cover the base—they should take 5–8 minutes. Drain and discard any that are still closed. You can use plain water, but for the best flavor use wine, hard cider, or fish stock (or mix these half and half with water), to which you can add fresh herbs, sliced onion, chopped garlic, and seasoning as in the classic French *moules à la marinière*. A modern Asian alternative is to use fish stock flavored with soy and/or sesame, chilies, and garlic, or

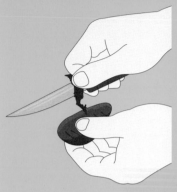

DEBEARDING MUSSELS

TIPS AND TRICKS: MOLLUSKS

- *Clams and mussels on their half shells wobble when you are broiling or baking them. To keep them stable, wedge them in a bed of rock or sea salt.*
- *When removing steamed mussels from their shells, check any large ones for a rubbery ring surrounding the central part of the flesh. This can be chewy, so pull it off and discard it.*
- *Always keep the juice from clams and mussels, tipping it into soups and stews for extra flavor.*

coconut milk flavored with lemongrass and cilantro.

■ Once the mussels are open you can either serve them as they are, or remove the top shells and detach the mussels from the bottom shells, then drop them into soups, sauces, and stews for a few minutes just to heat through (take care not to overcook or they will be chewy). Or you can put them back in their bottom shells and coat them in a stuffing, herb butter, bread crumbs, or a sauce and broil them until hot for 2–3 minutes, or bake them in the oven at 375°F (340°F in fan ovens) for 5–7 minutes.

■ Another way to cook them is to drop them straight into soups and stews with their shells on, cover the pan, and cook them for a few minutes until the shells open. They can be cooked this way in rice dishes such as risotto and paella, and in pasta sauces.

Oysters

The ultimate in style and luxury, oysters are an acquired taste—not everyone likes their slippery texture and salty flavor.

CHOOSE

■ Oysters are available all year round, but they are at their best when there is an "r" in the name of the month,

especially in winter. There are two main types—American and Pacific oysters. Both are sold live, graded according to size—the bigger the better. American oysters are regarded as the finest, and are the most expensive.

■ The best way to buy oysters is in their closed shells, so they will be as fresh as possible when you open them, but you can ask the fish store to do the job for you. Once they are open, keep them covered in the refrigerator until just before serving, and eat on the day of purchase.

■ Shelled oysters are available frozen, and smoked oysters are sold in cans. Both are good for cooked dishes.

PREPARE

■ If you have bought live oysters, check the shells are closed with no cracks. Discard any damaged ones. Scrub the shells with a stiff brush under cold running water, then open them with a shucker or sturdy knife (see opposite).

■ Frozen shelled oysters should be defrosted in the refrigerator before use. Leave them for at least 4 hours or overnight.

COOK

■ Fresh oysters are very delicate and best eaten raw because they can overcook quickly and become rubbery, but they can be broiled in their half shells,

mussels–oysters

seasoned, and protected by bread crumbs and herbs, a light stuffing mix, or a splash of cream and/or some grated Parmesan cheese. They can also be tipped out of their shells and pan-fried in butter, poached, or steamed. For any of these cooking methods, allow 2–4 minutes at the most.

■ Shelled and smoked oysters are most often used in pies and stews, and are traditional in English steak and kidney pudding. They are also good in canapé-size tartlets and baby quiches.

■ To make angels on horseback to serve as a canapé, wrap raw shelled oysters in small pieces of fatty bacon, prosciutto, or pancetta and thread on skewers, packing them close, so they don't unravel and overcook. Roast in the oven at 400°F (350°F in fan ovens) for 6 minutes.

SERVING OYSTERS RAW

The usual serving is 6 per person, although oyster lovers think nothing of eating 9 or even 12. Opening the shells is safer and easier if you use an oyster shucker with a guard to protect your hands should the blade slip (see right), but you can use a short, sturdy knife with a sharp tip instead.

■ Serve on a bed of crushed ice with some seaweed if you can get it, lemon halves, and sea salt, black pepper, and Tabasco for seasoning.

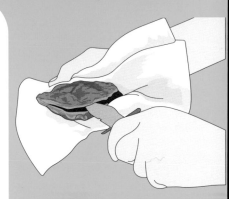

SHUCKING AN OYSTER
Insert the tip of the shucker or knife next to the hinge of the oyster's shell, holding the rounded end of the shell firmly in a cloth with your other hand.

■ *Work the shucker slowly between the two shells, twisting it from side to side until they are prized apart.*

■ *Scrape the oyster carefully from the top shell, then discard the top shell.*

■ *Detach the oyster from the muscle in the bottom shell, leaving the oyster sitting in the shell with its juice around it. Take care not to spill the juice—it is drunk from the shell after the oyster has been eaten.*

SHELLFISH:MOLLUSKS

Scallops

Also known by their French name of *coquilles St Jacques*, scallops are quick and easy to prepare, cook at lightning speed, and taste exquisitely sweet and tender.

CHOOSE

■ There are several types of scallop—bay, calico, and rock among others. You can buy large scallops in or out of their shells. The freshest are sold still in their shells, which your fish store will open for you. Allow 2–3 per person for an appetizer or 4–5 as a main course. The shells make attractive serving dishes, and the fish store will usually give them to you free of charge if you ask. Smaller scallops are cheaper, although their flavor is just as good as—if not better than—the large ones. They are usually sold out of their shells. You should allow 5–6 per person for an appetizer, 10–12 for a main course.

■ The roe or "coral" of a scallop is bright orange and considered a great delicacy in Europe. However, it is regular practice to discard it in the United States. Corals may be large and crescent-shaped or small and pointed. Scallops that are sold loose out of their shells will not have their corals attached.

■ Frozen or defrosted scallops are not worth buying. They are watery and tasteless compared to fresh, and some may have been soaked in water to plump up their flesh.

PREPARE

■ If the orange coral is attached, pull it away gently and set aside if you wish. Also pull away the little ligament that is attached to the side of the scallop—it is tough and will spoil any dish you are making. If it is stubborn, cut it off. Gently pat the scallops and corals dry with paper towels.

■ Small and medium scallops are best left whole. Large, thick scallops can be difficult to cook—the outsides may overcook while the centers remain raw. The way to avoid this is to cut them in half through their thickness. For stir-fries, cut each scallop into 4 chunks.

■ If you are using the shells, scrub them with hot, soapy water and rinse well, or put them in the dishwasher.

COOK

Only the briefest of cooking is needed, or the scallops will be tough. Pan-frying is the easiest method, and the one most chefs prefer—often described on menus as "seared" or "pan-roasted." Scallops can also be poached, stir-fried or broiled.

scallops

Pan-fry/sear/pan-roast: Season the scallops on both sides and brush with honey if you like (this helps give them a good golden color). Heat a splash of olive oil and a pat of butter in a heavy skillet over medium to high heat. When it's foaming, put in the scallops and cook for 2 minutes on each side for whole scallops, 1 minute on each side for halves and chunks. Press them flat with a metal spatula so they get nicely colored. Add any corals, if you wish, for the last minute. Lift out the scallops and corals, deglaze the pan with a splash of wine or balsamic vinegar, and drizzle over the scallops to serve. Or deglaze with white wine and make an instant sauce with steeped saffron and cream.

Poach: Bring fish or chicken stock to a gentle simmer, lower in the scallops, and poach for 4 minutes. Drain and serve warm or cold in salads (they taste very good with a balsamic or lime vinaigrette), or slice, and add to pasta sauces at the last minute.

Stir-fry: Heat sunflower or peanut oil in a wok until very hot, add the scallops cut into fourths, and stir-fry for 2–3 minutes maximum.

Broil: Wrap scallops in small pieces of fatty bacon, pancetta, or prosciutto, thread them on skewers, and cook under a hot broiler for 6 minutes, turning halfway through the cooking time.

SCALLOP

Squid

Inexpensive and available all year around, squid deserves to be eaten more often. It is quick and easy to cook, and has a pronounced shellfish taste. The smallest squid are the sweetest and most succulent.

CHOOSE

■ You can buy whole squid complete with its ink sac, but it is messy to clean, so ask your fish store to do the job for you. Cleaned squid tubes (the pouch or body of the squid) are readily available from fish suppliers and supermarkets, as are squid rings, which save you doing anything. Allow 2 small tubes or 4 ounces rings per person.

PREPARE

■ Rinse tubes and rings, drain well, and pat dry with paper towels.
■ For charbroiling or stir-frying, cut tubes along one of their sides and open them out flat, then score in a criss-cross pattern on the inside of the flesh. If you wish, marinate before cooking in olive oil and lime juice with finely chopped chilies and garlic.

COOK

■ Tubes can be stuffed and braised in a sauce (a tomato sauce spiked with chilies goes especially well). They are good filled with a bread crumb or couscous stuffing, to which you can add chopped onion, bell peppers, herbs, cured ham or cooked bacon, or crumbled, cooked bulk sausage. Fill them only two-thirds full to allow for expansion during cooking, and fasten the open ends with wooden toothpicks. Pan-fry in olive oil and butter for a few minutes until nicely colored on all sides, then cover with your chosen sauce, and braise on top of the stove or in the oven at 340°F (300°F in fan ovens) for 30–45 minutes, until tender when pierced with a skewer.
■ Rings can be deep-fried in batter, but they are healthier when pan-fried. Use them as they are or cut into strips, and pan-fry in hot olive oil—they take only a few minutes. Good flavorings for squid are chili, garlic, fresh ginger, and lime, and they are especially tasty served with a dipping sauce. They can also be cooked and added to paella, pasta sauces, and seafood salads.
■ To charbroil scored squid, brush it lightly with olive oil (or its marinade) and cook on a preheated stove top grill pan for 3–4 minutes, pressing down with a spatula. Cut into strips to serve—they look and taste good in salads. Or cut the squid into strips and add to stir-fries (Chinese black bean sauce is a favorite with squid).

Octopus

For novelty value, this is hard to beat
—and it tastes good too.

CHOOSE

■ Available fresh and frozen.
■ The smaller, the better—large
octopus can be tough. A whole
2-pound octopus will feed 4 people.

PREPARE

■ Frozen octopus usually comes ready-
prepared. If buying a fresh octopus,
ask the fish store to prepare it for you
so that it is ready for cooking, without
its innards, beak, and eyes.
■ Blanch in boiling water for 4 minutes, drain, and peel off the skin (with
a very young octopus this may not be
necessary).
■ To help tenderize the flesh, pound
it with a rolling pin, the smooth
side of a meat bat, or the base of a
heavy pan.
■ Cut into strips.

COOK

■ Braising in a thick, flavorsome sauce
is the best option, after browning in
hot oil over a high heat. Onions, garlic,
tomatoes, wine, and herbs all suit
octopus well, and the cooking time
should be about 1½–2 hours in the
oven at 340°F (300°F in fan ovens).

SQUID INK

*If you buy fresh squid from the
fish store, they may ask whether
you want the ink sac (it is inside
the squid and is very black). In
Spain they cook squid in its own
ink, and in Catalonia they use it to
color and flavor paella. Italians
color their pasta with it, and use
it to make a sauce to serve with
pasta. As well as buying it fresh,
you can also buy it in plastic
envelopes at some fish stores, delis
and supermarkets.*

SHELLFISH

WHAT'S IN A NAME?

■ **Crayfish** are miniature fresh-water lobsters, about the size of a jumbo shrimp, that are sold live or frozen. Poach them in fish stock (see page 409) or court bouillon (see page 411) for 5 minutes if fresh, 7 minutes if frozen and serve hot or cold as an appetizer, allowing 8–10 per person. Only the succulent and flavorsome tail meat is eaten. The heads and shells are good for making stock. Crayfish is not the same creature as the **crawfish**, although the names are often confused. Crawfish is simply another name for the spiny or rock lobster, also known as the *langouste* in French.

■ **Langoustines** belong to the lobster family and are also closely related to lobsterettes. The tail meat is sometimes sold as scampi (the Italian name), especially when coated in bread crumbs for deep-frying. They are usually sold frozen, either raw or cooked, and are pale pink in color even when raw. Poach or charbroil for 1–2 minutes (don't overcook) and serve hot or cold as an appetizer. Allow 6 per person. They can also be cut in half length-wise, brushed with melted butter, and cooked for 1–2 minutes under a hot broiler. Serve sprinkled with chopped herbs and slices of lemon for squeezing.

Milk, Cheese, and Eggs

MILK

INVALUABLE AS A FRESH AND NATURAL INGREDIENT IN COOKING, MILK IS ONE OF OUR MOST NUTRITIONALLY COMPLETE FOODS. IT CONTAINS PROTEIN AND FAT, CARBOHYDRATE IN THE FORM OF MILK SUGAR (LACTOSE), AND MINERALS AND VITAMINS IN ABUNDANCE —ESPECIALLY CALCIUM, ZINC, MAGNESIUM, VITAMINS A AND E, THIAMINE (B1), RIBOFLAVIN (B2), AND B12—ALL ESSENTIAL FOR GOOD HEALTH.

CHOOSE
Cow's milk

There are three main types, each containing a different amount of fat. All are pasteurized, which means they have been heat-treated to kill any harmful bacteria and extend shelf life. **Whole milk** is sometimes described as "full-fat" milk because none of its natural fat has been taken away. It has more vitamin A than other milks. Fat content is about 4%.

Low-fat milk has had about half of its fat taken away, which makes it less rich in vitamins A and D, but it has slightly more protein and calcium than whole milk. Fat content is about 1.7%.

Skim milk has had virtually all of the fat taken away, together with fat-soluble vitamins A and D, but on the plus side it contains slightly more calcium than whole milk. Fat content is 0.1–0.3%.

Specialty milks

Not all milk comes from cows, and most can be drunk and used in cooking in the same way. Check the label for exact usage.

Goat's and sheep's milk are both available fresh, either whole or low-fat, and have similar fat contents to their cow's milk equivalents.

Oats and rice are used to make long-life, lactose-free "milks" that are low in fat and cholesterol. They are good for the lactose-intolerant, or if you need to restrict your intake of animal fats for health reasons.

Soy milk is made from soybeans, and is available in fresh and long-life, plain, sweetened, and flavored varieties. Lactose-free and low in fat, soy milk is often calcium-enriched.

STORE

Fresh milk must be stored in the refrigerator to keep it fresh and out

of direct light, which can cause valuable vitamins to be lost. For storage
times, check the "use-by" date on the
bottle or carton—it is usually about
5–7 days from the day you buy it.

Freeze

Low-fat and skim milk can be frozen
for up to 1 month, although they may
separate when thawed. For best
results freeze homogenized milk (it is
less likely to separate) and defrost
overnight in the refrigerator.

Long-life milks

Fresh milk keeps for several days, but
there are alternatives with longer
shelf lives that are useful for times
when you run out of fresh. They are
especially suitable for cooking.

Coconut milk comes in many
different forms. See Pantry Staples,
page 80, for how to choose and use.

Condensed milk is cow's milk that
has been concentrated by being heated
and homogenized, then sweetened, and
evaporated. Sold in cans, it is very
sweet and sticky, with a thick, spoon-
able texture that is velvety smooth. Use
for making caramel (as in millionaire's
shortbread), fudge, and desserts.

Dry milk is produced by evaporating
the water from cow's milk. It comes

LABELS ON MILK— WHAT THEY MEAN

■ *BREAKFAST MILK comes from
fawn-colored, short-horn cattle
(Jersey), or brown and white cattle
(Guernsey). It is a whole milk that
is available homogenized (see
below) or with a visible layer of
cream on top. Both types are very
rich and creamy, with a fat content
of about 5%.*

■ *HOMOGENIZED is whole or
low-fat cow's milk with its fat distributed evenly throughout so the
cream does not rise to the top.*

■ *ORGANIC comes from cows that
have grazed on pastures that have
had no chemical fertilizers, pesticides, or agrochemicals used on
them. Producers must be registered
with an approved organic body.
Research indicates that organic
milk has more vitamins A and E
than nonorganic milk, and is
richer in antioxidants and essential
fatty acids.*

MILK:CREAM

in powder and granules, and can be made from whole or skim milk. Virtually fat-free, nonfat dry milk is not so vitamin-rich as whole dry milk, but it reconstitutes more easily when mixed with water. Dry milk keeps for a year, but once reconstituted it must be treated as fresh. It can be used as a substitute for fresh milk in recipes.

Evaporated milk is cow's milk that has been evaporated at a high heat, then homogenized. It is twice as concentrated as fresh milk, and can be used as a substitute in cooking to give extra richness, as long as you like its distinctive flavor. It can be whipped.

Oats, rice, and soya beans are used to make long-life milks (see page 442).

Sterilized milk is available whole, low-fat, and skim, in bottles and cartons. It is heated to a very high temperature that destroys virtually all bacteria. You either love or hate its very distinctive taste. It keeps for several months without refrigeration if unopened, but once opened it should be used within 5 days. Sterilized milk can be used for drinking and in cooking as a substitute for fresh milk, but it has slightly less of the B group vitamins and vitamin C.

UHT stands for ultra-heat-treated milk. Available in cartons as whole, low-fat, and skim, it is similar to sterilized milk in that it has the same keeping qualities (see above), but it has a milder flavor and more nutrients. It can be used instead of fresh milk for drinking and in cooking.

COOK

■ When heating milk, don't get it too hot or it may boil over and/or scorch on the bottom of the pan. Scorched milk tastes unpleasant, and will spoil the flavor of any sauce. The same is true of milk that has boiled over, which may also have lost many of its nutrients. To scald milk, heat it gently to just below boiling point, when bubbles start to appear around the edge, then remove the pan from the heat before it has a chance to scorch or boil over.

■ To flavor milk, scald it with aromatics such as vanilla beans or citrus zest, then remove from the heat, and leave to steep for about 20 minutes. Remove the flavorings before use.

■ Don't use skim milk in a recipe unless it says so, especially if it is to be heated with acidic ingredients such as citrus juice or raw onions. Acid can cause milk to curdle or separate, particularly low-fat, skim milk. To prevent milk curdling when using milk with these ingredients, keep the heat very low, and cook any onions first.

■ For a quick all-in-one white sauce, see page 461 and omit the cheese.

CREAM

Whether cream is used in cooking or for serving at the table, it will always add a luxurious touch. There are many types to choose from, and many different ways to use them in recipes.

CHOOSE

The fat content of cream determines its uses, so it helps to know this when choosing.

Clotted cream is more yellow in color than other creams, and nearly as thick as butter. Made by heating the cream of whole milk, which gives it a rich flavor and a slightly grainy texture, it has the highest fat content of all the creams, at around 65%. Traditionally made in Devon, Cornwall, and Somerset in the southwest of England, it is not widely available in other countries. It does not whip, and is not recommended for cooking.
USE INSTEAD Heavy or whipping cream.

Crème frâiche originated in France, and some of the best brands are imported from there. It is fairly thick, with a smooth texture and comes in full-fat, low-fat, and half-fat versions—the full-fat has 40–50% fat

WHICH CREAM FOR WHICH JOB?

- *COOKING—crème fraîche, half-and-half, heavy, light, sour, whipping*
- *POURING—half-and-half, heavy, light, whipping*
- *SPOONING—clotted, crème fraîche, heavy, sour, whipping*
- *WHIPPING—crème fraîche, heavy, whipping*

MILK:CREAM

content. The flavor is tangy, similar to that of sour cream but not quite so sharp. It becomes thinner when stirred or added to hot liquids, but thickens well when whipped. Use as a spooning cream for desserts (it goes especially well with fruit and chocolate), and in cooking to enrich mixtures and sauces—the full-fat version does not curdle when heated to a high temperature.

USE INSTEAD Sour cream or plain yogurt, or a half-and-half mix of one of these with heavy or whipping cream. Take care when heating, as sour cream and yogurt curdle if they get too hot.

Half-and-half is a cross between cream and milk, like top of the milk. It has a 12% fat content, and is good for pouring over desserts and break-fast cereals (especially porridge), and for making drinks and sauces when you want a richer taste than that of ordi-nary milk. It can be heated without curdling, but it can't be whipped.
USE INSTEAD Light cream or break-fast milk.

Heavy cream is luxuriously thick, with a full-on rich flavor and a fat content of 54%. This is the most versatile cream because it can be boiled without curdling and is good

as a pouring or spooning cream. It will whip to one and a half times its volume. It is ideal for floating on top of hot liquids such as soup or coffee, or folding into mousses, fools, and soufflés. Extra-thick heavy cream is homogenized, and best used for spoon-ing over desserts, not for whipping.
USE INSTEAD Whipping cream, crème fraîche.

Light cream is a smooth pouring cream with an 18–24% fat content. It is a good table cream to serve with desserts, and it can be used in cooking for enriching sauces, soups, custards, omelets, and quiche fillings, but it should not be boiled or heated to high temperatures as this will cause it to curdle. It cannot be whipped. Extra-thick light cream is homoge-nized. This makes it thicker than ordinary light cream, but it cannot be heated to a high temperature, nor can it be whipped.
USE INSTEAD Half-and-half or breakfast milk.

Sour cream is light cream that has been treated with a culture of bacteria to make it thicker and tangier. (It is not just cream that has "gone off.") It has an 18–21% fat content. It is mainly used as a topping for things like baked potatoes, blini, bortsch,

choose

goulash, stroganoff, and chili, and it is also good in dips and dressings, and spooned over desserts when ordinary cream is too rich. It separates when overheated, so take care when stirring it into hot liquids—do this with the pan off the heat when the liquid has cooled down a little. It cannot be whipped.

USE INSTEAD Plain yogurt or smetana (see right). Or make your own sour cream by stirring 1 tablespoon lemon juice into 1 cup heavy cream and leaving it to thicken at room temperature for 10–15 minutes.

Whipping cream is thick, but not so thick and rich as heavy cream as its fat content is lower, around 35–40%. It makes a good alternative to heavy cream whenever you want a lighter feel and taste with less fat and fewer calories, but it will curdle if boiled. It is best heated very gently, or used for pouring or spooning over desserts, or for whipping and decorating desserts and cakes. When it is very cold, it will whip to double its volume and become light and fluffy. It holds its shape very well, so it is good for piping, spooning, or floating on top of soup or coffee. It makes good ice cream.

USE INSTEAD Heavy cream mixed with light cream in the ratio of 2:1.

UHT CREAM

Ultra-heated-treated (UHT) cream is a useful standby because it keeps for up to 3 months without refrigeration if unopened. (Once opened it should be treated like fresh cream.) It tastes slightly different from fresh cream, but it has the same enriching qualities, and the flavor can easily be disguised by combining it with other ingredients. It is useful for adding richness to custards, soups, sauces, quiche fillings, and omelets, and it makes good Chantilly cream when whipped with vanilla extract or sugar.

SMETANA

Smetana, also spelled smatana, originates from Russia and Eastern Europe. A sour cream with a tangy flavor, runny texture, and fairly low fat content (around 10%), it can be used as a low-fat alternative to sour cream, or in place of plain yogurt. Use it as a spooning or pouring cream, or for adding to sauces and stews at the end of cooking. It will curdle if overheated, and will not whip thick. If a recipe calls for smetana and you cannot get hold of any, use whipping or light cream mixed half and half with sour cream or plain yogurt.

MILK:CREAM

STORE

All cream must be kept in the refrigerator and used by the "best before" or "use by" date. Once opened it should keep for up to 3 days. Creams with a fat content of at least 35% can be frozen, but they should be used within a month. For best results, whip heavy or whipping cream lightly before freezing and thaw overnight in the refrigerator. Thawed frozen cream does not whip so well as fresh, but can be used for spooning onto dishes and in cooking. To make it smoother, whip gently before use.

USE

There are a few tips and tricks for using cream that will help you get the best results, but choosing the correct type of cream for the job (page 445), is the best guarantee of success.

ADDING CREAM TO HOT MIXTURES

Heavy cream is best because its high fat content will prevent it from curdling even when it is boiled, but you may prefer a lower-fat alternative. Full-fat crème fraîche is the next best thing, as it too can be boiled without risk of curdling, but if you use any of the other creams, you need to take precautions.

■ Remove a few spoonfuls of the hot liquid to a bowl and stir in the cream, then return this mix to the bulk of the liquid a little at a time, stirring well to combine before adding more. Keep over a low heat until just warmed through, and don't let it boil.
■ As an extra precaution, stabilize the cream with cornstarch, allowing ½ teaspoon for each 4 tablespoons cream. Mix the cornstarch to a paste with a few drops of water before adding to the cream, then cook for 1–2 minutes over low heat, stirring all the time, to get rid of any raw flour taste.

WHIPPING CREAM UNTIL THICK

For speed you can use an electric whisk (see Kitchen Kit, page 60), but you will have more control and get greater volume if you use a balloon whisk (see Kitchen Kit, page 68). If you haven't got either of these, you can use a table fork, but it is hard work. Both whipping and heavy creams will then hold their shape for several hours in the refrigerator. Whipping cream will double its volume, heavy cream will increase by one and a half times. Crème fraîche can be whipped until thick, but it will not increase in volume.
■ Chilled cream whips better than

store–use

warm or room-temperature cream,
so keep the cream in the refrigerator
until just before you are ready to
whip, and don't use a warm bowl
or whisk. The colder everything is,
the better.

■ Pour the cream into a deep bowl
and start whipping, slowly at first,
moving the whisk in a circular motion
from the bottom of the bowl to the
top so the blades cut through all of
the cream and incorporate as much
air as possible.

■ As the cream starts to thicken there
will be less likelihood of splashing, so
you can increase your whipping speed
slightly. Don't go too fast—cream has
a nasty habit of separating and
becoming grainy very quickly. If this
happens, the cream is described as
"turned" or "split."

■ When a recipe calls for cream to be
lightly whipped to a soft peak, stop
whipping as soon as the cream will
hold a floppy peak shape when the
whisk is lifted—the top of the peak
should fold over on itself and not
stand upright.

■ If a recipe specifies that the cream
should be stiffly whipped or whipped
to a stiff peak continue whipping a
little longer, until the peak stands tall
when the whisk is lifted. Don't go
beyond this stage or the cream will
start to turn grainy and buttery look-

MILK:CREAM | YOGURT

ing. If this happens, the cream will still be edible but it will not look good as a decoration and it will not fold in properly. Use it in a warm sauce where it will melt.

■ Whipped cream will hold its shape for several hours in the refrigerator.

FOLDING CREAM INTO ANOTHER MIXTURE

For some cake batters, or when making mousses, fools, and soufflés, recipes often tell you to "fold in" the cream. Folding is a technique that insures two or more mixtures are evenly blended together without losing air and volume (see also Terms and Techniques, page 25).

■ With a rubber spatula or a large metal spoon (whichever you feel most comfortable using), stir a couple of spoonfuls of whipped cream into the main mixture until it is completely mixed in.

■ Now tip the rest of the cream on top and fold it in using the edge of the spatula or spoon. Cut down into the mixture until you reach the bottom of the bowl, then scoop, and roll the mixture over. Cut down again and repeat in a figure-eight action, turning the bowl around with your other hand until all of the cream is evenly incorporated and there are no streaks.

YOGURT

Made from milk, yogurt is a staple in many places such as India, other parts of Asia, Eastern Europe, Turkey, Greece, and the Middle East. Yogurt is made commercially by adding a harmless culture of bacteria (*Lactobacillus bulgaricus* and *Streptococcus thermophilus*) to milk after it has been pasteurized (heat-treated), then cooled. This creates the characteristic refreshing tangy taste and, under the right conditions of temperature and moisture, causes the milk proteins to set and become yogurt. The milk can be from cows, goats, ewes, and buffalos, the most common being cows, and can be skim, low-fat, or whole.

CHOOSE

There are many varieties and flavors of yogurt to choose from, including those with sugar, fruit, cream—even with gelatin added. Plain, natural yogurts that have no added flavorings, sweeteners, or colorings are the most versatile, healthiest, and the most useful for cooking with. These are some of the types available:

Bio: Uses a particular type of bacterium thought to help digestion. It is the mildest-tasting yogurt, less acidic in taste and creamier than others. Bio

use–**c**hoose

is short for probiotic (from the Greek word meaning "in favor of life").

Whole milk: Made with whole milk, this yogurt combines all the benefits of this milk (which is a rich source of vitamin A, vitamin E, niacin, and biotin), with the benefits of harmless bacteria.

Strained: Made from whole cow's milk (sometimes ewe's milk) and cream, this is a thick, especially creamy yogurt, with a fat content of about 10.2%. There is also a 0% fat variety made with skim milk and milk proteins.

Live: Most of the yogurt that we buy is live, which just means that the harmless bacteria added to the milk are still alive. The only yogurt that is not live has been heat-treated after production. This kills the bacteria, which gives it a longer shelf life, but a different taste and fewer health benefits.

Low-fat: Made with skim milk, this has less than 2% fat.

Organic: This is made from organic milk, and producers must be registered with an approved organic body.

Plain: Also called natural, this has no added flavorings or colorings.

Set: Made using traditional bacteria cultures, this is allowed to set in the pot it is sold in. This gives the yogurt a texture that keeps its shape.

GOOD FOR YOU
Since yogurt is made from milk, it has the same nutrients—protein, vitamins, and minerals—and is a rich source of calcium.

MILK:YOGURT|BUTTER

STORE

In its original container in the refrigerator and eat by the "best before"
date on the packaging. After this
date, the taste will start to become
much more acidic.

COOK

Yogurt is used a lot in many cuisines,
especially in Indian cooking, when
it is often added to a savory dish
toward the end to make a creamy,
tangy sauce. Yogurt can, however,
separate when heated, which spoils
the look and texture of a dish rather
than its flavor. To help prevent this,
use the yogurt at room temperature,
and when adding at the last minute,
beat it until smooth, then stir in just
a spoonful at a time to ease it into
the hot mixture. If the yogurt is
going to cook in the dish for longer,
stabilize it before adding, by making
a paste of cornstarch and water
and stirring this into the yogurt. (To
4 tablespoons yogurt, stir in a blend
of ½ teaspoon cornstarch and 1 teaspoon water.) Gradually stir the
combined yogurt/cornstarch into your
hot mixture, cooking gently for a few
minutes to get rid of the raw taste of
the cornstarch—but don't let it boil.
Alternatively, you can add the yogurt
gradually, straight into the pan, at
the beginning of cooking. If you wish
to add it to frying onions, for example, stir in 1 tablespoon of the
required amount of yogurt at a time,
and let it get absorbed before adding
the next.

USE FOR

■ Adding a spoonful or two to a spicy
curry to make it creamy and tone
down the heat.
■ Making a drink or sauce (such
as Indian lassi or raita, or Greek
tzatziki).
■ Marinating meat and poultry (it
helps tenderize at the same time).
■ A low-fat substitute for cream or
ice cream: use with fresh fruit in a
pavlova—you'll never guess that it's
not cream.
■ Making biscuits—it will lighten the
dough.

BUTTER

If you churn cream until it goes solid, you get butter. It is a totally natural product, unlike margarine, which is a processed food that contains additives. Butter contains a minimum of 80% fat with no more than 16% water.

CHOOSE

Most butter is made from cow's milk, but you may also see it made with other milks such as sheep's or goat's. France, particularly Normandy, produces some very fine butters such as *beurre d'Isigny*. Made with crème fraîche, it has a different taste and texture—very light and creamy. Sweet Italian butter is delicately flavored, pale, and just slightly sweet, similar to American butter.

Buy the best-quality butter that you can afford, as cheaper butters (often blended), tend to have a stronger, more overpowering, taste. Use butters interchangeably for spreading, depending on your taste. Sweet is often favored for cooking.

Lactic (cultured): Made by adding a culture of harmless bacteria to the cream, this has a very slight tartness and removes the need to add salt, although it is sometimes added for flavor. Many Danish butters are lactic.

TIPS AND TRICKS: BUTTER

If you have hot hands and find it difficult rubbing butter into flour when making pie dough, here's a solution. Firm up the butter by putting it (wrapped in foil or waxed paper) in the freezer for about 30–45 minutes to get it really hard. Then, holding it in its peeled back wrapping, coarsely grate it into the flour before mixing in the water. Wrap and chill the dough for 20 minutes or so before rolling out. This gives a slightly flakier pastry—with no rubbing in to do and no messy hands.

BUTTER v. MARGARINE

Some recipes call for using either butter or margarine. The choice is yours, but if it is flavor you are after, choose butter as it has more. A low-calorie margarine is not suitable for cooking, as it contains a high proportion of water.

MILK:BUTTER|OTHER BUTTER PRODUCTS

Slightly/lightly salted: This has less salt than salted butter, usually about 1%. Therefore, it doesn't keep as long as salted, but it is a good choice if you like the taste of salt yet are concerned about the amount you eat.

Salted: Butter which has salt added —the amount varies from 1–2.5%. Years ago salt was added as a preservative; today it is added for flavor. Salted butter is fine to cook with and great for baking, but it burns more easily than sweet butter when used for frying.

Spreadable/easy spread: This is not pure butter but a blend of dairy fats and vegetable oil. Low-fat versions are not suitable for cooking.

Sweet: Butter without added salt, this has a sweet, delicate taste and is good for cooking (especially frying), as it can survive higher temperatures without burning as much as salted butter. Also good for baking and for greasing cake pans. Many European butters are sweet.

STORE

Keep, well wrapped, in the refrigerator, away from any strong-smelling food as butter absorbs flavors easily. Use by the "best before" date on the packaging. Or store in the freezer for up to 6 months.

PREPARE

If using for baking or any dish where the butter has to be very soft, leave it at room temperature for 1–2 hours before using it, so it is easier to work with.

COOK

Butter can add creamy texture (in baking and sauces) plus flavor and richness to all cooking.

FRY To keep butter from burning, don't have the heat too high, although sweet butter can be heated to a higher temperature than salted. Or use half butter and half olive or vegetable oil. That way you still get the flavor but there's less chance of the butter burning. This all changes when you make "brown butter" as you heat it until it actually turns a golden brown to give a nutty taste. Good for pouring over fish or vegetables. Don't let it get too brown, though, or the butter will end up with a burnt taste.

BAKE When making cakes, the butter may need to be creamed (see Terms and Techniques, page 17) with the sugar to give a light texture, so the butter should be very soft (see Prepare, above)—check for softness by pressing your finger onto the wrapping.

OTHER BUTTER PRODUCTS

▪ Ghee

This is a form of clarified butter that is used a lot in Indian cooking. Clarifying is a process that makes the butter clear by removing the milk solids. Clarified butter and ghee have higher burning points (ghee has the highest), so are particularly good for frying. Both can be used interchangeably, but ghee has a stronger, nuttier flavor. This is because, after the milk solids have been separated out, the liquid is simmered to drive off more moisture, which turns the milk solids slightly brown. You can find ghee in Indian stores as well as some supermarkets, or make your own clarified butter (see below).

▪ How to clarify butter

Melt some butter in a pan until it is completely liquid. Let it stand so the white milk solids settle on the bottom. Skim off any foam with a slotted spoon, then strain off the yellow liquid, keeping the white solids behind. The clear yellow part is the clarified butter. Let it cool, then chill. Use for cooking only, as it has a grainy texture.

▪ Buttermilk

This used to be a by-product of butter-making, but is now made by adding to skim milk the cultures that ripen cream to make butter. This gives it a silky thickness and a tangy taste. It is sold as cultured buttermilk. Buttermilk is ultra low-fat (just 0.1% per 3.5 ounces) and, because its slight acidity reacts with rising agents, it is good for giving a light texture to biscuits, teabreads, pancakes, and muffins. Or try it instead of milk in a smoothie or milkshake.

CHEESE

CHEESE IS AN INCREDIBLY VERSATILE INGREDIENT FOR COOKING, AND BECAUSE OF THE RANGE OF STYLES, SOME ARE SUITED TO GRATING AND MELTING, OTHERS TO CRUMBLING AND BAKING. THIS SECTION LOOKS AT SOME OF THE MOST SUITABLE CHEESES FOR COOKING AND HOW THEY CAN BE USED.

Cheese is made from milk (mainly from cows, goats, and sheep) which is usually first heated (pasteurized) to kill off any harmful bacteria. Specialist artisan cheese makers tend to use unpasteurized milk, which can give cheese loads of character and flavor. Starter cultures (special friendly bacterial cultures) are added to sour the milk, thicken it, and develop the flavor, then an ingredient called rennet is added, which curdles and coagulates the milk, separating it out into solid curds and liquid whey. Most cheeses are made from the curds, but some, such as ricotta, are made from the whey. Salt is added, and the cheese is then stored and left to ripen and age, and to let the flavor develop. The time ranges from 1 month to 3 years. There are, however, certain fresh, unripened cheeses that don't go through the maturing process at all. Instead, these are ready to eat as soon as they have been made, such as mozzarella and fresh young goat cheeses.

CHOOSE

There are many cheeses available, from soft, mild, and creamy to strong, hard, and pungent. The differences result from the sort of milk used to make the cheese, the animal it comes from, and how it is made. Cheese made from cow's milk tends to be richer and fattier, goat's milk is sharper in taste, and sheep's milk is nuttier. The choice is down to personal preference and how you are going to use it. Look at the texture of the cheese, how strong its flavor is, and how it will behave when heated. There are many ways to classify the styles of cheeses—and the following categories are listed to help you choose the right one for your cooking needs.

Blue

The blue veins running through this style of cheese are created by harmless molds being introduced into it while still young. As the cheese ages, the

blue–hard cheese

blue veins grow, creating a complex labyrinth of tunnels and trails.

CHOOSE For their unique taste and richness, which can transform many dishes, including sauces and salads.

TYPES
- Mild and creamy such as mild (*dolce*) Gorgonzola and Maytag Blue.
- Powerfully assertive such as Roquefort and Danish Blue.
- Sharp and rich like Stilton, Irish Cashel blue, and Bergère Bleue.

USE FOR Melting and crumbling, and in salads.

GOES WITH Steak, bacon, Belgian endive, leeks, apples and pears, nuts, pasta.

USE INSTEAD Interchangeably within each type.

Hard

These have been pressed, so they are firm with a thick rind that may be waxed, oiled, or clothbound. The older they get, the harder and more powerfully flavored they become. Some are aged for several years.

CHOOSE For being good all-rounders.

GOOD FOR YOU
Cheese has a concentrated form of all the nutrients in milk, so it is rich in calcium and has protein and vitamins A and B. Full-fat cheese is, however, high in saturated fat.

STYLISH CHEESEBOARD
Rather than offering a board loaded with lots of different cheeses, try offering just one or two, with pieces of fresh fruit such as figs with a creamy blue cheese, or slices of apples or pears with a ripe wedge of Brie or Camembert. Drizzle the figs with some honey and walnuts, or tuck a few crisp lettuce leaves under the apple or pear slices, sprinkle with toasted pine nuts, and squeeze with some lemon juice. Give each person their own individual platter and it makes a very easy dessert— or lunch, served with some interesting bread.

VEGETARIAN CHEESE
Traditionally, animal rennet was used in the cheese-making process. Nowadays, a large proportion of the cheese produced is made with non-animal rennet, so it is suitable for vegetarians. Check the label to make sure.

TYPES

Cheddar: Originated in England and now produced in the United States, Canada, Australia, and New Zealand. It can be mild and sweet or sharp and nutty, depending on its age.

Traditional such as Dry Jack, Idaho Goatster, and Plymouth.

White crumbly cheeses such as Cheshire, Toscana, feta (authentically made in Greece from 85% goat's milk, 15% ewe's milk—gets its salty taste from being kept in salted brine).

Hard cheese for grating, such as Italian Parmesan (*Parmigiano Reggiano*) and Grana Padano.

Tangy sheep's cheese such as Spanish Manchego (good for nibbling), Ossau Iraty from the Basque country, and Italian romano.

Swiss-style melters like Emmental, Gruyère, Appenzeller, Fontina (made in Italy). All are stringy and stretchy when melted, perfect for sauces and fondues, or for dropping in cubes into soups.

USE FOR Grating, shaving, slicing, and melting.

GOES WITH

Classic hard cheeses: bread, bacon, apples, lettuce, tomatoes, potatoes.

Parmesan and Grana Padano: prosciutto, salad greens, pine nuts, bell peppers, basil, pasta, spring vegetables.

Swiss-style: chicken, cured ham, potatoes, mushrooms.

USE INSTEAD Use interchangeably within each type.

Semisoft

These are mostly cheeses that haven't been pressed, so are supple and more pliable. Aged gouda can get very hard.

CHOOSE For elasticity when melted.

TYPES

■ Dutch for grating and slicing, such as Gouda and Edam (lower in fat).

■ Soft sliceables such as Italian taleggio (fruity flavor), Californian Teleme.

USE FOR Grating, melting, slicing.

GOES WITH Pork, bell peppers, tomatoes, asparagus, potatoes, squash, mushrooms.

USE INSTEAD Use interchangeably within each type.

Soft

They tend to be milder in flavor when youthful, but some can become pungent with age. May be easy to spread (ricotta), tear (mozzarella), or slice (Brie).

hard–soft

CHOOSE For tossing into pasta, melting into sauces, crumbling or slicing over salads, tarts, and pizzas.

TYPES

Young, fresh cheeses such as goat, also called *chèvre* (there are so many varieties that flavors vary, but they are generally sweet and tangy, with a natural rind); mozzarella (mostly made from cow's milk, but the original version made with buffalo's milk is still considered the best)—very elastic when cooked); ricotta (mild and slightly sweet)—use it instead of mascarpone (see right) for a lower-fat alternative; halloumi (salty taste)—mostly eaten cooked, it doesn't lose its shape when fried, broiled, or grilled (cut in chunks for making kabobs).

Soft, creamy cheese like Brie and Camembert. Best sliced or chopped for melting, both go runny when ripe. Use them interchangeably.

USE FOR Melting, baking, and crumbling.

GOES WITH Try goat cheese with beet, asparagus, tomato, salad greens, herbs. Try other young, fresh cheeses, such as mozzarella and halloumi, with Mediterranean vegetables. Brie and Camembert are good with red berries such as cranberries and raspberries.

ONE-OFFS FROM AROUND THE WORLD

■ *GJETOST: This cheese from Norway, with its caramel-sweet taste and color (made with cow's or goat's milk), tastes rather fudgy and like no other. Its smooth texture means it can be shaved beautifully. Traditionally served at breakfast.*

■ *MASCARPONE: Considered a cheese, this is really a thickened cream with a high fat content, about 46%, less than heavy cream which has 54%. Originally from southern Italy, it has a texture similar to that of clotted cream. It can be used instead of cream and is best known for being a main ingredient of tiramisu. It melts easily too, to give rich, creamy sauces.*

■ *PANEER: An Indian low-fat cheese with a texture similar to that of tofu. Like tofu, it has a bland taste, but absorbs other flavors well. It is usually diced into curries, and is used a lot with spinach and peas.*

CHEESE

More fresh soft cheeses

Fresh cheeses tend to be the mildest and softest as they are sold when young, often only a few days old. Because of this, they also have no visible rind and are usually high in moisture. Most of them are especially useful for cooking, although some can also be served as table cheeses.

Boursin: A fresh cream French cheese, often flavored with chives and garlic or coated in crushed pepper. It melts easily, so use it to create a quick creamy sauce for pasta—stir into hot, drained pasta, slackened off with a few spoonfuls of the cooking water, and toss in a handful of basil to serve. Or spoon Boursin onto baked potatoes instead of butter.

Cottage: Creamy in taste, lumpy in texture. As it is made from skim milk (so very low-fat), it is popular with dieters. Usually eaten raw.

Farmer's: is like cream cheese but lower in fat. Ideal for blending into mixtures such as cheesecakes to make them lighter.

Full-fat soft (cream cheese): A very smooth, mild cheese with a silky texture made from heavy or light cream. Adds a richness to desserts like cheesecakes. A low-fat version is also available.

Quark: The German version of farmer's cheese. Made from skim milk, so very low-fat, light, and tangy. Use it for sweet or savory dishes—if counting calories, put a spoonful into mashed potatoes instead of butter, or on a bowl of strawberries instead of cream.

STORE AND SERVE

Buy cheese little and often and you can enjoy it at its absolute best—look at the "best before" date on the pack. If you buy cheese cut from a wheel, try to use it within a couple of days or it will dry out. Rewrap carefully with fresh wrapping when you put it back in the refrigerator. For pre-wrapped cheese, keep it in its original wrapping and store it in the lower part of the refrigerator. After opening, it is best loosely wrapped in waxed paper, then put in a plastic bag so it can breathe without drying out. Or wrap it in foil, but not plastic wrap as it makes the cheese sweat and go moldy more quickly. It's best not to put a mix of cheeses in a plastic box as their flavors may taint each other. An important point to remember is that if cheese is served cold, much of the flavor and aroma will be lost. So, to let the flavor develop, bring the cheese out of the refrigerator about 1–2 hours before you are going to serve it.

FREEZE Freezing is not an ideal way to store cheese as the flavor can be affected. If you have too much hard cheese, it's best to freeze it grated.

COOK

A few dos and don'ts:

DO
- Use good-quality cheese—it won't necessarily be more expensive, as the stronger the taste, the less you will need to use.
- Experiment with different flavors— don't just stick to the ones you know.
- Substitute if you need to, but only with a similar style and type of cheese.
- Use cheese straight from the refrigerator when grating for cooking, as it's easier and quicker.

DON'T
- Overcook cheese as the taste and texture will spoil. So, if making a sauce, add the cheese at the end, with the pan removed from the heat, stirring until it has melted.
- Broil cheese on too low a heat. Have the heat high and position the broiler rack not too far away from the heat. The cheese will then melt quickly before it has the chance to ooze lots of oil.

EASY CHEESE SAUCE
This is a simple all-in-one sauce that you will find handy for all sort of dishes—mixing into pasta, pouring over leeks and cured ham, or serving with broiled fish.
Takes about 5–10 minutes
Makes 1¼ cups

2 tablespoons butter (cut in pieces)
¼ cup all-purpose flour
1¼ cups milk
¾–1 cup grated firm cheese, such as Cheddar or Swiss

Tip all the ingredients, except the cheese, into a medium pan. Stir constantly over medium heat with a wooden spoon or balloon whisk. If little lumps start to form, the whisk is great for breaking them up. As the sauce comes to a boil it will start to thicken and become smooth and glossy. Once it has, let it simmer for a minute or two to cook off the flour. Take the pan off the heat and stir in the cheese until it has melted.

OPTIONAL EXTRAS: Add any of these with the cheese—1 teaspoon Dijon mustard, a handful of snipped chives or chopped parsley, or a splash of Worcestershire or Tabasco sauce.

EGGS

QUICK AND EASY TO COOK, EGGS ARE THE ULTIMATE CONVENIENCE FOOD—KEEP A SUPPLY IN THE REFRIGERATOR AND YOU WILL NEVER BE STUCK FOR AN INEXPENSIVE AND NUTRITIOUS MEAL. EGGS ARE ALSO ONE OF THE MOST USEFUL INGREDIENTS IN COOKING—WITHOUT THEM DOING THEIR QUIET JOB OF THICKENING, EMULSIFYING, AND AERATING, MANY RECIPES WOULD JUST NOT BE POSSIBLE.

CHOOSE

There are several things you need to know before buying eggs.

Age: The "best before" date is 28 days after the eggs have been laid. Check the date before you buy, and make sure you eat the eggs by then.

Color: Shells come in a variety of colors, from white through pale to dark brown, speckled, and blue. The color of the shell depends on the breed of the bird, not the quality of the egg, nor what the bird has been fed on.

Condition: Check that no shells have been broken or cracked, and don't buy them if they have.

Size: Eggs are graded according to weight (see opposite). Supermarkets insist on strict adherence to this grading, but you can buy oddly sized eggs from farmers and markets. If a recipe does not specify a size, it is best to use large or extra large. Most recipes are tested with one of these sizes.

Type: The breed of the bird may be specified, but it is more important to know how the birds were reared. Organic eggs are the most expensive, followed by farm-fresh and barn eggs. Eggs from intensively farmed hens are the cheapest. Organic eggs are expensive as they are produced according to strict criteria: They are farm-fresh, fed on a diet of organic produce, and ranged on organic land.

Some different eggs

Hen's eggs are the most popular, but eggs from other birds are worth trying too, and an increasing number of different types are becoming available. Farmers' markets and farm stores are often the best source and their eggs must be labeled appropriately.

Bantam: Weighing no more than 1½ ounces, these small eggs are ideal for children. If serving to adults, allow 2 per person. They look and

choose–store

taste similar to hen's eggs, and can be used and cooked in the same way.

Duck: Large in size with pale blue shells and a strong flavor, these eggs are good mixed with hen's eggs in omelets, scrambled eggs, and fresh pasta. Use 1 whole duck egg or 1 duck egg yolk to 2 or 3 hen's eggs, for the right balance of flavor.

Goose: Very large, rich-tasting eggs that have a very short season from mid February to the end of May. One goose egg is equivalent to 3 hen's eggs, so it is the perfect size to make scrambled egg or an omelet for one person. The deep buttery yellow yolk gives a good color, which is also the reason why bakers love using goose eggs in sponge cakes. If you are making a 3-egg layer sponge cake, 1 goose egg is all you need.

Quail: Tiny, speckled eggs that are good softly boiled, hard-cooked, or fried. Children love them for their size, which is also perfect for canapés, appetizers, and salads.

STORE

Eggs must be stored in the refrigerator, and should be eaten by their "best before" date. The shells are quite porous and easily absorb flavors from other foods, so keep them covered if you can.

SIZES OF HEN'S EGGS

MEDIUM	under 1⅞ ounces
LARGE	1⅞–2¼ ounces
EXTRA LARGE	over 2¼ ounces

SALMONELLA

If you buy good-quality eggs from a reputable source, the risk of salmonella contamination is minimal because the hens will have been vaccinated against it. In the unlikely event of an egg having bacteria, the risk of food poisoning is greater if the egg is eaten raw or very lightly cooked. For this reason it is inadvisable to serve raw or lightly cooked eggs to babies and very young children, pregnant women, the sick, and the elderly.

■ *Salmonella bacteria are destroyed at 148°F. Recipes that are likely to use raw eggs or eggs cooked below this temperature are mayonnaise, hollandaise sauce, egg custard, meringues, mousses, soufflés, frosting, marzipan, and ice cream.*

■ *Cooking times are given on pages 466–7 for boiled, fried, poached, and scrambled eggs, to insure that both the yolk and white are set and any bacteria destroyed.*

■ Store eggs with the pointed end down, so the air pocket in the rounded end is at the top.

■ You can test an egg's freshness by cracking it onto a plate and checking the yolk and white. A fresh egg will have a domed yolk and the white will have two distinct parts—thick near the yolk, thinner at the edges. A stale egg will have a flat yolk and the white will not have two distinct parts.

■ Eggs are always best used at room temperature, so remove them from the refrigerator 30 minutes before using.

FREEZE Eggs cannot be frozen in their shells, but if you crack them into a rigid container and beat them lightly, they can be frozen for up to 6 months. You can also freeze the whites or yolks separately (again you need to beat them lightly first).

PREPARE

Eggs are the ultimate convenience food and there is very little to do in the way of preparation.

CRACKING AN EGG

There is no guarantee that you will not break the yolk, but the following method is the most successful. Always crack each egg into an empty bowl, just in case one has gone bad.

■ Sharply tap the middle of the egg at its widest point against the rim of a bowl.

■ Hold the egg over the middle of the bowl and insert your thumb tips into the crack.

■ Prize the two halves of the shell apart and let the egg drop into the bowl (see opposite, above).

■ If any pieces of shell have dropped into the egg, scoop them out with the tip of a teaspoon.

SEPARATING AN EGG

Whites are needed for meringues and for folding into mousses and soufflés. Yolks are used for mayonnaise and for enriching and thickening mixtures like batters, sauces, and soups.

■ Crack the shell and prize the two halves apart as above, keeping the egg in one half of the shell.

■ Tilt the shell so that the white runs out into the bowl, then tip the yolk into the empty half-shell and tilt again, using the edge of the empty half-shell to cut off any white that clings (see opposite, below).

■ When all the white has gone, tip the yolk into a separate bowl.

■ If you are separating more than one egg, use a clean bowl to catch each white, just in case the yolk breaks. Whites will not whisk stiff if they have even the tiniest trace of yolk in them.

store—prepare

WHISKING EGG WHITES

Egg whites are whisked to a stiff peak (for a description of a stiff peak, see page 449) for meringues, and to give volume and lightness to cakes, mousses, and soufflés.

■ Start with a clean, dry bowl and whisk, and egg whites at room temperature that have no trace of yolk in them. For the greatest volume, chefs traditionally use a large copper bowl and a balloon whisk, but you can also get good results with a stainless-steel or glass bowl and electric beaters.

■ Tip the whites into the bowl and start whisking slowly, working the whisk against the bottom of the bowl to break up the whites and get a foam going.

■ As the foam increases, lift the whisk up to the top of the bowl in a circular motion and sweep it around the sides of the entire bowl—this incorporates air and adds volume.

■ Keep whisking in this way until the whites turn into a pure-white snow, then keep the whisk low in the bowl, and move it vigorously from side to side until you feel the whites tighten. When ready, they will stand in stiff peaks when the whisk is lifted.

■ Use immediately to make meringues or to fold into mousses and cake or soufflé mixtures. The folding technique for whisked egg whites is the same as for whipped cream (see page 450).

CRACKING AN EGG

SEPARATING AN EGG

FIX IT: EGGS

If you overwhisk egg whites, they will turn grainy or watery. To put them right, tip in a fresh egg white and whisk for 30 seconds.

COOK

Eggs cook most successfully at room temperature, so take them out of the refrigerator about 30 minutes before you start.

BOIL

■ One at a time, lower the eggs on a spoon into a small pan filled two-thirds full with simmering water. Don't boil more then 4 eggs at a time or the timing will not be accurate.
■ Bring the water up to a simmer again, then start timing. Allow 4 minutes for a softly boiled egg with a runny yolk, 7 minutes for a set yolk and white, 10 minutes for a hard-cooked egg.
■ When the time is up, remove the eggs from the water with a slotted spoon.
■ To cool hard-cooked eggs, plunge them straight into cold water and leave for 5 minutes, then drain, and peel. Leave them in fresh cold water until ready to serve.

FRY

■ Heat 2 tablespoons peanut or sun-flower oil in a skillet until hot (you should feel the heat rising when you hold your hand over the pan).
■ Crack the eggs one at a time into a cup or small bowl, and slide each one into the hot oil.

■ Fry over medium heat, spooning the hot oil over the yolk until it is covered in a white film. For a soft yolk and set white to serve sunny side up, allow 3–4 minutes. For an over easy set yolk and white, turn the egg over and fry for another 2–3 minutes.

POACH

■ If you have an egg poacher (see Kitchen Kit, page 54), bring some water to a gentle simmer in the bottom of the pan, drop a small pat of butter into each cup, then crack in the eggs. Cover and poach for 3 minutes for a runny yolk, 5 minutes for a set yolk.
■ If you don't have an egg poacher, fill a wide, shallow pan two-thirds full with water, add 1 tablespoon vinegar. and bring to a simmer. Crack the eggs one at a time into a cup or small bowl and slide each one into the water. Turn the heat down to low and cook the eggs gently for 3 minutes for a runny yolk. For a firmer set, cook for 4 or 5 minutes. Remove the eggs with a slotted spoon and drain well.
■ If you are making poached eggs on toast or eggs Benedict, rest each egg on a crust or slice of bread after removing it from the water. The bread will soak up excess water from under the egg and your toast or muffin will not be soggy.

cook

SCRAMBLE

- Whisk the eggs in a bowl (with a fork or coiled whisk) with cream or milk and some salt and pepper. Allow 2 eggs and 1 tablespoon cream/milk per person.
- Melt a pat of butter in a pan. When the butter is foaming, tip in the egg mixture, and cook over a low heat for 1–2 minutes, scraping the bottom of the pan and stirring all the time, until the eggs come together as a soft creamy mass.
- Remove from the heat and continue stirring for another 30 seconds until the eggs are softly set.
- For a firm set, cook for 3–4 minutes before removing from the heat.

USING EGG YOLK TO THICKEN

For enriching and thickening a hot mixture, such as a sauce, soup, or stew, at the end of cooking, mix egg yolks and cream to make a liaison.

- Mix 1–2 egg yolks with up to 4 tablespoons heavy cream, crème fraîche, or sour cream.
- Whisk a few spoonfuls of the hot liquid into the egg mixture. With the pan off the heat, pour the egg mixture slowly back into the hot liquid, whisking constantly.
- Return to a low heat and cook, whisking constantly, until the liquid thickens.
- Take care not to let it overheat or boil, or the egg yolk may curdle.

MAYONNAISE

Makes 1¼ cups
Ready in 30 minutes

INGREDIENTS
2 large egg yolks
1 teaspoon mustard, such as Dijon
2 tablespoons white wine vinegar
salt and ground black pepper
1 cup sunflower oil (or half sunflower and half olive oil)

Whisk the egg yolks, mustard, 1 tablespoon of the vinegar, and a little salt and pepper, until thick. Whisking constantly, beat in the oil drop by drop. After about 2 tablespoons of oil have been added and the mixture has started to thicken, slowly trickle in the rest of the oil, beating steadily. Season with more vinegar, salt, and pepper to taste.

Mayonnaise can also be made in an electric mixer, food processor, or blender. Combine the egg yolks, mustard, 1 tablespoon vinegar, and a little salt and pepper in the machine. Turn it on and slowly drizzle in the oil. Adjust the seasoning to taste.

If the finished mayonnaise is too thick, thin it by beating in a little warm water.

EGGS

Cooking in the microwave

You will get good, quick results in the microwave when poaching or scrambling eggs. Never cook them in their shells in a microwave because pressure will build up inside the shell and the egg may burst inside the oven, or when you take it out.

POACH

■ Crack an egg into a microwave-safe cup or ramekin containing 1½ teaspoons water.

■ Pierce the yolk and white in a couple of places with a toothpick.

■ Microwave on High for 40 seconds in a 750-watt oven, or for 60 seconds in a 650-watt oven. Let it stand for 1 minute before serving.

SCRAMBLE

■ Beat the eggs as for conventionally cooked scrambled eggs (see page 467) in a microwave-safe pitcher or bowl.

■ Cover with plastic wrap.

■ Microwave on High for 1½ minutes in a 750-watt oven, or for 2 minutes in a 650-watt oven.

■ Uncover and stir the eggs.

■ Microwave for another 30 seconds.

■ Let the eggs stand for 30 seconds before serving.

WHAT'S IN A NAME?

■ ALBUMEN is the white of the egg, and has two consistencies. The thick white stands up around the yolk and the thin white runs toward the edge.

■ CHALAZAE are the ropey strands that connect the yolk to the thick white. If they stand out prominently, this is an indication that the egg is fresh. You can eat the chalazae, but if you don't like the look of them, strain them out.

GOOD FOR YOU

Eggs are extremely nutritious and easy to digest.

■ They are an excellent source of protein.

■ One egg contains as many as 18 vitamins and minerals, including calcium, iodine, iron, phosphorus, zinc, and vitamins A, B, D, and E.

■ They are a good source of folic acid and the antioxidant selenium.

■ Relatively low in saturated fat, one large egg provides around 76 calories.

Conversion Tables and Index

CONVERSION TABLES

PLEASE NOTE THAT ALL CONVERSIONS GIVEN HERE ARE APPROXIMATE. YOU SHOULD FOLLOW EITHER THE METRIC OR IMPERIAL SYSTEMS THROUGHOUT A RECIPE, NOT A MIXTURE OF THE TWO.

WEIGHTS

Ounces	Grams
½	15
¾	20
1	30
1½	40
2	60
2½	75
3	90
3½	100
4	125
5	150
6	175
7	200
8	250
10	300
12	375
16/1 lb	500
1¼ lb	625
1½ lb	700
2 lb	1000/1 kg
3 lb	1500/1.5 kg

SPOON SIZES

Spoon	Fluid ounces	Millilitres
1 teaspoon	⅛	5
1 dessertspoon	⅓	10
1 tablespoon	½	15

°F	°C	Gas Mark	TEMPERATURE
275	140	1	
300	150	2	
325	165	3	
350	180	4	
375	190	5	
400	200	6	
425	220	7	
450	230	8	
475	240	9	
480	250	—	

Cups (US)	Fluid ounces (UK)	Millilitres	VOLUME
⅛	1	30	*Please note that*
¼	2	50	*there are 16 fluid*
—	3½	100	*ounces to a pint in*
½	4	125	*the US, but 20 fluid*
—	¼ pint	150	*ounces to a pint in*
—	7	200	*the UK.*
1	8	250	
—	½ pint	300	
1½	14	400	
—	¾ pint	450	
2	16	500	
2½	1 pint	600	
3½	1½ pints	900	
4	1¾ pints	1000/1 litre	
—	2 pints	1.2 litres	
—	2½ pints	1.5 litres	
—	3 pints	1.8 litres	

INDEX

ENTRIES FOR INDIVIDUAL FOODS INCLUDE FULL DETAILS OF
PREPARATION AND COOKING TECHNIQUES. THESE ARE NOT
NORMALLY INDEXED AT THE SPECIFIC TECHNIQUES. PAGE
NUMBERS IN BOLD INDICATE RECIPES.

AUTHOR BIOGRAPHIES

Angela Nilsen's career has always involved food, either teaching or writing about it for books, magazines, newspapers, both in England and North America (here she was a food writer with the Vancouver *Sun* newspaper, Canada for 7 years). From May 1994 to July 2004, she was Food Editor of *BBC Good Food Magazine*, and is now a freelance writer and editor. In 2003 she was short-listed for the Glenfiddich Cookery Writer Award, and is the 2004 winner of both the Glenfiddich Cookery Writer Award and The Guild of Food Writers' Cookery Journalist of the year Award.

Jeni Wright Jeni Wright has been writing about food and cookery for over thirty years, and has published as many cookbooks in that time —her first book was the best-selling *All Colour Cookery Book* for Marks & Spencer in 1976. Cooking techniques are her speciality, and she is the author of three cookbooks for Le Cordon Bleu School, most notably the acclaimed *Le Cordon Bleu Complete Cooking Techniques*. For four years she was a colleague of Angela Nilsen's at *BBC Good Food Magazine*, where she worked closely with many of Britain's top chefs.

ACKNOWLEDGMENTS

The authors would like to thank the following for their expertise and valuable advice given during the research for this book:

Fiona Beckett; Alistair Blair at The Fish Society (www.thefishsociety.co.uk); The Dairy Council (www.milk.co.uk); Roz Denny; British Egg Information Service (www.britegg.co.uk); English Beef and Lamb Executive (EBLEX); Sarah Jane Evans; Nichola Fletcher (www.fletcherscotland.co.uk); Flour Advisory Bureau; Game-to-eat (www.gametoeat.co.uk); Lee & Phyllis Harper at The Highgate Butchers, London N6; Steve Hatt Fishmongers, London N1; Dr Beckie Lang, Public Health Nutritionist; Dan Lepard; Norma MacMillan; Meat Livestock Commission; Mushroom Bureau (www.mushroom-uk.com); Douglas Pattie at the Fresh Produce Consortium; British Potato Council www.britishpotatocouncil.co.uk); Alan Porter, Managing Director of the Chocolate Society; British Poultry Council (www.poultry.uk.com); Judy Ridgway; The Seafish Industry Authority (www.seafish.org); Emma Sharp, Jamaican chef and cooking teacher; Claire Symington, Seldom Seen Farm (Geese), Billesdon, Leicester; British Turkey Information Service (www.britishturkey.co.uk); Kate Williams; Carol Wilson, Cookery Consultant to Billingtons Unrefined Sugars.